THE SOVIET AMBASSADOR

THE MAKING OF THE RADICAL BEHIND PERESTROIKA

CHRISTOPHER SHULGAN

EMBLEM

Cloth edition published 2008
Emblem edition published 2011

Emblem is an imprint of McClelland & Stewart Ltd.
Emblem and colophon are registered trademarks of McClelland & Stewart Ltd.

Library and Archives Canada Cataloguing in Publication

Shulgan, Christopher
    The Soviet ambassador : the making of the radical behind Perestroika / Christopher
Shulgan.

Issued also in electronic format.
ISBN 978-0-7710-7997-9

    1. Yakovlev, A.N. (Aleksandr Nikolaevich), 1923-2005. 2. Gorbachev, Mikhail
Sergeevich, 1931–. 3. Perestroika. 4. Soviet Union – Politics and government – 1985-1991.
5. Soviet Union – Economic policy – 1986-1991. 6. Ambassadors – Canada – Biography.
7. Ambassadors – Soviet Union – Biography. 8. Canada – Foreign relations – Soviet Union.
9. Soviet Union – Foreign relations – Canada. I. Title.

DK290.3.I25S58 2011   947.085'4092   C2010-905277-3

We acknowledge the financial support of the Government of Canada through the
Book Publishing Industry Development Program and that of the Government of Ontario
through the Ontario Media Development Corporation's Ontario Book Initiative.
We further acknowledge the support of the Canada Council for the Arts and the
Ontario Arts Council for our publishing program.

Typeset in Electra by M&S, Toronto
Printed and bound in Canada

McClelland & Stewart Ltd.
75 Sherbourne Street
Toronto, Ontario
M5A 2P9
www.mcclelland.com

1   2   3   4   5   15   14   13   12   11

CONTENTS

"Each step in one's spiritual development is the result of definite experiences . . ."

ARTHUR KOESTLER, *Darkness at Noon*

PART

1

WHISPERING REVOLUTION

1991

THE TARGET

ONE CLEAR SUMMER DAY in August 1991, on a quiet residential street not far from Moscow's Belorusskaya metro station, a small, bald figure in a boxy suit made his way down the sidewalk. The knee of his left leg stayed stiff through each pace, as though it was encased in some unseen cast or an unforgiving brace. His eyes searched the sidewalk from behind thick, plastic-framed spectacles. Soon he was joined by another, younger man, several inches taller, with blue eyes and thinning, neatly side-parted hair. He, too, was dressed in a suit.

The two men hugged. After the customary inquiries about health and family, they walked along the usually sedate sidewalk. Around them the neighbourhood seemed suddenly to come to life. Cars cruised by along usually empty pavement. More pedestrians than usual suddenly were about, some of them walking apace with the pair for several steps before passing. "The hell with them," the younger man said. "Let them do their jobs." Several years later, the men would discover that more than 70 Soviet counterintelligence agents were assigned to monitor their encounter.

The younger man was himself well-versed in counterintelligence. He was 56-year-old Oleg Kalugin. During a 32-year career with the KGB he rose to become the head of the organization's Directorate K, the foreign counterintelligence section that battled enemy spies outside Soviet borders. He made KGB history in 1974 at the age of 40, when he became the youngest agent ever to make the rank of general. He'd participated in kidnappings and umpteen other plots against the West, including helping to arrange one of the most notorious assassinations of the Cold War, the 1978 murder of the émigré Bulgarian dissident Georgi Markov, killed by an agent who poked Markov with a poison-tipped umbrella at a London bus stop.

By August 1991, however, Kalugin no longer worked for the KGB. In fact, the Soviet secret police despised the former spy. When Soviet leader Mikhail Gorbachev took power in 1985, Kalugin supported the leader's democratizing initiatives of glasnost and perestroika. Disillusioned with his employer, which was a potent opponent of the sweeping changes, Kalugin retired from the agency in 1990 and soon joined the then-nascent Soviet democracy movement. On June 16, 1990, Kalugin astonished the audience at a gathering of the Communist Party's democratic wing by denouncing his former employer. He became a fixture of international media by revealing many of the spy agency's secrets, including its extensive infiltration of the democracy movement.

His companion was one of the few figures the KGB reviled more than it did Kalugin. The older, limping man was Aleksandr Yakovlev, a Communist Party politician who had, until recently, anchored the democratic wing of the Politburo, the central policymaking and governing body that ran the Soviet Union. Depending on their sympathies, many Russian insiders alternately blamed or credited Yakovlev as much as Gorbachev for the reforms of perestroika.

It had been Yakovlev who'd requested the meeting.

"Why don't you come over?" asked Kalugin during the initial telephone call.

"No, it makes no sense," replied Yakovlev. "Our homes are bugged."

They picked the street near Belorusskaya station because it was near Yakovlev's apartment; it was also public and exposed, the better to convince any onlookers that there was nothing untoward about their discussion. Soon after they met, Yakovlev explained he wished to draw on Kalugin's extensive knowledge of the KGB's murderous history. Speaking in barely audible tones, and only in the vaguest of terms, the politician described a rumour he'd recently heard that the KGB was planning to assassinate him – to target him in a faked automobile accident. Now, he wanted to know: What did Kalugin think? Could the rumour be true?

Kalugin ruminated a moment. He talked about Yuri Andropov, and how the former general secretary and KGB head had disliked political assassinations. But Andropov was long dead, and these were different times. A power struggle was threatening to rip apart the Soviet Union's ruling Communist Party. As Gorbachev manoeuvred to keep the Party intact, Yakovlev and other liberal-minded party members waged a secret war against the orthodox Bolsheviks, such as Vladimir Kryuchkov, the chief of the KGB. In this atmosphere of simmering revolution, Kalugin said, who could predict anything?

"Kryuchkov is a madman, and there's no telling what he might do," Kalugin said. "He might resort to anything."

Yakovlev nodded. Kalugin was only confirming what he felt. Yakovlev said he'd written a letter detailing the rumour as well as his suspicion that it was Kryuchkov himself who was responsible for the plan. "I put it in a safe," Yakovlev said. "I wanted you to know in case anything happens to me."

Before the men parted, Yakovlev shared with Kalugin another worry, that the hard-line orthodox communists like Kryuchkov were preparing a coup – an attempt to wrest the Soviet Union from Gorbachev's hands so they could erase the effects of perestroika. Just days would pass before his prediction would be proven accurate.

2

THE TRAITOR

F OR MOST OF HIS TIME atop the Union of Soviet Socialist Republics, Mikhail Gorbachev preferred not to work at the Kremlin. Gorbachev regarded himself as a man of the people, and the quarters there were too formal for him. For day-to-day affairs he preferred the comparatively proletarian chambers in the nearby head-quarters of the Communist Party's Central Committee, the labyrinthine office building everyone referred to by the name of the square its edifice faced, Staraya Ploshchad. The building, set over a secret subway station designed to shuttle its staff to safer locales in the event of a nuclear attack, was decorated in the peculiarly Soviet motif of expensive materials, poorly maintained: worn wood panelling, chipped unpolished marble, ornate mouldings set onto peeling plaster in cavernously tall chambers.

One day about a year before the meeting between Yakovlev and Kalugin, KGB Chairman Vladimir Kryuchkov walked into Gorbachev's office along with Valery Boldin, Gorbachev's chief of staff. The two high-ranking Communist Party officials were there in an attempt to distance Gorbachev from his counterpart in perestroika, Aleksandr Yakovlev.

The meeting was Kryuchkov's idea. Like Yakovlev, Kryuchkov resem-bled the stereotype of the typical Soviet functionary lampooned so well by Stanley Kubrick in his film, *Dr. Strangelove*. Both shared blinking, weak eyes shielded from the external world by thick spectacles, and a propensity to clothe their soft bodies in shapeless suits. But where Yakovlev's external conformity cloaked the mind of a radical revolutionary, Kryuchkov fit the stereotype his appearance portrayed. He was the epitome of the Communist Party official, a sycophantic sort the Soviet intelligentsia disparaged as a "careerist" – sacrificing his own thoughts, his own conscience and morals, in a perpetual bid to forward his career.

In addition to running the KGB, Kryuchkov was a member of the Politburo and the de facto representative among Gorbachev's inner circle of the Soviet elite, the powerful bureaucrats in the army, the KGB and the Communist Party. The country's political system concentrated a tremendous amount of power in the hands of these men and women. The USSR was in geographic terms by far the world's largest country, encompassing one-sixth of the world's land mass and 293 million people. From the Bering Strait to the Baltic Sea, its territory sprawled across 11 different time zones. Under the tenets of communism, the state owned everything the country contained. Consequently, during the empire's 70-year history, the Party's elite, referred to as the *nomenklatura*, developed the privileges and powers of royalty, as compared with the lives of the downtrodden Soviet masses. Their lifestyle was a clear violation of the egalitarian Marxist-Leninist philosophy on which the Soviet empire had been built. The nomenklatura shopped in well-stocked stores regular Soviet citizens weren't allowed into. They vacationed in beautiful state-owned dachas. Even liberal members of this exclusive caste gloried in their privilege. "The *nomenklatura* is another planet," observed Len Karpinsky, a Yakovlev friend who belonged among their ranks until 1975, when his anti-Stalinist sentiments prompted his expulsion from the Party.

It's Mars. It's not simply a matter of good cars or apartments. It's the continuous satisfaction of your exclusivity; it's the way an army of bootlickers allows you to work for hours. All the little apparatchiks are ready to do everything for you. Your every wish is fulfilled. You can go to the theatre on a whim, you can fly to Japan from your hunting lodge. It's a life in which everything flows easily . . . You are like a king: just point your finger, and it is done.

Gorbachev and Yakovlev, as well as such reformers as the Soviet foreign minister, Eduard Shevardnadze, intended their reforms of perestroika (a Russian term that translates as "restructuring") and glasnost ("openness") to limit the power of the Communist Party. Their military spending cutbacks and nuclear arms agreements ended the Cold War. They freed the press, experimented with market reforms and introduced democratic elections; they also attempted to increase the independence of the judiciary. And they allowed formerly subservient Eastern Bloc countries such as Czechoslovakia and East Germany to decide for themselves whether they wished to remain under Soviet control. Many didn't, leading to such historic events as the toppling of the Berlin Wall on November 9, 1989. The same year, citizens throughout the whole of the Soviet Union had a hand in selecting their leaders when they voted for representatives to the Congress of People's Deputies, which, in turn, had elected Gorbachev in March 1990 as the first president of the Soviet Union.

By the time Boldin and Kryuchkov walked into Gorbachev's office, perestroika was seriously imperilling the nomenklatura's lifestyle. The nomenklatura hated the reforms. In fact, by the early months of 1990 many of these Communist Party functionaries were intent on stopping perestroika at all costs – as were millions of orthodox communists throughout the Union who regarded the reforms as a surrender to American imperialism, and a wholesale retreat from the superpower status the USSR had held since Stalin and the Great Patriotic War. Kryuchkov was a menacing leader of this conservative faction. Armed with intelligence derived from the KGB's information-gathering capabilities, which included listening devices and informants at the highest levels of the Communist Party, Kryuchkov decided on a strategy to halt perestroika: distance Gorbachev from his radically democratic advisor, Aleksandr Yakovlev.

Kryuchkov realized long before anyone in the West that Yakovlev had exceptional influence on the first president of the Soviet Union. "One of the most ominous figures of our history," Kryuchkov would later say of Yakovlev. "His main feature is exceptional secretiveness . . . " To Kryuchkov's mind, both Gorbachev and Yakovlev were to blame for perestroika. He called them the reforms' "foremen." But it's evident he placed the greater portion of the blame on Yakovlev; he portrayed Yakovlev as an "anti-Soviet" influence who successfully corrupted Gorbachev. Kryuchkov figured that if he could get Gorbachev away from Yakovlev, and his "anti-Soviet" influence, then he might be able to stop perestroika's democratizing reforms.

Once in Gorbachev's Staraya Ploshchad office, Kryuchkov revealed to the Soviet leader that he'd been investigating Yakovlev since 1989. Russians had an expression they used when someone was a nonconformist, or had beliefs that differentiated him from others: they called him a "white crow." And so far as the upper ranks of the Soviet Communist Party were concerned, Yakovlev was about as snowy a crow as it was possible to be. Unlike many high-ranking Soviets, he believed in personal freedom and self-determination. He believed in a free press and the right to artistic self-expression. And he believed a nation's laws should apply equally to all its citizens, regardless of social class or wealth.

Kryuchkov's investigation was intended to establish where Yakovlev's beliefs came from. How had this senior official come to believe in concepts and ideas that so contrasted with Communist Party dogma? Now, to Gorbachev, Kryuchkov revealed the results of the investigation: Kryuchkov said he believed Yakovlev, one of Gorbachev's best friends, was an American spy – an "agent of influence" controlled by the CIA. During their investigation, Kryuchkov and his agents had examined the whole of Yakovlev's career, from the 10 years he'd spent in Ottawa as the Soviet ambassador to Canada, to his rise though the ranks of the Communist Party in the 1960s as a speechwriter for Soviet leader Leonid Brezhnev, when he also worked as the acting head of the department of propaganda, which managed the media. The investigation turned up several interesting facts, Kryuchkov told Gorbachev. The first dated from Yakovlev's time in Canada, where the Canadian intelligence agency's dossier on Yakovlev concluded the then-ambassador "had a negative attitude toward

Moscow." The second piece of evidence, the chief said, was Yakovlev's participation in the first Cold War-era academic exchange between the United States and the Soviet Union. Back in 1958, Yakovlev had been one of 17 Soviet students selected to study at American colleges. Yakovlev attended Columbia University in New York City along with three other Soviet students. While there, he'd had improper, unsupervised encounters with American students. Far more damning, however, was the fact that one of the other Soviet students who attended Columbia with Yakovlev was the KGB traitor Oleg Kalugin.

It was too much of a coincidence for a conspiracy theorist like Kryuchkov. To him, it was clear that both Yakovlev and Kalugin had been turned by the FBI while they were studying in New York, back in 1959. Then they'd bided their time until they could be of use to the West. The story Kryuchkov peddled to Gorbachev was a Soviet version of one of history's most successful espionage rings, the Ring of Five, a group of upper-class British men who as young university students became spies for the Soviet Union, then rose to high positions within the British government, disclosing Western secrets to their KGB contacts all the while. One of them, Kim Philby, had even been in charge of the British government's anti-Soviet intelligence unit. Together, the men had been tremendously valuable sources for their Soviet masters.

Kryuchkov told Gorbachev he was convinced Yakovlev and Kalugin were potentially even more damaging to the interests of the state. In his memoirs, Kryuchkov shares Gorbachev's reaction to the news, which sounds suspiciously overblown; either Kryuchkov is exaggerating, or Gorbachev, who had a background in theatre, was displaying his acting talent. "One had to see Mikhail Sergeyevich!" Kryuchkov writes. "He was in a full confusion – he could not get in control with his feelings . . ."

"How reliable is this information?" Gorbachev asked.

"Absolutely reliable," Kryuchkov replied. "But the object of this information is so extraordinary, it should be verified one more time."

Gorbachev paced his office before Boldin and the KGB chief. "Columbia University," he mused. "Is it really that old?"

Another long silence passed. The general secretary seemed to be thinking. "Listen," he said finally. "You talk to Yakovlev. Let's see how he responds to all of this."

Kryuchkov was shocked. The response, he complained later, was characteristic of Gorbachev's inability to act decisively. The KGB chief never would confront Yakovlev with his suspicions. He didn't want to warn an American spy that he was on his trail. Instead the KGB began moving against Yakovlev in other, more duplicitous ways.

3

THE DOOMSAYER

SHORTLY AFTER Kryuchkov began trying to break up the partnership that spawned perestroika, Yakovlev walked into the Staraya Ploshchad office of Gorbachev's foreign policy advisor, Anatoly Chernyaev, to vent. Yakovlev's exterior demeanour seldom revealed his interior state. Like many who grew up under Stalin, he kept his emotions locked deep inside. But today it took only a glance at Yakovlev's furrowed brow for Chernyaev to realize that Yakovlev was agitated.

The Soviet state didn't recognize religion, so the big holidays in Moscow all had to do with historic anniversaries, such as the start of the October Revolution that birthed the Soviet Union. Speaking at such celebrations was a much-coveted honour, a mark of the power of the speaker, and Yakovlev was the longest-serving Politburo member who hadn't yet spoken at such an event. As the seventy-second anniversary of the October Revolution approached, Gorbachev knew Yakovlev had been hoping to speak at the celebration. But this event was well after Kryuchkov launched his campaign to discredit Yakovlev – and apparently the campaign was working. Rather than assigning the speech to Yakovlev, Gorbachev gave it to Kryuchkov. Soon after Yakovlev heard about Gorbachev's choice of speaker, he flew into Chernyaev's office and let loose with a rant that had been building since Gorbachev took power in March 1985.

The tirade illustrates much in the tumultuous relationship between Yakovlev and Gorbachev, who often seemed more like a bickering married couple than the world-changing duo who triggered the end of Soviet Communism. In fact, Yakovlev had been nagging Gorbachev for years to split the Communist Party in two, into a democratic and a conservative wing, as a precursor to staging democratic elections that would allow the people a direct hand in choosing the country's course. "What are you afraid of?" Yakovlev would ask Gorbachev. "It's impossible to continue the reforms with these people [the conservatives]. They have to be cut loose."

According to Chernyaev, Yakovlev began complaining to him that Gorbachev never once thanked him for his work. "I didn't even feel any gratitude from him for the fact that the idea of perestroika was born in our first conversations in Canada – back when I was ambassador."

"A friendly and trusting attitude – though not without some game playing – such were our private relations. But to publicly acknowledge my contribution?" Yakovlev continued, "Never! No way. I understand he's close to me in spirit. But he leaves a distance, doesn't want to identify with my views, either before the Politburo or Central Committee, who hate me, or before society, for this would put him in clear opposition to [such orthodox figures as] Ligachev and company. So he keeps me for personal use – to ask for suggestions, to consult with, to analyze or write something. Since perestroika began, all the Politburo members have given speeches on the anniversary of the October Revolution or Lenin's birthday. All, except me. And now again, look, he just appointed Kryuchkov, a new Politburo member, to deliver the [October Revolution] report."

And here, Yakovlev came to his point: Should he resign?

Chernyaev interpreted the question as a bluff – Yakovlev often got carried away, in the moment. But he indulged his friend all the same by treating the question seriously. Chernyaev told him that by resigning he'd just harm the reforms he'd helped Gorbachev unleash. "If you leave now, everyone will think that glasnost is over," he said.

That, at least, was what Kryuchkov was hoping. Kryuchkov was shuttling to Gorbachev anything that might serve to separate the duo behind perestroika. Kryuchkov indicated to Gorbachev that Yakovlev was preparing a putsch that would topple Gorbachev in favour of a more reform-minded leader. He indicated that Yakovlev was conspiring to take all the credit for perestroika. And he kept up his inferences that Yakovlev was spying for the CIA.

Did Gorbachev believe Kryuchkov's disinformation? Likely not; at least, he never followed up on the KGB chief's espionage charges. "I am not inclined to think that Gorbachev believed Kryuchkov's denunciations . . . But just in case, he began to be wary of me," Yakovlev wrote in his memoirs. "In essence, he delivered me into the hands of Kryuchkov, and scoundrels like him . . . they continued to whisper to him: Yakovlev is letting you down, get rid of him – and the tension in the party and society will ease."

There was a powerful irony in Kryuchkov's machinations. Kryuchkov spent the first three years of Gorbachev's leadership, from 1985 to 1988, toadying up to Yakovlev. That gambit was successful. Yakovlev became so convinced that Kryuchkov was the rare progressive official in the KGB that when Gorbachev consulted with Yakovlev about possible appointees to replace outgoing KGB chief Viktor Chebrikov, Yakovlev recommended Kryuchkov. It wasn't until Kryuchkov was firmly installed as KGB chief that he transferred his obsequious attentions from Yakovlev to Gorbachev – at Yakovlev's expense. "If I had known about Kryuchkov's duplicitous games, I would have acted in a completely different manner," Yakovlev lambasted himself later. "I would have shown the twits my mettle . . . I would have thrown out all the hesitations, doubts, and emotional stress that came from loyalty to Gorbachev . . . I trusted Gorbachev so much that I did not admit to myself even the possibility of his double game."

As Gorbachev cozied up to conservatives like Kryuchkov, Yakovlev noticed his friend consulting him less frequently. A previously unending stream of up to 150 coded memos per day dropped to 10 or 15. Gorbachev showed signs of suspicion toward Yakovlev. One day while he was mushroom hunting with his children and grandchildren, Yakovlev's car phone rang. It was Gorbachev, who sounded agitated. After Yakovlev told him where he was, Gorbachev demanded, "What are you doing there?"

"We're gathering mushrooms," Yakovlev said.

Then Gorbachev named two other powerful pro-democracy politicians, and demanded to know what they were doing in the forest with Yakovlev. Bewildered, Yakovlev said they weren't in the forest. So far as he knew, they weren't anywhere near him.

"Don't try to pull one over on me!" Gorbachev said. "I've been told they're with you. What's going on?"

"Mikhail Sergeyevich, I don't understand what you're talking about," Yakovlev insisted, finally realizing Gorbachev thought that Yakovlev was planning his own putsch. "It's very easy for you to check up on who is where. And your informant probably should be taken to the woodshed – and you should think about why he's provoking you."

The covert campaign against Yakovlev grew more serious in November 1990, as he was among the leaders arguing against the use of force to control such increasingly independence-minded Soviet republics as Lithuania and Latvia. One day Yakovlev's 37-year-old son, Anatoly, boarded a commuter train several hours outside of Moscow, intending to return from a visit with his daughter, who worked as a restorer at a nearby monastery. As the train was pulling from the station, Anatoly bent down to tie his shoelaces and heard a sharp crack. It was only after he straightened and noticed the spidery pattern of broken glass through windows on both sides of the train that he realized someone had just shot at him. Anatoly told police and his father, who interpreted the incident as a warning from the KGB. "It was a sign for me," the elder Yakovlev told his son. "If they had meant to kill you, they would have."

All of these episodes were taking place amid an empire-wide orthodox communist counterrevolution targeting perestroika. Protesters at anti-democracy demonstrations accused Yakovlev of working for the usual Soviet bugaboos, such as "Zionists" and "Masons." Echoing Kryuchkov, they also said he was working for the Americans. In an apparent reference to the Anatoly incident, one particularly chilling placard bore the elder Yakovlev's face with a target emblazoned over it, and the proclamation "This time we won't miss!"

The situation grew overtly murderous in mid-January 1991, when the KGB's elite Alfa commando force responded to independence demonstrations in the Lithuanian capital of Vilnius by attacking the state broadcasting centre, killing 13 and wounding 604. If the operation lacked Gorbachev's express assent, the leader was implicated in the aftermath for failing to punish Kryuchkov, or anyone in the KGB, for the bloodshed. The incident encouraged what little democratic support Gorbachev had to migrate to other, more liberal Russian leaders, such as Boris Yeltsin.

At the end of January, Gorbachev once again appealed to Yakovlev for advice. "What should we do?" Gorbachev asked. "Radicals on one side, social democrats on the other, and while their destructive pounding continues the economy keeps worsening and people are stretched to the limit . . . " Yakovlev was also feeling the pressure. His health was suffering. He was hospitalized for high blood pressure and other cardiac ailments. But he counselled Gorbachev to quit stalling, to continue the revolution the two men had started just five years before. And when Gorbachev balked, Yakovlev did what he had done throughout his friend's leadership. He encouraged him to think more radically. After all, Yakovlev said, "That's what revolutions are all about!"

Gorbachev didn't listen. In March 1991, when a pro-Yeltsin demonstration stood to attract hundreds of thousands of people to Moscow's city centre, Yakovlev begged Gorbachev not to repress the protest, but Gorbachev insisted, saying he had heard – from Kryuchkov, Yakovlev believed – that the demonstrators would attempt to storm the walls of the Kremlin with hooks attached to long ropes, the way medieval soldiers might once have attacked a castle. Shortly after Yakovlev recounted the rumour to one of the demonstration's leaders, Moscow mayor Gavriil Popov. "That's ridiculous," Popov exclaimed. Then, in a reference to the empty store shelves across Russia, he said, "Where would we get the rope?"

On March 28, the day of the Yeltsin demonstration, approximately 50,000 military troops and a sizable contingent of plainclothes KGB operatives flooded into Moscow in a bid to intimidate the demonstration, which nevertheless attracted a peaceful turnout of more than

150,000 people, none of whom were reported to have attempted to scale the Kremlin walls. The military presence was, for Yakovlev, yet another sign that the orthodox Communist Party functionaries were attempting to erase the effects of perestroika. He'd lived through a similar process before, in the 1960s, when Khrushchev's thaw gave way to Brezhnev's stagnant police state. As in the past, the process made him heartsick.

By mid-1991, Gorbachev was hoping to save perestroika, and the Soviet Union, with a "Union Treaty" that transferred some of Moscow's power to such republics as Belarus and Ukraine. Russia had previously been a kind of "Big Brother" to the other republics, in the Orwellian rather than fraternal sense. Yakovlev repeatedly warned Gorbachev that the conservatives would rather start a civil war, or stage some other sort of coup, before they allowed the treaty to take effect. Each time, Gorbachev ignored him. Yakovlev even took his concerns public. "These are toadies," Yakovlev told David Remnick, an American journalist. "They will look at you with these honest blue eyes and say, 'We're with the people, we're your only saviors, the only ones who love and respect you.'"

But Kryuchkov's scheming had worked. By this time Gorbachev no longer accepted Yakovlev's counsel; Yakovlev characterized his situation as isolation; he was an advisor to a man who neither sought, nor acted on, his advice. Despite the leader's protests, Yakovlev resigned in July as Gorbachev's senior advisor. "The people around you are rotten. Please, finally, understand this," Yakovlev told Gorbachev just before he left. "You exaggerate," Gorbachev replied.

Finally, Yakovlev did himself what he had long suggested Gorbachev do: he turned his back on the Communist Party and founded a new political organization, along with Eduard Shevardnadze and about 20 other leaders of the Soviet democracy movement, called the Movement for Democratic Reforms. In retaliation, the Communist Party announced its intention to expel Yakovlev, a move Yakovlev countered by releasing a letter announcing his resignation from the party he'd belonged to for almost a half-century, since 1943. That letter, dated on Saturday, August 16, 1991, contained yet another warning of the approaching coup.

THE PUTSCH

EARLY THE MORNING OF Monday, August 19, 1991 one week after Yakovlev's meeting with Kalugin, the telephone rang in the Yakovlev apartment. Nina, Yakovlev's wife, was the first to wake and pick up the receiver.

"Is Aleksandr Nikolaevich available?" asked the voice on the other end, referring to Yakovlev by his first name and patronymic, a Russian sign of respect.

Nina looked over at her husband. Then she looked at the clock. It read 6:20 a.m.

"No," Nina said. "He's still asleep."

"Listen," the voice said. "Do you know there's a coup taking place?" The voice identified himself. It was Kalugin, and he suggested they turn on the radio. Nina handed the phone to her husband.

"Oleg, what is it you're saying?"

"There's a coup – it's on the radio."

Yakovlev had been predicting it for months, of course. But sometimes a prediction proven right is difficult to believe, even for the sage who made it.

"Are you sober?" Yakovlev asked Kalugin.

"Soberer than sober."

Yakovlev thought a moment. What he said next was as much for his sake as Kalugin's. He said, "We must be prepared for anything."

The radio was broadcasting a statement by Gorbachev's nominal second-in-command, Vice-President Gennady Yanaev: "In connection with the inability for health reasons of Mikhail Sergeyevich Gorbachev to perform the duties of the President of the USSR, effective 19 August 1991 I have assumed the duties of the President . . . " This was nonsense, of course. Gorbachev and his family were under house arrest at their vacation compound in the Crimea, their phone lines cut to prevent contact with the outside world. Behind the coup was KGB chief Kryuchkov and seven of his fellow hard-line Communist Party conservatives, including the strategically important minister of defence and minister of the interior, who, along with the KGB, controlled the Soviet military capability.

The irony was that these were Gorbachev's men. During the last year he had relied on their advice as he ignored the counsel of such liberal reformers as Yakovlev and Shevardnadze. But Gorbachev's politicking had backfired on him. Weeks before, at a meeting at his dacha, with Yeltsin and others, Gorbachev agreed to Yeltsin's demand to fire Kryuchkov. Unbeknownst to Gorbachev, the KGB man in charge of the Soviet leader's protection had the room bugged. The information made its way to Kryuchkov, who couldn't allow his job to evaporate. Hence the coup.

At Yakovlev's apartment, the first hours of August 19 passed amid an atmosphere of danger. They checked the television: instead of normal programming, Tchaikovsky's *Swan Lake* came over the airwaves. Family and friends gathered and reported that columns of tanks and armoured personnel carriers were entering the city. One visitor reported that KGB vehicles were parked on either side of the Yakovlev's apartment building. The phone rang with journalists requesting interviews. "I feel shame for my country," Yakovlev told them. "For the fact that it has been possible, this kind of primitive, medieval happening, this coup." Everyone expected some sort of assassination attempt from the KGB. Yakovlev's daughter, Nataliya, wanted to spirit him out of Moscow in a little Lada she brought for the purpose. His son, Anatoly, argued hiding would serve no purpose. The KGB would track him down. If Yakovlev was going to go down, Anatoly argued, he should go down fighting.

Then Yakovlev noticed his nine-year-old grandson, Sergei, tying bottles and jars to the apartment's entryway. "As soon as someone starts to open the door, we'll hear it," the young boy said. Rather than hiding under a bed somewhere, Sergei was devising defensive measures to warn the apartment's occupants of intruders. Soon the adults also found their fight. Yakovlev got in touch with Russian President Boris Yeltsin, who helped to dispatch to the Yakovlev's apartment a heavily-armed detachment of Spetsnaz, special-purpose troops loyal to the democracy side. The KGB vehicles left soon after the troops' arrival. For the moment Yakovlev was safe.

The first task was to determine for themselves what was happening. Yakovlev and 38-year-old Anatoly snuck out of the apartment building and into a family friend's Lada – a little wreck of a car chosen for the fact that it was unremarkable. Together the two men drove around the city, to get some sense of the prevailing mood. In the main public squares, anti-coup protesters set up traffic blockades by flattening the tires of city buses and trolleys, or other trucks and cars, to prevent the troops from controlling the key access points. Elsewhere, Yakovlev happened to pull up alongside a tank. He asked the young, bored-looking tank commander whether he would fire on the Russian people. "No," the boy said. "And besides, we don't have any ammo." The next stop was the Mossovet, Moscow City Hall, where members of the Movement for Democratic Reform were gathering to plot strategy. But it soon became apparent that the centre of anti-coup force was the majestic, marble-clad White House, the seat of Russia's democratically elected parliament. By the time Yakovlev arrived at the White House, the building was ringed with a ridge of urban debris, a barrier constructed of buses and concrete and scrap wood that aimed to protect the activists from the Red Army's tanks. Thousands ringed the building. Yakovlev would have to push through a thick throng to get to the barrier, climb it, and then push through more people to get to the White House. It would have been difficult for a healthy man. For Yakovlev, whose one leg was fused straight at the knee thanks to an old war wound, it would have been impossible.

The crowd recognized him. Word spread that Yakovlev had arrived, and the crowd parted to provide a path for the limping old man, a veteran who started his fighting career as one of Stalin's soldiers, in the Second World War, only to become one of the rare high-ranking Communist Party officials to turn against the political system Stalin represented. Once he reached the barrier dozens of people cooperated to give him a hand, a boost, anything to get the famous reformer over the hill of cars and debris. Soon he was inside the building and helping Yeltsin, the Russian president, stave off the forces of conservatism and repression.

They wrote declarations. They gave speeches. They issued statements to the media and called for a national strike. As far as coups went, this one was poorly planned – more Marx Brothers than Marxist-Leninist, newspapers quipped. But it was less the quality of protest than the fact there was protest at all. Kryuchkov and his cronies seemed not to have expected any opposition; if they did expect opposition, they certainly didn't expect the protesters to be willing to risk their lives for freedom.

Later, people would debate the exact moment the coup failed. Some said Kryuchkov lost his nerve. Others, that Yeltsin made some sort of backroom deal with the KGB. What is certain is that Kryuchkov and his associates made a bet that the Russian people would accept the illegal attempt to seize power the same way they'd tolerated 70 years of Bolshevik rule. Kryuchkov lost that bet. At various times on August 20, the crowd protecting the White House is estimated to have numbered up to 100,000. They weren't just protecting Yeltsin, Yakovlev, and the other politicians, they were protecting Russia's first, tentative steps toward democracy.

By Tuesday's end, tank detachments were overrun with Russian babushkas bringing food to the troops inside and beseeching them not to shoot their guns. During the standoff, news filtered in from St. Petersburg, Russia's second-largest city, that the city centre was thick with protesters, with troops avoiding any confrontation. At one point, one of the conspirators appeared on television drunk. Particularly key was the signal from two generals, one from the army, one in the KGB, that soldiers needn't obey orders from the putschists. The coup essentially dissolved on the third day, when Kryuchkov and his henchmen flew to Gorbachev's vacation compound in an attempt to convince the leader to support them. Gorbachev declined. Realizing his was a lost cause, Kryuchkov capitulated. He was imprisoned along with most of his other conspirators. One of his associates shot himself before he could be arrested, the first of several suicides among them.

Gorbachev returned home to Moscow at 2 a.m. on Thursday. He seemed stunned as he descended his airplane's staircase. His wife had to be helped down the steps. Rather than going straight to the White House, where hordes of people awaited his appearance, Gorbachev went home to care for his family. It wasn't until later that day, at a press conference, that Gorbachev demonstrated how out of step he was with the rest of the country. Public opinion considered the Communist Party leadership to be almost as culpable as Kryuchkov in the coup; after all, many of the Party's top members supported Kryuchkov. Gorbachev didn't seem to realize that. At the press conference he signalled his intention to "reform" the Party. "You have given the worst press conference of your career," said Yakovlev, who returned to Gorbachev's side as an advisor soon after his return. "The Party is dead. Why can't you see that? Talking about its 'renewal' is senseless. It's like offering first-aid to a corpse!"

Gorbachev was forced to confront the Party's duplicity the next day. At a session of the Russian parliament Yeltsin forced him to read aloud the minutes of a meeting in which many of his closest associates in the Party came out in support of the coup. Chastened, Gorbachev agreed to resign as the Communist Party's general secretary. The Party that had used cruelty and violence to rule the country for more than 70 years underwent several other humiliations that day, including the banning of such party newspapers as *Pravda* and the dissolution of its ruling Central Committee. At the televised meeting where these events occurred, Gorbachev later noted that he caught several of his associates "gloating." He mentioned only two of them by name: Boris Yeltsin and Aleksandr Yakovlev. Four months later, at midnight on December 31, 1991, as a direct result of the policies Yakovlev pushed Gorbachev to institute, the Soviet Union ceased to exist.

PART

2

QUESTIONS

1939–1973

5

"THE BLOW THAT EXPLODED MY HEAD"

IN THE INTRODUCTION to Yakovlev's *A Century of Violence in Soviet Russia*, University of Massachusetts professor Paul Hollander marvels over the ideological transformation Yakovlev experienced during his life. As Hollander wrote, "It is hard to think of any other Communist official of comparable rank and distinction who so explicitly, sweepingly, and powerfully repudiated the system he was a part of." That's true. Yakovlev was until well into his thirties an enthusiastic supporter of Stalin. But by the time he turned 60 he was whispering revolution into Gorbachev's ear – a revolution that ultimately would disassemble the state Stalin killed so many to build.

What happened in between? How did Aleksandr Yakovlev evolve from Stalin's acolyte to Stalinism's nemesis? Was Kryuchkov correct – was Yakovlev, in fact, an American spy who brilliantly betrayed the Communist Party? In a word, no. Despite his harnessing the full resources of the KGB, Kryuchkov was never able to establish any but the most circumstantial of evidence linking Yakovlev and the CIA. Nor did Yakovlev's ideological evolution begin during the year he spent studying at Columbia University in 1958–59. In fact, Yakovlev's about-face follows a more complicated and interesting chronology than Kryuchkov imagined. It also suggests valuable lessons for policy makers in today's fraught international climate. It begins 17 years earlier than Kryuchkov alleged, in the marshland surrounding the city then known as Leningrad, during the fight against the Nazis that the Russians call the Great Patriotic War.

HITLER'S FORCES INVADED an unprepared Soviet Union on June 22, 1941, just three days after Yakovlev's family and friends threw the 17-year-old young man a party to celebrate his school graduation. Weeks later, on August 6, 1941, the Soviet military called up Yakovlev. Recruiters shunted him into the naval infantry – the marines, basically – and from there to officer training school, where he excelled at marksmanship and passed his eighteenth birthday on December 2. ""We hid our sense of doom with bravado, songs, boastful audacity, and inane arguments about how quickly we would defeat those fascists," Yakovlev recalls of this period. "But we were sick in our boyish hearts, and at night we dreamed of our mothers."

Eight weeks after his birthday, Yakovlev learned he had performed well enough in the course to become one of the rare trainees to earn the rank of lieutenant. The February after his graduation, Yakovlev travelled to a snowy military base in Chuvash, 700 kilometres east of Moscow, to meet the platoon under his command. He was by any estimate an unlikely commanding officer. He was born in 1923 to a Russian peasant couple who lived in a series of rural settlements set in the pine forests around the ancient city of Yaroslavl, about a five-hour drive northwest of Moscow. Yakovlev had been so sickly as an infant his parents waited for two years to register his birth. His father, Nikolai Alekseyevich Yakovlev, was a logger who fought for the Bolsheviks in the Russian Revolution; his mother, born Agafya Mikhailovna Lyapoushkina, was an illiterate homemaker devoted to the Orthodox church and subscribing to the peasant notion that too much learning could drive a person mad. She was also tough, bringing up Yakovlev and his three younger sisters in an era when that job also meant tending to such family livestock as a cow or a goat, as well as to the small garden that provided the family with vegetables. Skinny but broad-shouldered, Yakovlev grew into a headstrong youth whose playground was the wooded hills and valleys of the Kotorosl River, a tributary of the Upper Volga. In adolescence he turned studious. Rather than playing sports he was more inclined to devour the classics of Russian literature, or write poetry in attempts to woo female classmates. What would serve him well in the military, however, was his democratic spirit, a sense of equality among men he would later speculate he inherited from Nikolai, who, unusually for a Russian peasant, avoided physically disciplining his son. The only time Nikolai spanked young Aleksandr, so far as Yakovlev could recall, happened after the boy and his friends spent an afternoon swimming, then, to dry their clothing, set a fire and accidentally incinerated their shirts and pants. The spanking happened after Nikolai caught Aleksandr scampering homeward through the woods outside the family home, totally naked.

The platoon commanded by this poetry-writing lieutenant consisted of about 30 Chuvash peasants, surly, inexperienced, and, frighteningly middle-aged – Yakovlev was by several years the youngest man in his platoon. Most of the men were 15 or 20 years older than their commanding officer. They didn't speak much Russian. And none of them had ever before served in the military. They obeyed Yakovlev's orders, but with irony, with smiles or expressions that suggested their compliance was only an indulgence. Worse, any leadership skill Yakovlev had was corrupted because he was forced to act as a conduit for the absurdities of war. Fashioning his charges into lethal warriors entailed teaching them how to handle firearms, for example – a difficult task, considering that a weapons shortage meant the soldiers didn't have any guns. Much of training was spent slithering on elbows and knees across frozen fields.

After their training in Chuvash and a day's worth of travelling by rail, Yakovlev mustered his men at a camp 16 kilometres from the city of Leningrad, now St. Petersburg. It was March of 1942, and this was the front. Novel sensations replaced the boredom that plagued the soldiers during their training. The German artillery graced the sky with a dramatic theatre of flash and fire serenaded by the rumble of artillery fire. When that grew stale the soldiers occupied themselves figuring out how to stay warm. The area's low-lying land and umpteen bodies of water meant winter's usual snow and ice had a dampness that crept up sleeves and down collars, bringing the men to the verge of frostbite.

Soon a dense cube of a man approached Yakovlev's unit. He introduced himself as Commissar Pyotr Ksenz. He examined them – a group of dull-eyed grunts led by a kid barely out of high school, a lanky, bookish, thin-framed lieutenant with a ruddy complexion and a buzzcut. Ksenz barked at Yakovlev's men to wipe the snot from their noses. Then he provided the unit with their name, their mission, and their weapons. They were the third platoon of "submachine-gunners" under Ksenz's command in the 6th Separate Naval Infantry Brigade. Leningrad was surrounded and under siege by the Nazis, who were dug into the marshland around the city. Like the rest of the Soviet's Baltic fleet, it was the mission of Ksenz's brigade to attempt to break through Nazi lines before the Soviet citizens still inside the city died from starvation and cold.

Conditions for the Soviet infantry were harsh and unforgiving. Stalin forbade any soldier from being captured. Retreats, too, were forbidden. Yakovlev belonged to a brigade with a reputation for bravery that verged on insanity. Their nickname was Black Death. Ksenz assigned Yakovlev's platoon the function of probing, of reconnaissance – a suicidal form of hide-and-seek that saw them creep across mine-thick frozen marsh to locate Nazi machine gun nests and fortifications. Sometimes Yakovlev's men saw the Nazis first, and in those cases they tried to kill the enemy with sniper rifles. Other times, it was the Nazis who found the third platoon, and then Yakovlev and his men relied on their semi-automatic rifles to shoot their way back to camp. Sometimes Yakovlev returned with only half his men, the other half left on winter's battlefield to freeze solid and disappear under the snow, forming anonymous hillocks. Insubordination remained a problem until after the brigade's intelligence section assigned the young lieutenant a sensitive mission. They gave him a map, showed him a young woman, and explained he was to select a squad of his best men to help him spirit the woman to a certain cemetery behind the Nazi lines. And if something happened to her before they accomplished the mission, the intelligence people said, Yakovlev might as well shoot himself rather than return, because his punishment would be execution.

The cemetery was several day's hike away. They travelled only under cover of night. When it was light they hunkered into bush or grove and rested. Once they made it to their destination, the young woman gave Yakovlev a code word meant to indicate the mission's success, and then the squad of Soviet soldiers promptly got lost. Conscious of being surrounded by Nazis, the men hissed whispers at each other as they squabbled about which direction to go. Yakovlev was the ranking officer. He also was the youngest among them. His word didn't carry much weight. But once he spent some time with the map and the compass, he became confident he knew which direction was safe. It took a while to convince the men, but Yakovlev was able to lead the group to almost the exact spot they'd set out from days before. The feat earned him the respect of his men.

The winter of 1942 broke and the warmer weather melted the swamp's frozen topography. Snowdrifts dissolved to reveal long-dead faces and broken bodies. Their wounds sometimes weren't apparent, so that Yakovlev found his battlefield disturbing as much for its landscape as for the violence that happened there. The dead soldiers seemed "on the verge of getting up from the ground, smiling, and beginning to talk," he said in his memoirs. Through the previous months the survivors tried to forget the dead; now, with the thaw, the dead returned, as lifelike as the living.

"Who sent them to their death? Why were they killed? For what sins?" Yakovlev wondered. "I imagined myself lying under the snow all winter long . . . Before this incident, everything was somehow different: we fired, they fired. We hunted people and I was part of it, in the firing line with the sniper rifles. And then the war was turned to me with its young face, already dead. It was awful." Did he recognize a friend, a fallen comrade, or perhaps, an enemy dead from his own bullet? Yakovlev doesn't say. He says only it was this image that triggered his life-long hatred of violence – this image, and the associated memories of creeping through mine-sown spring muck amid a winter's worth of accumulated death. For months, images of spring's lifelike corpses would plague him whenever he pulled his trigger. Years later, the antipathy for violence they provoked would lead Yakovlev to dissuade Gorbachev, and more aggressive members of the Politburo, from using force to maintain Soviet control over breakaway Eastern European republics. Of the image of spring's recently thawed fallen soldiers, Yakovlev wrote, "That was the blow that exploded my head."

But the war was unavoidable. Through summer, Yakovlev's mind ignored the horror around him to focus on survival. He grew to respect Commissar Ksenz as a man who treated his soldiers fairly, regardless of rank. In turn, Ksenz grew to appreciate Yakovlev's bravery; the commanding officer presented the young lieutenant with a Walther pistol as thanks. The skirmishes dissolved into one another. So did the men; Yakovlev's platoon suffered more than 90 casualties, requiring reinforcements many times over. Then one foggy morning in August 1942, Yakovlev became a war hero.

His platoon joined a mission to blast a hole through the Germans' Leningrad ring. The plan was for the Soviet artillery to distract the enemy machine gunners while Yakovlev and the other infantry crept toward the nests on the ground. A pair of flares would signal the end of the artillery barrage, and the Soviet marines would sprint forward and overrun the Nazi positions before the enemy machine guns could cut everyone down. On the mission's eve Yakovlev and the other soldiers drank themselves to sleep with their hoarded vodka rations. They woke hours later, hung over. A thick mist obscured the 150 metres of swampland separating their camp from the German positions. If they began the mission immediately, the mist would cover their approach, allowing the Soviet soldiers to sneak toward the German fortifications unseen by sentries or lookouts. But as the sun rose the mist began to lift. The result was a strange weather effect: a narrow, clear band in which everything – tree branches, swamp reeds – seemed to have a heightened fidelity. Yakovlev and another junior officer rushed to the major overseeing the mission. If they attacked immediately, Yakovlev urged, the Soviets would retain the advantage. Because the Germans were on higher ground they were blinded by the mist. If the fog lifted any farther, the Soviet force would be slaughtered. But the major wouldn't take advice from a younger officer. By the time he got around to ordering the artillery to begin their barrage, the fog was gone.

Yakovlev directed a sergeant and a half-dozen infantrymen to the platoon's left flank, to provide covering fire, while he led the rest of the men on their messy, awkward approach. The whistle and thuds of the artillery were constant. Mines littered the ground. Yakovlev and his men duck-walked and crawled their way across the bog, slapping at gnats and other flying insects. If pools blocked their progress, they put their guns above their heads and waded through the stagnant water.

When the attack flares hissed above, 30 metres separated Yakovlev's platoon from the German line. Had they attacked hours before, when Yakovlev wanted, the fog could have protected them. Now in the clear air of daytime there was nothing to do but charge. Masking their fear in roared aggression, Yakovlev and his men surged forward. After just a few steps Yakovlev was down.

He was hit by four bullets – three shattered the bones around his knee. One punctured his ribcage and stayed lodged in his lungs. Some of the men tried to drag him back. Several of them were also shot. One succeeded in pulling the lieutenant clear. Yakovlev rode in a wagon on the eight-kilometre ride to the brigade hospital, passing out each time the wagon hit a bump. What followed was a long and painful journey away from the front, by train and army plane, to a larger hospital that could perform the surgery Yakovlev required. But by that point, days had passed and the skin around Yakovlev's leg wounds was black with gangrene. An attending medic decided his leg would have to be amputated. A drugged Yakovlev signed a paper consenting to have it removed at the hip. They pulled him into the operating theatre – a canvas tent that accommodated several different surgeries at once. The last thing Yakovlev remembered before the anaesthetic took effect was a different doctor, a surgeon, asking him how old he was.

"Eighteen," he replied.

"You," the surgeon said, "have some dancing yet to do."

When Yakovlev woke the first thing he did was to look down at the space left by his absent limb. There was a cast where there was supposed to be nothing. And poking out from the end of the white cast, like a dis-coloured cherry on a vanilla ice cream sundae, was a single, pale yellow bulb. It was Yakovlev's big toe – and he could move it.

A few minutes later, the surgeon paid him a visit. He gave Yakovlev's toe a tug. "Does it hurt?" the surgeon asked.

Yakovlev shook his head.

The surgeon smiled. "You're going to dance," he promised.

During surgery, instead of cutting off the limb, the surgeon cleaned out the infected tissue and fused together Yakovlev's knee joint, leaving him with a leg that was permanently locked straight. For the rest of his life, Yakovlev's gait had a hitch to it. He had to prop up his leg when he sat. And the bullet in his chest stayed there, sealed up in his lung, for the rest of his life. He was lucky; half his platoon had died in the battle. For Yakovlev's service, Commissar Ksenz recommended Yakovlev for the Order of the Red Banner, the Soviet state's second-highest mil-itary decoration after the rarely given Order of Lenin. He also received the more common decoration for valour, the Order of the Red Star. Ksenz demoted the major for not taking advantage of the fog. For years afterward Yakovlev would regret losing, along with the rest of his posses-sions as he travelled from the front, the Walther pistol Ksenz had given to him. Not because he wanted the firearm; after the war, he vowed never again to fire another weapon. Rather, Yakovlev considered the pistol as a memento of Commissar Ksenz, whose fairness would guide Yakovlev's sense of justice for the rest of his life.

YAKOVLEV LEFT THE HOSPITAL in February 1943. He travelled by train to Yaroslavl equipped with crutches and a knapsack of canned food. He caught a ride from a car owner happy to help a returning veteran. He crutched across his front yard and into the back, where he found his mother toting a pair of pails from the barn where they kept chickens and their single cow. The pails dropped. Next came the tears. Her reaction was partly one of relief. Yakovlev's father had also joined the war; the latest word from the front had him in a military hospital somewhere, fighting a nasty case of purulent pleurisy he'd picked up on a frigid battlefield. Now Agafya had one of her men back. Another part was worry. She was struggling to feed three daughters. How could she manage to provide for another dependant, as Yakovlev, with his crutches and war wounds, seemed to be?

Like everyone except elite Party officials, Agafya had had a brutal time during the war. Stalin had directed the nation's harvests to feed the military; what remained after that went to the cities. Practically nothing was left for the people like Agafya and Yakovlev's sisters, in the countryside. Anyone caught holding back a beet or an ear of corn for their own family's use was shot for crimes against the state. Fighting starvation, Yakovlev's mother had been forced to creep at night into the fields to dig through furrows in search of overlooked potatoes.

Once the first flush of their reunion passed, Yakovlev and his mother argued. Agafya tried to encourage her son to sign on at the local distillery, where workers received extra agricultural waste from the distillery process – precious food for the cow. But Yakovlev worried that his infirmities would prevent him from making a living as a labourer. He wanted to attend college, to learn a profession. He applied to Moscow State University and the Gorky Shipbuilding Institute, both of which turned him down for health reasons; they thought him too frail. Yakovlev ended up attending the Yaroslavl Pedagogical Institute, where the deputy director encouraged him to study history. The war's demand for soldiers meant Yakovlev was one of only five male students among a class of 1,200. The attention from the female students leavened the discomfort caused by Yakovlev's meagre student stipend, which allowed for only one meal a day. He began the laborious process of joining the Communist Party in 1943, and the following year his marks won him a Stalin

Scholarship, which increased his stipend fourfold; now he was able to send some money home. He also lucked into a job heading the school's department of military and physical training, putting the 21-year-old into the role of head gym teacher for hundreds of similarly aged girls, and earning him more help financially.

He began dating a young woman named Nina Smirnova, another student at the university. She was a good-looking girl, confident, intelligent and such a good dancer that she won prizes for her waltz. Yakovlev serenaded her with songs he wrote himself. He wrote her poetry. And when the war ended on May 9, 1945, the pair were caught up in the mass delirium that greeted peace. Yakovlev called the Soviet people's reaction to the news "a thunderstorm in May"; it created a roar that rivalled the noise of the shelling that had plagued them for four years.

The war exacted a terrible toll on the Motherland. An estimated 26 million Soviet citizens perished. Many were killed by the Nazis; many others froze to death or died of starvation. Both sides conducted scorched-earth retreats, when they burned everything in the territory they left to prevent the enemy from gaining supplies. Thousands of towns and tens of thousands of villages were incinerated. Along the front, literally nothing remained.

As bad as things were, the postwar years were marked with a near-universal optimism. In beating the fascists the Soviets demonstrated the superiority of their society to any other. Propaganda proclaimed that no other country had single-handedly defeated the Germans. Yakovlev shared in his countrymen's patriotic fervour. Four months after the war ended, on September 8, 1945, on a day marked by gentle rain, Yakovlev married Nina. The highlight of the ceremony was the surprise return of his father, whom Yakovlev hadn't seen for four years.

War proved a formative experience for Yakovlev, particularly because, at 17, he was younger than most when he joined the fight. War provided Yakovlev with a confidence born of surviving overwhelming danger with wit and luck. It gave him a standing in society and shaped many of the beliefs that would guide him for the rest of his life. He was a killer who resolved never again to kill, or even to sponsor violence. Similarly, war

helped develop his sense of fairness, his belief in the overarching sanctity of justice among all human values. War also introduced Yakovlev to
the notion that Stalin's system was fallible; indeed, that it could commit
injustice. Three separate incidents confirmed this perception. The first
happened on the battlefield, where the lieutenant from Yaroslavl witnessed the unfairness of the Soviet system for rewarding war heroes.
Drunken commanders whose mistakes sacrificed half their units earned
medals for bravery, for surviving bloodbaths caused by their own short-
sighted mistakes, while canny officers whose sober planning allowed
them to execute missions without loss of life went unrecognized.

The second incident Yakovlev heard about soon after he arrived
home. It had happened to his mother during one of the war's long,
hungry nights. The family's sheep pulled up the stake to which it was
tied and wandered into a field, where it gnawed on a few precious
heads of cabbage. For not securing her animal properly, and allowing
food to be wasted, Agafya was hauled into court. She narrowly escaped
imprisonment. When Yakovlev heard about this episode he was troubled. Surely, he wondered, it couldn't be right to treat struggling
people so harshly?

But the injustice that most troubled Yakovlev came to him as a
rumour in the months following war's end. Friends whispered about
certain locomotives with special freight moving through northern Russia
at night. Apparently one could spy these mystery trains at a certain local
station. Curious, Yakovlev went one evening, to see for himself, and was
treated to a sight straight out of Dante. Belching steam, a locomotive
rolled into Vspolye station to refuel while great masses of women went
up and down the cinder-strewn tracks intoning the names of the lost –
of husbands and brothers and fathers they hadn't seen for years. They
directed their attention at the boxcars, slat-sided compartments of wood
and steel, and as soon as the women pressed forward, small objects began
falling from the gaps between the slats. The boxcars seemed to be leaking
little balls of cotton. Yakovlev limped forward through the women. He
bent and picked up what turned out to be a scrunched-up piece of paper.
On it was a man's name and an address. Yakovlev picked up another,

then another, and discovered to his dismay that these mounting drifts were built of messages from men who were believed to be dead. Each message was a request to send word to a certain scrawled address that Alekei or Ivan or Sergei was still alive and wrongly imprisoned. Yakovlev looked up into the car's black interior – and saw himself.

Crowded into these freight cars were Soviet prisoners of war. The prisoners were the result of a controversial agreement Stalin had made with British Prime Minister Winston Churchill and American President Franklin Roosevelt at Yalta, in the war's dying days. The agreement required the Allies to return all Soviet citizens found in European prisoner of war camps to the USSR. Some of these men and women, aware of the repressions Stalin committed against the Soviet people, had fought on the side of the Germans. But the vast majority were former Soviet soldiers. Like Yakovlev, these men had fought along the front. Like Yakovlev, they were wounded, but not killed. Rather than being pulled from battle by their comrades, these men were captured by the Nazis, who herded them into large concentration camps and slave-labour facilities in Germany, where the survivors kept alive with hopes of reuniting with their wives, girlfriends, sons, daughters, parents. They celebrated the end of war like everyone else.

But then Stalin decided that the Soviet citizens taken prisoner by the Nazis weren't trustworthy. They might contain spies. They might have been infected with dangerous, foreign ideas. History provided Stalin with a lesson here. The officers from the Russian Imperial Army who occupied Paris after the Napoleonic Wars returned to Russia intent on reform, later triggering the Decembrist Revolt. In Stalin's threat-obsessed mind, the soldiers who weren't traitors before they were captured certainly would be once they mixed with prisoners from such capitalist nations as Britain and France.

So Stalin's secret police, the NKVD, scoured the work camps seeking Soviet soldiers. When they found someone who spoke Russian they convinced the soldier to return by painting utopian visions of impending reunions with families and loved ones. But as this postwar harvest moved by train from Europe to the Motherland, the secret police halted its progress at so-called filtration camps where the prisoners were required to fill out forms and undergo interrogation designed to separate the traitors from the faithful Bolsheviks. Anyone who seemed remotely suspicious was transferred to a work camp while the secret police investigated their cases. More than 400,000 citizens were imprisoned in these camps. When the filtration camp system was disbanded, in January 1946, 228,000 were detained "for further investigation" – a euphemism that, for some, meant forced labour and sometimes death in the Gulag.

Before the war, perhaps Yakovlev would have convinced himself that the cattle cars contained genuine traitors, and attributed his doubts to a misunderstanding of the way things worked. But the war had changed him. He had a confidence now, a belief in his ability to reason and an awareness that people in positions of authority could make mistakes. As he stood on the train platform surrounded by the names and addresses of POW-camp survivors now headed for the Gulag, Yakovlev wondered whether only luck had allowed him to avoid capture by the Germans as he lay wounded in the marsh outside Leningrad. Whether only luck had separated his lot from that of the soldiers who would remain prisoners long after war's end. "These were the first serious cracks in my heart, the first disappointments," Yakovlev wrote in his memoirs. "Like sulfuric acid, they ate away my dogmatic beliefs, slowly, but relentlessly."

6

THE SECRET SPEECH

CRISES OF FAITH are funny things. Take religious faith. Christians, Muslims, Jews, believers of all stripes and creeds can proceed through their lives weathering an awareness of famine and war, the injustices of nature-created catastrophes, the carnage of terrorist attacks. One's faith can endure the death of a spouse, a child, a parent. Then, thanks to an aligning of external circumstance and personal situation, some sequence of events prompts a comprehensive re-examination of a long-held belief system. In Yakovlev's case such an alignment didn't occur until more than 10 years after the war's end. Then, when it did happen, its effect was altogether different from what one might expect.

For Yakovlev, the decade between war and crisis of faith featured its share of evidence that the system was flawed. But it's a long way from a belief in the perfection of a system to a conviction that the whole system is corrupt. Party propaganda convinced Yakovlev and most others of the intellectual superiority of Stalin and the rest of the nation's leadership. This was a remarkably effective psychological tool that perpetuated Yakovlev's idealistic fervour until he rose to a position where he had first-hand access to the country's leaders. While he remained a relatively junior party member in the Russian provinces far from Moscow, he was able to dismiss most injustices he saw. He might not understand why an apparently unfair policy was necessary, but the Party's leaders plainly did, and they were smarter than him. Yakovlev passed the postwar decade confident in the glorious leaders' benevolent concern for the well-being of the Soviet citizenry, and the Party's capability to steer the superior system of Marxist-Leninist socialism on a course toward a workers' paradise. "What was I like in those days?" Yakovlev asks in his memoirs.

> I was a young man, and my belief in Marxist-Leninist teachings in socialism had not yet vanished; I got through the Great Patriotic War with that belief. I passionately hoped for the promised arrival of an earthly paradise . . . Of course, nebulous doubts and uncomfortable questions were already stirring in my head, like that of many others, but I convinced myself that these problems were not all that important. I drove them aside, since belief in the "greatness" of what the Party had accomplished and admiration for the "wise men of the Kremlin," who knew better than anyone else what had to be done, reigned supreme in my consciousness.

The postwar decade passed with a steady rise in Yakovlev's social stature. His career path followed a route similar to that of many war veterans, who became known, in a term that could be used disparagingly, as *frontoviki* – literally, those from the front. It was soon after the war that Yakovlev became a willing participant in the inherently unjust system overseen by the Communist Party. This period does not come up much in his memoirs. Indeed, in the post-Soviet era Yakovlev took pains in his books and media interviews to chronicle the extent he combatted the Party's injustices. However, it's important to realize that Yakovlev certainly would have been forced to compromise his morality to ascend through Soviet society, as he did during the postwar years. He would have had to choose silence over protest. He would have had to carry out orders he knew were unjust. Just as problematic, Yakovlev enjoyed the perquisites and privileges the Soviet system accorded to a select few. This exceptionality began with the privileges accorded to the frontoviki. Many were young Russian men from the provinces who

studied Soviet history at a post-secondary institution and then, upon graduation, became party bureaucrats, a class known as the apparat. Many
eventually moved to Moscow, where the city's sophisticated intelligentsia poked fun at their parochial accents and manners. These party
bureaucrats were a class apart from the rest of the Soviet populace and
they received the usual treatment accorded to ruling classes in other
countries. They shopped in stores stocked with a more diverse selection of better-quality food. They received access to superior medical
care and became part of a network of influence peddling where the
rules everyone else had to follow could be bent with a phone call to
the appropriate party member.

Soon after the war, while still a student, a party worker selected
Yakovlev to be educated in Moscow for a year at a special facility, the
Higher Party School, reserved for members who showed potential for
senior positions in the apparat; in Western society, one analogue would
be an MBA program. After he returned to Yaroslavl, he began working
in the Party's media section, supervising the operation of the area's small
community (rayon) newspapers. From there he spent three years working
as a journalist at the newspaper distributed throughout the whole of the
Yaroslavl region. Although in later years Yakovlev would dismiss his journalism as hack work, it was while at the newspaper that he learned to
express himself through writing. Another promotion made him the
region's deputy head of agitprop – the regional equivalent of the position he would one day hold for the whole of the Party. Next he became
the party member in charge of the Yaroslavl region's schools and higher-
education institutions. The rules now allowed him to attend meetings
where classified information was discussed. His perspective allowed him
to perceive a gap between the way things were and the way the Party
portrayed things.

One year, for example, the Yaroslavl area wasn't filling the crop allot-
ments it was supposed to send to the Party. The Party assigned Yakovlev
and many of the region's other senior officials to go to the farms and
find out what was happening to the crops. He went out into the country
with a mission to pester farm workers. Had they sent all their potatoes?

All their wheat? Why weren't they able to fulfill the state delivery plan? So far as detective work went, this mystery was less than Sherlockian: the problem was, there *weren't* any crops. Too much rain had fallen, and the crops had failed. Yakovlev was pestering farm workers to send Moscow their food when the farm workers weren't even able to feed themselves. Their children were starving. As if that weren't bad enough, the KGB was going around arresting anyone who talked about the food shortage – the "slanderers," they called them, who were "spreading rumours about some kind of famine." Here was the Party, his party, the party that was supposed to improve the situation of the farm workers, making things tougher.

Another incident represented his career's first major snag. One day in 1952, when Yakovlev was 28, his boss informed him that the Party's disciplinary body, the Committee for Party Control, had summoned him to Moscow for a meeting with Matvey Shkiryatov, the organization's chairman. That was all the information they provided. This was bad. Stalin was in power, and although low-ranking members of the nomenklatura such as Yakovlev would have discerned only a vague elevation of unease, of latent tension, Stalin's paranoid fantasies were growing acute. There was more talk than usual among party officials of conspiracies against Soviet society. Stalin described Moscow as "teeming with anti-Party elements." It was in this period, too, that Stalin manifested the fantasy of the Doctors' Plot, a supposed scheme by the mostly Jewish physicians of the Kremlin to poison the Motherland's senior-most officials. People braced themselves for another round of instability. Everywhere, the labour camps, the torture chambers, the rifles of the firing squads, the whole of the state's vast punitive mechanism poised for another round of deployment.

And meanwhile, here was Yakovlev on his way to the Committee for Party Control, where the staff could destroy careers at a whim; their decrees resulted in executions by firing squad or long sojourns in prison camps. But it was worse: Yakovlev was heading for a meeting with the committee's *chairman*, the so-called "conscience of the Party." An already frightened Yakovlev grew more worried upon entering the chairman's office. There was no smile, no explanation that Yakovlev was simply being interviewed for an investigation concerning some other poor soul. Instead, in sombre tones, Shkiryatov explained that Yakovlev stood accused of promoting "cosmopolitanism" in the schools he oversaw. Specifically, in typically wordy Soviet style, the charge faulted Yakovlev for "failing to display the requisite energy in the struggle against the domination of 'cosmopolites.'" Yakovlev deduced from the sheet of paper before Shkiryatov that the accusation had come from an anonymous letter. It could have been written by anyone. Nevertheless, the Communist Party treated the accusations in such letters as fact. Under the classic Soviet ethic of "better safe than sorry," the Party figured it was advisable to separate the accused from his job, his family, even his life, purely because of the possibility he was guilty of the misdeeds mentioned by his accuser.

And the charge was ridiculous. "Cosmopolite" was a pejorative but vague term used by the Party, often as a euphemism for Jews, but in this context it described members of the intelligentsia so pumped up with education that their faith in communism was compromised and replaced by capitalist sympathies. But weren't the people running the academic institutions *supposed* to be highly educated? One way to interpret this charge is that Yakovlev stood accused of placing in the institutes of higher education people who were too highly educated. In response, Yakovlev only managed to stammer something about how there wasn't any cosmopolitanism in his district. "Go," grumbled the conscience of the Party. "We'll decide."

The meeting had gone about as poorly as possible. Others had been sent away for lesser charges. Others had been *shot* for lesser charges. Exiting the office took Yakovlev longer than it should have. In such a situation, emotion overwhelmed the habits he'd evolved to conceal his crippled knee. His leg betrayed him. He winced as he lifted himself from his chair. His limp grew into something more serious, something with yaw, with pitch.

Watching him leave, Shkiryatov called out to Yakovlev one last question.

"Why are you limping?"

The condemned man turned.

"I was wounded. At the front."

"Where did you fight?"

"Near Volkhov."

"What branch?"

"The marines," Yakovlev said.

Apparently, Shkiryatov thought highly of veterans. He motioned Yakovlev to return to his desk. Speaking now in a more kindly tone, Shkiryatov began a monologue about capitalism's danger, how it could infect even the most stalwart believer. The danger required constant vigilance, he said. And with that warning, he let Yakovlev go.

In this faithful communist, the incident introduced an abiding distaste for "the struggle against cosmopolitanism." Who had written the letter? Why the accusation? And were others, similarly unjustly accused, doomed on equally flimsy grounds? Such questions troubled Yakovlev. But these questions were doubts about Bolshevism itself. And good communists didn't allow anything to compromise their zeal. If they did, they were strengthening the enemy overseas. Whenever such doubts occurred to him, Yakovlev quickly tried to distract himself with other thoughts. It was a trick he would practise a lot throughout the 1950s. "I took everything the leaders said, with some exceptions perhaps, as truth, not subject to doubt. To be precise, I was unwilling to waste effort on those doubts," Yakovlev explained.

LIKE ANY MEMBER of the Communist Party in the early 1950s, Yakovlev was a Stalinist. He attributed the best things about the Soviet Union to the Great Leader. The tenets of state propaganda had Stalin's predecessor, Lenin, founding the Soviet Union. Stalin, meanwhile, was said to be responsible for making the country into a world superpower. It was Stalin's vigilance that saved the country from the supposed counterrevolutionary conspiracies of 1937 and 1938, when subversive agents of foreign intelligence services were said to be found even in the highest ranks of the Communist Party. It was Stalin's mastery of military strategy that saved the country from the Nazis during the Great Patriotic War. It was through

Stalin that everyone in the Union was able to have free housing, education, and medical care. And it was thanks to Stalin's industriousness that the country would, one day soon, beat the imperialist capitalists of America and introduce the whole of the world to the wonders of Bolshevik revolution.

And then, on March 5, 1953, Stalin died.

The event, for Yakovlev, was tied to his move to Moscow. Deep in the winter of 1953, the Communist Party promoted Yakovlev to a position in its administrative headquarters, the so-called Central Committee apparat, considered to be the Soviet Union's organizational brain stem. At the age of 29, Yakovlev would be one of a few thousand functionaries running the whole of the Soviet Union. He would work in the department of schools, supervising a significant chunk of the nation's educational infrastructure, including the teaching of history and foreign languages. The position required he move away from his extended family in Yaroslavl to Moscow, and his mother unsuccessfully tried to dissuade him from accepting the position. Grasping for any excuse, she said his family was too young; Yakovlev's eldest child, Nataliya, was just six, and his son, Anatoly, was born shortly after the new year, on January 12, 1953. But the position was too much of an honour not to accept.

Stalin died while Yakovlev waited for the promotion to be confirmed. To say the event shocked the nation doesn't accurately describe the disorder it caused. One analogue for North American baby boomers might be the assassination of John F. Kennedy, Jr., 10 years later. But this trauma was deeper. People in the United States were certain the country would continue to exist without their leader. The same couldn't be said for the Soviets. During his quarter-century leadership, but especially during and after the Second World War, Stalin constructed around himself an aura of omnipotence. Propaganda depicted him as the greatest living human being. The Soviet people regarded him as a deity, an all-knowing superman whose mastery of military strategy and domestic policy ensured the Soviet Union would persist despite the great threats surrounding it. Stalin also had convinced everyone that the United States was waiting for the first sign of weakness to attack the Soviet

Union. Some interpreted Stalin's death as the harbinger of the promised war between capitalism and communism. And how could the Soviet Union prevail without its glorious leader?

Tens of thousands of Soviets converged on Red Square to see Stalin's body. Overcrowding caused a panic in which hundreds died. In the Yaroslavl region, the reaction was no less intense. Yakovlev's memoirs recount the meeting convened after Stalin's death by the Yaroslavl regional party committee. "Everyone was silent. Lida Zharova, the secretary of the city party committee, was sobbing. Others were too. Everyone was thinking the same thought: How will we go on with our lives? It seemed life had ended – that is how much we all had been brainwashed."

It was into a Moscow riven by the instability of Stalin's death that Yakovlev moved his family. A country boy, Yakovlev found Moscow bewildering. He had no friends, no mentors to offer guidance. "I felt quite uncomfortable in Moscow . . . Compared to my native Yaroslavl, life in Moscow shocked me with its artificiality . . . There is a constant feeling that someone or something is just on the point of crushing you: a building, a chimney, a car, your boss . . . To this day I do not enjoy walking around Moscow. With all my might, I try to see Moscow's beauty, but evidently I lack sufficient imagination. A strange imitation of life."

STALIN'S SUCCESSOR was Nikita Khrushchev, whose bowling-ball frame and irrepressible nature hid a gift for Machiavellian scheming that served him well in party politics. On February 25, 1956, Khrushchev disclosed many of the crimes of the Stalin era, simultaneously discrediting the dead leader and his still-living associates, many of whom were Khrushchev's rivals.

It is customary for historians to describe this disclosure, known as Khrushchev's Secret Speech, as a beginning, a seminal event in any communist's ideological journey toward disillusionment – to talk about how much the disclosures contained in the speech shocked or astonished, prompting disquieting questions about the system that controlled the lives of 200 million Soviet citizens. This too was Yakovlev's reaction. However, in the long run, Khrushchev's Secret Speech actually prolonged Yakovlev's faith in communism. Yakovlev had been quelling troubling thoughts about his country for more than a decade at that point. The speech provided an explanation for his doubts and misgivings. It provided him with a scapegoat, as well as an enemy he would spend the rest of his life fighting.

Yakovlev was one of the few who received an early indication of Khrushchev's willingness to criticize Stalin, the so-called "leader and genius for all times and peoples." In October of 1954 the young Central Committee instructor was dispatched to Vladivostok, where Khrushchev was due to make a stop. Yakovlev was assigned to help the leader, if he needed it. There was a meeting with the local party officials, and during it, Khrushchev displayed a disturbing predilection for criticizing the Soviet system. "We have become like priests who preach; we promise a celestial kingdom in heaven, but for right now there are no potatoes," Yakovlev recalled Khrushchev saying.

Khrushchev's fullest criticism would happen a year and a half later, almost exactly three years after Yakovlev moved his family to Moscow. Yakovlev was a non-voting guest of the 20th Party Congress, the gathering that saw a diverse sample of the Communist Party plotting the country's course. It was the first congress since Stalin's death, and aside from being party members' first glance at the way the new leader, Nikita Khrushchev, would handle his post, this was pretty dull stuff. The speeches amounted to public relations, the leaders getting the message across to the senior membership, who were then supposed to pass it on down the chain. For the most part, the message was "business as usual." The only major breaks with the past came in foreign affairs. Contrary to the Stalinist rhetoric about the inevitability of all-out class war with the West, the new speeches raised the possibility of peaceful coexistence. And there were a couple of lines that could have been interpreted as veiled criticisms of Stalin, vague disparaging references to "the cult of the individual" and past "lawlessness." But it was not until an unmentioned, secret session on the last day of the congress that Khrushchev came out with the real news.

Khrushchev's speech, "On the Cult of Personality and Its Consequences," exposed an abbreviated list of Stalin's crimes against the Soviet people. Even in their condensed form, there were a lot of them. The speech lasted more than four hours. Transcriptions run on for more than 20,000 words. Khrushchev went through a topic-by-topic list of Stalin's sins. He consistently held Lenin up as the standard of communist behaviour, using Lenin's writings, and to a lesser extent those of Marx and Engels, to contrast with the crimes of Stalin. Khrushchev's first topic was the personality cult, the state practice of glorifying Stalin. "It is impermissible and foreign to the spirit of Marxism-Leninism to elevate one person, to transform him into a superman possessing supernatural characteristics, akin to those of a God," Khrushchev said. "Such a man supposedly knows everything, sees everything, thinks for everyone, can do anything, is infallible in his behaviour . . . Such a belief about a man, and specifically about Stalin, was cultivated among us for many years."

Next came Stalin's crimes of repression:

Stalin originated the concept "enemy of the people." This term automatically made it unnecessary that the ideological errors of a man or men engaged in a controversy be proven . . . On the whole, the only proof of guilt actually used . . . was the "confession" of the accused himself. As subsequent probing has proven, "confessions" were acquired through physical pressures against the accused . . . This led to glaring violations of revolutionary legality and to the fact that many entirely innocent individuals . . . became victims. . . . there were often no sufficiently serious reasons for their physical annihilation.

Referring matter-of-factly to Stalin's abuses of power, to his criminal murders, his fabricated court cases, Khrushchev noted, "It was determined that of the 139 members and candidates of the Central Committee who were elected at the 17th Congress, 98 persons, i.e., 70 percent, were arrested and shot . . . When the cases of some of these so-called spies and saboteurs were examined, it was found that all their cases were fabricated . . . with the help of cruel and inhuman tortures . . . Many thousands of honest and innocent Communists have died as a result of this monstrous falsification of such cases."

For frontoviki like Yakovlev, Stalin's greatest deed was saving the country from the Nazis during the Great Patriotic War. But even this, Khrushchev said, was a lie: "The tactics on which Stalin insisted – without knowing the basics of conducting battle operations – cost much blood until we succeeded in stopping the opponent and going over to the offensive." Stalin's errors were more grave than simple strategic weakness, Khrushchev said. Shortly before the war Stalin purged the military's upper ranks; the "Great Leader" was in fact responsible for weakening the Red Army to the point that it was dangerously susceptible to Nazi aggression. Worse, he ignored indications from both British and Soviet sources that a Nazi attack was imminent. Rather than being the Soviet Saviour, Khrushchev told the 20th Party Congress, Stalin was nearly responsible for the Soviet defeat.

Khrushchev went on:

After the war . . . Stalin became even more capricious, irritable and brutal . . . his suspicion grew . . . His persecution mania reached unbelievable dimensions . . . He completely lost consciousness of reality . . . Let us also recall the affairs of the doctor-plotters . . . Actually there was no "affair" . . . Stalin personally called the investigative judge . . . and advised him on which investigative methods should be used. These methods were simple – beat, beat and beat again.

Khrushchev's accusations didn't seem real to the 32-year-old Yakovlev, immersed as he was in a sea of propaganda depicting Stalin as a benevolent, all-knowing leader. Sitting in the auditorium, Yakovlev recalls, "Everything was shattered into tiny little pieces, like fragmentation rounds in the war." Official reports ended with Khrushchev graced with a standing ovation and tumultuous applause. Not so, said Yakovlev.

People were stunned into silence. As they left the hall, "No one looked at anyone else . . . We left the session with our heads bowed low."

Copies of Khrushchev's speech were dispersed among party organizations throughout the Soviet Union. Somehow, the text made its way to the West. The *New York Times* reprinted it on June 4, 1956. The Secret Speech shocked those who came across it, as much for what it said as for the fact that it was said in a relatively public forum. It set off turmoil in the USSR's satellite republics. It caused heart attacks (in the leader of the Polish Communist Party, for one). It touched off revolutions. (In Hungary in 1956, the Soviet army crushed an uprising at the cost of 20,000 Hungarian lives.) People wondered whether the Communist Party could survive. Did it bear any culpability for Stalin's crimes? Khrushchev said no, but even he had trouble bridging the cognitive dissonance caused by his speech. A month later, Stalin's portrait still hung in Khrushchev's office, just as the monuments of the dead dictator glowered over downtown squares across the Union. Like many faithful party members, Yakovlev would grapple with Stalin's legacy, and his own complicity in Stalin's crimes, for the rest of his life.

7

THE PARANOID STYLE

SOVIET ATTITUDES toward their leaders were profoundly different from those in the West. Most patriotic Americans, Brits, or Canadians are able to criticize their political leaders because their own personal identities aren't tied to their leaders, or to institutions of government. A distance existed between an American's identity, and President Eisenhower's, for example. A similar span didn't exist for the Soviets. Yakovlev grew up believing the Communist Party was Stalin, and Stalin was the Communist Party; as a zealously enthusiastic party member, Yakovlev's identity was intimately tied to both.

So Khrushchev's Secret Speech forced Yakovlev into the mental equivalent of advanced yoga. His reasoning twisted itself into impossible positions. Stalin was the Communist Party. Stalin was corrupt. Therefore, the Communist Party was corrupt. But that couldn't be, Yakovlev thought; he, himself, was a party member.

The speech was a turning point for Yakovlev, as it was for many members of his generation. His hero, Stalin, was no hero. He was a murderer. "The speech turned my soul inside out," he wrote. "My enthusiasm for work began to wane, and at times I felt apathetic toward everything that was happening." The trauma from Stalin's betrayal of the Soviet people made it difficult for him to trust Khrushchev or other, more immediate superiors. Rather than blindly following orders he began to wonder about the motivations behind them: "I started to really pay attention to the bosses' speeches and unexpectedly began to uncover in them a mass of stupidities, lies, and hypocrisy. I grew more and more vigilant, breaking through my psychological curtain, and more frequently noticed in the conduct of the nomenklatura signs of careerism, grovelling, and intrigue."

In the days, weeks, and months that followed those hours in the Kremlin auditorium, events from Yakovlev's past burbled into his thoughts, unbidden. He recalled how his father was forced into hiding for several days in the 1930s and realized his father was almost killed in one of Stalin's purges. He thought about the Great Patriotic War, how a young peasant boy like himself was put in command of a platoon, and he realized that happened because Stalin purged the upper ranks of the military in the years before Hitler invaded. He recalled the disturbing scene on the Yaroslavl train platform, when he spied prisoners of war in transit from German concentration camps to Soviet prison colonies. He considered his harrowing visits to Shkiryatov's office, when he himself escaped a trip to the prison camp on the flimsy evidence of an anonymous letter.

How had these incidents, and Stalin's crimes, arisen from a communist system? Stalin's crimes were proof that something was wrong. But where was the problem?

Across the world, the revelation of Stalin's crimes was causing Marxists of all backgrounds to wonder similar things. This period was a time of soul-searching and examination for Yakovlev and his fellow party members. The feeling of betrayal – Stalin's betrayal of the Party, the Party's betrayal of the people – was bad enough. Worse was Yakovlev's suspicion that he too bore some complicity for the Party's crimes.

He decided not to be fooled again. Considering his conception of communism to be corrupted by two and a half decades of Stalin's leadership, Yakovlev resolved to teach himself Marxism a second time, with fresh eyes uncorrupted by Stalin's influence. Only then would he be able to decide who was to blame for Stalin's crimes: Stalin or the Party and its ideology. Hundreds and thousands of party members did the same thing, studying the original thinkers, such as Karl Marx and Friedrich Engels, as well as the founder of the Soviet Union, Lenin himself. It was the intellectual adventure of Yakovlev's generation, with thinkers across the country combing dusty volumes of Collected Works to seek out the source of the Party's defects.

Never one to do something halfway, Yakovlev decided to leave his work in the Central Committee in order to devote himself to this intellectual exercise full-time. "I sensed a need to re-educate myself, to reread everything I'd read before, go back to original sources – Marx, Engels, Lenin . . ." he wrote. He applied to the Academy of Social Sciences and was turned down several times. Finally, after substantial badgering, Yakovlev succeeded in convincing his superiors to allow him to study toward a graduate degree in the academy's Department of the History of International Communism.

Soviet society was changing in other ways. Silent, wraithlike figures, pale and dressed in rags, were appearing in cities across the Union. These recently freed denizens of the Gulag called themselves *zeks* (inmates), and their sudden presence was a disturbing reminder to senior party members like Yakovlev of the crimes committed in the Party's name during previous decades. Meanwhile, in foreign affairs, Stalinist rhetoric about the inevitability of a global class conflict with the United States gave way to a grudging acceptance of the West's capitalist existence and, with that, a greater emphasis on diplomatic relations. Soon American President Dwight D. Eisenhower pitched the Soviets a novel idea. The two sides had conducted a silent treatment that lasted years thanks to the Cold War. Improved relations would come if only the two countries could get to know each other better, he said. What about some sort of cultural exchange? Eisenhower's notion bypassed the dour government bureaucrats who usually handled Cold War diplomacy. The old general was thinking about regular citizens getting a sense of how the other side lived, and like a typical military man he thought big – the number he bandied about was 10,000. This plan sounded a little audacious to the slower-moving Soviets, who finally acquiesced to a limited, experimental version of Eisenhower's idea, in January 1958. By then the idea had evolved into an academic exchange funded by such private groups as the Ford Foundation, as well as the U.S. State Department, which was to administer the program. Scholars would study at a foreign host university and, during their off-time, do some travelling. In contrast to the hordes Eisenhower initially envisioned, the first cohort totalled 17 students from each country. The Central Committee selected Yakovlev as its representative among the group.

Citizens of today's globalized world might have a difficult time imagining how alien the United States seemed to the average Soviet bureaucrat, circa 1958. Yakovlev and his fellow exchange students bore similarities to cosmonauts off to explore the hostile environment of Planet America and its alien life forms. By 1959, the Soviet Union was one of the most isolated societies the modern world has ever known, thanks to Stalin's xenophobic drive in the postwar years to cleanse the country of any external influences its soldiers picked up during the war. Marriages to foreigners were forbidden and all relations with foreigners were barred for all Soviet citizens except those who worked for the Ministry of Foreign Affairs and the Ministry of Foreign Trade. Travel outside the Soviet Union was forbidden. Constant propaganda in the Soviet media portrayed any interest in the West as "kow-towing to bourgeois culture." Consequently, few of Yakovlev's associates in the Central Committee had been outside the Soviet Union, let alone to the United States.

Khrushchev's first trip there the following year, in September 1959, would inspire excitement and anxiety in the Soviet leader. Indicative of Soviet anxiety about the United States was the hubbub over Khrushchev's meeting place with Eisenhower. "Kemp Da-vid?" Khrushchev asked suspiciously when he first saw the trip itinerary. "What's that?" No one in Moscow could tell him; it was only after consultation with Washington that the Kremlin learned that Camp David was the president's Maryland "dacha."

Yakovlev is bound to have felt similar anxiety. Would a simple peasant boy be able to match wits with top American scholars? And how would the trip affect him? Extra-Soviet influences of any sort, including the influence of travel, were thought to have a corrupting effect on faithful communists, confusing previously correct thinking and possibly turning comrades against the Motherland. Yakovlev was to become one of a few dozen Soviet citizens who had actually lived among the enemy. He would have to be away from Nina, five-year-old Anatoly and 11-year-old Nataliya for the whole of the academic year – nine months. It was bound to be a lonely, and frightening, time.

In early September of 1958, the America-bound students gathered in Moscow at the headquarters of the Komsomol, the Party's youth wing, to endure orientation sessions that amounted to propaganda. Toward the end of September they flew in a converted TU-104 bomber to Copenhagen, then took a 14-hour commercial flight to New York's Idlewild Airport. The students were then broken up into smaller groups to be scattered among such top American schools as Harvard and the University of Chicago. Yakovlev was one of four students bound for Columbia, in New York City, where he and three comrades would live for the rest of the academic year among business students in dorm rooms on the twelfth floor of Columbia's John Jay Hall. Unlike the 34-year-old Yakovlev, all of his companions were in their mid-twenties. Gennady P. Bekhterev was studying local U.S. government. Y.N. Stozhkov was examining Soviet–U.S. relations before the Second World War. The youngest, 24-year-old Oleg Kalugin, was studying journalism. But Yakovlev's three companions' IDs were covers. They weren't scholars. They were on secret missions to learn about their enemy's lifestyle and develop contacts. Of the four Soviets enrolled at Columbia, Yakovlev was the only one who wasn't a spy.

BY THE LATE 1950s *Homo sovieticus* had certain defining characteristics, among which was a craving for conformity. Stability, law and order, security and predictability were elements that party propaganda encouraged its citizenry to value. Self-assertion was frowned on, individualism decried. Consequently, America was a scary place for the faithful party member. The scariest of its cities was New York, the scariest of New York boroughs, Manhattan. And in Manhattan, among the scariest of streets was the avenue called Broadway.

One dark evening during the 1958 holiday season, faithful party member Aleksandr Yakovlev braved Broadway. This was north Broadway, uptown Broadway, slum Broadway – in the pre-gentrification era, a cacophonous neon canyon filled with honking horns and the come-ons of catcalling pimps and prostitutes. Marquees shouted the names of filthy movies and strip-bar barkers beckoned into dark clubs and derelicts oozed defeat in the doorways of flophouses rentable by the hour, the night, the week, and the month: your pick. Buskers juggled or sang, or juggled *and* sang. Prostitutes jiggled. Junkies quaked. Newspaper sellers brayed. Meanwhile, independent operators navigated the pavement, hawking wares from pockets sewn into blazer liners, from wooden boxes slung around their shoulders, from broken-down shopping carts.

The scene was like something out of Dostoyevsky's St. Petersburg, a modern-day version of the urban tableau Raskolnikov might have witnessed in *Crime and Punishment*. Yakovlev's limp made him an easy mark. He could manage short bursts of speed across a room, but this was a long walk: 10 blocks from dorm room to destination, meaning, 10 blocks of stepping and lifting, stepping and lifting, with a stop maybe once a block to catch a breath. The vendors were at him to buy this, sample that, or go upstairs for a roll with something else – sometimes, it was difficult to decide just what that something else *was*. Plus all this variety threw him. It was so unlike home. There was a sense here that anything could happen. This, after all, was America. This was *capitalism*. He felt every metre of his 8,000-odd kilometres from home.

Luckily, Yakovlev had company, an American graduate student from Columbia named Loren Graham. Yakovlev clutched his parcel under his arm and kept close to the side of this American student. At Yakovlev's request they stopped into a florist and Yakovlev came out bearing a paper cone of cut flowers. When the nocturnal denizens of Broadway approached Yakovlev, Graham would place a hand on Yakovlev's back, or step in front of him, or get a handful of Yakovlev's suit jacket, and pull him along on his way. In this way they made it to the strangely tri-angular corner of 105th and Broadway, where Graham lived at 248 West 105th Street. Before Yakovlev went in he looked up at the building. It wasn't much. A wedge-shaped, five-storey, cockroach- and rat-infested tenement. Yakovlev took a breath, and went in.

THIS WAS EXACTLY the sort of unsupervised situation Yakovlev had been counselled not to get himself into. A little more than 30 years later, KGB Chief Vladimir Kryuchkov would use such an "unsupervised" encounter to accuse Yakovlev of working for the Americans. It was at a meeting like this, according to Kryuchkov, that the FBI or the CIA turned Yakovlev into a deep-cover mole working toward the destruction of the Soviet Union. During his pre-departure orientation he and his fellow students were warned to be vigilant for "provocations" of all kinds. This was a carry-over from Stalin's portrayal of the Soviet Union as a besieged fortress threatened on all sides by hostile capitalist conspiracies. For decades now the secret police had been uncovering supposed imperial-ist plots directed at all levels of Soviet society, from the Politburo on down to the lowliest collective farm. Never mind that most of these plots were little more than the paranoid fantasies of Communist Party bureau-crats or, even worse, simple quota filling; the "uncoverings" did their jobs. By the late 1950s, the psychology of encirclement was so effective, the few Communist Party members who realized Soviet living standards lagged behind those in the West blamed capitalist conspiracies rather than deficiencies in their own economic system. Now, this same psychology caused the Party to counsel Yakovlev and his fellow students to be on the lookout for provocations from everywhere – be it friend, classmate, teacher, whomever. Everyone was suspect. Some attractive young lady might lure one of them into a sexual situation and suddenly a week later a stranger reaches into his trench coat to produce eight-by-ten glossies that could be sent back to Moscow if they didn't procure the appropriate level of cooperation. Or money might be offered. Or the provocation might come from other, more creative methods of barter: improved grades, Western fashions. What was certain was that the provocations would come and, when they did, the Soviet students would have to remain steadfast in their communist faith.

This manic suspicion of Western conspiracy profoundly affected Yakovlev's American experience. When they first arrived, he and his fellow students were astonished by Manhattan's wealth. They couldn't get over the variety of everything, from fin-tailed automobiles to breakfast cereals, fur coats to the skin tones of people on the street – black, white, and everything in between. Symbolic of American power was the height of its skyscrapers. In 1958, the tallest building in Moscow was the 32-storey spire at Moscow State University. Dozens of Manhattan's buildings were that tall; the Empire State Building rose 102 stories. Western readers might be tempted to suppose that this realization alone might have inspired epiphanies in Yakovlev about the superiority of the capitalist system. But that's to misconstrue the extent that Soviet values were different from those in the West. Yakovlev's first reaction to Manhattan's wealth was resentment. An African slave might have had a similar reaction upon seeing the wealth of early nineteenth-century Atlanta. Here, Yakovlev thought upon seeing Manhattan's skyscrapers, were the proceeds of capitalist exploitation of workers.

The communist explorer settled into his dorm room. He enrolled in graduate-level American and Soviet history courses and learned to navigate the campus. But as he limped along Columbia's sidewalks and walking paths, the psychology of encirclement struck again. He felt as though he was being watched. And he was. The Columbia student newspaper wrote about the Soviet exchange students, as did local media, so Yakovlev and his three fellow pupils were unwitting low-level campus celebrities. Many students stared when they recognized the limping figure with the Russian accent. Worse, the FBI correctly expected spies to be among the Soviet exchange students. Because Yakovlev was the oldest of the group at Columbia, they figured him for the spy cell's ringleader, and in the early days of his studies they followed him incessantly.

To a Soviet citizen who treasured conformity, such attention was difficult to bear.

Then, in October, the Pasternak Affair exploded. The legendary Russian poet and writer Boris Pasternak had worked hard to get his novel, *Dr. Zhivago*, published in the Soviet Union, but the Party disliked its realistic portrayal of the Russian Revolution. They also thought the book championed the rights of the individual over the glory of the state. After he learned of the Party's refusal to publish the book in the Soviet Union, Pasternak sent the text to a publisher he knew in Italy, who arranged for translations in Italian, French, and English. The first printing reached American shelves in August 1958, the month before Yakovlev arrived in New York. On October 23, the Swedish Academy awarded Pasternak the Nobel Prize for Literature. When Pasternak accepted, the Soviet media went shrill with slander, calling Pasternak "a tool of international reactionaries" for his "traitorous conduct." Fellow writers called for him to be shot, or exiled. The Soviet Writers' Union expelled him. The Party also prevented Pasternak from going to Stockholm to accept the prize.

In Yakovlev's Manhattan, Pasternak seemed to be on the front page of every paper. *Zhivago* seemed to be advertised in the window of every bookstore. The whole affair was profoundly disturbing to Yakovlev. A voracious reader, he was justifiably proud of the Russian reputation for crafting some of the world's best literature. Plus, he was a big fan of Pasternak's Shakespeare translations. He read *Zhivago*'s English translation. He didn't think much of it. He was expecting something more powerful from one of his favourite authors. More troublingly, Yakovlev couldn't find anything anti-Soviet about *Zhivago*'s contents. His faith in the Communist Party was such that Yakovlev blamed himself for not being able to find the offensive portions of the book. It wasn't that the censors had been wrong, that the book wasn't, in fact, anti-Soviet. The problem was that Yakovlev's mind was too unsophisticated to ferret out the offending sentences. Yakovlev doesn't say so explicitly in his memoirs, but the reaction of Nikita Khrushchev to the affair may shed light on Yakovlev's reaction as well. "They gave Pasternak the Nobel Prize?" Khrushchev said. "Then they clearly did it to spite our country."

Many Soviet citizens believed the book's publication and the award were a scheme by the West to discredit the Soviet state. Consequently, Yakovlev reacted with irritation each time an American asked him which parts in *Zhivago* had so offended the censors. Were these provocations? Were they innocently curious questions? Or were the American students lobbing these questions at him to shake his faith in the Party?

Some American students sought out Yakovlev to debate him. These types seemed to regard conversations with Yakovlev as Cold War skirmishes; they tried to corner Yakovlev into disagreeing with the Soviet leadership or get him to concede American superiority over the USSR. And why not? Antipathy toward the Red Menace was widespread among the American public in 1958, exacerbated by Senator Joe McCarthy's fear-mongering exposure of homegrown communists earlier in the decade, and both sides' propensity to test an increasingly powerful series of nuclear bombs. In American schools, children rehearsed what to do in the event of an atom bomb attack. Owners of suburban split-level homes were digging up their newly sodded backyards to install subterranean bomb shelters. Housewives woke up during the night worrying about the pinkos and commies and whether their children would avoid nuclear Armageddon long enough to graduate high school, get married, and have children of their own. These attitudes manifested themselves in encounters Yakovlev had with his fellow students. Students asked him why the Soviet Union wanted to drop bombs on the United States. Another time, a shop clerk asked the Soviet scholar to remove his hat – because the clerk wanted to see Yakovlev's devil's horns. It's likely the man was joking, but in a measure of the hostility he felt in the States, Yakovlev took him seriously. Such encounters were persistent reminders that he was a foreigner in enemy territory. Internally he felt the same psychology of encirclement that plagued Stalin's foreign policy. Yakovlev felt besieged on all sides by these enemies, these Americans.

Even among the other Soviet students at Columbia, Yakovlev felt out of place. He could sense they thought him a little stodgy, a little backward, a little old. He was. Just five years removed from Yaroslavl, Yakovlev still spoke Russian in an accent that sounded provincial to urban speakers. He had already lost much of his hair. He was heavier than his fellow exchange students. And thanks to his limp, he found it difficult to conduct the long exploratory walks that familiarized the other three with Manhattan's layout. In contrast to Yakovlev's paranoid hibernation, the other exchange students swan-dove into America's melting pot. They took in the sights with the enthusiasm of tourists. They were game for any experience. Within weeks of arriving, they had American friends who accompanied them on trips to Yankee Stadium or jazz clubs. They trolled Greenwich Village strip bars, cruised the Bowery, and sat zombie-like in cinemas for hundreds of hours of Hollywood films. All three became fixtures at the student pubs around Columbia's Morningside Heights neighbourhood, but Kalugin in particular succeeded in blending in. He wrote for the student newspaper. He even ran for election to student parliament – and won.

The difference, of course, was that Yakovlev was at Columbia to study. The other three were only posing as students. They were under orders to experience all things American, to learn as much about the American way of life as they could, so they were outgoing to an almost absurd extent, seeking out conversation and companionship wherever they could find them.

Socially ostracized by the other Soviets, and feeling besieged on all sides by Americans, Yakovlev researched Franklin Roosevelt's New Deal among other topics. He kept to his dorm room, or the stacks of Columbia's Butler Library, with the only company available to him during those early days in New York: books.

LOREN GRAHAM MANAGED to break through Yakovlev's suspicious carapace. Graham was a Midwestern transplant in his first year of graduate studies at Columbia. Because he was studying Soviet history, Graham met all four of the exchange students. In Professor Alexander Dallin's class on Soviet foreign policy, he sat between Kalugin and Yakovlev. Despite the fact that Graham was, like Kalugin, 10 years younger than Yakovlev, Graham gravitated toward Yakovlev. There was a superficiality about Kalugin, Graham felt. He was like a frat boy, more interested in partying than studying. He said what he thought you wanted him to say, rather than what he felt. Yakovlev was different. He avoided social situations. He was reserved to the point of being bashful. But when he did speak, he seemed honest and introspective. Fascinated by the opportunity to speak with a party functionary, Graham would buttonhole Yakovlev after class and attempt to draw him out.

For his part, Yakovlev wondered whether Graham was an FBI agent. He hoped not; he liked that Graham didn't badger him about Soviet policies. The two men developed rules for their discussions. One asked a question, one answered. Neither hounded his counterpart into coming round to an opposing point of view. This was exploration by conversation, each student probing the attitudes and ideas of an alien society.

By late autumn, the pair was grabbing after-class meals at Broadway diners. Graham noticed Yakovlev was apt to defend even Stalin, so he asked about Khrushchev's Secret Speech. Yakovlev deflected the question back to him: What did *he* think about it? Graham said he thought Stalin was a criminal, and the speech an astonishing list of Stalin's crimes. Yakovlev just nodded. In turn, Yakovlev quizzed Graham about Harlem, the predominately black neighbourhood just east of Columbia then legendary in the Soviet media for its poverty. As they talked, Graham realized Yakovlev hadn't yet walked its streets. Minutes later the pair were on their way. They saw drug addicts. They saw drunks. Yakovlev talked about how disgraceful it was, that America allowed its citizens to live in such squalor. Graham conceded his embarrassment. Harlem's poverty was a problem.

As Yakovlev's only real friend, Graham found himself the de facto sounding board for the Soviet scholar's research about the New Deal, the series of social programs instituted by President Franklin D. Roosevelt in the 1930s. With his voluminous reading, Yakovlev learned about the New Deal origins of Social Security, the pension each American gets after the age of 65, and the Securities and Exchange Commission, the organization that regulates U.S. stock markets and the publicly traded companies listed on them. He came to understand that Roosevelt's New Deal amounted to a tempering of America's almost unregulated capitalism and its capacity to create social inequalities, and he learned how opposition critics lambasted Roosevelt as a communist in response. And he came to see Roosevelt's actions within the context of the Great Depression, the deep economic recession that struck the United States in the wake of the stock market shocks of 1929. One day Graham came upon Yakovlev in the stacks of Columbia's Butler Library. He spoke quickly. His usually bashful demeanour was gone. "Loren, I've been reading FDR's right-wing critics," Yakovlev said. "They all said Roosevelt was a traitor to his class, that he was destroying capitalism in America. But it's obvious to me that Roosevelt was not destroying capitalism at all. He was saving capitalism when it was on its knees."

Such discussions created a bond between two profoundly different scholars. Graham noticed as the first term passed that Yakovlev sometimes spoke of his family. By the holidays it had been three months since he had seen or spoken with his wife, daughter, and son. Seeking to ease his friend's loneliness, Graham invited Yakovlev to dinner at his apartment on Broadway. Yakovlev accepted.

GRAHAM'S APARTMENT was at the vertex of the apartment building's unconventional wedge shape, on the third floor. After the American unlocked his imposing deadbolt, Yakovlev followed his friend into the apartment's entrance, a dark, cramped hallway. To the right was a small bedroom that overlooked Broadway. In the darkness of December's early evening, it was illuminated by the flashing red neon sign outside: LIQUOR. They passed another bedroom door before the hallway opened up into the living area. Graham and his wife were both history graduate students, and money was tight, but with a few cheap posters and some plants they'd managed to create a homey oasis in contrast to the squalor outside. With the smell of the tuna and potato chip casserole cooking in the oven, it was an inviting scene. Yakovlev presented Graham's wife, Patricia, with the bouquet of flowers they'd picked up along the way. Meg, Graham's two-year-old daughter, received a children's book of Russian fables. His friend was a little stiff, Graham noticed, and chalked it up to his nervousness.

Yakovlev had been suspicious of his American classmate, at first. But over time Yakovlev watched the answers Graham gave the instructor during their classes together, and Graham's obvious hard work on school essays. Both indicated to Yakovlev that Graham was a genuine student. But if Graham ever was going to come out and reveal his affiliation with, say, the FBI, this dinner would be a perfectly private time. Perhaps to stave off conversation, Yakovlev spent the time before dinner playing with Meg, who, he told Graham, reminded him of his own daughter. Yakovlev found it easy to charm children. His great, glowering eyebrows and bald pate encouraged kids to expect him to be serious. So when he stuck out his tongue or waggled those thick caterpillar brows, he was sure to get a smile. Crossing his eyes earned a giggle. Within moments he'd made friends with Meg.

Once dinner was ready, Yakovlev managed to arrange his straight leg in front of him at the table and everyone tucked into the tuna casserole. Conversation touched on the Grahams' interest in visiting the Soviet Union. There were a couple of tense moments, such as Patricia quizzing her dinner guest on such Soviet sore points as the Pasternak affair. (The struggle required sacrifices on everyone's part, Yakovlev said, even artists like Pasternak who might be forced to alter their work.) Most of the discussion involved their professors. Yakovlev's teachers were an impressive lot, including such academic luminaries as the two-time winner of the Pulitzer Prize, historian Richard Hofstadter, whose writings eloquently illuminated the problems of American populism; specifically, the tendency of U.S. politicians to harness fear and xenophobia to achieve their policy aims – a trait to which Soviet politicians were equally susceptible. Another of Yakovlev's well-known teachers was David B. Truman, author of the definitive study on political pluralism in the American Congress, who provided Yakovlev with informed advice regarding worthwhile books on American politics. Truman then encouraged Yakovlev to think critically about the analysis the books contained.

No provocations happened at the dinner. Neither of the Grahams asked for secret information about the USSR. No one disclosed any undercover status as an agent of the FBI. What the dinner did was provide Yakovlev with a window into an everyday American household – a household not all that different from his own.

JUST BEFORE HIS American exchange ended in May of 1959, the State Department sent Yakovlev and the other three Soviets at Columbia on a three-week tour of America. Throughout, they were billeted at the homes of American families; in Vermont, with a Protestant minister; in Chicago, with a university professor. They also saw Philadelphia, Chicago, New Orleans, and Washington, D.C. During their travels, the Soviets dined at a Louisiana plantation whose owner declared that, despite the civil rights movement, Negroes would always be his slaves. Everywhere they saw the hallmarks of segregation; schools, drinking fountains, and wash-rooms reserved for use by whites or blacks.

About halfway through the trip they stopped for four days at an Iowa homestead. After a hearty breakfast each morning, the three younger Soviet students went off with the farmer to learn about tractor operation and sowing corn. Thanks to his knee, Yakovlev stayed behind at the farm-house and passed his days studying. One afternoon, bored and lonely, he heard the farmer's children playing outside in the yard, and on an impulse decided to join them.

Maybe it was his limp. Or perhaps their parents had warned them not to bother the communist visitors. In any event, when Yakovlev hobbled out onto the lawn toward the children they quickly grew quiet. But then Yakovlev made one of his faces, or performed some other trick that charmed them, and soon the lot of them were giggling through non-sense games.

After some minutes of this the farmer's wife came out of her house.

"I see you love children," she called out, tentatively.

"Yes, I have two children back home in Moscow. I miss them," Yakovlev said in his thick Russian accent.

"But in your country," said the mother, looking confused, "don't you have common children? And common wives?"

It took some discussion for Yakovlev to realize what she meant. The young woman thought the Soviets gave up their children, who were then raised by the state. Wives, too, she thought, were shared communally.

"Who told you that?" Yakovlev asked. He was appalled.

"The pastor."

Yakovlev explained about his living arrangements, how his family lived in a flat in a Moscow apartment building; there were no communal children, and certainly no communal wives.

Later, in front of her husband and everyone else at the dinner table, the American woman had Yakovlev go through it all again. But this time she had more questions. At her urging, Yakovlev described his first years, how he and his parents had lived in the Russian countryside, far from the nearest town, in his paternal grandfather's home, a building crowded because its other occupants included the families of his two uncles. Young Aleksandr spent his childhood running wild through hayfields, hunting raspberries in the woods, or tending to the family's horse, sheep, and cattle – similar to the lifestyle experienced by Iowa children.

As churchgoers, the Americans were particularly interested in religion, which they'd heard the Soviet Union had outlawed. Religion was suppressed, Yakovlev acknowledged. But his mother was a believer. She once brought a bottle of holy water home from church for her son to swallow, but Aleksandr refused – his teacher had taught him religion was nonsense. Angry, his mother banged him on the forehead with the spoon. His father broke it up. "It's his life," he told his wife. "Let him make his own choice."

Filled with such stories, dinner lasted long into the night. Yakovlev had never experienced such grateful, patient listeners. He felt these Americans understood him. Unfortunately, the experience was rare.

ON MAY 11, 1959, at the conclusion of the first Cold War-era student exchange between the U.S. and the Soviet Union, the *New York Times* examined the experiment in international diplomacy in a front-page story and declared it a success. A photo of Yakovlev and the other three Columbia students was prominently featured on the front page. Yakovlev was asked by the reporter to sum up his thoughts about his experiences in the West. "This has been a brilliant example of international cooperation," Yakovlev said. The reporter asked what he thought of American girls; Yakovlev responded that he hadn't had much time to consider them – he spent all his time with his books. He could say one thing with certainty, however: "Now I know that the American and Soviet peoples can live together peacefully. I wasn't sure before I came here."

Yakovlev flew home to Moscow a less dogmatic, but still faithful, member of the Communist Party, slightly more apt to separate his identity from the communist system, slightly more apt to wonder whether its policies accurately reflected Marxist-Leninist ideology. His year in America influenced him more than he admitted to the *New York Times*. It did not, however, affect his belief that Soviet socialism was a system of living superior to American capitalism. If anything, Yakovlev's experiences in America served to confirm his preconceptions. Soviets at that time thought of the United States in a manner similar to the way Americans thought of Russia in the Yeltsin years – as a wild, scary place, morally depraved, spiritually corrupt, where greed was the universal human value and money could buy all services and goods. Sure, Yakovlev thought, Americans could buy dozens of different cars in dozens of different paint shades. But what did that matter when illness could strike them down at any moment and the absence of state-provided medical care could leave them unable to afford a hospital visit? Who cared how many homes had televisions when many students couldn't afford to go to university?

Yes, Yakovlev thought, many people in the United States were better off than the people back home. But Soviet values counted moral considerations as more important than financial ones like personal wealth, and Soviets considered their country a more *moral* society than America.

State-run racism like the segregation of the American South was illegal in the USSR, although anti-Semitic behaviour was a hallmark of the KGB, among other Party organizations. The Soviet Union also was further ahead in equality for women, Yakovlev felt. And besides, when it came to the conflict between communism and capitalism, the momentum was on the Soviet side. Communism still seemed to be spreading across the globe. The same year Yakovlev was at Columbia the university invited as a speaker Fidel Castro, who had just established a new communist country in Cuba, just 150 kilometres south of Florida. Most Soviet citizens including Yakovlev expected their country to catch up soon to American living standards. After decades of unimaginable difficulty – Lenin's death and the farm collectivization of the 1920s, the purges of the 1930s, the Second World War famines of the 1940s – the 1950s were a time of comparative luxury, when Khrushchev lifted many of the restrictions imposed by his more authoritarian predecessor. Soviet technological prowess foretold more advances in living standards. The year before Yakovlev left for the States, Soviets launched the world's first Earth-orbiting satellite, the beachball-sized Sputnik. Weeks later the Soviets sent Laika into orbit, making the space dog the world's first orbiting creature. The Soviets would continue to best America in the space race well into the next decade.

Considering the effect of the exchange in his own memoirs, Yakovlev's classmate, Oleg Kalugin, reflected sentiments likely shared by Yakovlev:

My first year in New York actually strengthened my faith in Communism: I believed that although we were far poorer than the United States, we at least tried to offer all our citizens a decent level of education, housing and health care. Odd as it looks now, it seemed clear to me then that the United States didn't have the Soviet Union's vitality. Our achievements in science and the triumphs of our space program convinced me we would overcome our relative poverty and our Stalinist past and – by the end of the century – become a far better place to live than America.

Yakovlev remained critical of America after his visit, writing several books during the 1960s that accused the democracy of an aggressive, overly imperialist foreign policy stance. For example, sounding a little like his Columbia professor Richard Hofstadter reflected in a funhouse mirror, Yakovlev writes in the introduction to his book *Pax Americana* about the way American "propaganda" prepares "the people of the USA for a new world war . . . the ruling forces of the state create in the country an environment of hysteria and fear, persecute dissidents, instigate chauvinist instincts and feelings, implant military ways of thinking and prepare people psychologically for wars and the conquest of the world, along with the annihilation of socialism." This wasn't just lip service to the party line; in later decades Yakovlev would confirm he believed what he wrote, although he said he regretted his sometimes sneering tone.

America changed Yakovlev. His encounters with people like Loren Graham and the Iowa farming family taught him that shades of grey existed in the Cold War. Once one got past the misinformation and ignorance, Americans could be downright friendly, even to their enemies. His studies no doubt helped to plant the seeds of his conversion. He learned about the legislative leeway that federalism granted to American states. David Truman's classes on the American Congress taught him the mechanics of a two-party political system. The research he conducted on the New Deal may also have set an example. He learned in those Butler Library stacks how President Roosevelt had tempered his capitalist system with measures his critics decried as "communist." It's intriguing to wonder whether Yakovlev considered which "capitalist" measures might temper the excesses of communism. Yakovlev's friend Loren Graham would go on to become a renowned scholar of Soviet scientific history and a professor of the history of science at the Massachusetts Institute of Technology. He stayed in contact with Yakovlev, and would in later years wonder how the New Deal research had affected Yakovlev. In his memoirs, Graham argues that "the example of Roosevelt suggested an intriguing possibility [to Yakovlev]: a reformer was not necessarily a traitor." The research may have affected Yakovlev in another way. At Columbia professors such as Hofstadter and Truman encouraged him to think critically about America. Back in Moscow, Yakovlev is certain to have employed his new tools for critical thinking when examining Soviet politics as well.

8

POWER STRUGGLE

IN 1960, after four years of studying American history and the origins of communism, Yakovlev finished his dissertation, which detailed the manner that American "bourgeois" literature criticized that country's foreign policy. The Academy of Social Sciences awarded him the degree of kandidat nauk, approximately equivalent to a Western Ph.D. Sometime during this period, he also concluded the intellectual exercise that had sent him back to school in 1956. He now believed he knew the source of the Party's problems. The Party's obsession with cruelty and punishment, its extreme sensitivity to criticism, and its perpetual struggle with inefficiency and corruption – all these, and more besides, Yakovlev decided during his four-year sojourn in academia, were Stalin's fault. Now Yakovlev was inspired to return to work in the Central Committee administration, to attempt to cleanse the Party of Stalin's corrupting influence and bring in a more pure form of communism.

He soon found himself embroiled in a secret war – a power struggle that would take years to resolve, a power struggle that would define the direction of the Soviet Union for the remainder of its existence. For much of the Cold War, Western Kremlinologists knew very little about the secretive world of the Central Committee. Party insiders, the ones who really knew what was going on, didn't speak frankly to Westerners. Because one never knew who was an informant of the KGB, few insiders even spoke frankly to their trusted friends. So to determine power dynamics and succession plans, Kremlinologists in London and Washington resorted to such exercises as analyzing where party officials stood to watch parade processions in Red Square – the closer you stood to the leader, the higher you were in the pecking order. Everyone but the most sophisticated of watchers thought of the Central Committee bureaucrats as an indistinguishable blob of grey suits and pale skin. Like the *Star Trek* enemy the Borg, all its members were supposed to hold basically the same opinions, to unfailingly support and enact the policies that came from the Presidium.

That was nonsense. The Central Committee apparat was as thick with betrayal, secret allegiances, and fractious intrigue as Washington's Congress, London's Parliament or, for that matter, Caesar's Senate. The only difference was that very little of this acrimony ever reached Western ears.

On one side of this power struggle were the Stalinists. Their creed, Stalinism, was less a set of ethics than a state that suspends ethics. Like "militant philosophers," the Stalinists depicted themselves as high-minded soldiers fighting to create a workers' paradise where the state provided for all, and all citizens were liberated from poverty's prison. Revolution was the means to attain this workers' paradise. Seen in this way, the revolution that created Communist Russia was the first stage in a worldwide class war between the working proletariat and their capitalist masters, the bourgeoisie, who controlled the United States and its Western allies. In keeping with this war mentality, the Stalinists advocated a system of Machiavellian ends-justifies-the-means ethics that permitted the sacrifice of individuals for the greater good of the Party. Censorship and hyper-punitive practices that sent thousands to the Gulag or psychiatric hospitals, and any number of other repressive measures, were necessary under Stalinism because the Party was at war. Stalinists tended to portray this scenario as temporary. Once the revolution ended in victory for the workers, the paradise would arrive and such peacetime concepts as human rights and personal freedoms could be eased back into society.

The Stalinists' enemies, referred to as reformists or liberals, either didn't think Soviet society was on a wartime footing, or didn't think a wartime footing justified the suspension of human rights. They favoured a cessation of Cold War militarism abroad, while closer to home they advocated easing censorship and permitting comparatively greater political pluralism. Because they often favoured experimenting with private property and other market reforms, this group was castigated by the Stalinists as "Westernizers." Battling toward this form of socialism meant limiting the glorification of Stalin, or any single individual leader, and cleansing Stalin's influence from the Party – a process called de-Stalinization.

At his most ethical moments in the 1960s, Yakovlev acted like a reformer fighting the Stalinists in the Central Committee. But he was not without his lapses. Aside from the ideological battle over Stalin's legacy, interfactional rivalries were perpetually breaking out in the corridors of Staraya Ploshchad, the Central Committee headquarters. Often in these battles for power, Yakovlev aligned himself to factions that backed propositions he knew were wrong. By this time, the Party's edicts no longer sent hundreds of thousands of zeks rolling east in cattle cars toward Siberia to fill the purge quotas of the secret police. Still, this period saw the Party crush the Novocherkassk worker uprising in 1962, the arrests of the writers Andrei Sinyavsky and Yuli Daniel in 1965, and the invasion of Czechoslovakia in 1968. There were also countless injustices against dissident members of the intelligentsia such as the legendary nuclear physicist Andrei Sakharov and the crusading writer, Aleksandr Solzhenitsyn. Thousands of Soviet citizens who sought to join relatives abroad were denied permission to leave the country. Thousands of others were imprisoned for disagreeing with the policies of the Soviet state, and the Party's ruling elite colluded to exert illegitimate control over 250 million lives.

To what extent was Yakovlev complicit in these injustices? Years later, such figures as the Soviet dissident turned Russian politician Vladimir Bukovsky would castigate Yakovlev for aiding the Party in human rights violations. Meanwhile, such Yakovlev associates as the well-known Russian journalist Genrikh Borovik insisted that even during the 1960s Yakovlev acted as a force for glasnost and the democratization of the country.

In a way, they're both right. Yakovlev was not a crusading defender of human rights in this period. It was not possible to rise as far as he did in the Party without compromising one's ethics, especially when one possessed a moral compass as sensitive as Yakovlev's. Sometimes he was a force for good in a profoundly corrupt institution, but in seeking to gain power and further his career, he did ally himself with those who committed injustice. And he committed injustice himself.

For what it's worth, Yakovlev devoted his post-Soviet life to righting the wrongs perpetrated by the Communist Party. Even before the collapse of the USSR, he became chairman of a commission to rehabilitate victims of political repression. He pored through long-locked archives, examined the fates of those sent to their deaths by firing squad or in the Gulag, and painstakingly overturned their convictions for invented crimes against the state. Although he never came out and said so explicitly, it seems possible he was motivated by the guilt he felt over this 13-year period, from 1960 to 1973, when he was most complicit in the crimes of the Communist Party.

WHEN HE REJOINED the Central Committee in 1960, Yakovlev set to work for Leonid Ilichev, who acted as Khrushchev's ideologue; in other words, Ilichev helped Khrushchev ensure that the Party's actions corresponded to Marxist ideology. Ilichev assigned Yakovlev to the Department of Agitation and Propaganda, typically shortened to AgitProp. Ilichev wanted Yakovlev to work on the Agitation side, which was sort of an institutional cheerleader for Marxism. Not being the cheerleading sort, Yakovlev asked for and was granted a job in Propaganda. This side oversaw sports and education, but its main task was to ensure that the media reflected and encouraged the same party-endorsed opinion toward everything, called the "party line." Yakovlev began as a bureaucrat in the newspaper division, where most of the work involved investigating

)

complaints that poured in when the occasional article reflected an opinion that strayed too far from the party line. Only months later, Ilichev promoted Yakovlev to head up AgitProp's radio and television division.

It was the warmest period of the thaw – an atmosphere sometimes referred to as glasnost, or openness. The term dated back to the time of the tsars, when it described easing state censorship to allow some criticism of the government. Similarly, Khrushchev loosened restrictions on cultural and intellectual matters. As an avid reader, Yakovlev was particularly excited by the liberation happening throughout literature. Stalin had demanded literature serve as propaganda; short stories, novels, and poetry were required to feature exclusively positive, educational depictions of Soviet life. Now, writers and other artists were experimenting with portraying the world as they saw it. Leading this movement was the literary magazine *Novy Mir*, whose editor, the poet Aleksandr Tvardovsky, published a poem that was a clarion call for sincerity in art, bewailing a literature "so indigestible, you feel like screaming." The poem ends with the writer vowing to go over the past "with a white light" to determine where he went wrong, to avoid writing "the cold smoke of lies," and to "ignore all judgments and all consequences."

Tvardovsky followed his own advice, publishing countless stories that dispensed with positivity or educational value and depicted Soviet life *as it was*, most famously in November 1962 with *One Day in the Life of Ivan Denisovich*, Aleksandr Solzhenitsyn's first published story, which exposed the harships of life in the Gulag system, which was only then beginning to be acknowledged by the state. Tvardovsky's backing would help the writer win a Nobel Prize only eight years later.

Yakovlev, too, felt the exhilaration of the thaw. He joined the cultural scene that revolved around the daring anti-Establishment poetry readings given by some of *Novy Mir*'s most famous poets, including Yevgeny Yevtushenko, Bella Akhmadulina, Robert Rozhdestvensky, and Andrei Voznesensky. At such events the audience watched in suspense to discover how far the poets dared to stray from the party line. One writer compared the liberation in this way: "Probably the students of Galileo experienced the same joy as they escaped the cramped, tightly locked universe of Ptolemy." Yakovlev sums up the atmosphere a little more succinctly: "We all grew a little younger."

Inspired by the thaw, and his experiences in America, Yakovlev shook up the Soviet media scene. In the early 1960s Soviet radio was dominated by just two stations, where programming content was limited to political propaganda and some classical music. Western broadcasters, including Voice of America, the BBC, and Radio Liberty, sent into the USSR more diverse, contemporary programs as a form of informational warfare, but the Party jammed the Western stations, preventing Soviet listeners from receiving the signals, especially in urban areas. Yakovlev seems likely to have had some influence on the curtailment of jamming in June of 1963, allowing Soviet radio owners to pick up Western broadcasts unimpeded. He then reorganized the Party's second radio station to compete with the Western programming by founding Radio Mayak, or "Beacon," which offered listeners a comparatively human alternative to the stern cadences and iron Marxist propaganda of the main broadcast channel, Program One. Mayak had news around the clock, interspersed with contemporary music and, eventually, some limited lifestyle and literary programming. Its debut on August 1, 1964 was a major event in the thaw; today it remains a popular Russian radio network. Yakovlev also pushed to found a newspaper that would act as an informative companion to existing propaganda-ridden publications, but the initiative went nowhere.

While Yakovlev favoured increased freedom of speech and of the press, it's important to realize he also participated in the dissemination of party hypocrisy. Mayak, and the other media overseen by the Propaganda Department where Yakovlev worked, either lied overtly or presented a distorted picture of events to Soviet listeners, to secure the Party's hold on power. The general rule dictated that nothing on the airwaves or in print could generalize negatively about the Soviet system. Newspapers were allowed to report on a functionary who had committed a particularly inexcusable alcohol-related gaffe, say, but they could never bemoan the epidemic proportions of Soviet alcoholism.

The media also were prevented from reporting on crime or disasters, either manmade or natural, because the Soviet system was supposed to be flawless. Hedrick Smith, a onetime Moscow correspondent for the *New York Times*, recounts a remarkable and possibly apocryphal story that nevertheless illustrates the system's absurdities. The story begins with a young woman flying from the Central Asian city of Karaganda to spend a week in Moscow to write her entrance examinations for Moscow State University. Three days after she should have returned home her worried father contacted friends in Moscow, who hadn't heard from her. He flew to Moscow; the university said she didn't write the entrance exam. Police had heard nothing. It was only after the father consulted with airline officials that he discovered his daughter hadn't ever arrived in Moscow. Her plane crashed en route. Thus, two weeks after the accident, the father realized his college-bound daughter was dead. The kicker: airport officials who informed him of the accident also told the grieving dad he wasn't to disclose to anyone how his daughter had died. Nothing was printed in the papers. Nothing appeared on radio about the crash.

Such policies perpetuated the power of the Communist Party. They also fooled its own members, like Yakovlev, into thinking the system was less corrupt than it was. During one of the ill-conceived schemes that marked Khrushchev's leadership, the Party in late spring of 1962 raised food prices throughout the Union just as the wages of some workers were cut. On June 1, 1962, the move spawned demonstrations in the industrial town of Novocherkassk. A crowd assembled before the town's party headquarters and speakers demanded lower food prices and wage increases. The Party called in special forces, which shot into the unarmed crowd, killing 23 protesters. A wave of arrests led to the conviction of 116 people, with seven sentenced to death and others subjected to jail terms between 10 and 15 years.

But for a perverse reference in *Pravda* praising the working spirit of the labourers at the locomotive plant, the Soviet media ignored the incident. In his memoirs, Yakovlev mentions that his boss spoke of it when it happened but said the demonstrators fired first on the soldiers. At this point, however, Yakovlev was almost 40 years old. He had a decade's worth of experience amid the hypocrisy of the Central Committee. He is certain to have sensed there was more to the story.

So Yakovlev was enjoying the life of a senior party bureaucrat in Moscow – eating specially prepared meals in the Central Committee cafeteria, vacationing at luxurious sanitaria, and recuperating, when one of his war wounds periodically acted up, in the best state-run medical facilities. All while hapless workers from Novocherkassk were executed for participating in demonstrations to make a living wage, and millions of others bore their own private injustices because they felt powerless, and feared the consequences of agitating for change.

But what were Yakovlev's options? He was a faithful Marxist who favoured some liberalization of Soviet politics. When the Party behaved as it had under Stalin, should Yakovlev have shouted the crimes out at some plenum? Should he have insisted exposés appear in state media? Should he have advertised his disagreement to every available party member? Or should he have done instead what he did, which was keep his head down, do his job and, when he felt able, use his influence to nudge the Party toward glasnost?

9

IRON SHURIK

SOON AFTER REJOINING the Central Committee bureaucracy, Yakovlev moved into the orbit of an exciting new force for change in the Party's upper echelons, a group led by Aleksandr Shelepin, whose good looks and city-boy sophistication encouraged devotion in his followers similar to that shown toward John F. Kennedy in the United States. Shelepin was as dynamic and glamorous a politician as the Soviet system produced. Some similarities exist between Shelepin's position in the early 1960s and Gorbachev's position two decades later. The fact that Shelepin was born in 1918 made him a full generation younger than the power brokers of the Presidium and just five years older than Yakovlev. (In contrast, Khrushchev was born in 1894, and his successor, Leonid Brezhnev, in 1906.) Shelepin was educated at the Moscow Institute of History, Philosophy, and Literature, and his power base was the Party's youth movement, known as the Komsomol, a 19-million-member organization that Shelepin first began leading at age 34. Think of the Komsomol as a more militant, Marxist version of the Boy Scouts and Girl Guides. Once Shelepin tightened discipline in the Komsomol by, among other things, disparaging "shirkers" and those who pursued "alien" tastes like "vulgar dancing," the group became a fearsome force for Khrushchev's policies. For example, to help the leader's Virgin Lands Campaign to render unfarmed land fertile, one of Shelepin's volunteer drives dispatched more than 300,000 young men and women to Kazakhstan in 1954. When in 1958 Khrushchev was looking for someone to lead the secret police out of its Stalinist past, it was Shelepin who got the job. The new KGB chief filled the spy agency's ranks with old chums from his Komsomol days. Then, three years later and now nicknamed "Iron Shurik," Shelepin was again promoted, this time to the Central Committee Secretariat, and provided with a mandate to do with the whole of Soviet society what he had previously done with the Komsomol – to whip it into shape, to combat "humbuggery, spoilage, bureaucratism and all that is negative and alien to the socialist system."

In the early days Shelepin spoke as though he was a reformer. At a party gathering in 1961, Shelepin condemned Stalin and his compatriots in unusually harsh language: "How can these people sleep in peace?" he said at the congress, speaking of Stalin's former associates, many of whom still occupied senior positions within the Party. "They must be haunted by nightmares, they must hear the sobs and curses of the mothers, wives and children of innocent comrades done to death." But as one Kremlinologist noted, "Neither that speech nor his earlier ones can be taken as a key to his deepest convictions." Like all adept party bureaucrats, Shelepin was known "to be nimble at zigging when the party line zigs and zagging when it zags."

Indeed, while publicly disavowing Stalinism, Shelepin was engaging in typical Stalinist behaviour. For example, when he headed the KGB he approved the murder of the Ukrainian guerrilla nationalist leader, Stefan Bandera. An assassin did it with a device that belched a cloud of poisonous prussic acid into Bandera's face, creating symptoms that mimicked a heart attack. Shelepin personally received the assassin at KGB headquarters to congratulate him on his success, and awarded him the Order of the Red Banner, a prestigious honour.

It's not clear exactly when Yakovlev become one of Shelepin's "Young Group." Yakovlev's immediate superior in AgitProp, Vladimir Stepakov, was a Shelepin man, thanks to Stepakov's earlier work in the KGB, where he became head of the Moscow detachment. Regardless of the work connection, Yakovlev might have gravitated toward Shelepin anyway. Through the early 1960s Iron Shurik was gathering around himself the youngest, most intelligent and dynamic members of the Central Committee, the people who could really get things done; the men who, as Yakovlev notes in his memoirs, wanted to "awaken the sleeping capital." Yakovlev certainly belonged to this group, many of whom felt that Shelepin's leadership was only a question of time. What was certain was that everyone was tired of Khrushchev, whose increasingly capricious nature was alarming the Central Committee.

Khrushchev's fate is relevant to Yakovlev's. Indeed, Khrushchev is one of a handful of topics that causes Yakovlev to shift, in his memoirs, into a melancholy but no less eloquent prose – and why not? "L'homme Nikita" started the job of glasnost and perestroika that Yakovlev and his fellow reformers saw themselves finishing. Interestingly, much of what Yakovlev writes about Khrushchev can apply to Yakovlev himself. "Crafty, but also naïve in a childlike way," Yakovlev says of Khrushchev. "He sought to go beyond the horizon . . . He had no idea at all what lay beyond the horizon." In attempting to reform the Soviet system, Khrushchev ran afoul of the party apparatus, the powerful minions who distrusted change because it threatened their own private fiefdoms, regardless of whether it would improve the country.

One of Khrushchev's reforms proposed abolishing the system of special stores where party bureaucrats selected their groceries and other goods from a wider selection than that available to common Soviet citizens – a move that alienated him from the Party bureaucrats. Khrushchev's decision to give peasants passports provided a whole class of people across the Soviet Union with more freedom of internal movement. Suddenly the passport-equipped farmers had some choice in where they wished to live. A market economy's ability to quickly change labour prices might have tempered such a shock. But in the Soviet Union's centrally planned economy, millions took their new passports and stampeded for the cities, which in turn caused rural labour shortages and other chaos. The system exacted a revenge on Khrushchev, as it would a quarter-century later on Gorbachev and Yakovlev: it blamed Khrushchev for the food shortages.

Other grand schemes backfired. Storing nuclear weapons in Cuba, a Soviet client-state, brought the world to the brink of apocalypse with the Cuban Missile Crisis in 1962. Then Khrushchev alienated Russia's most powerful ally, China. By 1964, Khrushchev had alienated party bureaucrats with his unpredictable behaviour and wild policy shifts. Shelepin, Brezhnev, and other heavies decided to force him out on October 12, 1964. Khrushchev became the first Soviet leader to depart from office alive. In recognition for his role in the putsch, Shelepin was named to the Presidium (better known today as the Politburo), which selected as Khrushchev's successor Leonid Brezhnev. The new leader was a chain-smoking Ukraine-raised ethnic Russian so dependent on the suggestions of others he'd been nicknamed "The Ballerina," because anyone could turn his opinion. While he publicly pledged service to the goals of socialism, Brezhnev would prove to care more about his own personal enrichment and the accretion of power. But on the morning of October 14, when one of Brezhnev's assistants called Yakovlev to request his help writing the new leader's first official speech, none of that mattered. It mattered only that Brezhnev was not Khrushchev. When Yakovlev met him three days later, Brezhnev seemed no match for Iron Shurik. Shelepin's succession seemed inevitable.

WITH SHELEPIN IN THE PRESIDIUM, with his protégé Vladimir Semichastny atop the KGB, the Young Group parachuted and promoted other friends into key positions. The head of AgitProp, Ilichev, was fired and replaced with Yakovlev's immediate superior, Vladimir Stepakov. Soon Stepakov promoted another Shelepin man to be his second-in-command: 41-year-old Aleksandr Yakovlev. His sphere of control extended now to the whole of the Soviet propaganda apparatus – not just radio and TV, but newspapers and sports programs as well as educational facilities. In his day-to-day duties he was something like an über-editor; he devised the spin Soviet media placed on current events.

Yakovlev also increasingly found himself writing speeches for Brezhnev and other top figures.

He also helped Shelepin's group in their sorties against Brezhnev and his supporters. "Why are you working so hard for him?" Yakovlev once asked two of Brezhnev's speechwriters. "Do you want to turn this ignorance into a cult?" The summer after Brezhnev took power, Yakovlev played a key role in discrediting one of Brezhnev's associates. The affair started when Arkady Sakhnin, the editor of *Komsomolskaya Pravda*, the Party youth wing's official organ, published a juicy exposé about one Captain Alekei Solyanik. Problem was, Solyanik was a Soviet celebrity renowned for his exploits. He was the hero who ran the country's most famous whaling fleet. He'd been the subject of adventurous profiles in the party press. He was a Hero of Socialist Labour, among the USSR's highest distinctions. And he also happened to be Brezhnev's man; during his visits to Moscow, Solyanik often provided the general secretary with expensive gifts.

The exposé said Solyanik was involved in some distinctly unsocialist labour practices. According to the report, Solyanik ran an illegal but highly lucrative bone-carving operation on his whaling vessels. When the crews put in to ports in such countries as Australia and New Zealand, Solyanik traded the whalebone carvings for expensive carpets and other goods, which he then brought back home and sold. That he was running what amounted to an illegal, privately owned import-export operation was bad enough. But particularly egregious to communist readers were the working conditions of the whalebone carvers. The good captain was apparently working his men like slaves. Conditions on the boats were so bad that one sailor committed suicide. Instead of being a hero of socialist labour, Solyanik was exploiting workers as cruelly as the capitalist robber-barons of America.

The article generated attention. Solyanik's friends demanded an official inquiry, and Yakovlev drew the assignment. The politically safe move would have been to clear Solyanik. Yakovlev could have fired a few people, slapped Solyanik on the back, and returned to business as usual.

But here was an opportunity for Yakovlev's private beliefs – his belief in the need for a more independent press – to intersect with his political interests. Solyanik was Brezhnev's man. That made him the enemy of Yakovlev's patron, Shelepin. By making Solyanik look bad, Yakovlev was scoring points for his faction and furthering the cause of the press. So once the canny bureaucrat completed his investigation, he filed a report defending the story to the Central Committee. The matter was placed on the agenda of the Central Committee's Secretariat, a body to which such bigwigs as party leader Leonid Brezhnev, his Politburo associate Mikhail Suslov, and Aleksandr Shelepin all belonged. Brezhnev didn't usually attend these meetings, preferring to leave administrative details to his older, more experienced associate, Suslov. Still, Yakovlev went into it feeling significant amounts of trepidation. He grew more nervous when Brezhnev showed up to occupy his usually empty chair. Then Yakovlev noticed that none of the other Secretariat members would meet his gaze.

Once the meeting began it turned into a pile-on against the press, and by extension Yakovlev. Speakers said the *Komsomolskaya Pravda* article had stained the whole of the country by slandering a prominent man of the state. The Department of Propaganda – read: Yakovlev – should never have allowed the newspaper to publish the article. By the end, even the disgraced Solyanik felt secure enough to display his indignation, complaining the exposé damaged his ability to lead the whaling fleet.

Shelepin was the second last to speak. What are the facts? he asked. If the facts in the story are wrong, then let's punish the editor-in-chief, and those who supported him. But if the facts are correct, then why punish anyway? In the Central Committee, in an era when no one ever quite came out and said what they meant, Shelepin's words amounted to an endorsement of Yakovlev and the exposé.

So most of the Secretariat was supporting Brezhnev's man, Solyanik. And Shelepin was standing up for his own junior ally, Yakovlev. Brezhnev might have piped up here, to tip the scales either way, but the leader disliked confrontation. He kept quiet, and the room's attention shifted to Suslov, the old man of the Politburo. Would Suslov align with

Brezhnev? If he did, Sakhnin, the newspaper's editor, would certainly be fired. Yakovlev's job, too, could disappear.

Suslov began with the usual boilerplate about managing employees, describing "the need to care for the staff." Yakovlev exchanged glances with Sakhnin. This didn't sound good.

"Everyone here was correct –" Suslov said.

Yakovlev's mood must have plunged at that point. *Everyone* had piled on to him. *Everyone* wanted him fired. But in the weird logic of Soviet politics, what *everyone* said didn't matter. With the Solyanik debate evenly balanced between Brezhnev's cronies and Shelepin's defence of Yakovlev and the media, Suslov went with his gut instinct. And in contrast to Brezhnev's pragmatic embrace of the fruits of corruption, Suslov was a faithful, orthodox communist who despised extravagance of any kind. In this instance, it was Suslov's will that won out.

"Everyone here was correct," Suslov continued, "that we can't leave Solyanik in his job."

Yakovlev exchanged a glance with Sakhnin. Were they hearing correctly? No one had said Solyanik should be fired. However, party leaders weren't known for their fidelity to historical accuracy. Apparently, Suslov was deciding to ignore the room's previous toadying. "Bad things are happening in the fleet, and one man has committed suicide," Suslov continued. "Of course, the newspaper could have sought advice before publication, but, judging by the investigation results, everything stated in the article was true . . . Solyanik must be dismissed from his job."

Yakovlev was elated. Shelepin's support had been crucial. This time, he had squeaked through. As the meeting broke up, Brezhnev stopped the editor and Yakovlev. "Now you quit whistling the same tune!" he said. The deputy Propaganda chief had been saved – this time – by Kremlin intrigue.

AMID ALL THESE POWER GAMES, Yakovlev often had to perform tasks he found repugnant. A few months after the putsch, in February 1965, Shelepin contradicted his earlier thaw rhetoric by speaking at a party gathering about the "tightening up" required by Soviet society, an allusion to a return to the stability and order that existed under Stalin. In private, he went further, speaking of the need to rehabilitate the dead dictator's reputation – in other words, to cleanse Stalin of the stain caused by Khrushchev's Secret Speech. Was he showing his true colours? No. Someone like Shelepin didn't have true colours. He had only the will to power, and a desire to say whatever he thought would help him attain his goal of supreme leadership. Shelepin's Stalinist rhetoric was a ploy to win the support of the Central Committee where, in the wake of Khrushchev's chaos, lots of party members felt Soviet society needed some "tightening up." More discipline. More stability. More control. It was amid this context that the Communist Party began a clampdown on the most exciting literary magazine of the Soviet thaw, *Novy Mir*, and its editor, Aleksandr Tvardovsky.

A month after Shelepin ratcheted up the Stalinist rhetoric, a series of senior party officials showed up to a meeting of the Russian Writers' Union, Soviet literature's governing body. The speakers were bigwigs; one of them, Andrei Kirilenko, belonged to both the Presidium and the Secretariat, the first and second most powerful groups in the USSR. In fact, he was one of the party bigwigs who ordered the massacre of the workers at Novocherkassk. Now, he was about to execute a similarly hamhanded response. *Novy Mir's* crime was publishing "one-sided" and "confusing" stories that reflected negatively on Soviet life, said Kirilenko and his cronies. From now on, the magazine would have to publish stories that were faithful to Leninist principles. All this foretold a return to Stalin's censorship, a return to the time when all opinion reflected the party line. Sensing the repressions to come, Tvardovsky fell into a depression so serious he required hospitalization.

Vladimir Stepakov, the Propaganda chief, and Yakovlev's boss, supported the crackdown on Tvardovsky. In public, at least, to adhere to party discipline, Yakovlev had to do the same. This troubled him. Tvardovsky was 13 years older than Yakovlev, but Propaganda was one of two Central Committee sections that regulated the magazine. (The other was Culture, also headed by a Stalinist.) The men had many mutual friends, including the high-ranking liberal deputy in the Party's Culture department, Albert Belyaev, and the writer and onetime *Novy Mir* editor, Konstantin Simonov. But even aside from their personal connections, the censure of *Novy Mir* would have troubled any Soviet citizen who loved literature.

Tvardovsky was a big, blustery man with translucent blue eyes and thick white hair combed into a side part. In his youth he was such a fervent believer in communism that he stayed loyal even after his father was denounced as a "kulak," or wealthy peasant, and sent to his death in the Siberian labour camps. Tvardovsky first became famous after he served as a war correspondent in the Great Patriotic War. His service provided him with the material to write an epic poem, *Vasily Tyorkin*, about the wartime experiences of a low-ranking soldier. It was published to acclaim in 1946. (Yakovlev counted it among his favourite poems.) The notoriety helped Tvardovsky win the editorship of *Novy Mir* in 1950.

The courage Tvardovsky displayed in that role – discovering Solzhenitsyn and countless others – exacted a cost on the poet, who battled alcoholism throughout his life. He was fired for four years, from 1954 to 1958, after he missed – due to drunkenness – a meeting that the Party called to discuss the magazine's "excesses." He was rehired after his successor, Yakovlev's friend Konstantin Simonov, also offended the Party. By 1965, after seven uninterrupted years of audacity, Tvardovsky's reputation in Soviet culture had no American equivalent. His stature as an editor combined the literary cachet of *The New Yorker*'s William Shawn in the 1950s with something like the political influence of the *Washington Post*'s Ben Bradlee in the Watergate-era 1970s. In fact, Tvardovsky discovered and published so many of the best-known dissident writers that some said the thaw should be called the "era of Tvardovsky." To its fans, the work Tvardovsky printed in *Novy Mir* was inspiration for them to be more honest and open in their own lives; to his enemies, Tvardovsky's honesty was blackening the Soviet reputation.

IN SEPTEMBER OF 1965, a few months after Yakovlev's Solyanik triumph, the KGB under the charge of Shelepin's protégé, Vladimir Semichastny, began an offensive against the liberal literary intelligentsia of Moscow. Tvardovsky and *Novy Mir* bore the brunt of the attack. In almost simultaneous raids the KGB searched two apartments that housed much of the unpublished work of *Novy Mir's* most famous writer, Aleksandr Solzhenitsyn; when he found out what happened, Solzhenitsyn figured he was headed back to the Gulag. Instead, the same week as the Solzhenitsyn raids, the KGB arrested two of *Novy Mir's* writers. Their names were Andrei Sinyavsky and Yuli Daniel. Both were known to oppose any return of Stalinist repression; Sinyavsky in particular was a highly regarded critic with enemies in the Party's orthodox wing. Sinyavsky and Daniel were also writing satirical stories about Soviet life – uncleared by Soviet censors, and without approval from the Party – and sending them to the West, where the stories were published under pseudonyms in foreign literary journals. The KGB accused the two writers of disseminating anti-Soviet propaganda.

This business put Yakovlev in a tough spot. Sinyavsky and Daniel's "crimes" evoked his complicated experiences with Pasternak in New York. The writers' arrests seemed a transparent attempt to discredit Tvardovsky by connecting the gentle satire and criticism in *Novy Mir* with treason. Yakovlev's friends in the Writers' Union were rallying around the imprisoned writers. But the Propaganda Department was in the thick of arranging how the trial was to be covered by the Soviet press – deliberations in which Yakovlev would certainly have participated.

Suslov assigned Yakovlev to sit in on the trial of Sinyavsky and Daniel, the better to manage the press response. Yakovlev would have been a natural to go. He was the number two man in AgitProp. The presence of such a senior party bureaucrat would show the writers and editors in the courtroom the import that the state placed on the proceedings. But Yakovlev was against the trial, seeing it as a clumsy, unsophisticated attempt to rein in the country's best-known forum for literary art. So to Suslov, Yakovlev provided excuse after excuse explaining why he couldn't go. He wasn't familiar with the case. He hadn't read Sinyavsky's and Daniel's stories. Besides, this was more of a literary than a media matter. Someone should go from the Department of

Culture. That one stuck; Suslov, ever obsessed with following bureau-cratic job descriptions, arranged for a Culture bureaucrat to go. The trial ended in a conviction, and Daniel and Sinyavsky were sent on long sentences – five and seven years, respectively – to the labour camps.

The Sinyavsky–Daniel trial was just one sign among many that the Party was regressing back toward the totalitarian state that existed under Stalin. The anti-Tvardovsky rhetoric peaked at a major gathering of the Communist Party the month after the trial's end, in March 1966, when the Party yanked the editor's membership in the Central Committee. Military histories once again were glorifying Stalin's role in the war; members of the military were discouraged from subscribing to "anti-Stalinist" publications, such as *Novy Mir*. Meanwhile, progressive news-papers editors were fired and replaced with quieter functionaries. The orthodox party organs once again began talking about that old Stalinist bugbear, "cosmopolitanism" – and using it to mask increasingly preva-lent anti-Semitism. Censors clamped down on talk of the Gulag and most other realistic depictions of Soviet life, prompting the flourishing of the self-published literature known as samizdat. Only the protection of Yakovlev and other liberal members of the Central Committee prevented Tvardovsky from losing his job in this period. Nevertheless, Tvardovsky remained defiant. Truth, Tvardovsky wrote, could escape the strongest barriers, the way water seeped through the strongest dikes: "Through con-crete, through woven steel / It will burst – all your labour in vain."

How could the reform-minded Yakovlev, an avid reader, an ardent fan of Tvardovsky, align himself with a cabal of Stalinist law-and-order enthusiasts like Shelepin's group? Several different factors were at play. Shelepin's cadre amounted to a covert, internal opposition aligned against Brezhnev and the rest of the leadership. Russian oppositions have a history of tolerating alliances of convenience until they attain power. For example, what little opposition the secret police allowed to exist in Putin's Russia formed a scrappy coalition that saw a liberal demo-crat like Garry Kasparov working alongside members of the far-left National Bolshevik Party; similarly odd matchups existed in pre-Revolutionary Russia. The Young Group that Shelepin gathered around him in preparation for an anti-Brezhnev putsch probably harboured a similar range of political sentiment. In the secretive environment of the Party, members tended to base their alliances on pragmatic calculations rather than political beliefs, which mostly went undiscussed. Which war unit you fought in, the fact your sister was married to somebody's brother, your comparative youth – within the Party, these factors were considered more important than how you felt about Stalin's legacy. And above all these factors was power. Participants in the Party's political games allied themselves with the most powerful faction they could find. Then, once they were cozily ensconced in a clique, they sought opportunities to pull the party line in the direction they wanted. By aligning himself with the up-and-coming faction thought to be destined to control the Party, Yakovlev was making it more likely he could influence policies in years to come. Becoming a Shelepin man was a bet that, once Shelepin succeeded Brezhnev, Yakovlev would have a chance to push the party line toward a socialism that was more accommodating to dissent and a free press.

And finally we come to what is perhaps the most important element to consider when discussing conflicts between faction membership and personal sentiment. If Yakovlev failed to budge the party line – if the Party, despite Yakovlev's arguments, went ahead and did something Yakovlev found personally despicable – then party practice said Yakovlev had to fall in line. He had to zag when the Party zagged. He had to sacrifice his personal beliefs for the good of socialism. The edict meant Yakovlev did many things he found personally repugnant when he worked in the Central Committee. He did them anyway, because he was a good communist, yes – and also possibly for less noble reasons.

A FIST TO THE JAW

I N JUNE 1966, four months after the Sinyavsky–Daniel trial, Aleksandr Shelepin led an official delegation on a trip to visit the Soviet ally of Mongolia. Far from the oft-stifling atmosphere of Moscow, where KGB bugs lurked in every corner, Shelepin and his friends relaxed, perhaps a little too much. During one typically toast-filled dinner, an associate with whom Yakovlev worked closely in Propaganda, Radio Committee Chairman Nikolai Mesiatsev, proposed a toast to Shelepin. Except that wasn't the way he phrased it. Instead, he toasted Aleksandr Nikolaevich Shelepin – *the future general secretary*.

In a society where everyone was supposed to display absolute loyalty to the supreme leader, the toast was an indication of the Young Group's swaggering confidence. In Stalin's time, such an act would have resulted in torture and execution for Shelepin and Mesiatsev, as well as anyone remotely connected to them: co-workers, family, friends, friends' friends – possibly even pets. Just for good measure. That wasn't the style of the current, confrontation-averse, caution-obsessed Politburo, where the emphasis was on collective leadership and rule by consensus of all members. In such a hyperpolitical environment Shelepin's confidence stood out. The older men of the Politburo aligned against him to teach a lesson. In May of 1967, Stalin's daughter, Svetlana Allilueva, defected from the Soviet Union through the U.S. embassy in New Delhi – a tremendously embarrassing blow for the Soviets. Using the defection as a pretext for the move, the Politburo fired Shelepin's protégé, Vladimir Semichastny, from his post atop the KGB, replacing him with Yuri Andropov. A month later, while Shelepin was in hospital for abdominal surgery, the Politburo removed *him* from his post atop the immensely powerful Party-State Control Commission. A few months later, Brezhnev's faction arranged for him to lose his spot in the Party Secretariat. Shelepin's only consolation at this point was his seat on the Politburo – a difficult perch from which to stage any major power plays against an increasingly powerful Brezhnev.

Brezhnev and his Stalinist underlings killed the fresh hopes of the thaw. People realized the future would be much like the past. This progression from idealism to cynicism was tough for anyone who enjoyed their previous freedoms, as Yakovlev had, just as blindness is a tough disability to manage for one who has enjoyed sight. One member of the intelligentsia said the artistically stifling atmosphere in Moscow felt as though the air had been pumped from the city.

"The country swam with the current," Yakovlev writes in his memoirs.

Any absence of leadership breeds many negative, even vile, phenomena in public life . . . Deception, exaggerated reporting of results, and false information abounded, as they all competed to catalogue their successes: Oh, what splendid work we're doing, what excellent results! . . . I too signed such notes. The reports on agitation and propaganda work looked especially absurd. We announced how many propagandists and agitators were working day and night in this or that region and in the country as a whole, and we reported their effective influence on people . . . Everyone knew that it was a lie. But everyone pretended that it was the truth. Falsehood penetrated the system to the core. Supposedly the productivity of labor and the quality of production were growing quickly. Nobody believed that, and what is more, nobody could have believed it, for the store shelves were reminiscent of dinosaur skeletons . . . It was a theatre of the absurd.

Yakovlev kept busy in this period. On top of apparat work, he wrote a second dissertation, a survey of American writing on foreign affairs in the period 1945 to 1966, earning him a 'doktor nauk' degree. (It doesn't really have a western equivalent but can be considered a kind of "super" Ph.D. that qualified Yakovlev to run his own research institution.) Despite his esteemed rank, he was not above deriving amusement from these absurdities. The Party handed awards to particularly productive workers. The Central Committee apparat were supposed to forward candidates for awards to the Secretariat. Once he forwarded a few editors' names Yakovlev realized no one ever checked the list of honourees, so he decided to have a little fun with the system. Soon, astonished newspaper editors were finding themselves receiving awards for growing potatoes or tractor plowing. One of Yakovlev's deputies, a man whose alcohol consumption sometimes affected his work, received an Order of the Red Banner for excellence in the growth of hops.

ON AUGUST 20, 1968 Yakovlev drew his most formative assignment yet. His superior Pyotr Demichev asked him to meet at his office. Demichev was a crony of Brezhnev and only slightly older than Yakovlev. But as the Central Committee secretary in charge of ideology, he was Stepakov's direct superior – the boss of Yakovlev's boss. At the meeting, Demichev assigned Yakovlev to lead a contingent of about 20 Soviet journalists to provide propaganda support for the "liberation" of Czechoslovakia.

According to the rhetoric circulated in the Soviet media by Yakovlev's department, this should have been an exciting, invigorating assignment – the sort of thing that reignites a communist's youthful spirit. Soviet troops had liberated Prague from the Germans in the Second World War. Three years later, in 1948, Czechoslovakia became a communist state – and, thanks to its location on the western edge of the Eastern Bloc, a bulwark against the forces of capitalism. For years, it had been run by a puppet of

Moscow's named Antonín Novotný. But then, in early 1968, Novotný was toppled. According to the newspapers that Yakovlev managed, the perpetrators were a conspiracy of Western provocateurs and the nation's Jewish intelligentsia. The official Soviet line said Novotný's replacement, Alexander Dubček, was a puppet of the West. Dubček was doing rash things like pulling back state control of the press and considering market reform. He even discussed the possibility of lifting one-party rule and instituting some sort of democracy. According to the reports of the Soviet ambassador to Prague, Czechoslovakia's working classes were desperate to be rescued from this nefarious traitor.

There was another take on what was happening in Czechoslovakia, one favoured by observers in the West as well as members of the Soviet intelligentsia, who heard about the "Prague Spring" through Voice of America and other foreign media. All were celebrating Dubček and the Prague Spring. They depicted Dubček's reforms as a continuation of Khrushchev's thaw. Dubček's government was seen to be humanizing the repressive Soviet flavour of communism, moving Czechoslovakia toward intellectual freedom, toward freedom of expression, toward freedom of art and of mind. The Moscow intelligentsia hoped the Prague Spring was contagious. If the economy in Prague and environs improved, they speculated, perhaps the Party could be convinced to try something similar at home.

As the reforms continued, the Soviet Politburo decided on a "rescue mission." Demichev informed Yakovlev that troops from the Soviet Union and four allies were to descend on Czechoslovakia that night, liberating Prague just as the Red Army had done 23 years earlier. Yakovlev made an attempt to wriggle out of this assignment in much the same way as he had the Sinyavsky–Daniel trial. He protested that he didn't know anything about Czechoslovakia. Besides, he'd need things like leaflets and posters for the propaganda effort.

"All that's been done," Demichev said, waving away Yakovlev's protests. "The military has everything in place."

Yakovlev and his team flew first to Poland, then to an airport outside of Prague. His first impression of Czechoslovakia was the sight, visible from the airport, of an improvised gallows. Hanging in effigy from a noose was a Soviet soldier. Aside from the Soviet ambassador and a handful of frightened Czech Communist Party bureaucrats, no one in Czechoslovakia welcomed Yakovlev or the other 225,000 members of the occupying forces. There wasn't much actual fighting. The "liberators" were far too strong for that. Of the 50 people who died in the invasion, the majority were Czechs or Slovaks killed when the liberators fired on unarmed civilians. With little trouble the Soviets and their allies set up tanks and artillery fortifications at key transportation points – bridge entrances, railway stations, major intersections – and in front of strategically important buildings, such as radio and TV stations, government ministries, and universities. And then the resistance began.

Here's what the Czech people did to the Soviets: they *shamed* them. This was a resistance fought not with bullets, but with propaganda. Like some sort of virulent moss, anti-Soviet slogans spread over every available surface of the city: cathedral walls, the stones of the Charles Bridge, on posters and placards and, thanks to some brave youths, on the outside of Soviet tanks. After 20 years of being forced to learn Russian in their schools, the Czechs were delighted to finally find a use for the hated language. Painted, sprayed, printed or daubed, they used their knowledge of Russian to insult the "uninvited guests" and bade them to return to their homes. The slogans also arrived by air: pirate radio stations broadcasting insults. Some were ironic, absurdist takes on Marxist slogans. Others subverted Soviet propaganda. "Proletarians of the world unite – or I shoot!" There was the ironic "Long live USSR–CSSR friendship!" (which used the Soviet abbreviation for Czechoslovakia). Biblical references cited the supposedly fraternal relationship enjoyed by Moscow and Prague: "Abel and Cain were also brothers!" Others equated the behaviour of the Soviets with that of their foreign, historic enemies: "Vietnam – CSSR: U.S. imperialism – USSR imperialism." All the messages tried to force the occupying force to confront the coercive nature of the occupation.

The tactics of the resistance troubled Yakovlev. Some graffiti suggested Dubček and the other reformers were the true Leninists; by invading, the Soviets were executing a crime of Stalinist proportions. Particularly galling to Yakovlev, thanks to his experience fighting the Germans, were the swastikas Czech citizens scrawled on Soviet tanks and the cartoons in newspapers and newsletters that compared the invasion to the Nazi occupation of Czechoslovakia during the Second World War. "Dubček is our Lenin," read one poster. "Hitler's successor – Brezhnev!"

The liberal party member and former Pravda writer Len Karpinsky wrote in samizdat that the Soviet invasion was "a fist to the jaw of thinking society." Yakovlev in turn describes his reaction to the Czech resistance in similarly violent terms. Such protest hit him, he said, "like a truncheon in the head." As the chief propagandist for the occupying forces, Yakovlev held the role of commanding officer in this war of slogans and placards – a task so opposed to his personal sentiments that it was like assigning Bill Clinton to head the public relations team of George W. Bush's presidential campaign. But disciplined communist that he was, Yakovlev put aside his personal sentiments and set about following the party line. He led his editors, broadcasters and writers as they did their part to crush the Prague Spring.

Yakovlev is certain to have come across the "Two Thousand Words," the clarion call for reform from writer and Czech party member Ludvík Vaculík, which was reprinted in newspapers across the world as well as copied, printed, and posted on walls and surfaces across Prague. "The leaders' mistaken policies transformed a political party and an alliance based on ideas into an organization for exerting power, one which proved highly attractive to egoists itching to wield authority, to cowards with an eye to the main chance, to people with bad conscience . . ." wrote Vaculik. "We all of us bear responsibility for the present state of affairs. But those of us who are communists bear more than others, and those who acted as component parts or as instruments of unchecked power bear the most of all."

Did these words prompt in Yakovlev any internal crises? Did they trigger any self-examination? Did he look at himself and ask whether he was an egoist, a coward, a person "with bad conscience"?

His memoirs don't say. They do indicate that he worked hard to provide propaganda support for the "rescue mission." Yakovlev helped coordinate military helicopters to drop leaflets over Czech cities. "The Soviet government," the leaflets said, "proceeding from the principles of inseparable friendship and co-operation, and in accordance with existing contractual commitments, have decided to meet the request for rendering necessary help to the fraternal people of Czechoslovakia."

Acting "from the principles of inseparable friendship," Soviet troops attempted to shut down Czech media by parking tanks and artillery guns outside Prague's main newspapers and radio stations. They stationed troops with guns by the printing presses. But with many members of Czechoslovakia's Communist Party, and many government ministries, staying loyal to the values of the Prague Spring, the resistance was able to get around the measures, often with the help of contingency plans developed by the Party in preparation for attack by the West. Resisters found mothballed antique printing presses the Soviets didn't know about, smuggled out the lead type and templates from their setting rooms, and cranked their newspapers out by hand. Pirate radio stations beamed slogans into the sky. When the Soviets seized their antennae, the pirate broadcasters connected their transmitters to utility wires. Yakovlev's colleagues brought in a trainload of jamming equipment to scramble the pirate stations, but word went out over the airwaves and before the train reached Prague the resisters arranged to block the tracks with disabled locomotives. Eventually, the Soviets resorted to using a helicopter to transport the jammers. Another incoming train was loaded with enough radio equipment to set up a broadcasting station for Soviet propaganda, but somewhere between Poland and Czechoslovakia the Czech crew "lost track" of the freight. In the days before the freight was tracked down, the pro-occupation station Radio Vltava beamed in their Czech-language broadcasts from East Germany.

"They have guns and rockets. Our weapons are chalk, pen, word, and the consistent ignoring of them!" crowed the newspaper, *Rude Pravo*. That hurt, too; "them" of course, meant Soviet troops. And *Rude Pravo* was the official organ of the Czechoslovakia Communist Party, which was supposed to be loyal to Moscow. But aside from its editor-in-chief figurehead, the *Rude Pravo* staff were loyal to the cause of the Prague Spring. Yakovlev and his men discussed printing their own version of *Rude Pravo*, possibly at the old headquarters. But the pro-Soviet editor was too afraid to attempt it. They did try to print the newspaper in Dresden, in East Germany, and succeeded in producing an edition, but on the return trip the helicopter transporting the print run was shot down. One of Yakovlev's most resourceful colleagues was killed in the crash.

Doing *anything* was difficult for the Soviets. Defiant locals caused interminable nuisances for the occupiers. Travel was difficult because resisters took down every navigational aid available, including street signs, house numbers, and the placards that identified buildings. When lost Soviet troops asked for directions, the Czech people pretended not to hear their requests, or feigned misunderstanding. Yakovlev experienced this and many other signs of local displeasure. He watched a sit-in at Prague's Wenceslas Square. He heard the well-organized, ear-splitting 15-minute blast of noise in which the citizenry used bells, whistles, horns, and any other noisemaker they could to signal their resentment. There were subtler symbols of resistance. At one restaurant, Yakovlev placed an order in Russian. The waitress disappeared. A half-hour later Yakovlev was still waiting. Then he tried an experiment. He signalled to another server and gave his order this time in his rusty English. His food arrived just two minutes later.

After a week in Prague, Yakovlev flew home to Moscow. The good communist had done his job. Radio Vltava was up and running. Two days after his departure, Yakovlev's fellow propagandists succeeded in arranging the publication of a Soviet newspaper, *Zpravy*, to represent the interests of the Kremlin. Back home, Yakovlev found such Politburo members as Suslov, Chernenko and Brezhnev hungry for information from Czechoslovakia. During a meeting with Brezhnev, Yakovlev told the general secretary about the slogans, the posters, and the radio broadcasts protesting the presence of Soviet forces. He outlined the nearly universal resentment of the Czech and Slovak people. And he told Brezhnev that "he had to support Dubček, that he had no alternative . . . To criticize Dubček endlessly for having surrounded himself with the 'wrong people' was senseless . . . Otherwise, hostility in Czechoslovakia toward the USSR would continue to grow."

Yakovlev's entreaties had little effect. Occupation troops peaked at about 500,000 soldiers and settled in for a long stay. Almost five months after the invasion, with a return to Stalinist repression looking inevitable, a Czech student named Jan Palach walked into Prague's Wenceslas Square carrying a jerry can of gasoline, a set of matches and a letter that specifically mentioned Soviet propaganda. Speaking for Palach's resistance cell, the letter said, "We have decided to express our protests and awaken the people of this country . . . Our group is composed of volunteers . . . I have had the honour to draw the first number . . . Our demands are: 1. The immediate abolition of censorship. 2. The prohibition of the circulation of Zpravy (an illegal newspaper . . . produced and circulated by Soviet propagandists working with the occupation forces) . . . Signed: Torch No. 1." Palach drenched his clothes with gasoline, struck a match, and set himself alight. He died of his burns three days later. More such self-immolations followed.

These actions were perhaps the most startling symbols Yakovlev had of the harm perpetrated by the system he worked in. As months passed, the Soviets regained control of Czechoslovakia, setting a precedent that became known as the Brezhnev Doctrine, which advocated exerting military pressure to secure Soviet control over its allied republics.

"The Prague Spring taught me quite a lot," wrote Yakovlev. The republics of Eastern Europe weren't willing members of the socialist brotherhood, as his Propaganda Department suggested. They were coerced into their alliance with Moscow. The supposed brotherhood of international socialism was instead a dictatorship imposed by strong Moscow over its weaker allies. In the mind of the Soviet invasion's chief propagandist, Red Army bullets and brawn may have won this military war, but the placards and slogans of the Czech resistance scored a victory on another plane.

ONE TRAGEDY LIKE ANY OTHER

IN CERTAIN QUARTERS of the Soviet Union, the Prague Spring trig-gered a militant patriotism similar to what struck the United States after the World Trade Center terrorist attacks. Yakovlev's conserva-tive colleagues in the Central Committee worried that Alexander Dubček had almost succeeded in hijacking one of the jewels of the com-munist bloc with his talk of "socialism with a human face." And in Moscow, there were signs the intelligentsia was growing similarly uppity. What if the spirit of the Prague Spring flourished in Moscow? *What was to be done?*

Even before the Soviet tanks rolled into Prague, the Stalinists had their share of evidence that repression was overdue. Four years after Khrushchev, the shop shelves were as empty as they'd ever been. Meanwhile, technology and urbanization were making it more difficult for the Soviet leaders to regulate what their citizens knew. Ever-greater numbers of shortwave radios were increasing the awareness of Western culture. Young Russians were sprinkling English words and phrases into their speech. The prospect of the communist bloc overtaking the West in material prosperity, which seemed inevitable in the 1950s, seemed less likely than ever. Worse, the Americans had by that point overtaken the

Soviets in the space race. And just the year before Prague, in 1967, the U.S.-backed Israelis easily bested the Soviet-backed Arabs in the Six-Day War. The Russian way of life, it seemed, was under threat.

In response, the ever-present undercurrent of xenophobia in Russian society showed signs of strengthening. The heritage-obsessed All-Russian Society for the Preservation of Historic and Cultural Monuments (VOOPIK) grew explosively after it was founded in 1965, until the group counted seven million members by the early 1970s. In literature, strapping Russian peasant characters known as muzhiks were perpetually going to heroic lengths to repel foreign invaders from their villages. When the muzhiks left the village for the city, they succumbed to alcoholism or other spiritual weaknesses. The meaning of these fables was clear: the peasantry derived its strength from the old ways of Russian culture, the rural traditions of the village; removing the peasants from these supports was akin to cutting off Samson's hair.

Three weeks after the invasion of Czechoslovakia, this anti-modernist xenophobia received its guiding manifesto when *Molodaya Gvardiya*, the official monthly of that orthodox legion of communist boy scouts, the Komsomol, published an essay by a critic named Viktor Chalmaev. Titled "Inevitability," Chalmaev's essay was one of a series that appeared in *Molodaya Gvardiya* reflecting a similar line of thought. Russia was special, said this school. The harshness of the northern climate bred in Russian peasants a uniquely fervent spirit that, again and again, proved unconquerable – against the Tatars, against the Swedes, against Napoleon. This special Russian character explained why Russia was the first place where communism took root. That same character explained how the Soviet Union was the only country to single-handedly turn back the Nazis in the Second World War. The source of this Russian strength was the peasant village and its lifestyle. In the world depicted by Chalmaev and his brethren, the old hamlets were paradises full of strong, hard-working, ethnically pure Russian men and women who lived moral lives within the safety of their cultural traditions. Western influences were luring Russian peasants from the old villages to the cities, and corrupting the peasant spirit with consumerism. Russia was in trouble? The thing to do, Chalmaev said, was to cut off the country from Western influences. Key to returning the upper hand in the Cold War to the Soviet Union, then, for Chalmaev, was a move *away from* modernity, a mass cleansing of everything in Soviet society that was Western or foreign or, for that matter, Jewish. In other words, the radical nationalists wanted the Russian culture to turtle – to go isolationist, to sever ties with the West and patch up the Iron Curtain so tightly that not even foreign shortwave radio broadcasts could penetrate it.

Although they didn't say so explicitly, Chalmaev and the other radical nationalists were attempting to rehabilitate a line of thinking popularized most recently by Yakovlev's hated enemy Stalin, who appealed to Russian patriotism to keep morale high during the worst days of the Great Patriotic War. Now, many ethnic Russians in the Central Committee apparat sympathized with the views of the radical nationalists. Such department heads as Culture's Vasilii Shauro, Science's Sergei Trapeznikov and Yakovlev's own boss in Propaganda, Vladimir Stepakov, particularly subscribed to this line of thinking. To the handful of liberal members remaining in the upper ranks of the Communist Party, all this talk of heritage and racial purity was disturbing. A corollary to the radical nationalist logic required the repression of non-Russian ethnicities, which the nationalists felt were corrupting the *Rus* way of life. And principal among these harmful ethnicities, of course, was every fascist's favourite whipping boy, the Jews, whom a *Molodaya Gvardiya* essay disparaged as "educated shopkeepers." These anti-modernist tendencies replicated the ancient Russian thinking that gave rise, in tsarist times, to the era of the Black Hundred movement and the anti-Semitic pogroms, when mobs executed entire villages of Jews.

Yakovlev especially was disgusted by this radical nationalist thinking, which seemed custom-tailored to earn his enmity. Yakovlev saw this as an example of Russian urbanites romanticizing life in the countryside, a tendency that seemed to crop up once every couple of generations. Few of the radical nationalists had much first-hand knowledge of the hardships of peasant life. They tended to come from intelligentsia families in the bigger Russian cities. Most were educated at Moscow State University. Yakovlev had grown up in a peasant village. He hadn't even seen a railway station until he was 13 years old. In contrast to the glorious traditions imagined by the radical nationalists, Yakovlev knew the countryside was full of ignorant, illiterate serfs who laboured like slaves (under the tsars they actually *were* slaves). Those old villages were bastions of superstition, beset by alcoholism and hunger. The poverty of the rural village was not something Yakovlev wished to romanticize.

Other things irked Yakovlev about the radical nationalists. Chalmaev and the rest disparaged the Jews? Yakovlev's much-respected commanding officer in the war, Commissar Petr Ksenz, was a Jew. The radical nationalists despised cosmopolitanism? So, apparently, had the letter writer who sent Yakovlev to his frightening appointment to see Shkiryatov in 1952. The radical nationalists wanted to use the danger of cosmopolitanism to restrict peasant education? But Yakovlev was a peasant who had greatly benefited from the existing Soviet educational system. Finally, the radical nationalists were criticizing consumerism among the peasants? Complaining about consumerism among the peasantry was absurd, he thought. The peasantry weren't materialists – they just wanted enough to eat.

THE PARTY CLAMPED DOWN on Soviet society in the wake of Czechoslovakia. Libraries across the country were growing even more restrictive in granting access to foreign books. In the sciences, Jews and other non-Russian nationalities were finding their career prospects limited. Meanwhile, the Propaganda Department resumed jamming foreign broadcasting signals, preventing reception of Radio Liberty or other Western broadcasts.

Aside from writing the odd Propaganda Department memo arguing against Stalin's rehabilitation – particularly, in the months preceding the dead dictator's ninetieth anniversary – Yakovlev was not necessarily going out of his way to advertise his liberal beliefs. It was in this period that one of the Central Committee's key Stalinists, Science Department chief Sergei Trapeznikov, felt comfortable enough around Yakovlev to complain – as the two men rode in a car to the Kremlin – about the damage de-Stalinization was doing to Marxism. A cynic might point out that it served Yakovlev's job security to keep his anti-Stalinist beliefs to himself. That said, it also served the interests of the intelligentsia. For if Yakovlev's senior rank made him complicit in the Party's crimes, that same rank also allowed him to temper the Party's injustices from within. While Brezhnev's Stalinist advisors stifled dissent by firing liberal editors from their jobs, Yakovlev found himself atop a vast network of lesser-ranked liberals who sometimes called on him for protection. For example, in 1967, the journalist Len Karpinsky and the social scientist Fedor Burlatsky published an article in the newspaper *Komsomolskaya Pravda* condemning aspects of the censorship system, angering party conservatives. Yakovlev used his power and party connections to temper the punishment against the writers, who lost their jobs but eventually landed softly at a hospitable bastion of liberal socialist thought, the Institute for Concrete Social Research. Similarly, Burlatsky in turn used his own not-inconsiderable influence to help shelter dissident historian Roy Medvedev as he weathered the response to his anti-Stalinist work, *Let History Judge*.

Tvardovsky, too, was barely hanging on to his job at *Novy Mir*. That Tvardovsky was able to keep his post was thanks to the protection of Yakovlev and his fellow liberals in the Central Committee apparat. But for all the editor's absence of job security, the Soviet invasion of Czechoslovakia seems to have strengthened his will toward combat. Tvardovsky was alone among prominent Soviet editors in refusing to sign statements indicating support for the Czech invasion. And with Chalmaev and the journal *Molodaya Gvardiya* greasing Soviet society's post-Prague lurch toward fascism, it was Tvardovsky who published the first response that had any juice.

It came in the form of an essay by the journal's senior literary critic, Aleksandr Dementyev, and it criticized "the idea of national exclusiveness and the superiority of the Russian nation over all others" – ideas that were central to the thinking of the *Molodaya Gvardiya* crowd. Dementyev's most potent criticism pointed out that radical nationalism violated Marx's description of an international proletariat, in which all races were equal.

In fact, instead of interpreting history through the lens of class, the proletariat versus the bourgeoisie, as Marxists were supposed to do, Dementyev said the radical nationalists called for an East–West conflict based on race. Essentially, Dementyev was saying the radical nationalists weren't being good socialists – a line of argument that contained compelling irony. *Novy Mir*, that thorn in the side of the Communist Party, suddenly was decrying the radical nationalists for not being communist *enough*.

Yakovlev and the other liberals in the Central Committee endorsed the *Novy Mir* essay when they published a response in the official journal of the Writers' Union, *Literaturnaya Gazeta*. The essay was written under the byline of "V. Ivanov," described as a "highly-ranked member of the Central Committee." The essay declared the radical nationalists' arguments politically wrong, particularly Chalmaev's insistence that the peasantry's moral values were more important than its standard of living.

Typically, when the Party entered a debate such as this, the participants ceased their combat. Not this time. As 1969 waned, as autumn shivered and approached winter, it seemed Marxist theory no longer mattered to the Soviet leadership. Radical nationalism had lots of support in the upper reaches of the Party. Mikhail Suslov was rumoured to back it. Much of the KGB sympathized with its cause. Despite the fact that Brezhnev's wife was Jewish, the general secretary didn't seem to care one way or another; he recalled what happened when Khrushchev alienated the Party's rank and file. He wasn't about to make the same mistake.

So that July, 11 of the Union's best-known conservative writers published in the orthodox weekly *Ogonek* a letter titled "What Is *Novy Mir* Attacking?" In a sarcastic tone, the letter argued that the ideas espoused by Chalmaev and his fellow writers were the best way to fight the corruption of Soviet youth by Western ideology. Remember, the essay said, what happened in Czechoslovakia, where such American concepts as personal liberty and democracy had almost triggered the collapse of the Union. "Contrary to the zealous appeals of A. Dementyev not to exaggerate 'the dangers of alien ideological influences,' we assert again and again that the penetration of bourgeois ideology among us was, has been, and remains a very serious danger . . . [which] may lead to the gradual replacement of the concept of proletarian internationalism, by cosmo-politan ideas, so dear to the hearts of certain critics and writers grouped around the journal *Novy Mir*." That last line was the essay's harshest blow. It portrayed *Novy Mir* as a conduit for Western ideas into the minds of Soviet youth.

On another level, what the letter *said* didn't really matter. By allow-ing the criticism of *Novy Mir* and, by extension, the essay Yakovlev and his fellow liberals put in *LitGaz*, the Party was signalling that it no longer cared about Marxist theory. Anyone who knew anything about socialist theory realized propaganda that portrayed Russian heritage as superior to other races was anti-Marxist. The idea of universal brotherhood, the concept of equality for all – in fact, any of the ideals on which social-ism was founded – they were anachronisms that no longer applied. What mattered to the Party now was power. Anyone who caused a fuss, anyone who criticized or lampooned or did anything else that threatened the power of the Politburo, would be subject to penalties. Solzhenitsyn, for example, was expelled from the Writers' Union in November 1969, a radical step that signalled the authorities were, essentially, firing him; he would no longer receive income from the state.

Meanwhile, *Novy Mir*'s Tvardovsky was being summoned daily to the Writers' Union and encouraged to resign "for health reasons." Tvardovsky wouldn't. He was a loyal socialist, a man so devoted to the Communist Party that he had a lifelong aversion to samizdat publica-tion because he saw publishing outside the parameters of the Party as disloyal to the Soviet Union. Tvardovsky attempted to get Brezhnev and the other Politburo leaders on the telephone, to argue his case, but no one would take his calls. Sometimes the stress made him collapse into an alcoholic puddle, but usually he stayed defiant. If the Party wanted him gone, then it was the Party's job to fire him, he said.

But Brezhnev and the rest of the Politburo didn't dare risk that. If they were seen bullying a poet as renowned as Tvardovsky from his position, they risked making him a martyr, a cause célèbre for the intelligentsia. So in the end, they did something underhanded: they used Tvardovsky's loyalty to the Party against him. As he combatted the Stalinists,

Tvardovsky was also trying to secure for Soviet publication his poem "By Right of Memory," which the nearly 60-year-old poet regarded as the conclusion to his life's work. It dealt with his guilt over his father's death, and the tension between loyalty as a communist and the writer's duty to speak honestly; in the end, he opted for honesty. "Faced with the facts of the past / You have no right to act against your conscience – / After all, for those facts / We paid the highest price." His first attempt to publish a fragment, in the magazine *Yunost* (Youth), happened in 1967, but it was rejected by censors. Through 1969 he submitted the full version numerous times to the censors for publication in *Novy Mir*. More rejections.

Then the old fragment dating from the *Yunost* submission appeared in *Posev*, an anti-Soviet Russian-language émigré magazine published out of Frankfurt, West Germany. To most, it seemed that Tvardovsky had done the same thing that had doomed Pasternak, Sinyavsky, and Daniel: He had turned his back on the censorship system and published his work first in the West. But Tvardovsky denied any involvement with the poem's publication. His friends believed him. They knew the loyal communist wouldn't send his poem to an anti-Soviet journal; he *certainly* wouldn't have sent an out-of-date version. It was clear someone, some enemy of *Novy Mir*, had leaked the poem in a bid to discredit Tvardovsky. However it happened, the poem's publication abroad provided the Central Committee with the pretense it required to move against one of the Soviet Union's best loved poets. "How are things?" visitors to *Novy Mir* would ask. "We're still in work *today*," Tvardovsky's staffers would say, and then, superstitiously: "Touch wood."

INSPIRATION FROM AMERICA

A S THE MOSCOW INTELLIGENTSIA seethed about Tvardovsky's fate, Yakovlev conducted his second trip to America, where, among other adventures, he found himself embroiled in a tense discussion with the American film star Jane Fonda. He was one of a delegation of high-ranking Soviet journalists conducting a tour of their Cold War opponent at the invitation of the American Society of Newspaper Editors. The trip's high point was a party Fonda and Steve McQueen hosted for the Soviet luminaries at a house in the Hollywood Hills, in a grand wood-panelled chamber illuminated by picture windows and the soft, subdued light from a tropical aquarium. Peter Sellers was on the invite list, as was Beatle Ringo Starr, the Canadian film director Norman Jewison, and other Hollywood royalty, such as Kirk Douglas, Lee Marvin, Doris Day and McQueen's neighbour, James Garner. Most of the celebrities had been gathered by the event's organizers, Nick Williams and Robert Gibson, editor and foreign editor, respectively, of the *Los Angeles Times*.

It was the end of January 1970, and America was poised between the free love and acid-dropping era of the late 1960s and a strengthening tide of more cynical political activism. Bookended by the 1968 assassination of Martin Luther King, Jr., and the start of the Watergate scandal in 1972, this was precisely the moment when the intergenerational schism created by the baby boomers exhibited itself most keenly. America was just three months away from the Kent State shootings, when the Ohio National Guard fired on student protestors demonstrating against the U.S. invasion of Cambodia, killing four of them. The American public had recently found out about the My Lai massacre, in which a platoon of GIs herded together a village of Vietnamese civilians and slaughtered them, inflaming antiwar sentiment. Meanwhile the white middle-class was moving out of American downtowns to the suburbs after a wave of race riots in Watts and Detroit, among other cities.

Amid all this social, racial and generational turmoil, Yakovlev and the Soviet journalists whizzed through eight different cities over 18 days, meeting everyone from the Reverend Jesse Jackson to Nixon's national security advisor, Henry Kissinger. The trip, a journalism exchange designed to reciprocate a similar visit made to the Soviet Union by American editors the previous year, was intended to provide the Soviet journalists with a first-hand course in Americana, to see for themselves things weren't quite so dire as Soviet propaganda portrayed. In fact, thanks to late subway trains, mechanical mishaps, cancelled flights and the political climate of the era, the opposite happened.

YAKOVLEV LANDED JANUARY 19, 1970, at John F. Kennedy Airport in New York City along with 10 of the most senior figures in Soviet journalism. Lev Tolkunov, the editor of the Soviet government daily, *Izvestia*, was with him, as was A.I. Lukovets, deputy editor of *Pravda*. Norman Isaacs, the president of the American Society of Newspaper Editors, met the contingent at the airport and shuttled them into a bus bound for the Algonquin Hotel. Their tour guide was a Russian-speaking United Press International reporter, Nicholas Daniloff, who would cause a crisis during the Reagan presidency in 1986, when he was arrested in Moscow and held for a year because the KGB suspected he was a CIA agent.

Before they dove into their meeting-heavy schedule, the Soviet journalists did some editing to the itinerary the Americans had arranged, cancelling a trip to Disneyland, a flight on Hugh Hefner's corporate jet, *Bunny*, and a visit to the headquarters of *Playboy* magazine. "Business before pleasure," one of the Soviets exclaimed. The tour's first stop, New York, was a frigid maelstrom of meetings in which the visiting journalists noted some of the Americans admitting anxiety over the country's future. Executives at the American television network CBS, for example, worried that Nixon's vice-president, Spiro Agnew, was restricting free speech with his criticisms of American media. A subterranean voyage into what was then the grimy depths of the New York subway system had the visitors boasting about Moscow's cleaner stations. A train that was 22 minutes late brought them to the offices of New York Mayor John Lindsay, who didn't sound optimistic about America's prospects for the coming decade. "Our country is at the threshold of spiritual and maybe even physical collapse," Lindsay told them. On the way back to the hotel, the mayor's chauffeur also was critical, complaining about the city's unwillingness to fund public services. Later, in the storied four-teenth-floor board room at the *New York Times*, the paper's financial editor shared his concerns about the U.S. gross national product, which had failed to grow at all in the previous quarter.

Yakovlev and company's impression of America did not improve the next day, in Chicago, when on their way up to visit Mayor Richard Daley their elevator abruptly ceased its ascent between the floors of City Hall. Long moments passed as the visitors stifled claustrophobia and discussed their war wounds and heart conditions. It was a foul-tempered bunch who confronted Daley, who quickly grew defensive with Yakovlev and company's persistent questioning about racial inequity and the riots at the 1968 Democratic Party convention. Then, as unlikely as it sounds, the delegation was stuck a *second* time in the elevator at the headquarters of the *Chicago Tribune*. The cause may have been the tendency of the 12-plus delegation to cram everyone into the same elevator. That time, the unlucky Soviets passed the minutes before their rescue debating America's much-vaunted capitalist efficiency. "If this happened in our country, I would fire everybody who had anything to do with the elevators," grumbled one of Yakovlev's companions.

After a quick trip up to the American heartland of Wisconsin, the Soviets were back in Chicago to watch the Reverend Jesse Jackson preach a sermon during a voter registration campaign, which led to lots more discussion about American racial inequality. Two days later, after the Soviets flew to California, the notion of inequality was thrown back at the Soviets by protesters demonstrating – with Soviet hammer-and-sickle flags emblazoned with Nazi swastikas – against communist repression of Jews, a demonstration the Soviets interpreted as a government-sponsored "provocation" against them. And there was a bomb scare during a visit to New Orleans.

The trip wasn't a complete debacle. A visit to Sacramento allowed Yakovlev to meet California governor and former Hollywood star Ronald Reagan, providing an important first impression; decades later, Yakovlev's briefing notes to Gorbachev would help lay the groundwork for the trusting relationship between the two world leaders, allowing them to negotiate the arms control agreements that would end the Cold War. Yakovlev and the rest of the Soviets were taken aback when Reagan walked into the room with a pronounced limp and explained that he'd injured his leg in a fall while breaking a horse at his ranch. Reagan spent most of the meeting explaining his conversion, in 1962, from Democrat to Republican. And a hectic swing through Washington, D.C., in a caravan of black Cadillacs, had the Soviets interviewing Nixon's secretary of state, William P. Rogers. Highlights included their visit to the West Wing of the White House for the meeting with Henry Kissinger, who mused about the concept of "sufficiency" in nuclear arms limitation talks, and assured the Soviets he favoured improved relations between the two Cold War combatants. The biggest hit of this leg of the tour was Senator William Fulbright, the powerful Democrat and foreign policy expert, who was full of criticism for such American adventures in internationalism as Vietnam. "The great powers must rid themselves of the illusion that they are always right," Fulbright said.

Throughout the trip, the Soviet delegation experienced a view of America that confirmed their worst preconceptions. When Isaacs and other American editors had visited the Soviet Union the previous year, they were inundated with propaganda about the superiority of the Bolshevik system. Of course they were – the journalists who guided them during their trip were employees of the Soviet state. In America, though, the comparatively more independent journalists treated the Soviet scribes to a view of the most powerful nation in the free world, replete with all her blemishes. As if to ensure the Soviets left with a poor impression of their sworn enemy, the flight that was to transport the group from Washington back to New York, and then home, was cancelled at the last minute, forcing them to scramble to make a Manhattan-bound train.

CALIFORNIA, TOO, HAD ITS PROBLEMS. Friends of Steve McQueen and Jane Fonda had, in August 1969, been slaughtered by Charles Manson and his family of flower children in a gruesome quadruple murder. A young black professor, Angela Davis, had been fired from the University of California, Los Angeles for belonging to the Communist Party. And a couple hundred miles up the California coast, American Indians had just occupied the former penitentiary island, Alcatraz, to draw attention to their land claims.

But at the party in Hollywood, the glamour of the world's film capital prevailed. Thanks to such films as *The Thomas Crown Affair* and *Bullitt*, McQueen was soon to be voted the country's favourite film star – the living, breathing embodiment of American individuality. Fonda, too, was at an apex of her celebrity. Weeks later, on February 16, 1970, along with her brother, Peter, and father, Henry, she would grace the cover of *Time* magazine, an event that nearly coincided with her nomination for a 1970 Academy Award, her first, for her starring role in *They Shoot Horses, Don't They?*, marking her successful career transformation from *Barbarella* sex bombshell to serious actress.

At 46, Yakovlev had few of the attributes that typically made guests popular at Hollywood parties. He was nearly bald. His ears were prominent. He had full lips, a broad fleshy nose and above his brown eyes were magic-markered brush strokes of eyebrows, thick like Brezhnev's. Many of the Californians around him were tanned, stylish, and fit.

Yakovlev was none of those things. He'd earned his pallor working long days in Staraya Ploshchad. His broken body carried a few more pounds than it should. And yet, among all these radicals, among this diverse crowd, all so different and yet, all so universally American, Yakovlev and his fellow travellers were treated even by the celebrities as celebrities.

For many members of the west coast counterculture, the vast territory on the other side of the Iron Curtain was an object of fascination. The few Americans permitted to travel to Moscow came back with exotic stories about bugged hotel rooms and surveillance by KGB handlers. Now, on this Hollywood hill, some of these celebrities harboured Marxist sympathies. Their heroes were people like Fidel Castro and Che Guevara. Lenin held a special place in their hearts. It was fashionable among these members of the radical left to blame the Cold War on overly aggressive American foreign policy. They believed the United States would be well advised to become more like the Soviet Union.

So in the Los Angeles of 1970, a living, breathing Soviet citizen was an object of extreme curiosity. Even more thrilling was the ability to speak to someone like Yakovlev, who had intimate knowledge of the Kremlin. He also had some pull, some power. Consequently, Yakovlev attracted even more interest than his fellow Soviets. These actresses and rock stars and fast-talking film directors, they all had questions about Moscow, about Solzhenitsyn and Sakharov, and about life behind the Iron Curtain. Who *really* held the power in the Politburo? And less intelligent questions: Was it true they kept Lenin embalmed, in a public mausoleum, that his corpse was there for just anyone to see?

At some point in the evening, Yakovlev was confronted with the aqua-blue eyes of the party's co-host, Jane Fonda. Soviet politicians tended to be enthusiastic about Hollywood starlets; a decade before, Marilyn Monroe had made an admirer of Nikita Khrushchev when the two attended a party together. There is no doubt Yakovlev was charmed. Recalling their meeting later in his memoirs, he refers to the starlet as "Jane" and demonstrates a respect, rare coming from Yakovlev, for her intellect. Significantly to Yakovlev, Fonda was just then in the midst of a political awakening. Soon she would be organizing fundraisers to help jailed members of the Black Panthers, the militant African-American civil rights group. In just over a month, Fonda would be arrested herself when she helped American Indians occupy an Army base in an attempt to build support for an aboriginal cultural centre on the site.

Their conversation began with a surprise. The actress demonstrated a knowledge of Russian matters that astonished Yakovlev, until he learned that Fonda's soon-to-be ex-husband, *Barbarella* director Roger Vadim, was an émigré Russian. Five years earlier the pair had travelled through the Soviet Union, and Fonda charmed Yakovlev with anecdotes from the trip. What struck her, she said, was how much *kinder* the Russian people seemed than Americans. Endearing herself to Yakovlev, Jane agreed that the scramble for the almighty dollar was a corrupting influence on American life.

By this point a small crowd had gathered to watch the Soviet speak with the American actress. It was at this point, too, that Fonda put Yakovlev in a strange position. Fonda's biggest political cause was the antiwar movement; her efforts were considered subversive enough by the U.S. government that, later that year, FBI director J. Edgar Hoover placed her under surveillance that included wiretaps on her telephone and monitoring of her daughter's kindergarten class. These days, Fonda was thinking about the deployment of Agent Orange, a toxic defoliating agent the American military used to clear the Vietnamese jungles of vegetation, to make it easier to kill enemy soldiers. She worried about the jellied gasoline incendiary bombs, known as napalm, raining down on Southeast Asian villages.

Fonda outlined the dangers of American militarism – the way military contractors pushed U.S. foreign policy, rather than the other way around. She also accused the United States of following a "provocative" foreign policy – of spreading its imperialism to such continents as Asia and Africa. There was an irony here: in his books, Yakovlev often made the same point in harsher language. But Fonda was going further than *warning* the Soviet visitor. She *criticized* Yakovlev's country for underestimating the full danger of Washington's yen for provocation. Fonda didn't have to say what the U.S. was provoking. With both combatants in the Cold War possessing arsenals that could destroy the world many times over, everyone understood the risk of nuclear war.

This conversation dropped Yakovlev into strange waters. He was well acquainted with the danger of relaxing too much on trips outside the Soviet Union. It was standard procedure to infiltrate such trips with members of the KGB. His reply was certain to reach his superiors back in Moscow. On the surface, what Fonda was saying wasn't dangerous. She was criticizing American foreign policy. But the way she uttered this criticism, she was also rebuking Moscow – criticizing the Politburo for not understanding how dangerous the United States could be. In the possible presence of KGB, Yakovlev could not tolerate any criticism of Moscow. He would have to respond. But how? Unintentionally, Fonda had created a trap for him. If he disagreed with her in a certain way, people might think he was saying the U.S. wasn't dangerous. So Yakovlev opted for a classic Central Committee tactic: vagueness.

"International relations are complex matters," Yakovlev said.

But Fonda wouldn't be dissuaded. She was implacable. She reiterated her point.

"American militarism is dangerous," she said. "Moscow doesn't realize *how* dangerous."

Yakovlev tried again. "You're probably not right about everything," he muttered, conscious his reply meant nothing.

Upon their return to the Soviet Union, the journalists extrapolated their impressions into generalities that disproved the Americans' prized constitutionally protected freedoms. Freedom of speech? But Angela Davis was fired for saying she was a communist. Equality before the law? Perhaps for whites, but as they heard during the Jesse Jackson speech, black people still were treated differently in the United States. With the many glitches that struck their trip, it's easy to see how the journalists, Yakovlev included, failed to appreciate what most Americans then took for granted: the superiority of capitalist America over its communist Soviet counterpart.

As months passed, Fonda would continue her crusade against the Vietnam War, even travelling in 1972 on a solo trip to hostile

North Vietnam to document the American military's attempt to bomb dikes in a bid to flood rice paddies and starve the Vietnamese people. During the trip she unthinkingly posed at the controls of an anti-aircraft gun and recorded radio messages the North Vietnamese used as anti-American propaganda. While some on the left credited her with helping to stop the American bombing, saving thousands of lives, the conservative right called her a traitor. For years afterward, conservative-minded soldiers dropped Fonda portraits into urinals at U.S. Army bases so true American patriots could urinate on the actress's face. All too soon, Yakovlev would be subject to similarly crude castigation at the hands of his own party's conservative wing.

ACTING CHIEF OF AGITPROP

O N FEBRUARY 10, 1970, exactly five days after Yakovlev returned to Moscow from the United States, a grave man with a straggly brown beard appeared at the entrance to *Novy Mir*'s manuscript-littered offices on Moscow's Maly Putinkovsky Lane. There wasn't much room in the building. The already cramped office space seemed to be crammed with every writer in the city. Where writers didn't sit, winter coats and hats and scarves were heaped in mounds on any available horizontal surface.

But if there was anyone they'd move for, it was him – Aleksandr Solzhenitsyn, the best-known Soviet dissident writer. With small talk and lots of awkward sideways steps to get around the cordons of people blocking the hallways, Solzhenitsyn made his way through the corridors on the first floor, where the junior staff had their offices. Then up a flight of stairs to the cluttered, cavernous boardroom Tvardovsky used as his office. The editor was a big man with pale blue eyes, an unlined face and steely white hair swept back from his classically Slavic hairline. He kept a rough Russian cigarette perpetually pinched between his second and third knuckles. Tvardovsky got up when he spied his visitor. They hadn't seen each other for almost three months. They were currently quarrelling – as they always seemed to be lately. But this fight was bigger than bickering. During the first few days of February – interestingly, while Yakovlev was in the United States – the Writers' Union exercised what control it had over *Novy Mir*. It "strengthened" the eight-person *Novy Mir* editorial board by removing four of Tvardovsky's closest associates. It was bad enough that the replacements were party conservatives, none of whom, Solzhenitsyn said, had ever held a pen in their lives. As though to add an extra element of insult, however, one of the Secretariat's replacements was a longtime Tvardovsky critic. He'd accused the poet of representing the interests of the upper classes – accused him, basically, of betraying communism. By selecting this particular critic to advise the magazine, the Writers' Union was signalling that it believed the critic was right. To a loyal communist like Tvardovsky, a man who stuck with the Party even after it killed his father, the whole affair was a sign that his country considered him a traitor.

Solzhenitsyn and Tvardovsky shook hands, then embraced. Solzhenitsyn quickly made the point that was the purpose of his visit. Although the Writers' Union had fired half Tvardovsky's editorial board, several issues of the magazine were already finished – Tvardovsky should stick around for those, then see where things stood. Who knew? Perhaps something could change.

But Tvardovsky was done. "I'm tired of being humiliated," Tvardovsky answered. "Just sitting at the same table and trying to talk to them seriously. They've brought in people I've never seen before. They'll say 'resign!' and I shall."

It was clear Tvardovsky intended to stick with his path. Solzhenitsyn attempted to cheer his old patron. "You've done your share of donkey work," Solzhenitsyn said. "Now you can rest. Rostropovich and I will call for you and carry you off to his castle."

Soviet cellist Mstislav Rostropovich was at that point sheltering Solzhenitsyn in a wing of his cavernous dacha, located in the verdant hamlet of Zhukovka, on the outskirts of Moscow. For Tvardovsky, it was an appealing image: a relaxing holiday to mark his retirement with two other famed figures of the Russian arts. Tvardovsky appreciated the gesture, but stayed firm. The next day, on February 11, Tvardovsky's letter of resignation appeared in the official publication of the Writers' Union, *Literaturnaya Gazeta*.

The experience broke Tvardovsky. The great poet holed up in his dacha and sought solace in cigarettes and vodka. He emerged once to visit the dissident biologist Zhores Medvedev, whom the KGB had committed to a psychiatric hospital for circulating samizdat literature – a visit that touched Medvedev so much that it reduced him to tears. Later that summer a stroke damaged Tvardovsky's ability to speak and left him partially paralyzed. While in hospital, doctors discovered a large cancerous tumour in his lung. They gave him a month to live. Ever the fighter, he held out. When he later learned that Solzhenitsyn had won a Nobel Prize, he said, "That's our prize, too," meaning *Novy Mir*'s. In fact, along with Rostropovich, Solzhenitsyn visited Tvardovsky one last time and witnessed an almost motionless wreck of a man, barely able to speak. He died the night of December 18, 1971, of another stroke, at age 61. When the state-selected speakers at his memorial service made no mention of his fight with the Party, a young woman stood to protest. "Is it possible that no one is going to say that we are burying our civic conscience here?" With help from the crowd, she made it out of the hall before the secret police could grab her. But it was Solzhenitsyn who had the last word. "There are many ways of killing a poet," Solzhenitsyn wrote. "They killed Tvardovsky by taking *Novy Mir* from him."

THE SETUP WITH THE POEM published abroad, the ignored calls, the forced resignation: the Party's treatment of Tvardovsky troubled Yakovlev. One of the Soviet Union's greatest poets deserved better. Throughout the country Yakovlev had just left, citizens were criticizing President Nixon and his administration in the harshest terms possible. Such rhetoric acted as a check against the governmental abuse of power, Yakovlev realized. Meanwhile, his own party was so sensitive that it sacrificed loyal poets to stifle the merest suggestion of dissent. Yakovlev could do little at that point to save Tvardovsky. With the Stalinists growing in power, even Yakovlev had to watch his step.

Much of Yakovlev's time at this point was devoted to writing speeches for Brezhnev and the other Politburo members. Since he'd written Brezhnev's first official speech, Yakovlev had become one of the Central Committee's most highly regarded writers. The honour wasn't as glamorous as it sounds. Writing for Brezhnev was not quite the most boring job in the Union. The Soviet leader's public addresses were legendary for their ability to induce sleep. Brezhnev's genius, which he exhibited throughout his 18-year reign atop the Soviet Union, was his ability to maintain the status quo. His speeches helped. They included passages where he spoke vociferously, with much gesticulation. They could go on for hours. But for all that, Brezhnev rarely made any points of consequence. Providing the meaningless verbiage required by the general secretary was a peculiarly Sisyphean task.

For all the dullness, there were perks to the job. The speechwriters seconded themselves for durations of up to two months in dachas, or country houses, some of them formerly occupied by such Soviet luminaries as Stalin himself. There they were able to eat and drink all they wanted. Occasionally the leaders looked in to check on their work, and the writers would complain about the mysterious creative process that birthed a really first-class speech, and how long it took, and then they'd be left alone for another couple of days, to toil at their magic.

Among the most impressive of these dachas was Brezhnev's. Named after a nearby town, Zavidovo was a sprawling compound of residences set amid a forested hunting preserve located on a bend in the Shosha River, about 150 kilometres northeast of Moscow. Dubbed the Soviet version of Camp David by Kissinger, the first Westerner to visit the preserve, in 1973, Zavidovo had an Alpine motif with interiors decorated in what Kissinger called "velvet-covered Victorian opulence." Brezhnev's villa was the largest, of course, a two-storey chalet featuring cavernous ballrooms plus a dining room and a movie theatre. There was an Olympic-sized swimming pool and a fully equipped gym. And surrounding the residences was a territory of gentle hills covered in grassland, lakes, and forests of birch trees and poplars. It was here that Brezhnev took his visitors on hunting expeditions for wild boar, which Soviet guards lured near hunting stands to be shot by the exultant general secretary.

Typically, the speech-polishing labour at Zavidovo followed a set routine. Yakovlev and the other writers congregated to go over each other's drafts, dispersed to make changes on their own, and ultimately reconvened to knit together the best lines into a coherent, but ultimately meaningless, whole. Once the speeches were done, the general secretary joined the writers for long toast-filled culinary extravaganzas in the dacha's enormous dining room. While Yakovlev participated in these toasts, he claimed to despise the practice that inevitably devolved into a competition to give Brezhnev ever more obsequious plaudits.

One evening the month after Tvardovsky's resignation, Yakovlev was at Zavidovo relaxing in the billiards room with the other writers, after a day of work. It was the usual bunch. Aleksandr Bovin was there, as was *Pravda*'s editor-in-chief Viktor Afanasyev. Yakovlev was playing billiards with Georgi Arbatov, the expert in American affairs. With Yakovlev just back from New York, it's possible the two men were discussing some quirk of the American experience.

Yakovlev could never completely relax around this crew. He felt like an outsider among them. Many of the other writers were the scions of high-ranking party officials. Something about them made Yakovlev self-conscious of his peasant background, particularly his thick Yaroslavl accent, which he knew sounded provincial to the other writers – a little like a Maine accent sounds to someone from Manhattan. The other writers were constantly talking in shorthand and having to explain to Yakovlev, which made him feel like an uninformed rube. Meanwhile, Yakovlev regarded himself as a socialist true believer. Some of his colleagues seemed to him like toadying careerists, reluctant to speak their mind to the leaders because they were concerned more about saving their jobs than doing anything to help the Soviet people.

It was a typical night. Serenaded by the click of the billiard balls, sipping vodka in a room that was bigger than most of their apartments, the writers shared anecdotes they could discuss only with each other, such as the time that Brezhnev disparaged a speech as too "bourgeois," and handed it back to Yakovlev to rewrite. "This is more like it," the leader said, the next morning – apparently not realizing that Yakovlev's rewrite entailed little more than the sprinkling of the word "socialist" at a couple of key points.

One of the other writers came into the room with some news: "Stepakov's just been dismissed."

All conversation stopped.

The cue ball rolled across the felt.

The room's occupants contemplated the implications of the news.

Stepakov, of course, was Yakovlev's Stalinist boss. Yakovlev had been expecting something like this. Stepakov was too close to Shelepin and his scheming for Brezhnev to allow him to occupy a key role such as chief propagandist. With Brezhnev's power growing yearly, Stepakov was bound to be eased out sometime. In fact, Stepakov was bound for the foreign ministry, where he would work as the Soviet ambassador to Yugoslavia. The transfer sounded prestigious, but it was definitely a demotion. This was the style of the Brezhnev Politburo: velvet handcuffs, but handcuffs nevertheless.

In the billiards room, Yakovlev struggled to determine what Stepakov's dismissal meant to his own career. It was standard for any new head of department to hire his own first deputy, which meant Yakovlev would be out of a job. But Yakovlev was well-known to Brezhnev. He believed he and the general secretary had a certain rapport. Certainly, Brezhnev seemed to like his speeches. Perhaps Brezhnev would overlook his former association with Shelepin. Perhaps *Yakovlev* would be Stepakov's replacement.

Perhaps Yakovlev smiled. Perhaps it was only that he failed to look disconsolate at the news. In any event, something betrayed to the other writers Yakovlev's growing excitement.

"Sasha, there's nothing for you to hope for," Arbatov told him. "They'll never confirm you."

Yakovlev wasn't so sure. The next day he found it difficult to concentrate. Whenever his speechwriting hit an impasse his mind would turn to the position of AgitProp head, and whether Brezhnev might promote him to the now open spot. Was it, in fact, possible? Yakovlev had a reputation among the other apparatchiks as an unpredictable figure. The term applied to him was "ideologically dangerous." In an era when a man's excellence was a measure of his conformity, Yakovlev displayed a troubling tendency to think for himself, to act like a so-called "white crow." Usually such a man would never have made it to the Central Committee, or lasted in its ranks.

But Yakovlev was a war hero whose exploits had been written up in the military press. And then there was his knowledge of Marxist-Leninist thought. Every action conducted by the Communist Party was supposed to be dictated by the political theories of Karl Marx and V.I. Lenin. By the mid-1960s, few party politicians, Brezhnev included, were able to discuss the theories with any degree of expertise. In contrast, Yakovlev had an encyclopedic knowledge of Marxism-Leninism. The attribute had helped him to become prized for his services as a speechwriter not only by Brezhnev, but by most other members of the Politburo, who frequently asked Yakovlev to sprinkle Marx or Lenin quotes through their texts. Mikhail Suslov, in particular, Yakovlev knew, prized his services. And shouldn't the Politburo *want* the man in charge of party propaganda to be an expert in Marx and Lenin?

Throughout the day he swung from one extreme to the other; perhaps he'd get the promotion, perhaps he'd be fired.

That evening, Yakovlev, Arbatov, and the other writers were deep into one of their "tea-drinking" sessions, which involved more vodka than tea. This time they were in the winter garden, a sitting room set in what amounted to a tropical greenhouse stocked full of vegetation seemingly pulled by the roots from some steamy Congolese wilderness.

Brezhnev came into the room. After a few of his usually bombastic greetings, he turned to Yakovlev.

"Well," he said, "whom shall we appoint for Propaganda?"

Yakovlev felt the attention of the whole of the room. He looked toward the supreme leader. Brezhnev was smiling.

This was Brezhnev's typically non-confrontational way of informing Yakovlev that he wouldn't be getting the job. His face felt sunburned.

Afanasyev, the *Pravda* editor and one of the worst of the careerist writers, proposed a party secretary he knew from his old hometown. Out of respect for Yakovlev, the rest kept silent.

Yakovlev listened to a monologue in his head: *They don't trust you. They don't trust you. They don't trust you.* His situation stemmed from his alignment with Shelepin's men, and now he berated himself for that decision. Aligning himself with the Shelepin faction now seemed a miscalculation. Yakovlev's fate wasn't clear, but one thing was certain: what had been a meteoric ascent through the apparat was stalled.

YAKOVLEV WAITED ANXIOUSLY for something to happen. In what seemed certain to be the short term, he became the acting head of Propaganda. Weeks passed with him tensing up each time the telephone in his office rang. Would *this* call bring news of Stepakov's replacement? Or Yakovlev's own dismissal? Likewise, he braced himself before any encounter with Brezhnev, or the other "celestials." Various uncomfortable scenarios played out during Yakovlev's downtime – the elevator moments, the moments immediately before sleeping and after waking, or on the weekends, as he wandered the woods outside Moscow looking for mushrooms, a favourite occupation he shared with his family. *How would the news arrive? What were they waiting for?*

He asked his associates in the Central Committee apparat how he could secure his spot, but no one seemed to know anything. Yakovlev even suggested several candidates who might be suitable for the vacant post – people whose open minds might prompt them to keep Yakovlev where he was. Among the names he suggested was a young party secretary with a reputation for open-mindedness, from the southern Russian region of Stavropol, a guy by the name of Mikhail Gorbachev. Inquiries were made through the party apparatus, and Gorbachev turned down the offer because the post didn't have the job security Gorbachev wanted.

At this point Yakovlev decided he had three choices. He could become a careerist – he could set aside the misgivings of his conscience and do whatever it took to secure his position as the Party's chief propagandist. With Brezhnev secure in the leadership, and a coterie of Stalinists congregating around him, this sort of thing was happening all over Staraya Ploshchad. Former idealists once excited by the prospects of the thaw, now were participating in the creeping rehabilitation of Stalin's reputation because, it was thought, that's what Brezhnev's advisors wanted. Going this route would require putting away his conscience and toadying to the new class of power brokers, people like Brezhnev's advisor on agriculture and propaganda, Viktor Golikov, and Science Department head Sergei Trapeznikov. If Yakovlev chose this path he would have to start devising ever-more complimentary toasts for the general secretary. He'd force the journalists who worked under him to invent story after story glorifying Brezhnev's Second World War heroics, and ask the historians to spin textbooks detailing the leader's strategic brilliance.

Yakovlev didn't know whether he could stomach that. How could he look at his son, Anatoly, his daughter, Nataliya, or, for that matter, Nataliya's new baby daughter, Natasha? What sort of a country would he be leaving them?

He could leave the Central Committee, as some of his friends were doing. A few went to existing research institutes, like the Novosibirsk Institute of Economics and Industrial Engineering, whose distant location on the far eastern side of Asia insulated it from the political pressures of Moscow, or the closer Institute for Concrete Social Research. Yakovlev talked to associates, investigating whether he might be able to open his own research institute somewhere, or take over an existing one, but it seemed the Politburo was worried that if he had an institute he would use its academics to argue liberal opinions that could undermine the authority of the Central Committee. They believed he'd use it as a soapbox, in other words. It seemed the research institute wasn't an option.

The last course was to act according to his conscience, and to view Stepakov's dismissal as an opportunity. Yakovlev expected to be fired at any moment, anyway. He had little to lose. Why not regard his sudden, accidental promotion as liberation – as a chance to do what he liked? He would be like the archetypal condemned patient whose mortal diagnosis suddenly prompts him to live life to the fullest. With Stepakov gone, Yakovlev could run Propaganda the way he wanted.

With such choices whirling around his head, Yakovlev was called on business to the southern Russian city of Krasnodar. He happened to stay at the same party residence as another high-ranking apparatchik, Viktor Golikov. This was trouble. Golikov, Brezhnev's advisor on agriculture and propaganda, was one of the worst of the Stalinists. They'd tangled before. The rumour in Staraya Ploshchad had Golikov coveting the top spot in the Propaganda Department. Still, protocol dictated a night out with the local party secretary, an evening to which Golikov also was invited. Dinner passed without much incident. It was only once they got to the billiards table, once all three were well into the vodka, that things erupted. Golikov started complaining about *Novy Mir* and Tvardovsky, and other writers and artists whom Yakovlev regarded as among the most courageous members of the intelligentsia. All were guilty of "revisionism," Golikov said, implying they wanted to falsify history, an interesting label, considering the Party had for decades revised history to portray the state in the most positive light possible. Yakovlev managed to hold his temper until Golikov directed the invective toward him. The memos Yakovlev was writing to the Central Committee had lately been "confusing," Golikov said – a term Soviets used to describe something that didn't correspond to the consensus opinion. And what was Yakovlev doing supporting the "blackeners," those treasonous writers smearing history and the Party with negative depictions of the country's situation? Like that Konstantin Simonov, whose diaries from the Second World War were so obsessed with the stupidity of the army leadership? How unpatriotic!

Bringing up Simonov struck a nerve with Yakovlev. Simonov was a good friend, and Yakovlev had read the diaries and liked them. Simonov wasn't blackening anything, Yakovlev said. His diaries told of the horrors of war, what it was like in the chaos at the front. Yakovlev had served there, he said. It *had* been horrible. Reading the diaries made Yakovlev feel proud about his own contribution. What was disloyal about that?

Golikov came back at him with a line of argument often used to repress the media. At its heart, the argument was about whether, in times when the state was threatened, writers should portray things as they were, or as the state wished them to be. Golikov thought writers had a patriotic duty to portray things positively, to keep up morale. In contrast, Yakovlev thought writing that aimed at patriotic ends, rather than realism, was a recipe for bad art. Things grew so heated, in fact, that the local Communist Party secretary broke up the fight by suggesting the two combatants head to bed.

It wasn't much. But it amounted to Yakovlev's first face-to-face confrontation against the Stalinists. By arguing against Golikov in Krasnodar, Yakovlev effectively came out of the closet.

YAKOVLEV NEVER SAYS SO, but it seems likely that the three events – Tvardovsky's forced resignation, the trip to America, and Yakovlev's promotion, after the dismissal of his Stalinist boss, to the acting head of the Propaganda Department – played a role in inspiring him to redouble his fight against the Stalinists. Tvardovsky was gone. For the past several years party liberals had been dropping like the flies of the cliché; probably the most shocking conservative coup happened at the bastion for liberal academics, the Institute for Concrete Social Research, where conservative party elements had arranged the firing of director Alexei Rumyantsev and 140 of his staffers. The conservatives had done their job so well that Yakovlev no longer had anyone to protect. Rather than working behind the scenes within the upper ranks of the Communist Party to support the ones doing the fighting, it was time for Yakovlev to take up the fight himself.

His was not a highly visible march against Stalin's rehabilitation. He was not a dissident – at least, not a public one. Nor did Yakovlev conceive of himself as a subversive force within the Communist Party. He saw himself as a proud socialist, a loyal member of the Communist Party, and a devoted citizen of the Soviet Union working to improve his country. He wanted only for his superiors to run things the way the Party's ideological forebears – Marx and Lenin – had intended.

In this fight with the Stalinists over the country's direction, waged with newspaper articles and Central Committee memos rather than with tanks and artillery, Yakovlev was a guerrilla fighter who materialized only to strike against particularly strategic targets. He was forced to concentrate his resources where he thought his influence would have maximum leverage – or when the beneficiary was a particularly dear friend or admired figure. According to a story reported by the *New York Times*'s Bill Keller, one day during this period the famed poet Yevgeny Yevtushenko appeared in Yakovlev's office carrying page proofs from *Novy Mir* that were never to see print because the censor had blocked them. Yevtushenko's poetry had apparently violated some obscure edict. With the poet still in the office, Yakovlev picked up his phone and called the chief government censor, Pavel Romanov. "What is this fuss again with Yevtushenko?" Yakovlev said. "Look, if I call you, it means this is not only my opinion. Do you understand me? I think it will be better if you publish." When a cause was lost, when his influence could do little to stave off the Stalinists or radical nationalists, he did little to stop it. Sometimes he even cooperated. As late as 1972, Yakovlev and the Propaganda Department collaborated with the Stalinist-headed Science Department in a campaign to discredit the head of the Institute of Russian History for "reformist" (read "anti-Stalinist") actions.

Such complicity was necessary because by the early 1970s, Yakovlev was one of the only high-ranking Communist Party members still fighting Stalinism. Many of the leaders were thought to sympathize with the radical nationalists. Politburo member and onetime Khrushchev protégé Dmitri Polyansky, for example, was an anti-Semite. Yuri Andropov, the KGB head, tolerated nationalism amongst his agents and may have been one himself. Even Brezhnev fraternized with virulent ultra-patriots. Support at such high levels encouraged Yakovlev's enemies in the Central Committee apparat to conspire against his influence. Soon after Stepakov's dismissal, in April 1970, Soviet newspaper editors who should have sought the acting head of the Propaganda Department's approval to publish controversial articles were instead appealing to Stalinists in the party apparatus, such as Yakovlev's deputy, Anatoly Dmitryuk, or Yakovlev's nemesis, Viktor Golikov. Yakovlev spiked an article destined for the orthodox newspaper *Sovetskaya Rossiya* that decried the way pop musicians were corrupting Soviet youth, then was dismayed to discover the newspaper published the article anyway. Matters came to a head after Yakovlev opposed the publication in the same newspaper of a positive review of a novel by the Stalinist writer Ivan Shevtsov, called *In the Name of the Father and the Son*. Once again, *Sovetskaya Rossiya* published it anyway. Yakovlev called the newspaper editor, who countered that Dmitryuk had approved the article, as well as someone "a little higher up" – Golikov, it turned out. With such protection, the editor figured he didn't need Yakovlev's approval.

This was mutiny, and if the newspaper got away with it, Yakovlev would soon be pushed from his job. At this point, Yakovlev displayed his acumen for political manoeuvring. He appealed to Suslov, the Politburo's *éminence grise* and a fanatic about adhering to the most minute of party regulations. Bearing this in mind, Yakovlev avoided subjective labels like Stalinist and spun the problem as one of job description and party hierarchy – Golikov and Dmitryuk were making decisions that should have been Yakovlev's to make. Suslov put the matter on the agenda for the Central Committee Secretariat, where the proceedings turned into a trial of the Propaganda Department. The Secretariat brought up a letter Golikov co-wrote with the editor of *Sovetskaya Rossiya*, accusing Yakovlev's department of being too soft on "revisionist sentiments" in newspapers and magazines – "revisionist sentiments" being party jargon for anything that criticized the Party's supposedly perfect history. Worse, said Golikov in the letter, Yakovlev supported pop music, which impeded the production of "genuine art." But the key accusation, in a nod to the Tvardovsky affair, was Yakovlev's support for writers who instead of "principled" stands, published opinions that contradicted the official party line. To marshall support for the letter's accusations, Golikov implied to Suslov and the rest of the Secretariat that Brezhnev supported the letter's contents.

Matters of ideology and party discipline were Suslov's rubric, not Brezhnev's, and Suslov resented the implication that Brezhnev's opinion had any bearing on what was essentially his territory. Suslov also realized Golikov was angling for Yakovlev's job – angling not to Suslov, but to Brezhnev. Another strike.

Before the Secretariat, Suslov cross-examined each of the parties. During his turn, Dmitryuk admitted that he gave permission to publish the article without Yakovlev's consent.

"Comrade Dmitryuk," Suslov asked. "How can you work for the Central Committee when you so flagrantly violate party discipline?"

The editor made several excuses: he thought the article particularly important, and figured publishing was fine so long as he had the support of Brezhnev's office. Suslov snapped over that one. "Who did the Central Committee appoint to manage the press?" Suslov demanded. "As far as I recall, the Propaganda Department. What's going on?"

Suslov transferred Dmitryuk from Propaganda and fired two of *Sovetskaya Rossiya's* deputy editors. "It was a lesson," Yakovlev says in his memoirs, stifling the glee he must have felt. "Suslov reminded the nomenklatura just who was who in the party."

Good timing. With his position strengthened, Yakovlev wrote a memo for the Central Committee criticizing the increasing glorification of Stalin in newspaper stories, literary journals, and poems. "The topic of Stalin is becoming a special fashion," he noted in the document. "Many articles and literary works pay a great deal of attention to the description of his personal traits and achievements at the expense of the demonstration of the multifaceted work of the party, its Central Committee and the courage and labour heroism of the Soviet people. In such a way, the historical truth is being distorted."

But that summer, the Stalinists grew ever more audacious. The salvo came, of course, in essay form, in the August 1970 issue of *Molodaya Gvardiya*. This one was by a young writer named Sergei Semanov. It was an attempt to fashion Stalin as the patron saint of the radical nationalists; it was a paean to the dictator who was the first to encourage Russian patriotism, and who during the toughest years of the Second World War, while millions of Russians were dying at the front, used propaganda to convince the Russians of their innate cultural superiority over Nazi Germany. Victory was inevitable, Stalin told his masses, because the Russians were just plain *better* than the Krauts.

Had Semanov left it at that, he might have been fine. He didn't. "The turning point in the struggle against wreckers and nihilists took place in the middle of the 1930s," Semanov said. The writer said it was at that time that "all honest working people of our country were once and for all welded into a single and monolithic whole." Not only that: "This period exercised the most favorable influence on the development of our culture," he said. But the 1930s was the decade of the purges and the show trials, the worst of Stalin's repressions. While many Russians thought Khrushchev and the intelligentsia were too hard on Stalin, no one wanted a return to those frightening times, when millions died and millions more perished in the prison camps from hunger, hypothermia, or overwork. Semanov's essay sounded like the work of a zealot; his was the rant that exposed writers like Chalmaev for the fascist extremists they were.

The few knowledgeable observers in the intelligentsia realized Semanov's essay provided Yakovlev with powerful ammunition – an excuse to enact vengeance against the Stalinists for what they did to Tvardovsky. So did Yakovlev. "The adherents of chauvinism . . . overplayed their hand," he says in his memoirs. Letters of complaint poured into the Propaganda Department. To discredit the radical nationalists, Yakovlev bundled up the letters and sent them to party leaders, who, as Yakovlev hoped, assigned Propaganda to censure *Molodaya Gvardiya*. Yakovlev directed his staff to prepare the harshest criticism yet to appear in the Soviet press of radical nationalism. Once again, it appeared under the byline "V. Ivanov" – but this time Yakovlev arranged to run what one member of the intelligentsia called "the long-awaited salvo" in *Kommunist*, whose edicts on ideological matters were interpreted by party members to have the punitive force of legal precedents. "The reader should understand that the journal *Kommunist* never repeats what it has said," explained one observer. "It does not give lectures or deal out reprimands: it pronounces sentences – final and unappealable." Once it recapped the hubbub created by the articles of Chalmaev, Semanov, and their brethren, the article chastised *Molodaya Gvardiya* for ignoring previous reprimands. The journal, "Ivanov" declared, had a "clearly mistaken direction." Soon, *Molodaya Gvardiya*'s editor was fired.

Finally, it seemed that the leadership was coming around. Apparently caught up in the spirit of his victory, Yakovlev published later that same year, under his own byline, an intriguing article in *Kommunist*. It amounted toward an early call for glasnost, or transparency, in government. In it, Yakovlev described the government-media-populace feedback loop that exists in vital, healthy democracies, in which a government acts, the media reports, the people discuss, and the government, in turn, adjusts. "Information," Yakovlev wrote, ". . . makes the masses more competent to observe, react, and criticize – one of the conditions for the effective participation of millions of Soviet citizens in the government of their country. It would otherwise be impossible to have a normally functioning socialist system or a growth of consciousness and social participation on the part of the workers." Bear in mind that many party bureaucrats spoke publicly about the need for workers to participate in government. Most were hypocritical, of course. Simultaneously, across the Soviet Union, writers and academics were being turfed from their jobs or otherwise punished for publishing anything that approached an honest evaluation of government. Most party bureaucrats didn't want "the masses" to "observe, react and criticize." They wanted the masses to shut up, stay ignorant, and do what they were told. But as we know from his actions 15 years later, Yakovlev *wasn't* being hypocritical. Idealistic? Sure. Naïve? Certainly. Nevertheless, even back in 1971, Yakovlev was calling for glasnost in government.

Meanwhile, within months of its former editor's dismissal, *Molodaya Gvardiya* was up to its old tricks. With each new issue of the journal it became apparent that the new editor was just as much a radical nationalist as the old one. Now more magazines and journals were echoing this ultra-patriotism. Despite Yakovlev's work, the Stalinists in the Party's upper reaches were winning.

WHAT TO DO? The question obsessed Yakovlev. Marx and Lenin had pre-dicted an international proletariat – a future in which workers across the world overthrew the bourgeois capitalists, founding a new society where all comrades were free and equal, where allegiances of nation-alism were irrelevant or didn't exist. Lenin portrayed the USSR as the first incarnation of this paradise on Earth. Among all the repressive poli-cies to come out of the Politburo since Brezhnev succeeded Khrushchev, this nationalism was among the ones that most clearly con-tradicted Marxist-Leninist theory.

He kept at it. He wrote his reports to the Central Committee. He pub-lished another article in *Kommunist* under his own byline criticizing certain radical nationalist authors – he didn't mention them by name – for ignoring Marxist-Leninist teachings. At the beginning of 1972 he released to the whole of the Central Committee an expansive decree, *On Literary Criticism*, that called for Soviet culture to return to its Leninist (read "anti-nationalist") roots. And still the Soviet Union regressed toward restrictions that hadn't existed since the days of Stalin. Party journals hinted at tougher times to come for the intelligentsia and the Jews. Meanwhile novels persisted in glorifying the moral superiority of full-blood Russians.

There were reasons for hope. In the realm of foreign affairs, Brezhnev and the Politburo were making overtures of friendship toward the West. Yakovlev was thick in the preparations for an international ice hockey contest with Canada. U.S. President Richard Nixon even visited Moscow in May of 1972 in one of the most overt symbols yet of the fragile Cold War peace called détente. Meanwhile, Yakovlev's news-papers and magazines prepared for a full-scale celebration of all things Soviet to mark the empire's fiftieth anniversary at the end of 1972. All this alongside perpetual glorification of the Russian identity that threat-ened the whole of the USSR. Was Yakovlev the only party member who saw hypocrisy here? Who saw that encouraging Russian patriotism would encourage patriotism in Ukraine, and Georgia, and so on throughout the Union, until the whole of the Soviet empire whirled apart from the centrifugal pressures of its disparate ethnicities?

To silence the nationalists, to strike a killing blow against this Stalinist thinking, to attempt to pull the Politburo toward a reformist line once and for all, Yakovlev conceived an article that would sum up the whole of the controversy. It would make the points that he and *Novy Mir* had been arguing since just after the Soviet invasion of Czechoslovakia. It would be his manifesto, his masterwork, his ultimate polemic against Stalinism and its subsidiary ideology of radical nationalism. It would name names. More importantly, it would identify an insidious, dangerously anti-Marxist line of thinking that pervaded most aspects of Soviet culture. It would expose extremism hiding *in plain view*. In length, in tone, in its purpose of exposing Stalinism, it would be Yakovlev's own version of Khrushchev's Secret Speech.

The Soviet Union's chief propagandist wrote the article in the fall of 1972 and timed its submission for maximum effectiveness, for publication just weeks before the USSR's fiftieth anniversary. He chose to publish it in *Literaturnaya Gazeta*, which was read by Soviet literary fans of all stripes and creeds. When he handed it in, *Literaturnaya Gazeta's* editor, Alexander Chakovsky, was so astonished by what it contained that he risked insubordination by questioning whether Yakovlev knew what he was doing.

"You know you'll lose your job for this?" Chakovsky asked.

"I don't *know* it," Yakovlev said. "But I'm not ruling it out."

At this point, what did he have to lose?

THE ARTICLE APPEARED ON NOVEMBER 15, 1972. Titled "Against Anti-Historicism," it was 12,000 words splashed over two full pages of broadsheet. It was cut with the standard soporific rhetoric, but every so often, amid those narcotic paragraphs and Lenin quotes, came jabs of overproof potency. Clearly Yakovlev was settling scores. He castigated the writers congregating around *Molodaya Gvardiya*. He disparaged the "hysterical writings" of the Stalinist novelist Ivan Shevstov. Such "individual zealots of 'national spirit'" dealt, Yakovlev said, in "concepts that have long set our teeth on edge: 'the enigma of Russia,' 'the heavy cross

of national consciousness'. . . ." They glorify life in pre-revolutionary
Russian villages out of a "failure to understand the laws of life." In fact,
the old peasant settlements were marked by "hunger, poverty, shackled
muzhiks and the lash of serfdom." And anyone who said differently,
Yakovlev said, was contradicting basic principles of Marxism-Leninism.
For the first time, a senior party figure was accusing *by name* some of
Moscow's most famous writers of anti-Marxist nationalism. Years later,
characterizing its importance, an academic called the essay, "the
harshest criticism of Russian nationalism . . . written by an important
functionary of the Central Committee since the 1920s."

Its appearance caused a sensation. Upon first reading, both sides, the
Stalinists *and* the liberals, interpreted Yakovlev's essay as an official
decree of the Communist Party. They thought the leaders got together,
discussed the issue and decided to clamp down, Soviet-style, on the
nationalists, the way they had been clamping down on the liberals since
1965. Something big must have happened at the top levels of the Party.

Everyone buzzed with speculation and questions. Did Yakovlev's
article foretell some shift in power? Was Suslov finally flexing his
muscles? Were Brezhnev's days numbered? For the article to be as long
as it was, and for it to be written in such harsh terms, indicated that
Yakovlev's message had official support. Yakovlev was condemning the
nationalists in terms the Party reserved for *really* nasty people, like
American capitalists. The terminology he used was like something from
the days of Stalin. He accused the nationalists of polemics with Lenin!
That was the sort of blasphemy that rewarded guilty parties with long
stays in scenic Siberia. Among the 16 writers Yakovlev mentioned by
name in the article were Sergei Semanov and Viktor Chalmaev, who
were profoundly alarmed by its appearance.

Then something even more surprising happened. Had Yakovlev's
essay represented an official decree, after its publication the junior journalists toiling all across the Soviet media would have stampeded to
endorse the chief propagandist's argument. Countless news items would
have applauded Yakovlev's article and explained why it was perfectly in
line with Marxist-Leninist thought.

That didn't happen. There were a few mentions of it – *Pravda* mentioned it soon after it appeared, for example. But Yakovlev's essay was the equivalent of a car-sized boulder dropping into a swimming pool. The ripples should have been sloshing around the surface for weeks afterward. For *months*. One of the few responses that received public attention was a letter written to Suslov by Mikhail Sholokov, winner of the Nobel Prize for his story cycle, *And Quiet Flows the Don*. Sholokov was one of those arts and letters pets the Communist Party trotted out whenever it needed to show that it supported cultural figures – an establishment toady who seemed willing to do whatever the Politburo asked, so long as it helped him to maintain his considerable income and beautiful dacha. Sholokov *condemned* Yakovlev's article. And if *Sholokov* condemned it, that meant the leaders condemned it.

And *that* meant Yakovlev was acting on his own.

When everyone realized this possibility, the conversation redoubled. Recall that this incident occurred in the era of the Brezhnev leadership, when consensus was supposed to rule the Central Committee, when the convention was for any disagreements to be settled in advance, quietly, so when an issue came up in any public forum everyone simply agreed and the edict became the official party line. Disagreement frightened Brezhnev. It was supposed to happen behind closed doors, out of sight. To the external world, the Communist Party was supposed to be monolithic and united in thought, word, and deed. And yet, here was Yakovlev contradicting, in a public forum able to be read by Western eyes, beliefs that had currency with a significant portion of the Politburo. What on earth could have gotten into him? What on earth would *happen* to him?

SHORTLY AFTER THE ARTICLE APPEARED, Yakovlev headed to Brezhnev's conference room in the general secretary's quarters at the Kremlin with both reluctance and anxiety.

Much of the speculation was correct. Neither the Politburo nor the Secretariat endorsed the article. Demichev, his direct boss in the Secretariat, knew about it, but Demichev was a pushover who would later deny all knowledge. The two key powers among the leaders, Brezhnev and Suslov, had no inkling. Of course they didn't. They would never have allowed the essay to go to press. Even if they agreed with it, which they didn't, pragmatic reasons would have required its delay. It appeared two weeks before Brezhnev's speech commemorating the fiftieth anniversary of the Soviet Union. It appeared less than a week before Suslov's seventieth birthday. Yakovlev's essay sapped attention from both events.

Yakovlev had regrets. "I always placed my convictions, correct or not, over my own well-being," he says in his memoirs, sounding rueful. The Party received reams of letters in response to the letter. Golikov took the critical missives to Brezhnev. The positive ones went to Yakovlev until Suslov confiscated them. Attempting to zag with the Party, Yakovlev set up meetings with some of the writers he criticized, including Semanov, to make amends. The intent of his essay was grossly misunderstood, he claimed. He was simply trying to provoke an intellectual debate; he certainly wasn't trying to offend any honest patriots.

Naturally, Yakovlev was nervous the first time he encountered Brezhnev after the essay's appearance. Soon after Yakovlev sat down at the general secretary's conference table, Brezhnev came over to where Yakovlev was sitting. Through the cloud of cigarette smoke that always surrounded him, Brezhnev admonished Yakovlev for publishing the piece without first clearing it with him. The Soviet leader implied Yakovlev was lucky he wasn't being punished. "I'll forgive you – this time," Brezhnev told him. Brezhnev even gave Yakovlev a hug.

Yakovlev was relieved. He thought the matter settled. But then at the next meeting of the Secretariat, the matter came up again. The secretaries limited their criticism in front of Yakovlev, who at one time or another had helped write speeches for most of them. Still, it was a tense affair. Suslov didn't attend, which was a bad sign. At one point Yakovlev tried to cite Marxist-Leninist theory to justify the essay. But the member running the meeting, Andrei Kirilenko, cut him off.

"Sasha, don't get us involved in theory," Kirilenko said.

This was the final straw. The precepts on which Yakovlev's essay were based were basic Marxist-Leninist, the sort of thing schoolchildren

learned during their primary years. An international proletariat, sub-
suming nationality for the greater cause of the global revolution – this
was what communism was *about*. The Politburo was being hypocritical.
Moreover, as Kirilenko's comment suggested, it *knew* it was being
hypocritical. Had there ever been a clearer indication of the Soviet leadership's cowardice? Had there ever been a clearer indication of the
leadership's obsession with power?

Clearly, the Party was broken, Yakovlev finally realized. But how to
fix it?

Yakovlev went straight from the meeting to the office of his boss,
Demichev. The timing was bad; Yakovlev had trouble controlling his
temper; now he was particularly upset. He could be rash in such times,
saying things he didn't mean, saying things he'd later regret.

"Evidently," Yakovlev said, exhibiting this last characteristic in particular, "the time has come for me to leave."

This was rash. Yakovlev should have known something was brewing
from Demichev's reaction. Rather than insisting Yakovlev stay in the
Central Committee apparat, the spineless party secretary gave him an
option. "Would you agree to go to the Moscow Pedagogical Institute –
as director?" Demichev asked.

It was among the most prestigious teaching institutes in the Soviet
Union. But like most high-ranking posts, this one had a political dimen-
sion. As director of a large teaching institute, Yakovlev would be forced
to continue the creeping Stalinization he'd fought for the last several
years. He declined.

"Then what would you like?"

Yakovlev thought this was a private conversation. He thought they
were speaking hypothetically. "You know what?" he said to his boss. "I'd
like to go," he said, "to one of the English-speaking countries. To
Canada, for example."

Yakovlev didn't think anything would happen as a result of his conversation with Demichev. But unwittingly he'd provided his enemies with
the ammunition they required. As with Tvardovsky, a man of Yakovlev's
rank couldn't be overtly pushed from his position. But if he could be

shown to have gone willingly, he could be pushed anywhere. And Canada was perfect for the purposes of the Politburo. The country was so distant from Moscow that it would be impossible for Yakovlev to have any influence on affairs in the Soviet capital.

The next morning Yakovlev was admitted to hospital. He'd been having pains in his chest. Doctors figured the cause was a bullet fragment from his old war wound. Occasionally his body's natural processes moved a fragment to a spot where it caused him pain, or threatened a major organ. Surgery was scheduled.

While he was in hospital, the leaders discussed what to do with him. Dmitri Polyansky, the anti-Semite, pushed hardest to have Yakovlev removed. Brezhnev didn't say anything except to ask whether anyone had actually read the article. On his second day in hospital, Yakovlev heard the news: he was being exiled to Ottawa, where he would serve as the Soviet ambassador to Canada.

Since it kicked out Khrushchev and installed Brezhnev at the top, the Politburo had worked quietly and steadily to freeze the freedoms – of thought, of the press, of artistic expression – that had warmed the capital in the phenomenon everyone called the thaw. By expelling Yakovlev, they were ridding the Central Committee apparat of one of its final idealists. With Yakovlev gone, the Communist Party of the Soviet Union entered its last repressive epoch.

PART
3
ANSWERS
1973–1983

THE RELUCTANT DIPLOMAT

W HAT FOLLOWED were melancholy days. Yakovlev despised few things more than moving. He and Nina's last significant move of any distance happened in 1953, when the couple transported their lives a five-hour drive south, from their hometown of Yaroslavl to Moscow. That, too, had been traumatic. It took years for Yakovlev to feel comfortable in his bustling metropolitan home. But the inconvenience of that move was tempered by the flush of its impetus. What a contrast. Then, Aleksandr was not quite 30. He was called by the Party to its capital, a proud servant excited to begin work for the Central Committee. Almost exactly 20 years later, Yakovlev was a disgraced servant being thrown by the Party *away* from its capital. Then had been his career's greatest coup. Now came his career's first major defeat. Never had he faced such ignominy.

The Party officially named Yakovlev as the ambassador to Ottawa in mid-May, 1973. He was to leave in the third week of July. It wasn't much time to uproot a life. There were refresher courses in English. There was packing. He called up friends he hadn't seen for months to say goodbye. Before he left the Soviet capital, party protocol required Yakovlev to parade around and introduce himself to his new co-workers – the

Muscovites who would connect Ambassador Yakovlev in Ottawa to the Soviet bureaucracy back home. The roster of visits consisted mostly of staff from the Ministry of Foreign Affairs and the KGB. Humiliation shadowed Yakovlev through these appointments. He could feel each of these new contacts sizing him up. These functionaries treated him as if he were infectious. As his counterparts sat behind their desks, Yakovlev could see them evaluating him. He remembered other people Brezhnev had pushed into diplomatic service from senior positions in the Central Committee, such as his old boss, Stepakov, who became ambassador to Yugoslavia. People gossiped about Stepakov behind his back then; they gossiped about Yakovlev behind his back now.

A few managed charitable comments. For help with speaking English, Andrei Gromyko, the Soviet foreign minister, suggested watching religious broadcasts on television, where the enunciation was excellent. At least, people said, Ottawa's climate was a lot like Moscow's – as if that were a good thing. Or, at least he'd be able to come back once a year, for the annual leave usually taken in late summer. Some of these encounters were useful. Friends warned Yakovlev that many staff at foreign embassies in the West were KGB. (Typically up to two-thirds of the staffers in Soviet embassies worked for the intelligence agencies, such as the KGB or its military equivalent, the GRU – although to obscure this fact the agents were nominally assigned with other job titles, such as press attaché or consular officer. Even the ambassador himself might not know for certain the identity of the spies working under him.) Yakovlev's friends warned him these undercover operatives had instructions to report "on his every step and action, particularly on contacts with the press." Yakovlev realized he would have to adhere to the official party line far more strictly than he had in the Central Committee apparat. It was ironic: in Ottawa, he'd have to represent the very policies he'd once criticized.

Sympathy came from some unlikely sources. Just before they were to leave, Yakovlev and Nina took a week of vacation at the Barvikha Sanitarium, a spa reserved for Soviet elites. One day while Yakovlev and a friend were strolling in the countryside near the sanitarium, the pair happened upon one of the most legendary of the "celestials," a man who helped found the Soviet state. His name was Vyacheslav Molotov. He had been Stalin's foreign minister. He'd helped Stalin enact his campaigns of torture and bloodshed. Then, in Stalin's final years, the old dictator tested Molotov's loyalty by arresting his wife, who languished in prison until Stalin's death in 1953. "Was it you who wrote that article?" Molotov asked Yakovlev when they were introduced. Once Yakovlev confirmed it, Molotov congratulated him. "An excellent article, accurate and necessary," Molotov told him. Molotov recounted how in the old days Lenin himself warned Molotov of the destructive influence of radical nationalism. It was exactly the opposite reaction that Yakovlev would have expected from one of Stalin's henchman. The encounter added to his feeling of persecution. He'd been right!

That was the bit that stung the most painfully. It was like that European fairy tale about the emperor with no clothes. Yakovlev was the one to point out the hypocrisy, and instead of siding with him, the Party agreed it was better to pretend. And thanks to his stupidity, thanks to his hotheaded essay, Yakovlev wouldn't be around to fight back.

Back in Yaroslavl, his sisters and parents gave the couple a send-off party. Saying goodbye to his children was difficult, particularly given the fact that Nina had been helping their 26-year-old daughter, Nataliya, raise their first granddaughter, four-year-old Natasha. Leaving behind the Yakovlev's 20-year-old son, Anatoly, a fourth-year philosophy major at Moscow State University, also was difficult, given his recent hospitalization for a mysterious ailment that turned out to be a stomach ulcer. The treatment required a strict diet. Would Anatoly adhere to his diet? Could Nataliya cope with raising her daughter alone? Neither Yakovlev parent was certain. But the exiles had no choice: they had to go. In July, Yakovlev and his wife said goodbye to their children, and left.

YAKOVLEV AND NINA ARRIVED in Canada on July 19, 1973, along with the disgrace of his demotion and an intense anxiety about the future. They flew into Montreal, the closest international airport to Ottawa. Soon after

Yakovlev and his wife left the plane, they were confronted by a receiving line of the people with whom they would work closely in Canada – senior embassy staff, consular officials, plus the heads of station of the other Soviet commonwealth countries, such as Bulgaria and Czechoslovakia, and their wives, all of them lined up in the airport terminal like a military brigade waiting to be inspected by their commanding officer. After a gruelling 7,000 kilometres of travel, such an intimidating reception was the last thing they wanted.

The greeters called him "Your Excellency" and congratulated him on his new posting. Each repeated as if by rote how much they wanted to work together, their desire to offer assistance, to be of service when needed. Very little penetrated either of the Yakovlevs, who were exhausted from the flight, and paying more attention to protocol than dialogue. These diplomats put a lot of stock into knowing whose hand to shake first, with the proper number of hand pumps. The Yakovlevs didn't, but they were determined to make a good impression.

Yakovlev's new co-workers were prepared not to like him. Many of the major Canadian newspapers ran stories about the new ambassador, including the fact that this posting was a demotion. Through channels official and not, the Soviet diplomats in Ottawa had already realized their new ambassador was out of favour with the Soviet leadership. Even here, the reek of the pariah wafted around him. Worse, Yakovlev's predecessor had been popular with both embassy staff and the domestics who ran his household. The former Soviet ambassador to Canada, Boris Miroshnichenko, hadn't wanted to leave Ottawa. The Miroshnichenkos had recently lived for some months in temporary lodgings while they renovated the ambassador's residence. Just as they were due to move back in, the news had come from Moscow that they were being transferred – to Kuwait. The Soviet staff blamed Yakovlev for pushing their favourite out of Ottawa.

Still, they were diplomats, and they were trained to conceal their true thoughts. The welcoming ceremony was perfectly congenial. After some perfunctory conversation, Yakovlev and Nina made their way to the embassy car. Another 90 minutes of highway driving and they were at the home where they would live – for how long? For, Yakovlev hoped, as short a duration as possible.

His friends had been right: Ottawa did have some similarities to Moscow – a northern capital riven by temperature extremes, bisected by a river. Ottawa had little of Moscow's vitality or bustle. Its dullness was a perfection of the bland condition that afflicts some government towns. Apart from a few interesting Gothic-inspired government build-ings, the city centre was a monotony of modernist buildings. Still, this much smaller city had a connection to the outdoors that Moscow lacked. With its trees, its waterways, and its proximity to wilderness – the rapids of the Ottawa River, the hilled forests of the Gatineau – this Canadian city seemed to occupy territory it had not quite civilized.

The ambassador's residence at 390 Lisgar Road was in the middle of Rockcliffe Park, a moneyed Ottawa enclave of gentle rolling hills and winding lanes shaded by monumental elm trees. The governor general, Canada's nominal head of state, and the prime minister, the country's political leader, both lived only a short walk away, as did many of the city's diplomats. Cliffs nearby overlooked the rapids of the Ottawa River; a short walk in a different direction took Yakovlev to a smaller river, the Rideau. The official residence was a three-storey structure, bereft of char-acter but for the dormers that interrupted the peak of its roof. The walls were whitewashed cement. It hid from the road and the park across the street with the help of a high hedge. There was a garden where Yakovlev eventually would develop an amateur horticultural interest, especially in roses. The first floor had a sitting room, lounge and a dining area for smaller diplomatic functions. The Yakovlevs' living quarters were on the second floor, and the third was reserved for the domestic staff of a maid, cook, and driver.

The early days in Ottawa were hectic. Brooking no jet lag, Yakovlev went to work on his first full day July 20. His first order of business was a visit to Canada's Department of External Affairs, to introduce himself to the staff of the Soviet desk as well as to the protocol chief, where Yakovlev apologized for his rusty English and declared he would be fluent in two months. (Both he and Nina were taking lessons.) On Thursday, July 26, the new diplomat officially presented his credentials to Governor General Roland Michener, in a ceremony at Rideau Hall, Michener's sprawling residence. The proceedings included a police motorcycle escort and diplomatic speeches. Civilians wore morning coats to the event. Yakovlev wore his diplomatic uniform and the array of medals he'd won during his war service. A good deal of this speechifying came from Yakovlev himself. To Michener, Yakovlev said in heavily accented English, "It gives me great pleasure to say that I am taking up my duties at a time when the relations between the USSR and Canada have reached high-level and serious positive shifts toward détente."

Now officially recognized in Canada as his country's representative, Yakovlev began introducing himself to other government officials. He met Secretary of State for External Affairs Mitchell Sharp, who just that month had a summit in Helsinki with the Soviet foreign minister, Andrei Gromyko. And after the weekend's respite, more meetings followed on Monday. The scandal that preceded his arrival combined with the Sharp meetings to generate lots of interest from the Canadian press in the new Soviet ambassador, who, recalling his friend's advice about KGB monitoring, declined all requests for interviews.

Yakovlev quickly learned that boredom was the bane of his new position. Rather than negotiating trade agreements or business deals that were beneficial to the USSR, Yakovlev found himself immersed in tedium. At receptions around Ottawa he was often approached by Canadian politicians demanding to know why the rights of Sakharov or Solzhenitsyn, or some other dissident favourite of the protest press, were being trampled. As the living local embodiment of the Soviet government, Yakovlev had to reply with the official party line. There were endless Canadian enquiries demanding to know why the Communist Party prevented the emigration from the USSR of any number of citizens, many of them Jews or Ukrainians, many of them some Canadian's grandmother or aunt or second cousin once removed. Usually, Yakovlev couldn't do anything about such problems.

It was during Yakovlev's government meetings that he realized how far removed he now was from power in Moscow. Jean Chrétien, then minister of Indian affairs, told Yakovlev that Canada had heard the Soviet government wanted to repopulate its Arctic region with musk oxen. As a goodwill gesture, Chrétien said, the government wanted to present the Soviets with seven pairs of the enormous animals. The Canadians would get the animals to an airstrip in Winnipeg; the Soviets only had to fly them the rest of the way.

Yakovlev did some digging. He discovered Chrétien was right. The Soviets had been looking for musk oxen to repopulate the northern Siberian peninsula of Taymyr. He sent off a telegram to Moscow. No reply. He sent off another, then a flurry. Still no reply. He did some more digging, and discovered the Central Committee had already allocated money to buy the musk oxen. The purchase was to be made from the Americans, in Alaska, and it was bound to be quite expensive. Once he grasped that, Yakovlev also grasped what his problem was. In the Party's bureaucratic labyrinth, some official, or some cadre of officials, was intending to skim their share from the purchase money. Free musk oxen from Canada sounded like a good deal, and it was, but because it was a gift there was no exchange of funds to skim, which meant the party apparat favoured the more expensive U.S. arrangement.

Chrétien and his staff kept calling Yakovlev, badgering him about when the Soviets would pick up these animals. Reluctant to admit his country's endemic corruption was the reason for the delay, Yakovlev kept making excuses. Had he been confronted with a problem like this when he was still in Moscow, he would simply have picked up the telephone, made some calls, pulled in a few favours, done some blustering and threatening, and ultimately forced someone to arrange to get a plane to Winnipeg to pick up the damned animals. Things were different now. Distance made him easy to ignore, as did his fall from grace. And in a Moscow obsessed with the enemy of American imperialism, no one cared about relations with the sleepy northern country where Yakovlev had landed. The Canadian diplomats quickly developed a theory that the new ambassador was in Ottawa as a figurehead. He had come to

Ottawa in disgrace. Now, he didn't even have the pull to arrange for his country to receive a gift like these musk oxen. How was he to negotiate trade agreements, or anything else?

By the autumn of 1973, Yakovlev was getting it from all sides. His own staff acted disloyal. They questioned orders they should have obeyed. They seemed to distrust him. Relations between the Yakovlevs and their staff grew so bad that someone in the Soviet diplomatic colony sent a report back to Moscow accusing Yakovlev and his wife of wasting the embassy's money on lavish *objets d'art* to redecorate their residency. The head of the Soviet Ministry of Foreign Affairs Second European Division, Vladimir Suslov, the mandarin who oversaw relations with Canada as well as the United Kingdom, Australia, and New Zealand, flew to Ottawa on September 12, 1973 to look into the matter. This was yet another humiliation. Suslov actually went through the Yakovlevs' living quarters and examined each of the objects that supposedly were purchased with embassy funds. The inventory revealed to Suslov that most of the new items weren't so lavish, nor had they been purchased with the embassy's money. In fact, many of the new items had been purchased by the previous ambassador.

Then, still more humiliation. Suslov went to the Department of External Affairs to meet with the Canadian diplomats who worked on the Soviet desk. Suslov told them that Yakovlev was upset by the suggestions then going around Ottawa that he was out of favour with Moscow. Suslov insisted that Yakovlev had extensive contacts in the upper reaches of both the Communist Party and the Soviet government; he called Yakovlev "high calibre." Moreover, Suslov said, "[Yakovlev's] word will be listened to in Moscow."

The fact that Yakovlev's boss had to come to Ottawa to vouch for him may have damaged his reputation more than it helped. And the problems with the embassy staff continued. As was traditional for Soviet ambassadors across the world, the Yakovlevs threw a party for the diplomatic community on November 7, the anniversary of the October Revolution, one of the biggest Soviet holidays. The Yakovlevs regarded the event as their official entry to Ottawa society, and they badly wanted it to go well. They staged the party in three of the grand rooms on the first floor of the Soviet embassy and served such typical Russian delicacies as caviar, salmon, sturgeon, and vodka. But staff strife threatened to scuttle it: the Yakovlevs were astonished to discover most of the food had disappeared before the party was to begin. It had been swiped by the staff. And once the guests arrived and drinks began to flow, many of the vodka bottles turned out to have been emptied before the party and refilled with water, a fact the Yakovlevs learned from their Canadian guests. It was not an auspicious entry into Ottawa society.

Yakovlev had his problems, but he was more concerned about his wife, Nina, who was having a tough time adapting to the couple's banishment. Her homesickness was so acute it spawned physical symptoms. She missed their children. She worried about Anatoly and his ulcer. She missed Natasha, her four-year-old granddaughter, and wondered how Nataliya was coping. At a time before the Internet eased the distance between continents, when communication across the Iron Curtain meant censored letters or expensive telegrams, the Yakovlevs' posting meant missing out on sharing the little girl's infancy.

Back in Moscow Nina had stayed out of party politics, or any sort of spotlight. She taught English and brought up the children. Being an ambassador's wife was far more high profile; the diplomatic community considered Nina almost as much a representative of the Soviet Union as they did Yakovlev. The pressure was new to her. During receptions she felt shunned by the women from the Western countries. She was keenly conscious of her inexperience with protocol. And the wives of the ambassadors from the other Soviet bloc countries all seemed so much more worldly. In contrast to the other wives' talk of such places as New York and Berlin, she'd travelled little beyond Yaroslavl and Moscow. She had never been outside of Russia.

As winter approached, a female embassy secretary pulled Nina aside. The secretary told Nina the coat she wore to diplomatic engagements wasn't fitting for the wife of the Soviet ambassador. The ladies in Ottawa typically wore fur to ward off the chill; did Nina want to borrow the secretary's mink stole for her next engagement? Nina said she'd think about it; then, as soon as she was alone, she broke down.

The coat issue was a symbol. She felt she was letting down her husband, and her country, with her unsophisticated ways. The Soviet diplomatic community in Ottawa placed a lot of emphasis on appearances – as though fashion was just another Cold War battlefield in which they competed with their Western counterparts. Nina realized the secretary's offer meant many of the other women must have been talking about her. Perhaps they were saying that her coat was an embarrassment for all of them. Perhaps they considered *her* an embarrassment. There wasn't money for her to buy a fur, not now. Their food and transportation costs were provided by the Soviet government, but the Ministry of Foreign Affairs paid the Yakovlevs only $400 a month in spending money. She would have to wear the secretary's coat. The other ladies were certain to talk about it. It was just one more humiliation for the Yakovlevs, one in a year of many.

MIDWAY THROUGH that first Canadian winter, just as all these anxieties were becoming unbearable, the Yakovlevs heard from Moscow the news that Leonid Brezhnev was coming to Canada.

Twice.

For about 90 minutes each time.

The Soviet leader was flying to Cuba to meet with Castro. Midway between Moscow and Havana, he and his entourage planned to make a refuelling stop in Newfoundland, at the Gander airfield on the province's frigid northeastern shore. Despite the short duration of Brezhnev's stopover, protocol dictated the Soviet ambassador welcome the leader upon his arrival.

Yakovlev didn't know what to expect. His exile to Ottawa happened with Brezhnev's assent. Would it be awkward, this meeting between the leader and the man he'd condemned to this ignominious exile? How would Brezhnev act toward Yakovlev? Would he be reserved? Merely polite? Or would he be his usual overbearing and effusive self? Perhaps Brezhnev would provide Yakovlev with an explanation for the reassignment, an indication of how long his exile might last. Perhaps Brezhnev might even ask him to return to Moscow. It was all a mistake, he might say. We need you. Why not? Stranger things had happened in the Politburo.

Preparing for the visit was a nightmare. Yakovlev begged Canada's External Affairs department to arrange for some high-ranking member of the Canadian government to receive Brezhnev. Then he heard that the embassy's ranking KGB officer had picked up worrying intelligence about a terrorist group of anti-Castro Cubans, a group called Alfa 66, who were said to have assigned a sniper and a cell of support operatives to attempt to assassinate Brezhnev in Newfoundland. Yakovlev's staff passed on the rumour to the Canadians, who took it seriously. The Canadians were still smarting from a diplomatic disaster that happened during the visit of another Politburo member, Soviet Premier Alexei Kosygin, in 1971, after Canadian Prime Minister Pierre Trudeau took Kosygin on an impromptu and under-secured walk across Ottawa's Parliament Hill. A Ukrainian immigrant recognized Kosygin and, approaching from behind, leapt on the Soviet premier's back and rode him, piggyback-style, for several moments before police were able to pull off the man. With Yakovlev already on shaky ground, any similar mishap would be costly to his career.

Brezhnev was scheduled to arrive on his first refuelling stop on Monday, January 28, 1974. The day before, Yakovlev schlepped out to the North Atlantic shore along with several other Soviet embassy staffers. The contingent also included diplomats from Canada's Department of External Affairs and the Cuban ambassador to Canada. Monday morning dawned in a blizzard that was still raging as the first of the retinue's four planes, a Soviet-made IL-62, landed at Gander at 9:15 a.m. Everyone braced for the leader, but the most senior member on this flight was Brezhnev's translator. There was some question whether the remaining planes would be able to land amid the blowing snow. As Brezhnev's plane, another IL-62, descended, visibility was poor. Wind whipped the runway. The atmosphere in the airport verged on panic. The Aeroflot representative was swearing at the KGB representative; Aeroflot's rep said the KGB was forcing the plane to land on the wrong runway, one that hadn't been cleared of snow. In his memoirs Yakovlev floats the possibility that the KGB's act was deliberate. He wondered whether the agency was attempting to stage a fatal accident in such a way that the West, or at least Canada, would receive the blame for Brezhnev's death. The danger would have been apparent to Yakovlev. Yakovlev's career rested on this encounter proceeding smoothly. Stakes were much higher than that, however. If Brezhnev died in a plane crash, the conspiracy-obsessed Soviets were certain to rail about the accident resulting from some nefarious plot of the West. With both sides aiming nuclear missiles at each other, such an accident could trigger events far more serious than the loss of Yakovlev's job.

Then a power surge knocked out all the radio channels but one between the plane and the control tower. Yakovlev's Soviet associates reported ice on the runway.

The plane's wheels touched the runway. The pilots braked. The wheels skidded, then caught.

Brezhnev was safe.

Once the plane taxied to a stop, attendants wheeled a stairway alongside the exit. Yakovlev went out into the frigid North Atlantic blizzard and waited. Brezhnev must have made quite the appearance for the tense Soviets gathered to receive him, materializing on the gangway silhouetted by swirling snow and the usual cloud of cigarette smoke. He looked haggard and grey, with folds of skin hanging on his face as though he had recently lost a lot of weight. In fact, he was getting over a flu. Still, when Brezhnev reached ground, he wrapped Yakovlev up in a bear hug. Along with the other high-ranking passenger, Foreign Minister Gromyko, the whole entourage trudged through the snow into the airport reception area, where Brezhnev was received by the highest-ranking Canadian present, a mid-level diplomat on External Affairs' Soviet desk named Alec Chistoff. Brezhnev seemed impervious to any diplomatic slights. If anything, he was happily surprised at Chistoff's fluent Russian. Brezhnev gave Chistoff a short message for Prime Minister Trudeau, outlining the Soviet leader's best wishes and desire for continued "good neighborly relations of mutually beneficial cooperation . . .[to] serve the interests of both our countries and the cause of universal peace." He flirted with a female airport employee. He spent an hour on a secure line to Moscow. Then, at some undetected signal, he pushed his way out into the cold, returned to his plane, and departed for Cuba and Castro.

Brezhnev would touch down again in a week on his return flight to Moscow. Yakovlev would have to receive him on the second visit as well. There hadn't been an opportunity during the earlier touchdown visit for the ambassador to tie up any loose ends with the leader. Indeed, from Yakovlev's viewpoint, the first visit was disastrous. He warned Chistoff that relations between the two countries would be seriously compromised if no senior Canadian government ministers turned up for the return visit.

A worried Yakovlev stayed in Newfoundland, meeting with the province's lieutenant governor and other representatives. He learned too that a group of Jewish protesters from the Newfoundland capital of St. John's planned to picket Brezhnev's next stopover. The evening before Brezhnev's arrival, the local affiliate of the Canadian Broadcasting Corporation interviewed the protest leader, a doctor named Avrum Richler. This Richler said he expected 15 to 20 demonstrators, a sizable turnout for such a remote location. Their aim, Richler said, was to draw Brezhnev's attention to the plight of Jewish refuseniks, so-called because they were denied permission to emigrate from the USSR.

Soviets of the era did not deal well with protesters. They assumed any organized displays of antipathy were planned by host governments – as they would have been in the Soviet Union. Consequently, many of Yakovlev's staff, particularly his second-in-command, Vasilii Vakhrushchev, wanted to prevent the protest at all costs. Vakhrushchev even lodged an official protest with the Canadian government. If a protest happened, Vakhrushchev said, relations between the two countries would be seriously damaged. The Canadians said they couldn't do anything. As long as the demonstration was peaceful there was nothing they could do to prevent it.

Yakovlev arrived in Gander late that Saturday night, the evening before Brezhnev's return. At 8:30 the next morning, the protestors also arrived. There were 10 of them all told and they assembled in the terminal building with their signs. One said "The Right to Live, the Right to Leave." Another: "Solzhenitsyn: The Conscience of Russia"; a third, in misspelled Russian: "Freedom for Russian Jews."

Yakovlev was able to introduce a member of Canada's federal cabinet this time, a Newfoundlander named Don Jamieson who was the government's minister of economic expansion.

Brezhnev's plane arrived around 5 p.m. Richler and the protesters hurried out of the terminal to a fenced-in section with a view of the tarmac. As Brezhnev appeared on the gangway, the protestors began singing the Hebrew spiritual "Let My People Go." It was quite a soundtrack to accompany Yakovlev's climaxing anxiety. He wasn't certain how Brezhnev would respond to all this. It must have been some moment for the protesters, too. For Westerners at that time, Brezhnev's ignominy rivalled the way many post-9/11 Americans felt about Osama bin Laden or Saddam Hussein. In fact, Brezhnev was far more dangerous: the machinations of Saddam or Osama might kill thousands of Americans, but Brezhnev and the nuclear arsenal he controlled could have obliterated North America. This was a man who could have triggered total global annihilation.

"Well, what now?" Brezhnev asked, once he'd given Yakovlev the usual bear hug. This time he looked tanned and considerably more healthy. Brezhnev noticed the protesters. He asked his ambassador what the fuss was about. Perhaps the wise thing here would have been for Yakovlev to fudge things, the way he had about the absence of an official Canadian government reception, a week before. The language barrier might even have allowed him to get away with it. But the Canadians were watching; moreover, this was an opportunity for the Soviet leader to be confronted with opinions that contradicted the party line. Yakovlev had been arguing in favour of such a confrontation back home for several years. So Yakovlev told Brezhnev the truth: that the loud group was a delegation of Jewish Canadians who had gathered to protest the Soviet treatment of Jews. "They want to talk," Yakovlev told him.

Thinking perhaps of Alfa 66, the KGB officer interrupted and said a meeting was out of the question. But Brezhnev, buoyed by his week's vacation, was in a good mood. He looked back at Yakovlev.

"What do you think?" the leader asked. "Should I go over?"

"I think we have to go to talk to them," Yakovlev said. Brezhnev consulted next with the Canadian cabinet minister. Jamieson echoed Yakovlev – he didn't see any harm in an encounter.

"Then," said Brezhnev in his nicotine growl, "let's go talk to them."

Astonishing the assembled phalanx of Soviet security officials, Mounties, and External Affairs functionaries, Brezhnev marched over to the fence where the protesters were congregated, with Yakovlev and everyone else trailing behind. Several moments of astonished silence passed. Then, with only a few strands of cyclone fencing separating the protesters from one of the most powerful men on Earth, the confrontation began.

"The group was probably taken aback by Brezhnev's sudden appearance in front of them and were not really very well prepared for the encounter," judged Chistoff, the Canadian diplomat. Once they regained their composure, the protesters wasted some oxygen shouting at Brezhnev. "Why is the USSR preventing 500,000 Jews from emigrating?" demanded one female protester. Characteristically, Brezhnev chose to respond to her. Uncharacteristically, his answer had substance. He disagreed with the statistic; in fact, he said, only 3,000 Jews wanted out. (A reliable figure is difficult to determine but the larger figure is closer to being accurate.) And the USSR wasn't preventing their exit. The problem was Israel, where the Jews wanted to go – that country, Brezhnev said, echoing the incorrect party line, wasn't able to take them because it was embroiled in its own difficulties. Later, during a meeting with Jamieson, Brezhnev argued this logic again. Did Canada or the United States want the USSR's Jewish refuseniks? If so, Brezhnev said, they could have them.

Their composure recovered, the protesters began mentioning specific cases. A woman called Sylva Zalmanson was dying in prison of tuberculosis, they said. Brezhnev had never heard of this Zalmanson. After consulting with an aide, he responded that she was in prison for attempted hijacking. She was a criminal. Of course she couldn't leave.

Now more names came at him, dozens of them, and Brezhnev saw he was getting nowhere. Holding up his hands, he concluded the encounter with a request. He asked the demonstrators to send information about specific cases of Jews who wanted to emigrate to him, via the Central Committee. He would personally ensure they were looked into. Led by his aides toward the warmth of the Gander waiting area, Brezhnev muttered to himself, "You have to know how to talk to people."

Once in the building, Brezhnev endured the usual diplomatic boilerplate. Jamieson read Brezhnev a message from Prime Minister Trudeau, who was abroad on a diplomatic mission himself. "Please accept my own best wishes," Trudeau said, in a standard diplomatic greeting which nevertheless seemed to please both Brezhnev and Yakovlev. Jamieson ran through some of the outstanding trade negotiations between the two countries, mentioning in particular the stalled talks on a civil aviation agreement. Brezhnev suggested locking negotiators from the two sides in a room until they came up with an agreement. It was not clear whether he was joking.

Yakovlev managed this time to speak one-on-one with Brezhnev – a fact certain to be noticed by both his own staff and the Canadian diplomats. Out of nowhere, Brezhnev brought up Yakovlev's diplomatic exile. He asked how Yakovlev had come to be in Canada. This was a classic Brezhnev strategy: feign ignorance in an attempt to shrug off responsibility.

"It's beyond me, Leonid Ilich," Yakovlev shrugged, referring to the leader by his given name and patronymic, a sign of respect.

Both men knew that both men knew more than they were saying. But if Brezhnev was willing to put behind him the disputes that had culminated in Yakovlev's exile, then so was Yakovlev.

Brezhnev waved his hand, as if irritated, and made a disparaging remark about the "comrades" back home.

There was a bear hug, and Brezhnev was gone.

Brezhnev's friendliness could not be construed as an invitation for Yakovlev to return to Moscow. Nor was it an indication of how long his exile would last. But for an ambassador struggling with disloyalty among his staff, Brezhnev's affectionate treatment functioned like a *deus ex machina* – the hand of God descending from the clouds to put things right. Embassy staff members noticed the warmth Brezhnev had displayed toward Yakovlev. They also noticed the weight Brezhnev gave to Yakovlev's advice; the leader had listened to Yakovlev even when he contradicted the KGB officer about whether to approach the protesters. Word spread through the Soviet diplomatic colony in Ottawa that Yakovlev had sway with Brezhnev himself, and in the days following the Gander encounter, business with his staff grew a little easier for the Soviet ambassador.

THE NEW CANADA

M ANY WESTERN NATIONS besides Canada would have provided Yakovlev with a dangerous, broadening experience. As with any other dogma-based institution, belief in Soviet Communism suffered when its adherents were exposed to opinions that challenged its orthodoxies. As author Robert D. English says, "It is difficult to overstate the devastating impact that firsthand exposure to the West had on old beliefs and stereotypes." Yakovlev had experienced this phenomenon himself during his two trips to the United States, in 1958 and 1970. But while both trips changed Yakovlev – the first selling him on the benefits of a free press and freedom of expression, the second helping to inspire his outspoken calls for reform in Brezhnev's Moscow – neither exposure sold Yakovlev on the superiority of capitalism or democracy. Unfortunate timing had a lot to do with this. Yakovlev displayed a knack for visiting the West at low points in the functioning of America's democratic mechanisms. His Columbia exchange happened in the repressive period between McCarthyism and the civil rights movement. His second trip to the States occurred shortly after a wave of urban rioting and political assassinations (Robert Kennedy, Dr. Martin Luther King, Jr.) that saw America lurching toward a full-blown generational schism, with the shooting of student protesters at Kent State University and other such battles just months away. Similarly, Yakovlev's arrival in Ottawa in the summer of 1973 coincided with the Watergate hearings that would lead to the resignation of President Nixon.

Also contributing to his antipathy toward American democracy was the lingering effects of his education in Marxist-Leninist ideology, which predisposed Yakovlev to look for faults in an American system he regarded as a hostile enemy – while simultaneously ignoring its benefits. This combination of factors left Yakovlev confident that the American system was a mechanism for a government just as flawed, corrupt, and inhumane as the Brezhnev Politburo's version of communism.

His experiences with Canadian democracy, however, would yield a somewhat different opinion.

A LITTLE MORE THAN A YEAR before Yakovlev arrived in Canada, Prime Minister Pierre Trudeau's foreign policy advisor, Ivan Head, wrote an essay for the journal *Foreign Affairs* that mentioned many of the factors that would have made Canada more hospitable to Yakovlev. The article was called "The Foreign Policy of the New Canada." Yakovlev read it, probably during the research he conducted to prepare for his Canadian posting, and was intrigued. Then, during the endless rounds of introductions it was customary for a foreign ambassador to make at the beginning of a posting, Yakovlev met Head briefly, likely at Head's office in Room 214 in the Langevin Block, a blood-red Gothic Revival edifice set across the street from Ottawa's Parliament Hill.

Head occupied a role in Ottawa similar to Yakovlev's, in that both men were viewed with distrust by the diplomats in Canada's Department of External Affairs. "The Department," as it was called, still presented problems for Yakovlev. The organization's Soviet desk was populated with Cold Warriors, people who took the American attitude that the Soviet Union was an enemy entity that posed a threat to the free world. Representative among them was Yakovlev's counterpart, the Canadian ambassador to Moscow, Robert A.D. Ford, who saw himself as an expert in Russian literature but was suspicious of any measure that came from the Soviet Communist Party. Following Ford's lead, the Department's diplomats in Ottawa took a similar approach with Ambassador Yakovlev. This attitude presented a problem for Yakovlev. These Canadian diplomats were supposed to act as his first point of contact with the Canadian government. If the ambassador had a proposal, say, for a deal involving the purchase of Canadian power turbines by a Soviet electrical generating plant, then Yakovlev was supposed to approach the Department and request a meeting with the appropriate Canadian representative. Then, theoretically, the Department would see about setting up a meeting. This system placed all the power in the hands of Department diplomats, who often seemed to simply ignore Yakovlev. Time-relevant requests for appointments with cabinet ministers or other functionaries dragged out for weeks before they were turned down, usually with the request to send a memo instead. It is indicative of the Department's stance toward Yakovlev that, more than a year after his arrival, Canadian diplomats continued to speculate whether the ambassador was just a figurehead, and whether the true power in the embassy belonged elsewhere.

Luckily for Yakovlev, others in Ottawa were also frustrated with External Affairs' diplomats. Under the previous prime minister, Lester Pearson, the Department had been the federal government's glamour job, the beneficiary of a lavish new headquarters that opened two weeks after Yakovlev's arrival in Ottawa. Not coincidentally, the headquarters was called the Lester B. Pearson Building, and was located just a few steps across the street from the prime minister's residence.

But Pearson stepped down in 1968, and his successor, Pierre Elliott Trudeau, considered the Department an anachronism, a bloated and inefficient bureaucracy too obsessed with following protocol to move at the speed required by modern diplomacy. Among Trudeau's ideas for reform was a proposition to do away with the whole diplomatic system. In an age of instant communication, he said, who needed an intermediary to shuttle messages back and forth between world leaders?

Virtually ignoring the Department, Trudeau placed much of the authority for generating foreign policy outside of External Affairs, entrusting it instead to Ivan Head, a onetime law professor at the University of Alberta. Technically, Head was Trudeau's "special advisor." The vague term referred to a position Trudeau himself spoke of as a Canadian version of the influential U.S. National Security Advisor Henry Kissinger. Head accompanied Trudeau on diplomatic missions, briefed the prime minister before meetings with foreign leaders, and even accompanied him to those meetings – often displacing the host ambassador from his usual advisory role. Canada's diplomatic corps despised Head. They thought him arrogant. They resented his influence on Trudeau, viewing his counsel "as a competing source of advice whose quality they could not assess" and jealously monitoring his globe-trotting and meetings with foreign dignitaries.

Thanks to his experience in the Central Committee, Yakovlev was accustomed to using back doors to access power brokers. Yakovlev saw that Head represented a link to the prime minister that superseded the hostile mandarins in the Department of External Affairs. Protocol dictated that Yakovlev ask External's permission before talking business with Head. The jealous Department certainly would have found some reason to decline the request. However, protocol eased for social appointments. So one day Yakovlev called Head at his office and suggested an unconventional social engagement.

In his gruff, almost-impenetrable Russian accent, Yakovlev first apologized about his command of the English language. Yakovlev then disclosed to Head that he'd read the *Foreign Affairs* essay, and liked it. But he had some questions – questions that perhaps stemmed from his ignorance of Canadian affairs. Would Dr. Head come by the Soviet ambassador's residence for a drink, maybe a light supper, and they could discuss the essay further?

Head agreed.

YAKOVLEV MET WITH Head in the study of the ambassador's residence. It was a cozy chamber on the home's first floor, with a fireplace, a pair of couches, and a table on which were strewn the publications Yakovlev had taken to reading in Ottawa – *U.S. News and World Report* and *The Economist*, among them. Yakovlev's cook laid out a light dinner – likely including the Russian caviar that Yakovlev urged on many Canadian guests. The cook poured them drinks. And then Yakovlev pulled out the January 1972 issue of *Foreign Affairs*. He turned to Head's essay, which, Head saw, was thatched with underlining, the margins dark with exclamation marks and inscrutable scribbled notes. "If it's all right with you," rumbled the Soviet ambassador, "I'd like to read you certain passages, and then let's debate them." Minutes later, Yakovlev had his eyes fixed on the book and was reading the text aloud.

Inconveniently for historians, neither Yakovlev nor Head ever provided a line-by-line summary of the topics in Head's essay that twigged Yakovlev's interest. But taken as a whole, the essay seems almost custommade to win Canada the sympathy of its new Soviet ambassador. One of the essay's most intriguing notions is mentioned in its title: "The Foreign Policy of the New Canada." A similar line occurs in the essay's body, when Head quotes the prime minister: "We are building a new society in Canada [which] places increasing emphasis on the quality of life and the importance of human relations."

To explain this notion of "the new Canada," Head would have had to provide Yakovlev with some historical context. The idea germinated in the latter half of the 1960s, against the backdrop of Canadian centennial celebrations in 1967 and the internationally popular Montreal World's Fair, Expo '67. In roughly the same period, Canada retired its old flag, based on the British Ensign, and replaced it with a bold design dominated by a single red maple leaf. The thrill of national renewal had helped Trudeau get elected in 1968. The oil shocks of the early 1970s also contributed to this nascent patriotism, as Canada realized it was the world's only industrialized non-communist country that produced more oil than it consumed. It was the United States' largest foreign supplier of oil. Problem was, much of that oil was controlled by American entities, by "the whim and fancy of foreign producers and international cartels," as one politician complained. That epiphany spawned a greater realization of the extent to which America dominated Canadian life, or, as Head put it in the essay, "of the amorphous embrace of millions of American magazines and books, of hundreds of thousands of American investors, of thousands of American films and television programs, of the constant pressure – friendly yet overwhelming – of 200,000,000 talented, energetic, acquisitive Americans."

So "the new Canada" was a response to the domination of Canadian life by American influences. Head's essay uses the oft-quoted Trudeau characterization of the Canadian situation as "sleeping with an elephant." This drive toward a new Canada, then, was an effort to survive the night – an effort to define, preserve and protect a separate Canadian identity. Coinciding with this national coming of age was a blossoming anti-Americanism. The small country that had spent much of its independent existence emulating its southern neighbour was realizing its cities and towns were just as, if not more, pleasant places to live than the Chicagos and New Yorks of the era. "Our quarter-century old admiration of all things American exhausted itself in the blazing villages of Vietnam, the dark labyrinth of Watergate, and the long-overdue realization that the United States was crowding out not just our industries, but our way of life," wrote Canadian writer and editor Peter C. Newman. Such attitudes spawned a novel, a bestseller in Canada, that imagined the forced annexation of Canada by an energy-hungry United States. In an essay about the book (called *Ultimatum*) for the *New York Times Book Review*, Robert Fulford, another Canadian editor, referred to "the degree to which anti-Americanism has begun to dominate the way Canadians think about themselves and their place in the world."

"The race riots and the assassinations took place in our living rooms, too," Fulford noted. "At some point the Canadian perception of America changed – began, in fact, to be reversed . . . Where America had symbolized success, now it came to mean failure."

Across the nation, Canadians involved themselves in an existential debate on their identity, which usually dissolved into a discussion about how Canadians differed from their Yankee counterparts. Canadians proudly declared themselves more tolerant, more equitable, more communally minded – more civilized, darn it – than their neighbours to the south. The decade's turmoil and political activism affected Canada as it did other Western countries, most notably with the FLQ crisis of 1970 that resulted in Trudeau invoking the *War Measures Act*, a form of martial law. But rather than inflaming the populace, that crisis, spawned by Quebec separatists, provided Canadians with a sobering respect for the negative symptoms of ethnic nationalism. Once the crisis passed, Canadians attempted to regain their grasp on the international reputation for pragmatism and rationality they constantly told themselves they had; what the American politician Adlai Stevenson Jr. once referred to as Canada's "built-in gyroscope."

All this discussion of a Canadian national identity found a sympathetic observer in Yakovlev. He shared Canada's anti-American tendencies, and the swell of Canadian patriotism Head described was a far cry from the sort of nationalism Yakovlev rallied against in his fateful exile-causing essay. Instead of the Russian bear bellowing about its superiority, Canada was an underdog battling American money, culture, and power to establish the mere hint of a national identity. Given Yakovlev's crippling war wound and his rural peasant *cum* outsider upbringing, he tended to side with the underdog. His behaviour during his Canadian posting indicates he did in this instance, too.

ANOTHER FACT of the new Canada certain to pique Yakovlev's interest was its comparatively impartial position on the Cold War. Head in particular had a reputation for siding with the Soviets. As both Head and Trudeau pointed out frequently, Canada resided along the route missiles might follow if the Cold War went nuclear; Head later would call Canada "the meat in the sandwich between two nuclear powers." This uncomfortable position bred in both men a desire to cultivate warm relations with both Cold War combatants – a strategy designed to place the small nation in the political role of intermediary should relations between the two countries ever break down. "It was in Canada's interest, and seen to be consistent with Canadian traditions, to seek a more orderly state of world affairs, where tensions could be relieved and conflicts resolved through structured, non-violent means," Head and Trudeau would later write in a co-authored book. "Communication was the first step."

Head's essay charted a course for Canada somewhere between the Soviet East and the American West. "Canada's southern neighbor has been a traditional friend; it is in Canada's interest that her northern neighbor . . . be friendly as well," he wrote. "A nation of 22 million people cannot be regarded as a threat by either the United States or the Soviet Union. That fact places upon Canada a responsibility to search for areas of common interest within each. Those areas are well identified in one direction [the U.S.], but require considerable probing and examination in the other [the Soviet Union]."

Geography wasn't the only factor that placed Canada midway between the United States and the Soviet Union. Politically, too, Canada resided somewhere between the two enemies – more friendly to social- ism than America, far more capitalist than the Soviets. Political Canada has always resided several notches to the left, resulting in a system that encourages a socialist equality of situation rather than the individualist equality of opportunity favoured by Americans. Canadians were proud of their system of universal health care, a socialist innovation. Unlike Washington, Ottawa never outlawed her national Communist Party. Even the comparatively right-wing Canadian Prime Minister John Diefenbaker declined to join the U.S.-led economic embargo against Castro's Cuba. Similarly, Canada stayed out of the Vietnam War, which many Canadians regarded as an exercise in American imperialism.

In 1974 left-wing political forces were a powerful factor in the Canadian scene. Indeed, when Yakovlev arrived in Canada, the social- ist New Democratic Party ran three of the 10 provincial governments, and Prime Minister Trudeau's Liberal Party formed the federal govern- ment only in coalition with the New Democrats' federal arm.

This thinking was reflected in Canada's attitude toward the USSR, and toward the Soviet ambassador. Granted, his embassy was picketed by protesters throughout his posting, usually Ukrainians or Jews agitat- ing for family reunification. But high-ranking Canadians such as Head also provided Yakovlev with something else, something different from the hostility that provoked his "enemy camp" mindset during visits to the States. The difference may have opened Yakovlev to the benefits of Canadian democracy.

THEIR FIRST ENCOUNTER lasted perhaps a few hours, and by the end of it Head had arrived at a decision about this new Soviet ambassador. Working for Trudeau, Head had come to know quite a few Soviet diplomats. They tended to be gregarious and outgoing men who loved children, all of which applied to Yakovlev. But they could also be competitive in a way that prevented any real friendship from developing. They always seemed to want to score points against capitalism or democracy. They had a reserve that prevented them from wavering from their dogmatic, Party-dictated ideological script. If any disagreement became serious, their composure dissolved and they shifted to petulance, accusing the Canadians of absurd conspiracy plots and resorting to needlessly dramatic threats, such as the severing of relations between the two countries.

Relations with Yakovlev were professional, at first. Head referred to Yakovlev as "Your Excellency." Yakovlev referred to Head as "Professor." But under all the etiquette there was a level of engagement that Head had never experienced with any other Soviet diplomat. During the hour or so they talked, Head felt that his Soviet conversation partner expressed opinions and thoughts he'd reasoned himself, rather than memorized from some party textbook. Yakovlev displayed few signs of wanting to participate in some grand tennis match between capitalism and communism; he never seemed to be keeping score in his head.

Instead, Head found himself debating his essay, and Canada's place in the world, with an obviously intelligent man whose political system had led him to develop opinions very different from Head's own. What struck Head was Yakovlev's clear desire not to judge, not to badger Head into coming around to Yakovlev's viewpoint, but rather to *understand* why Head thought the way he did. In a non-judgmental, very open-minded manner, Yakovlev was trying to get inside Head's head. "This was an intellectual, professorial kind of tutorial he was expecting me to conduct with him," Head would say later. "He wasn't trying to get any additional information out. It was just . . . understanding the nuances in an article of that sort." Head, who found himself missing the peda-gogical aspect of academic life, experienced the satisfaction that came from teaching an adept, engaged pupil who genuinely wanted to learn.

So, after the first encounter, the two men again got together, again to debate some text Head had written, and soon their encounters were hap-pening semi-regularly, whenever both had a free evening and a yen for conversation. By autumn 1974 the relationship between Yakovlev and Head had grown close enough that Yakovlev had, through Head, a genuine back door to the corridors of Canadian government – a diplo-matic conduit that superseded the mandarins at External Affairs he'd earlier found so uncooperative. Yakovlev no longer sent important mes-sages through External. Now, Yakovlev simply called Head directly, on the telephone, or dropped into Head's office to pass along a note. The Department complained that this new method of passing information violated protocol. The diplomats painstakingly noted each encounter between the prime minister's foreign policy advisor and the Soviet ambas-sador. "I am concerned about the attempts by the Soviet ambassador to make end runs around this department," complained one diplomat.

In fact, something else was happening. Ivan Head was providing his new Soviet friend with an education in Canadian democracy. It would have astonished the Communist Party bureaucrats back in Moscow, but even in 1974 steps toward the Party's ultimate destruction were happen-ing in a fire-warmed study set just off the sleepy, tree-lined paths of Ottawa's Rockcliffe Park.

16

THROWING SNOWBALLS AT LENIN'S TOMB

B ESIDES YAKOVLEV'S RELATIONSHIP with Head, other factors made Canada a dangerous place for any vestiges of Communist Party dogma remaining in Yakovlev's thinking. Two such factors combined in September 1974 when Prime Minister Pierre Elliott Trudeau invited Ambassador Yakovlev to the Colisée de Québec, in Quebec City, where Team Canada was hosting the Soviets in the first match of the latest Summit Series between the two countries.

The idea behind several incarnations of Summit Series was to pit the world's two best hockey-playing nations against one another in a sporting spectacle that would provide the victor with the right to claim uncontested global hockey supremacy. The first happened in 1972. Because sports fell partly under the rubric of the Propaganda Department, Yakovlev was among the party bureaucrats whose support helped to overcome high-level doubt – Brezhnev and the rest wanted guaranteed wins – in convincing the Politburo to permit the series to happen. That September, the Soviets won the first game of the series, 7–3. Suddenly Canadians woke up to the possibility, never before considered by most, that Canada might lose. The whole of the nation became entranced by the eight-game contest. Newspapers, magazines, and television provided Canada with an education in all things Soviet-related. Canadians learned about the Soviet lifestyle, the culture, the character of the people. They learned, too, that the foreign wings, centres, and defenders could perform with just as much heart as their native boys. Some even professed to prefer the Soviet emphasis on passing plays and finesse, rather than the gritty, physical style used by the Canadians. When the eighth game began in Moscow on Sept. 28, 1972, the series was even, with three wins apiece and a single tie. This game, too, was an even affair, tied in the final minutes of the third period. Then, with just 34 seconds left, Canadian forward Paul Henderson picked up a loose puck in the Soviet end. Goalie Vladislav Tretiak saved the first shot, but the rebound skittered out of the goalie's control and Henderson flipped the black disc over the goalie's pancaked pads, for what remains the most famous goal in Canadian history. For the moment, Canada's hockey superiority was secure.

Two years later, on Sept. 17, 1974, Yakovlev was perched beside Trudeau in the Colisée for the first game of the second Summit Series. The sportswriters' consensus had the Soviets besting the Canadians this time around. Instead of NHL players this Team Canada was populated mostly by grizzled veterans selected from a new upstart league, the World Hockey Association, including such names as Bobby Hull, Gordie Howe, and the now-legendary Paul Henderson. Against a considerably more experienced Tretiak, Canadian Johnny McKenzie scored the first goal about halfway through the first period. The next third was a shooting gallery and by its end the Soviets were up 3–2. Then, with just five minutes left the Soviets drew a tripping call and during the ensuing power play Canadian forward Bobby Hull unleashed a slapshot that tied the game. The match concluded in a 3–3 tie.

Watching the series, which the Soviets eventually won, Yakovlev was proud of his players. "Our guys proved their worth on the ice," Yakovlev wrote. "They played with inspiration, selflessly, and they fought without sparing themselves. It is impossible to convey what Tretiak, Kharlamov, Yakushev and all our other hockey players were accomplishing. You had to see it. It was a celebration of will, courage, and beauty. Our hockey players did substantially more to improve relations between the two countries than the politicians did over the course of many years."

The Summit Series encouraged Canadian citizens to reassess their Soviet counterparts. Canadians who once feared the USSR as a nation of KGB agents and atom-bomb-crazed politicians now understood that Soviet citizens, too, were human beings. Thanks to these hockey matches, no one in Canada was going to ask Yakovlev to remove his hat, the better to see his horns. Instead, the discovery of Yakovlev's nationality was more likely to provoke some hockey-related comment of grudging admiration. "After [these games] it became easier to work for me," Yakovlev said, later. "It so happens in life – diplomats, politicians argue, accuse one another . . . but when hockey players play and all the country watches, gets excited, worried – and in Canada, as is known, hockey is a national disease – after that, they get to know your country better. And after that, no matter where I went, all conversations began and ended with hockey, already in a very friendly, interested tone. After such conversations it was somehow easier to come to terms . . . I think, in general, it had a very big impact on Canadian-Soviet relations."

Pierre Trudeau picked up on this hockey diplomacy. At the end of the match he watched alongside the new Soviet ambassador, the prime minister leaned over to Yakovlev. "You know, your guys are great players," he said. "But they're something else – they're diplomats."

TRUDEAU AFFECTED Yakovlev's time in Canada far more than hockey, however. The prime minister's personality dominated Ottawa through-out the whole of Yakovlev's Canadian posting. When Yakovlev arrived, Trudeau already had served for five years. He would still be serving after Yakovlev left; aside from an uneventful nine-month span that began in 1979, he governed Canada for the 16-year period from 1968 to 1984. He was a fascinating, impulsive and irreverent politician, a wealthy Montreal intellectual whose charisma drew comparisons to American president John F. Kennedy. "One of the wisest, most reflective and most articulate leaders in the Western world," appraised *New York Times* columnist James Reston. Trudeau also had some unconventional ideas about the Cold War – ideas that may have had a formidable influence on Yakovlev.

The Canadian leader's background couldn't have been more different from Yakovlev's. Trudeau was born four years earlier, on October 18, 1919, to Charles Trudeau, a Catholic francophone businessman, and his Protestant anglophone wife, Grace Elliott. Pierre was the eldest child; the couple had another son and a daughter before Charles died in 1935, when Trudeau was only 15. By that point, Charles had built and sold for $1.2 million a mechanic and gas station business, the Automobile Owners' Association. He also invested well. In contrast to Yakovlev's poverty-ridden life in northern Russia, the Trudeau family was wealthy by any standard. Young Pierre was schooled in private Catholic schools by Jesuit priests, where he displayed an early aptitude for debate and political philosophy. While Yakovlev was fighting Nazis under a Jewish commander in the Great Patriotic War, Trudeau was cruising a Harley-Davidson motorcycle around Quebec dressed in Nazi-style clothing – a temporary flirtation with fascism that grew out of a youthful affiliation with Quebec nationalists. He earned his law degree from the Université de Montreal, then did his master's in political economy at Harvard. Soon after he began a doctorate program at the London School of Economics. He passed his time managing the family's wealth, dabbling in politics and philosophy, and travelling. Between trips to such then unconventional destinations as the Soviet Union, India, and China, Trudeau helped to found a French-language political journal, *Cité libre* and worked for the federal government in the influential Privy Council Office, which advises the prime minister and his cabinet. In 1961 he won a gig as a law professor at the Université de Montréal, and finally got serious by successfully running for Parliament in 1965. Two years later the legal idealist was named minister of justice by Prime Minister Lester B. Pearson, and he embarked on a startlingly libertarian course that secured women's right to abortion and legalized homosexual behaviour, reflecting his oft-quoted statement that "the state has no place in the bedrooms of the nation."

Trudeau became Liberal Party leader in 1968, and his subsequent national election campaign capitalized on the protest spirit of the hippie decade by incorporating an individualist, anti-establishment vibe. As prime minister his militant response to the 1970 FLQ crisis shocked the nation, as did the 51-year-old bachelor's decision the following year to wed a 22-year-old raven-haired beauty named Margaret Sinclair. The couple's first state visit was to the Soviet Union, in May 1971. Margaret befriended Soviet Premier Alexei Kosygin's daughter, Lyudmila, on the trip. Trudeau for his part told Brezhnev that Canada wanted to reduce tensions in Europe, and committed to cut by 50 percent the number of Canadian troops stationed on the continent. He also signed a "Protocol on Consultations" that provided a dispute-resolution framework and committed the two countries to regular diplomatic meetings. Trudeau called the new protocol "an important step towards the establishment of the most autonomous foreign policy possible" – meaning, autonomous from the United States. Later, Trudeau said, "Canada and Canadians want very much to be able to look to the north, as they have long looked to the south, and see friends in each direction." The comment caused a flap among conservative voters, but the sentiment was clear: Trudeau hoped to set Canada on a course for Cold War neutrality.

CANADA'S PRIME MINISTER was nearly alone among leaders of Western democracies in sympathizing with the Soviet side of the Cold War. Those sympathies stemmed from a lifelong fascination with communism. Soon after he completed his studies at Harvard, the devout Catholic youth travelled to Paris, telling people he was researching a dissertation on the theme of Christianity and communism. The idea for this dissertation persisted into Trudeau's 1947 enrollment in the London School of Economics, where the topic drifted into a reconciliation of Catholicism with communism – something he felt was possible thanks to papal condemnation of "the great material inequalities in modern industrial capitalism."

Trudeau's thesis advisor at LSE was the renowned socialist Harold Laski, then nearing the end of a remarkable career. Laski had advised American president Franklin Roosevelt on the New Deal. As the Labour Party's chair he was the ideologue who guided socialist strategy in Britain, most famously during Labour's whipping of Churchill's Conservatives in the election of 1945. A learned figure who charmed his conversation partners with gossipy asides, real or imagined, about the politicians he advised, Laski could be a tremendously persuasive interlocutor. He is said to have converted Joseph Kennedy, Jr. to socialism but had less success with his younger brother, the future American president John F. Kennedy.

Central to Laski's appeal was his capacity for unconventional reasoning. At root he was a liberal democrat who believed in socialism because he saw poverty as a form of repression, similar to censorship. He wished to preserve such rights as freedom of speech, assembly, and religion while also favouring state redistribution of wealth among citizens. By the late 1940s, when Trudeau studied with him, Laski was judging American democracy to be flawed, thanks to the "ever wider divergence between the democracy it proclaimed" and "the reality of capitalist power," which, Laski believed, led inevitably toward working-class poverty. He was particularly troubled by racial inequalities and "the use of hired thugs to intimidate workers in labour disputes," believing that "American democracy was not only flawed, but also fundamentally hypocritical." How, he asked, could the United States "proclaim the virtues of freedom abroad while allowing its own system to deviate so totally from the liberalism, constitutionalism and democracy that it proclaimed?"

Meanwhile, Laski also was concerned about the Soviet Union. He met Stalin during a 1946 trip to the USSR, and came away impressed, but he considered Stalinism a phenomenon separate from the friendlier form of socialism he advocated. Laski wished to preserve human freedoms under the aegis of parliamentary democracy – a position that inherently criticized Stalin's one-party rule. He considered the Soviet Union "a non-democratic police state." Laski's reservations about either system led him to a troubled agnosticism on the Cold War, which he considered a conflict between two "Messianic philosophies," both of which deserved healthy portions of blame for the world-endangering conflict that resulted from their mutual animosity. He ultimately fell out with the Labour Party after Prime Minister Clement Attlee aligned Britain with the United States in the nascent Cold War, which Laski felt to be a betrayal of the Labour Party's socialist ideology. Trudeau was in London studying under Laski just as tensions between the U.S. and the USSR were coalescing into the Cold War. Trudeau's official biographer, John English, argues that Laski's perception of the East–West conflict would define the views of the future Canadian prime minister. "[Laski] became a major intellectual and, to a lesser degree, personal influence on the young Canadian . . . Harold Laski became, for Trudeau, a model."

By the time Trudeau left Laski's tutelage in the summer of 1948, the Canadian's lifelong romance with the Soviet Union was well advanced. Intent on experiencing Soviet Russia first-hand, he set out east from London on what would become an around-the -world trip that would last into the following year, travelling first through such Eastern European countries as Poland, Czechoslovakia and Bulgaria, but failing to make it into an increasingly isolationist USSR. After a swing through the Middle East and India, Trudeau did manage to visit China on the eve of Mao's victory. He actually met Mao during another trip, in 1960, the same year he set out on a quixotic, and unsuccessful, attempt to canoe to Cuba soon after Castro's rebels took Havana.

Trudeau's first successful trip to Soviet Russia happened in 1952, during what would prove to be the last year of Stalin's life. Trudeau was 32 and spent most of the spring and some of the summer there – a spate of time available to him thanks to his late father's fortune. Ostensibly his intention was to participate in an economic conference in Moscow. Others dismissed the conference as propaganda. Certainly, it attracted devout communists from around the world. Trudeau may have attended it purely as an excuse to see the USSR.

The trip provided its share of adventures. Bored by the conference, Trudeau spent much of his time hanging around the Canadian embassy, where he professed his admiration for Soviet living conditions to the embassy's chargé d'affaires, Robert A.D. Ford, who would go on to become a long-serving ambassador to Moscow. Trudeau travelled by train on a three-day journey to Tbilisi, Georgia. The only other occupant of his compartment was a beautiful Russian woman who, suspiciously for that era, spoke flawless English. Trudeau suspected she was a spy. Back in Moscow, Trudeau attended mass at the American embassy, where he met the wife of the American chargé. He told her that he was a Catholic as well as a communist; according to one account, he then attacked the United States and praised the Soviet Union. In 1952, to Americans, such conduct was tantamount to blasphemy. Angry American embassy officials confronted their Canadian counterparts, who insisted Trudeau was only joking. Another adventure saw Trudeau trudging through a snow-covered Red Square to lob snowballs at Lenin's Tomb. Eventually, such stunts earned him the enmity of the authorities. In late July, after almost four months in Russia, Soviet policemen appeared at his apartment, packed Trudeau's bags for him, and put him on a plane, homeward bound. He returned to Canada on July 23, 1952.

Was Trudeau a communist? The topic was debated around Montreal in the aftermath of his trip, as he wrote about his adventures and appeared on radio downplaying the threat represented by Soviet secret police. The military were too preoccupied exchanging salutes to terrorize the population, he said. Before student audiences at the Université de Montréal he praised the Soviet educational system and architecture, as well as funding for the arts. Conservative pundits in Quebec said he was naïve and ill informed. They called him a Stalinist mouthpiece. Another said he was "the Canadian Karl Marx."

Later in life, Trudeau didn't hide his affection for communism. The book he co-authored with Ivan Head, *The Canadian Way*, declared the Communist Revolution of 1917 the most significant event of the 20th century. He struck up a friendship with Fidel Castro. He didn't believe the Soviet Union represented a military threat to Western Europe. And after he became prime minister in 1968, "a rapprochement with Moscow became a top priority in his foreign policy," wrote Ford. Another observer noted, "He could not see the Soviet Union or the People's Republic of China in demonological terms, he had become bored with the un-thinking rhetoric of the Cold War, and his rational mind rejected the idea of a balance of terror founded on nuclear weapons." One key advisor speculated that if pressed to choose between the competing systems of capitalist America and communist Russia, Trudeau would have chosen the centrally planned communist system versus what he regarded as the chaos of the capitalist economy.

But that's a hypothetical dilemma. In truth, Trudeau was too much of an individualist to ever fully embrace anyone else's political system, including Lenin's, and too much a contrarian to subscribe to the good-versus-evil, us-versus-them mentality that characterized either side of the Cold War. Dating from his days at Harvard he was a zealot about protecting indvidual rights from the excesses of state power. "The sov-ereignty of the individual is the alpha and omega of Trudeau's political thinking," noted one Trudeau biographer. He was an expert in consti-tutional affairs; his passion for protecting the rights of the individual would result in the defining achievement of his later years in office, the institution of the Canadian Charter of Rights and Freedoms. Calling himself a "communist" to the wife of the American diplomat came out of a mischievous desire to provoke a reaction, a character trait he often displayed even as prime minister. (Passing a demonstration of truckers on Parliament Hill, he once rolled down his window and shouted a sug-gestion they consume excrement, a phrase that sounded much more rude in the French he used.)

What matters is that, in Trudeau, Yakovlev found an atypical juxta-position, a figure wary of any government's totalitarian tendencies and simultaneously sympathetic to the Marxist cause of social justice. This awkward combination was similar to that of his early mentor, Harold Laski: Soviet Communism was an admirable, if flawed, attempt to create an equitable society. So, too, was Trudeau persuaded of the evils of American imperialism. The best option was a middle way that resided somewhere between the ideological poles created by Soviet Communism and American capitalism. During that first trip to the Soviet Union in 1952, Trudeau said "his position is that of a neutralist-idealist and that it is possible for men of good will to try to act as a centre group which will eventually widen, and prevent the two extremes from clashing." Similarly, the book he co-authored with Head, *The Canadian Way*, cites Harold Laski's belief that capitalism and communism required an intellectual bridge to avoid "a catastrophic age of terror." The two statements summarize the international role Trudeau and Head were charting for Canada. They also explain why a friendship between Yakovlev and the pro-Soviet, social justice-crusading Trudeau might have been dangerous for the corrupt careerists running the Communist Party.

ONCE YAKOVLEV BEFRIENDED Ivan Head, a relationship with Trudeau was all but inevitable. Yakovlev displayed a gift throughout his career for strategic networking, and during his early years as ambassador no one held more of an allure in Ottawa than Trudeau. Similarly, Head is likely to have discussed with Trudeau the circumstances behind the arrival of this new kid in town. Trudeau is certain to have been intrigued. "What would have interested Trudeau about Yakovlev?" asks Allan Gotlieb, a onetime undersecretary of External Affairs, who refers in conversation to the "Yakovlev–Trudeau romance." "That he was the Soviet ambassador. That's it. That's all he needed to be for Trudeau to have made time for him." Others corroborate the prime minister's interest in meeting Soviet citizens. "He would refuse to see the foreign minister of Turkey, for example, but find time to have the Russian poet Andrei Voznesensky for lunch," wrote Ford.

The two men probably met two months after Yakovlev's arrival, in the fall of 1973, as Trudeau was due to leave on a state trip to China. Conscious of Moscow's perpetual jockeying for global positioning with Beijing, and wary of offending the Politburo, Head pushed for Trudeau to receive Yakovlev before the prime minister's departure. "The new

Soviet Ambassador has now been in Ottawa some two months," wrote Head to the prime minister. "Because of the hypersensitivity of the Soviets with respect to China . . . I urge you to receive the Ambassador prior to your departure for China."

Yakovlev and Trudeau's relationship quickly grew past that of a professional contact between ambassador and government leader. It helped that the two men lived close to one another; a park and a traffic circle is about all that separated their homes. During warmer weather, Yakovlev sometimes passed time tending to the roses that bordered his driveway. Similarly, Trudeau sometimes tooled around the neighbourhood in one of his cars, or on less conventional modes of transportation for heads of government – his bicycle or on foot. If he happened to catch sight of Yakovlev in his yard, Trudeau would often wave. Soon, Yakovlev was inviting the prime minister to drop by the residence for blinis, traditional Russian pastries. The PM did stop by, and after that the encounters grew more social.

Their families also got along. When the Yakovlevs first met her, Margaret Trudeau was a 24-year-old flower child, and as much of an outsider among the prim matrons of Ottawa diplomatic circles as Nina Yakovlev. During the Yakovlevs' first visit to the Trudeaus' home, Nina charmed Margaret with her lack of pretension. When introduced to the two young Trudeau children, Nina sat down on the carpet to meet Justin and Sacha at eye level, then pulled from her purse some candy. Nina's 50 years made her twice Margaret's age, and the two women developed a friendship with mother-daughter overtones. "Margaret treated my wife very well," Yakovlev noted. "[They] called one another on the phone. She treated my wife not as the wife of an ambassador, but as though she were her mother." The affection was mutual. "I regarded her as if she was my own daughter," Nina recalls.

In fact, one legend still believed by many – it was on Wikipedia as recently as late 2007 – had the Trudeaus naming their second son after Yakovlev. This is nonsense that nevertheless does have a factual foundation. Alexandre Trudeau was born on December 25, 1973, just months after the Yakovlevs' Ottawa arrival and far too close for Trudeau to have honoured the Soviet ambassador in this manner. According to Yakovlev's memoirs, Lyudmila Kosygina, the premier's daughter, suggested the name of Alexandre, and sometime after the young boy's birth the Trudeaus were discussing suitable nicknames. The prime minister said males with such first names could be called "Sacha." His wife didn't believe him, and to convince her Trudeau suggested she call Yakovlev to verify the name. Margaret did, and to this day Alexandre Trudeau is known as Sacha.

The two families grew closer with the arrival in Ottawa of the Yakovlevs' granddaughter, Natasha, a pretty, blond-haired, blue-eyed child who was two years older than Justin Trudeau. In Moscow Natasha's mother – Yakovlev's daughter Nataliya – was working to build a career in fashion. She didn't have much time to be a parent. And besides, Yakovlev thought, it might be good for the little girl to be exposed to a different country. It certainly was good for Nina, whose loneliness abated now that she had someone to look after. Now Yakovlev was one of the few men in the capital of Trudeau's age who also was parenting a young child. The two families socialized during skating parties on the nearby grounds of the governor-general's residence, Rideau Hall. The Trudeaus invited the Yakovlevs to 24 Sussex Drive for private dinners, just the two families together. When the Russian circus came to town the Yakovlevs invited the Trudeaus to attend a performance; the Trudeau boys were delighted by the appearance, just behind them, of a horse at the top of the bleachers, a surprise stunt that profoundly alarmed the secret service men charged with safeguarding the prime minister. Such encounters developed a bond between the two families. One staff member of External Affairs' Soviet desk who witnessed the Yakovlevs' relations with the Trudeau family was struck in particular by the affection the Trudeau boys had for the Soviet ambassador; the boys treated Yakovlev like an uncle or a grandfather.

Still, this was the Cold War. Contacts between the prime minister and the supposedly nefarious Soviet ambassador generated concern in Ottawa and in Washington alike. Jealously, warily, curiously, the

Canadian diplomats in Ottawa catalogued each instance the prime minister met with the Soviet ambassador. Was Yakovlev somehow influencing Trudeau, they wondered, encouraging the prime minister to come around to the Soviet way of looking at things?

IT SEEMS MORE LIKELY that the influence went the other way. If he respected your intellect, then conversation with the prime minister was a tremendously demanding business. He dispensed with social niceties, challenging suppositions, criticizing precepts, sounding opinions. Intellectual laziness and over-reliance on the conventional wisdom were abhorrent to him, and he would inform you if he thought you guilty of these sins. All in all, Trudeau approached conversation as though it were combat: "Why do you think that?" "Why not?" Or simply, "Why?" Few opinions weathered serious conversations with Trudeau unaffected. And over the years, Yakovlev and Trudeau conducted their share of serious conversations.

As time passed, the two men fell into a practice of getting together one on one. Not for business reasons. Simply to chat. The encounters typically happened at one of their homes, usually over a meal. Yakovlev prepared for these occasions the way a university professor might prepare for a lecture. Knowing that Trudeau liked Tolstoy and Dostoevsky – the PM could quote passages by heart – Yakovlev might brush up on the novelists' artistic *oeuvre*. Sometimes Yakovlev devoted their encounters to specific topics, such as more contemporary Russian literature, or writers of the countryside, with their implicit criticism of Soviet agricultural policies.

They talked together for personal pleasure and political interest. They asked questions out of curiosity or for professional consideration. Each wanted to understand the system that had nurtured his counterpart – and the sort of mind that system created. Thus, their conversations were wide-ranging discussions in which two extraordinarily well-informed men talked, sometimes about whatever came into their heads. Trudeau wasn't invested in proving capitalism's superiority to communism.

Because he didn't embrace either system, he posed for Yakovlev the ideal debating partner – an intellectual adventurer willing to explore any notion without condemnation for violating some ideological dogma. Human rights created some memorable discourse, as did nuclear arms control strategies and the idea of spheres of influence – a pet theory of Trudeau's that identified realms in which each of the great powers should be able to exercise control. Gradually, Trudeau used Yakovlev as a trusted source of information about Moscow's activities, consulting him whenever the Soviets did something that puzzled him, or when he was curious about how some event in the West might be viewed by the power brokers in Moscow.

In the early days of their friendship, for example, Trudeau was eager to hear about the health of Soviet leader Leonid Brezhnev, who, Yakovlev relayed to Trudeau, "was tired and his health less than it should be" – quite an admission for a Soviet ambassador to make to the leader of his host government. The prime minister also requested the ambassador's help on the matter of David Geldiaschvilli, a Soviet immigrant to Canada who had returned to the USSR to visit with long-unseen relatives. Then, without warning, Soviet authorities imprisoned Geldiaschvilli and sentenced him to death. It turned out that Geldiaschvilli was a veteran on a list of war criminals. After a series of heartbreaking entreaties to the prime minister from Geldiaschvilli's wife, who still lived in Montreal, Trudeau asked Yakovlev to look into the matter. Eventually, the sentence was commuted to 15 years – a fit of leniency almost unprecedented, Yakovlev informed the Canadians.

The relationship could work both ways; Trudeau also performed favours for Yakovlev. "As for my diplomatic requests, I would write them on little sheets of paper and pass those on to him," Yakovlev wrote in his memoirs. "Such notes had a magical power indeed; they quickly went off to be studied, and, as a rule, they were positively resolved." Solzhenitsyn, the writer, was finally expelled from the Soviet Union by the Communist Party in 1974. The crusading dissident visited Canada to investigate the possibility of settling there. Just days before Solzhenitsyn's arrival, Moscow ordered Yakovlev to prevent the prime minister from receiving the writer in an official visit. "I met with Ivan Head and told him all this," Yakovlev says. "Well aware of our political ways, he smiled, and at the end of the conversation he asked me to put Moscow at ease, declaring that [Trudeau's] meeting with Solzhenitsyn would be short and formal. In fact, it was a long meeting, but after it Head phoned me" – on an embassy phone line certain to be monitored by the KGB, both men knew – "to confirm that everything was brief and formal, just as he had promised."

Trudeau and Yakovlev came to form an East–West version of a mutual admiration society. The prime minister felt protective enough of his friendship with the Soviet ambassador that he insulated it from External Affairs – not allowing the Department's note-takers to attend many meetings, despite the pressure they applied to participate. In turn, in Yakovlev's memoirs and other writings, Trudeau draws praise reserved for few, if any, others. "He impressed me as a figure of world calibre," Yakovlev says of Trudeau. "An extremely well-educated man." Elsewhere, Yakovlev calls him, "the shrewd intellectual, the dreaded debater, who ascended the Canadian firmament like a bright star." And of Trudeau's September 2000 death, Yakovlev writes, "The death of Pierre Trudeau was not only the death of a great Canadian citizen, but also an irreplaceable loss for mankind."

Did Trudeau provide Yakovlev with a role model, similar to the way Laski provided Trudeau with an ideological mentor, years earlier? Yakovlev proved reticent throughout his life to discuss the extent the West influenced his political thinking. But Trudeau's belief in a state that protected human rights while redistributing wealth is intriguingly similar to Yakovlev's ideal at the end of his Canadian posting.

Yakovlev's behaviour while in Ottawa indicates he valued the opinion of Trudeau, and several of his closest colleagues, like Ivan Head. When Soviet dignitaries visited Ottawa, Yakovlev often hosted receptions at his residence. If the Soviet visitor was sufficiently liberal – someone like the expert on North American affairs, Georgi Arbatov, for example – then Yakovlev would invite a select few Canadians to stay behind, after dinner, for an intellectual salon that hopscotched along the flashpoints of the Cold

War, from the Middle East to Southeast Asia to Central and South America. Trudeau attended such salons, as did Head and other members of Trudeau's brain trust, such as Deputy Undersecretary of State for External Affairs Klaus Goldschlag. One Canadian who witnessed these salons believed Yakovlev was intentionally exposing the Soviet visitors to opinions that contrasted with the dogmatic thinking of the Communist Party. He was showing key Soviet ideologues how the Cold War was viewed by intelligent, informed and, most important, comparatively impartial interlocutors.

There is some evidence Yakovlev was less reticent about Trudeau's influence on him in private conversation. "Yakovlev told me that Trudeau had the same influence on him that Yakovlev would later have on Gorbachev – Trudeau showed him everything is possible," says Igor Zakharov, the Russian-language publisher of the pulp fiction of Boris Akunin (the pseudonym of Grigoriy Shalvovich Chkhartishvili) so wildly popular in post-Soviet Russia. Zakharov became an acquaintance of Yakovlev after he worked under the ambassador at the Ottawa embassy beginning in 1974. Zakharov's recollection of the conversation sounds like an oversimplification. The post-perestroika Yakovlev was reluctant to describe his influence on Gorbachev, and certainly not so bluntly as Zakharov quotes him. Still, it's an intriguing idea – that Canadian Prime Minister Pierre Trudeau forms a link in the causal chain toward perestroika.

EVEN WITHOUT THEIR CLOSE RELATIONSHIP, Trudeau might have presented Yakovlev with an education in democracy. Almost exactly a year after he began his posting, Yakovlev witnessed his first Canadian federal election. It was brought on by events in the Middle East. Seven years before, U.S.-backed Israel devastated the air forces of the Soviet-backed Arabs in the 1967 Six Day War. In 1973, Egypt, Syria, and other Arab nations struck back, destroying a significant portion of Israel's air attack capability on Yom Kippur. Many Arab countries also united in an oil embargo against the West in retaliation for the West's support of Israel.

The price of oil spiked, and with the spike came inflation. Between March 1973 and 1974, prices increased 10 percent in Canada. Workers across the world struck for wage increases to cope with higher expenses. Gas shortages caused long lines at service stations. And governments in the West teetered as voters blamed them for their troubles. In Canada, the Trudeau minority government's end happened in May 1974 after both the socialist NDP and the comparatively right-wing Progressive Conservative Party voted against a federal budget because it failed to include inflation protection.

The irony, noted by the *New York Times*, was that "things are going rather well for the average Canadian." Yes, people were dissatisfied by higher prices. But soaring commodities translated into more money and jobs in Canada's oil- and resource-laden economy. Compared to a U.S. mired in Watergate at home and Vietnam abroad, Canada seemed a comparatively stable and well-run nation. This new pride in country represented an opportunity for a re-energized Trudeau, who maintained a significant lead in approval ratings (46 percent compared to just 22 percent for his Progressive Conservative rival, Robert L. Stanfield). Trudeau's chartered DC-9 zoomed around Canada like a downtown taxi. He campaigned on Newfoundland streets, visited Prince Edward Island gymnasia, and sang along with Ontario senior citizens to the tune of "She'll Be Coming 'Round the Mountain." Then it was off to Vancouver.

Among the biggest factors helping Trudeau was the presence of Margaret, his 25-year-old wife, who injected the campaign with a *joie de vivre*. For reporters she donned a bikini and splashed around with Trudeau in a hotel pool. Microphone in hand, beautiful and stylishly dressed, she humanized the PM by declaring that her husband wasn't at all arrogant. "I can speak of him as a very loving human being who has taught me a lot about loving," she told one crowd. "Not just loving each other, which is pretty nice, but love for humanity and a love for each human being, a tolerance toward the individual."

"Campaigns are fun again," Trudeau declared.

The 1974 campaign was one of the more remarkable and exciting in Canadian history. It was about picking a leader, and establishing a mandate. But Trudeau turned it into more than that. Trudeau turned it into an election about the idea of Canada, a contest to define what Canada meant to its various peoples, and to the country at large. He ran on a platform of economic and cultural protection against the United States. In response to separatist talk in Quebec and alienation in the western provinces, Trudeau hammered during speech after speech that Canada's diversity was its strength, that a tolerance for other cultures was part of the Canadian way.

Yakovlev was fascinated. He attended political conventions; he listened as Trudeau's speeches whipped crowds into a frenzy. He witnessed the way political parties crafted their platforms to appeal to the greatest fraction of the electorate, and watched as competition in debates and before voters helped mould new policies. He saw, too, how Canada's two national television networks covered it all. In other words, he witnessed modern democracy in progress.

As election day approached, pollsters predicted another minority government. Given Yakovlev's later influence on perestroika, it's intriguing to wonder what might have happened had events turned out other than they did. Western democracies have had their share of voting controversies. The election of George W. Bush in 2000 is one notable example. In Canada, Quebec Premier Maurice Duplessis was frequently accused of electoral fraud. What if the 1974 Canadian contest had been sullied by accusations of fraud or other misadventures? Would Yakovlev have developed his influential enthusiasm for democracy had his first election experience been anything but a model exercise in electoral politics?

Canadians voted on July 8, 1974, and once the votes were counted, Trudeau won. But he didn't just win. With Britain, France, and Italy afflicted with weak leaders governing ineffectually, and the United States exactly one month away from the resignation of Richard Nixon, Trudeau's majority win was an impressive demonstration of democracy. The victory meant that Canada, alone among Western countries, had a strong statesman at its tiller. Where the House of Commons had been, before the election, riven by regional political blocs that polarized the nation, the 1974 election supplied the winning Liberals with support distributed across much of the country, providing Trudeau with the support of 141 of the House of Common's 264 seats, eight more seats than he required for a majority.

It is surely significant that Yakovlev's first impression of electoral politics in a free and democratic society was a vote that improved the stability of its nation. The results resounded even outside Canada's borders. "In a dramatic comeback, Pierre Elliott Trudeau's Liberal party has confounded the forecasters to win a robust majority in the House of Commons; and Canada has given the world an impressive demonstration of the health and vibrancy of its democratic institutions and practices," ran a *New York Times* editorial. Providing international context, the editorial noted, "At a time when democratic institutions are in retreat or under heavy pressures almost everywhere and when weak, minority governments are the rule rather than the exception throughout the Western world, the significance of the decisive outcome in Canada's general election can hardly be exaggerated." It was impossible for the *Times* to know how prescient those words would prove.

17

A TIME OF REST AND MANY THOUGHTS

O TTAWA WASN'T JUST prime ministers and political philosophy. Months passed, and the ambassador started getting the hang of diplomatic life. His English improved. His much-discussed friendship with Trudeau assisted his dealings with Canadian government mandarins. He grew accustomed to attending the diplomatic community's endless receptions – the embassy of Wherever having Whatever official soirée to honour Somebody or Something – an independence day, the birthday of a patron saint. He would go in, shake a few hands, crack a few jokes, then escape. Between the consul in Montreal and the various press attachés and trade officials in Ottawa, the Soviet diplomatic community amounted to maybe 100 families. Various brouhahas and diplomatic flaps occupied the ambassador's energy for a news cycle or two, such as ballet dancer Mikhail Baryshnikov's June 1974 defection in Toronto. But all those minister-counsellors and chargés d'affaires pretty much ran themselves, especially considering that more than half of them also were getting some instruction from the Lubyanka, the KGB headquarters, or from some other Soviet intelligence service. The truth was, once he figured out the mechanics and rivalries of the Canadian government, once he figured out whom to call for which problem, the ambassador's job wasn't all that demanding.

For the first time in his professional life, Yakovlev had time on his hands. His previous career had made him an absent father. When Nataliya and Anatoly were young he'd been working in the Central Committee, and often he left the apartment before they rose and didn't come home until after they were in bed. It went like that six or seven days a week when one was a high-ranking official in the Communist Party, and there were also trips to the various far-flung republics and that year on exchange at Columbia. By the time he was exiled to Ottawa, Yakovlev had realized he'd missed his kids' childhood.

He treated his exile as thought it was an opportunity to redeem himself. The once-absent father now doted on his granddaughter. They were an incongruous sight, the 51-year-old Soviet ambassador and the five-year-old schoolgirl, the limping war hero and his three-foot-tall companion. Neighbours could spy them sometimes in Yakovlev's yard, making snowmen or impromptu igloos on weekend afternoons. Other times they played among the banks the snowplows made, laughing and digging and pushing, constructing elaborate crystalline mazes on the lawn. In warm weather, especially on the weekends, the two Russians would be out among the rose bushes that lined their driveway, clipping and pruning and every so often tying an errant bloom so the branch didn't break under the weight of its petals. Big hand clasped in little hand, they wandered the park across the street. They had a route they'd follow – from Lisgar Road across Buena Vista and Rockcliffe Parkway, and then a slow stroll along the verdant lawns until they reached a certain point, a specific tree, a rock, a crook in the path, and then they'd turn and saunter back. They invented fairy tales along their wanderings. The best of them they recited into Yakovlev's office dictation equipment, and every so often when Yakovlev fumbled for a tape to record some matter of business, Natasha's voice would come out of his cassette player.

The Yakovlevs began building lives in their new home. They cultivated friendships with other diplomats. They organized various clubs to
entertain their sometimes homesick contingent of Soviet diplomats –
cooking groups that created Russian cuisine, impromptu musical groups
to play traditional songs. Once a week they showed Soviet movies. They
conducted ice-fishing trips in the Gatineau Hills, and mushroom-
hunting exhibitions to Fitzroy Park. Yakovlev had a sauna installed in
his residence, and he whiled away his time sitting on the humid boards,
drinking green tea, reading North American newspapers, and sometimes
dictating notes for a book he was thinking of writing about Canada. In
fact, he was so serious about the project that he undertook considerable
effort to get approval from the Department of External Affairs to bring
another Soviet citizen to the embassy, to act as a research assistant.
Unfortunately, Yakovlev never did complete the project.

Regardless, Canada became an object of study. He read up on
Canadian history, learning about such concepts as federalism and mul-
ticulturalism. Courts and the mechanism of an independent judiciary
became objects of fascination. The petty thieves, prostitutes, and drug
peddlers who populated certain benches in certain Ottawa courtrooms
might have been surprised to learn that the seat neighbour listening so
intently to the proceedings was the ambassador of the Soviet Union. And
whenever he had time he visited Canadian farms all over the country.
One of the USSR's perpetual problems was agricultural productivity:
despite the country's vast size, and the wealth and breadth of its natural
resources, the country still couldn't manage to feed itself. In the mid-
1970s, that wasn't such a problem for a country that sat atop vast oil
reserves. Flush with cash from exporting its energy resources, the Soviet
Union simply bought wheat and other agricultural commodities from
countries that were willing to export their supplies, such as Canada. To
Yakovlev, such purchases were a national embarrassment, an admission
that, despite the Soviet Union's vast fields of black earth, considerable
farming history, and sizable labour force, it still couldn't provide for itself.
Canadian crop production was far more efficient than the Soviets',

Yakovlev knew. And yet the two countries had similar soil conditions, with similarly short growing seasons. So Yakovlev set himself the task of finding out how Canada managed to create harvests so much more efficiently than the Soviet Union.

Yakovlev infiltrated the clucking caverns of Ontario chicken farms. He admired the Rocky Mountain vistas in Alberta cattle ranches and the endless golden plains of Saskatchewan wheat. Some trips were made under the auspices of trade missions. Others were billed as research for Yakovlev's book. At each one Yakovlev asked copious questions. How many head of cattle resided at the farm? How many labourers were required to tend them? He saw differences in insemination techniques that allowed Canadian cattle to produce healthier offspring. He saw differences in feeding techniques that allowed Alberta steers to gain weight faster than their Crimean counterparts. And these differences Yakovlev dutifully noted and transcribed in long memoranda he sent home to Moscow. He hoped they'd help the Party improve Soviet practices; in fact, he would discover, most of his memos were ignored.

But the key difference, Yakovlev noted, was the motivation of the Canadian workers. When foreign officials visited a Soviet collective farm, Yakovlev knew that the collective farm manager used the occasion to take the day off, to stage a tour along with an elaborate reception that involved lots of vodka toasts. Here in Canada, foreign officials received a different reception. When Yakovlev showed up outside a silo or corral, the farmer came over, gave him a handshake and spent a minute or two talking crop rotation or feeding techniques. Then the farmer invited Yakovlev to look around, and disappeared. Back to work. Farmers in Canada, Yakovlev realized, worked a hell of a lot harder than their Soviet counterparts. The difference, Yakovlev knew, was that the Canadian farmers owned their farms, their land, and the profits they generated. In contrast, the Soviet collective farm managers ran their operations for the state. They were paid a certain amount a month, regardless of whether they logged 10 productive hours a week, or 80.

Troubled, Yakovlev thought back to his childhood, to the days before the state took control of all farming, and how his parents farmed their little plot of land "from the morning till the dark." How his family had had enough to eat and how similar families today did not. "It was a time of both rest and many thoughts," Yakovlev would write.

THE JOB HAD ITS INCONVENIENCES. Protesters were constantly parading placards and shouting slogans outside the Soviet Embassy. Usually they were Ukrainians, or people upset about one Ukrainian in particular, the writer Valentyn Moroz, who was in prison for speaking out against the Soviet regime; in particular, he called for Ukraine to secede from the USSR. He'd been in jail for four years by the summer of 1974 when he began a hunger strike to protest against prison conditions that included attempted rapes and beatings by cellmates. Not wanting to create a martyr, Soviet authorities forced tubes down Moroz's throat to feed him. Rumours about Moroz's condition made their way to North America. Suddenly Yakovlev was seeing people outside the embassy every day, chanting in support of Moroz and every so often breaking a window with a thrown bottle or rock. There was no real danger, thanks to the high iron fence that surrounded the building. But it wasn't pleasant, having the demonstrators out there. Yakovlev complained to the Canadian government, and sometimes to the press, that the police weren't doing enough to protect the embassy. A few protesters were there all day and night, conducting their own hunger strikes in solidarity with the dissident writer. Once, when they learned the Soviet embassy was hosting a party, the protesters chained and locked shut the fence gates just as guests were starting to arrive. The guests had to wait for the fire department to cut through the chains before they could enter.

There were other irritants. The biggest embarrassment in those early years happened in November 1974, two months after Yakovlev attended the hockey game in Quebec City with Trudeau. The context was the slowly increasing hype for the 1976 Summer Olympic Games, in Montreal. By coincidence, the following summer games were to be held in Moscow. The head of the Soviet National Olympic Committee was an old acquaintance of Yakovlev's, a 37-year-old former decathlete named Alexander Gresko, with whom Yakovlev had worked on the first Summit Series between Canada and the Soviet Union. Gresko was always jetting back and forth between Moscow and Montreal to study the Canadian preparations. During one trip to Ottawa he visited with the prime minister, and the two men posed for a picture. Then, weeks later, a report on the front page of Canada's national newspaper, the *Globe and Mail*, disclosed the news that Gresko had been kicked out of London as an alleged spy only three years earlier. The paper ran the picture of Trudeau smiling alongside Gresko. Since Trudeau was already being criticized as too soft on the Soviets, the news that he'd shaken the hand and accepted a gift from a onetime KGB agent didn't help his political fortunes. Things grew worse when it became apparent that Gresko was let in to Canada against the recommendations of the RCMP; the implication seemed to be that Trudeau, or someone in External, had waived law enforcement concerns about the onetime spy. Yakovlev was appalled that any Soviet visitor might embarrass his powerful friend. He wrote a letter apologizing to Trudeau, and must have been relieved when Trudeau responded with a message telling him to think nothing of it.

There was friction with the bureaucrats in Moscow as well. Around the same time as the Gresko affair, Yakovlev was called back to Moscow for what amounted to a performance review. Relations with his employees had improved by this point, and the embassy was running smoothly. But the foreign affairs minister himself, Andrei Gromyko, showed up to the session. This was unusual; the attendance of such a senior official typically foretold some sort of conflict. And when things began, the bureaucrats began criticizing Yakovlev. They had ammunition: in addition to the Gresko affair, his embassy featured other irregularities. He arranged for his employees' children to attend local Canadian schools rather than segregating them in small classes behind embassy walls, as was more typical. And Yakovlev apparently wasn't displaying the requisite energy in distributing copies of Brezhnev's speeches to the Canadian media. For the bureaucrats in the Soviet ministry, Canada was considered a plum assignment. The bureaucrats were trying to push Yakovlev out of Ottawa so that one of their own could take the coveted spot.

But then Gromyko took the floor. Yakovlev liked Gromyko. When the foreign minister was in New York on United Nations business, he'd invite the Yakovlevs to private dinners. Yakovlev prepared for these encounters the way he did meetings with Trudeau; he read up on topics that interested Gromyko, so he'd have conversation ready in advance. Gromyko, too, is certain to have kept tabs on the perception of Yakovlev in Canada, likely inquiring about the ambassador during Gromyko's meetings with Secretary of State Mitchell Sharp and his successor, Allan MacEachen. "Tell me," Gromyko asked his fellow bureaucrats in the Ministry of Foreign Affairs, as he spoke in Yakovlev's support. "Where else do we have an ambassador on whom the country's prime minister, with his children, drops in at home without warning and says, 'Let's sit down and have a chat'?"

In Ottawa, Yakovlev's relationship with Trudeau was encouraging the ambassador to develop beliefs that would one day threaten the Party's control of the Soviet Union. Meanwhile, in Moscow, that same relationship was saving Yakovlev's job.

WAR MINUS THE SHOOTING

I N 1976, Montreal hosted the XXI Summer Games. The occasion would prove to be the last time for more than a decade that the Olympics would include athletes from both sides of the Cold War. The Games also forced Yakovlev to confront some disturbing realities about his relationship with the Communist Party.

The Montreal Games were of particular significance to the Soviet officials, since the next Summer Olympiad, in 1980, would be held in Moscow. The Soviets sent along an unusually large delegation – without Gresko, notably – aiming to study every aspect of the event's operation, from food services to athlete security. The swollen communist retinue placed Yakovlev in the role of a teacher whose principal decides to sit in on a class. In contrast to the supposed Olympic spirit, the Games were becoming one more political battleground. Both sides saw the Games as just another field of battle for the Cold War. The athletes were soldiers, their medal wins, combat victories. Medals were particularly important to the Soviets because, by 1976, sport was one of the few avenues the nation had left to demonstrate the superiority of communist USSR to capitalist America. Washington had won the space race. The propaganda about an impending socialist paradise to rival the richest areas of the United States had long since grown stale for many Soviet citizens. But in athletics, the superior sports budgets of the Warsaw Pact countries reaped the communists motherlodes of gold, silver and bronze. Both the Soviet Union and East Germany would win more gold medals than the U.S. in 1976.

So athletic supremacy was taken care of. As ambassador to the Olympics' host nation, it fell to Yakovlev to ensure the Soviets avoided embarrassment on the political front. It was an impossible job made worse by the fact that so many Soviets were so ready to be embarrassed. One major problem was defections – bids by communist athletes to remain in the West. In an era when any defection was a defeat, an indication life was better outside the Soviet Union than in, dozens of athletes had defected at the previous summer games in Munich. Defections were also expected in Montreal. Meanwhile, Ukrainian and Jewish protesters were preparing to draw attention to the plight of their countrymen kept behind the Iron Curtain – the refuseniks denied permission to emigrate, the nationalists in Ukrainian jails.

People labelled "provocateurs" by the Soviets distributed flyers written in Russian providing instructions to Eastern Bloc athletes on how to defect. Advertisements appeared in Canadian newspapers accusing the KGB of abusing the rights of Ukrainian dissidents. Events unrelated to Yakovlev elevated tensions. In a bid to engender relations with Communist China, the Trudeau government denied visas to the Taiwanese athletes unless they changed the name they planned to compete under, the Republic of China. Taiwan declined, and despite extraordinary pressure from the United States, Trudeau held his ground. Taiwan was out. Then, in a bid to convince New Zealand to sever sporting relations with apartheid South Africa, 28 African countries plus Guyana and Iraq boycotted the Games. Plus, these were the first summer games since the events of Black September, the bloodbath that ensued when Palestinian gunmen snuck into the Munich Olympic Village and took hostage and eventually killed 11 Israeli athletes.

Amid such international anxieties, the Olympic Village in Montreal seemed like a war zone. Reports had the security of the Games mobilizing Canada's largest military operation since the Second World War. Police and soldiers rivalled athletes in numbers – 16,000 drawn from almost every uniformed corps Canada had available, patrolling the Olympic Village, the public transportation, the airport, hotels, stadiums, swimming pools, equestrian facilities. The whole province of Quebec was under surveillance, it seemed.

As soon as the Games began the troubles started for Yakovlev. At first it was little things. At the many parties corporate sponsors held around Montreal, Yakovlev's countrymen engaged in what the ambassador considered shameful drunken misbehaviour. Worse, Ukrainian nationalist groups seemed to be in every velodrome and stadium with their protest-slogan T-shirts and their blue-and-yellow flags. They cheered whenever they spied an athlete they considered their own, such as the Ukrainian sprinter Valery Borzov, rumoured to be a prime candidate for defection from the USSR athletic team. And then there was the bonfire some demonstrators created with a Soviet hammer-and-sickle flag. Yakovlev's associates dreamed up all sorts of indignant responses. "However hard I tried to calm down the bureaucrats, it was useless – they called for official protests," Yakovlev wrote in his memoirs. Two KGB generals in Montreal to observe the Games wrote "panic-filled" telegrams to Moscow describing "an anti-Soviet orgy." Most damaging to Yakovlev, according to his memoirs, was their description of the ambassador's response. The embassy, the generals wrote, "remained unbothered." In a way, they were right. Despite his past as a propagandist, the Soviet ambassador couldn't muster up the energy to create the sort of response the Party expected. Pamphlets and press releases alleging conspiracies of Western imperialism, indignant tirades of sarcasm and invective over Uncle Sam's provocations – all that just seemed silly to Yakovlev now.

FOR YAKOVLEV, the Olympics climaxed two days before the closing ceremonies, with an incident involving an athlete named Sergei Nemtsanov, a platform diver from the Kazakhstan city of Alma-Alta. During previous diving competitions around the world, including several meets in North America, Nemtsanov became legendary for his "rip entries," a nearly splashless technique for completing the dive that required the athlete to expand his water displacement as he descended, causing a noise like tearing fabric – hence the name. Many observers pegged Nemtsanov for a gold medal. Despite his young age – he was only 17 – Nemtsanov's coaches placed an extraordinary amount of pressure on him. But Nemtsanov placed only ninth in the preliminaries, and ninth meant he wouldn't go on to the finals, a privilege accorded only to the top eight. His Olympics were over.

The tendency among athletes in such a situation is to cut loose. With months of disciplined Olympic preparation behind them, they crave a little fun, a little leisure. Such partying went against the regulations the provocation-wary Soviets imposed on their athletes. Enticed by the prospect of spending time with a 16-year-old female diver he liked, an American, Nemtsanov snuck out of the village anyway for a night on the town. His coaches caught him. Facing certain punishment on top of his disappointing performance, with mere hours to go before his plane was to depart, Nemtsanov consulted with other, non-Soviet divers, including the 28-year-old Canadian, Skip Phoenix. Minutes later, he decided to defect – a simple matter, as a temporary office of the Royal Canadian Mounted Police was quartered in the building where Nemtsanov was staying.

When they discovered Nemtsanov had missed his flight, the Soviet contingent exploded. This was on a Thursday evening, July 29. The Olympics were due to conclude that Sunday, and thus far the Soviets had avoided an onslaught of defections; aside from Nemtsanov, a few Romanians crossed over, but no one else from the USSR. Yakovlev was now in an awkward position. To his conspiracy-minded comrades, it was clear Nemtsanov's action was a plot to embarrass the glorious Motherland. "Unbelievable hysterics ensued," Yakovlev wrote in his memoirs. "The pressure on the embassy was colossal." The Soviets didn't just want Nemtsanov back; they wanted to retaliate, to embarrass the Canadians they saw as responsible for the defection. That evening, hours after Nemtsanov's disappearance, Yakovlev's hard-line second-in-command, Nikolay Makarov, placed a call to the home of a counterpart at External, the Canadian diplomat Alec Chistoff. In contrast to Yakovlev's liberal style, Makarov was an orthodox communist bureaucrat and a proverbial pain in Yakovlev's neck thanks to his propensity to send back to Moscow reports of the ambassador's slightest missteps. During the conversation with the Canadian diplomat, Makarov used words like "kidnapping" and "child-snatching" and threatened to report the Canadians' lack of cooperation if they didn't immediately return the boy. Later that evening, Yakovlev tried to decrease tensions with a more diplomatically worded memo. "Bearing in mind that S. Nemtsanov is a minor," his note said, the embassy requested "a prompt return of S. Nemtsanov to the Soviet Olympic team."

Yakovlev at this point wasn't certain what was going on. He'd heard that an Olympic official, at an emergency IOC session, had said that the diver was in "safe hands" and "under the protection of the Canadian government." Before he troubled the prime minister, Yakovlev attempted to go through the usual channels. The day after the defection, Yakovlev, Makarov, and another Soviet diplomat, Gennady Zolotov, went to External Affairs demanding a meeting with Allan MacEachen, the secretary of state. Instead, they were shown to André Bissonnette, an assistant undersecretary, to whom Yakovlev dutifully read a series of harshly worded memos provided by the Soviet Foreign Ministry. The Soviets, Yakovlev read, had "info at our disposal concerning the participation in this act of American special services" with the "connivance of Canadian authorities . . . The Embassy cannot but regard this fact as kidnapping of S. Nemtsanov." They threatened to sever sporting relations with Canada unless Nemtsanov was returned, "since our sportsmen are not ensured the proper safety . . ." At stake was Soviet participation in the Canada Cup international hockey tournament, due to be held in mid-September.

The assistant undersecretary pointed out that Nemtsanov's visa allowed him to stay in the country until August 31, 1976. Since he was legally in Canada, Bissonnette said, the young man was free to do what he wished. Then Bissonnette dropped the bombshell: as difficult as it might be for the Soviets to believe, the Canadian government didn't know Nemtsanov's location. And this was true. Once Nemtsanov signed the relevant paperwork – notably, an intent to apply for refugee status – the Mounties let him go, and Nemtsanov left with the Canadian diver, Skip Phoenix, in Phoenix's conversion van. Unbeknownst to any Canadian official, by Friday afternoon the pair were hunkered down in a home belonging to a friend of the Canadian diving coach, Don Webb, in Pointe Claire, Quebec, just west of Montreal. They didn't tell Yakovlev, but External Affairs could get messages to Nemtsanov by relaying them through Webb – and that was the extent of their contact with the young diver.

By now, Yakovlev was becoming convinced that this *was* a kidnapping. The ambassador implied that some American agency was responsible. The FBI, perhaps, or the CIA. In fact, Yakovlev said, some Soviet officials doubted whether the boy was still alive. Yakovlev insisted Nemtsanov be returned immediately. He wanted a medical examination conducted. And in a reference to what he thought was American involvement, Yakovlev wanted the third parties in this "dirty affair" to be punished.

As the Soviets were getting up to leave, Yakovlev mentioned appeals the Soviets were planning to make to the prime minister. Grasping at whatever might convince the Canadian officials, Yakovlev stooped to threats. He said he knew a Soviet sailor who had recently spent 10 days in a Canadian immigration centre. The sailor had some stories to tell about the treatment he'd received there. "Perhaps," the ambassador said, "that should be made public."

Yakovlev should be forgiven for this threat. He was under intense pressure from the party officials around him. Accustomed as they were to the extraordinary reach of their all-knowing secret police, the Soviet visitors couldn't imagine that the Canadians might simply let the boy go, on his own recognizance. Meanwhile, KGB agents were scouring Montreal and its suburbs, and rumour after startling rumour was coming out of the Olympic Village. The Soviets heard that the first target of the kidnappers was their star sprinter, Valery Borzov, who had received telephone death threats hours before his bronze performance in the 100-metre dash. According to another, Nemtsanov would be transported shortly to the United States. Still another rumour said he was under the influence of behaviour-modifying drugs. Meanwhile, Yakovlev's comrades were wondering why, if the Soviet ambassador had such great relations with these Canadians – if, as Gromyko had said, he was friends with the nation's prime minister – he wasn't able to convince this Trudeau to return the boy.

With his job hanging in the balance, Yakovlev did pen an appeal to the prime minister. "Only extraordinary circumstances force me to address a personal letter to you," he wrote on the Friday night after the Bissonnette meeting. "These circumstances are connected with a strange disappearance from the Olympic village of a 17-year-old Soviet school-boy Sergei Nemtsanov . . . In this case I would like to take advantage of your invitation to address you in difficult cases and seek your personal attention to this affair . . . " In the letter, Yakovlev also enclosed two telegrams, containing heartfelt pleas from Nemtsanov's grandmother and mother begging the return of the athlete to his Alma-Alta home. "I am turning 80, Sergei is my only grandson whom I have brought up and I simply do not imagine how I can live without him," the grand-mother wrote. "I have heard about you, Mr. Prime Minister, as of a highly humane and just man and sincerely hope that you will not reject my most humble request."

Later that Friday evening, at 9 p.m., Yakovlev again visited the Department of External Affairs to meet with the assistant under-secretary. Reluctant to blame Canada, and always eager to believe the worst of America, Yakovlev expressed his belief the Nemtsanov affair was the work of U.S. secret services by spinning the boy's disappearance as "not only an action against the USSR, but against Canada as well." The implication was that the U.S. was trying to damage Canada–Soviet rela-tions. All the same, Bissonnette had some good news. Apparently Yakovlev's letter to Trudeau had done its job. Bissonnette informed the ambassador that Canadian authorities were attempting to find Nemtsanov to set up a meeting between the young diver and Soviet officials. "We're doing our best to find the boy," Bissonnette said. "But we do have to work within our legal system."

The next day Trudeau called Yakovlev to discuss the matter. The prime minister explained that Nemtsanov had the legal right to request to stay in Canada if he pleased. Still, Trudeau said, the Canadians would pass on the Soviet request for a meeting, and the prime minister would, as Yakovlev later recalled, do everything possible to see that the boy returned to his home. Trudeau also had a couple of requests. According to Yakovlev's memoirs, he asked the ambassador to stop the KGB from snooping for Nemtsanov. He wanted the Soviets to ratchet down their rhetoric – all the talk about kidnapping and drugs would make it diffi-cult for the Canadian government to help arrange Nemtsanov's return. Also, Trudeau said, once the diver returned to Kazakhstan, "the Canadian public needs to know that Nemtsanov has not been put in prison."

"As I mentioned to you in our telephone conversation today every-thing has been done to locate the young athlete as you have requested," Trudeau wrote in a follow-up letter later that day. "I am sure you will understand, however, that such a meeting cannot take place as a result of coercion and that it is essential that no cause be given to anyone to believe that such has been the case." Trudeau included in the letter a vague handwritten postscript reminding Yakovlev to temper the Soviets' rhetoric: "In difficult situations, it is important not to upset the balance which is required between good friends."

So it was that early Sunday afternoon, three Soviets – Nemtsanov's coach, a fellow diver, and one of Yakovlev's consular officials – assembled at a Montreal RCMP station. By this point, a Canadian legal firm had volunteered to represent Nemtsanov, who went into the meeting along with two of the lawyers. The meeting lasted 40 minutes. Nemtsanov's teammate assured him that no harm would be done to him if he returned. But Nemtsanov stayed firm. He wanted to stay in Canada.

And that was it. So far as Yakovlev was concerned, Nemtsanov dis-appeared again. In a stunt certain to have embarrassed Yakovlev, the Soviets conducted a press conference where they spoke of signs

Nemtsanov had been "psychologically brainwashed by highly trained specialists." Meanwhile, a KGB-wary Skip Phoenix smuggled Nemtsanov to Ontario, to a Muskoka cottage where Nemtsanov stayed with relatives of another Canadian Olympic diver, Scott Cranham. Many expected him to snag a lucrative athletic scholarship to a wealthy American school. The rest of the Soviet Olympic team returned home, and Yakovlev embarked on a campaign of damage control. During an August 6 meeting with Secretary of State Allan MacEachen, the ambassador described his behind-the-scenes efforts to keep the situation cool. "The sooner the Nemtsanov affair is forgotten," Yakovlev said, "the better."

It was not to be. Two weeks later, without warning, Nemtsanov turned up at a Canadian immigration office in Montreal and asked officials there to arrange a meeting with Soviet consular staff. The meeting actually happened in Ottawa, in a Holiday Inn coffee shop, the next afternoon. Nemtsanov told members of Yakovlev's staff that he'd changed his mind. Unable to connect with the American diver (her father, a Cincinnati grocery magnate, had spirited her out of Canada as soon as the Nemtsanov hubbub started), a bored Nemtsanov decided he missed his friends and grandmother, and wanted to return home. He boarded an Aeroflot flight the next day. "All's well that ends well," a Soviet consular staffer remarked to a Canadian immigration official.

Once behind the Iron Curtain, Nemtsanov gave an interview to a Soviet newspaper that described how he was "forced into" defecting. Canadians injected him with drugs, he said, to "blunt and paralyze the brain." When Ivan Head heard about the interview he dashed off a memo to the prime minister suggesting they write to the Soviets to ask whether "this kind of activity is consistent with warm Canadian–Soviet relations." Trudeau's reply is scrawled on an archived copy of the memo. "Certainly not," the prime minister wrote. "Just tell the Soviet ambassador that we would understand if he was embarrassed by such B.S.!"

The Soviet ambassador was, indeed, embarrassed. The Nemtsanov affair, and the whole Olympic experience, would have long-standing effects on Yakovlev – he refers to the "special impression" left by the Games. The Olympics coincided with the third anniversary of his arrival in Canada. They afforded him with the opportunity to observe large numbers of Soviet officials in the West and, by extension, through Western eyes. His recounting of this period in his memoirs belies a frustration with Soviet histrionics and grandstanding, and a consciousness of the counter-productive nature of his comrades' obsession with Western conspiracy. Back home Brezhnev was showing signs of senility. Meanwhile, the Party was building a personality cult around Brezhnev to rival Stalin's. Independent thought and creativity were dying off, to be replaced with monotonous groupthink that only perpetuated the same old Soviet problems. Throughout this Nemtsanov affair Yakovlev had an opportunity to recognize the intellectual ossification plaguing his colleagues from home. Had he stayed in Moscow, had he never been exiled, Yakovlev too might have experienced this decreasing capacity for creative thought. "Only then," Yakovlev said, "I understood I was extremely lucky." Evidently, Yakovlev was recognizing the benefits of this banishment.

YAKOVLEV'S OLYMPIC EXPERIENCE has a footnote. Soon after the closing ceremonies, Yakovlev received a visit from George Cohon, the whip-thin, toothy-grinned president and chief executive officer of McDonald's Restaurants of Canada Limited. Cohon was a lawyer from Chicago who bought the franchise rights for eastern Canada in 1967 for $70,000. Less than a decade later he was a Canadian citizen, the chairman of McDonald's Canada, and one of the worldwide company's largest shareholders. In Yakovlev's office, Cohon described how one day at the Montreal Olympics he had approached a busload of Soviet bureaucrats, the organizing committee of the 1980 Summer Games, and convinced them to allow him to buy them lunch at the nearest McDonald's.

He did this, Cohon explained to Yakovlev, as a bit of a lark. It was a manifestation of the Olympic spirit, introducing all these Soviet visitors to the wonders of Big Macs and chocolate shakes. But he also had another reason for his invitation. Cohon wanted McDonald's at the next Summer Games in Moscow, serving large fries and apple pies to the international crowds. Then, once the Games were over, Cohon wanted to keep the restaurants open. In short, Cohon wanted to open the Soviet Union's first fast-food restaurant chain.

As he received Cohon's pitch, Yakovlev stayed impassive. Anyone who was familiar with the stagnation of Brezhnev's USSR would have realized this man's dream was insane. A central tenet of Bolshevik communism had the state owning everything. Soviet law didn't permit the operation of a privately owned business like a McDonald's franchise, at the Moscow Olympics or anywhere else. Privately owned business meant capitalism, and capitalism was the enemy.

And by the late 1970s, McDonald's was becoming the epitome of capitalism. The fast-food restaurant was spreading across the globe like some sort of large-scale kudzu vine. Cohon recited several paragraphs' worth of statistics that indicated the company's momentum. By the end of the decade the hamburger chain would be in 27 countries, operating 4,500 restaurants around the world – 300 of them in Canada. McDonald's work crews were serving 1.9 billion meals annually. In the United States, the company had just sold its 30 billionth hamburger. Meanwhile, few Soviet citizens even knew what a hamburger was.

One might imagine a born salesman like Cohon going into a pitch session with the Soviet ambassador and soft-pedalling his approach – describing his long-standing love for Lenin and Marx, say, while also complimenting the literary facility of Brezhnev and the adroit policy mind of Suslov. Cohon did nothing of the sort. In fact, Cohon did the exact opposite to Yakovlev: he proclaimed his faith in the capitalist system. "I believe in free enterprise and pay-based performance," Cohon said. "Competition and profit are not dirty words."

Cohon thought such provocative statements would capture Yakovlev's attention. Little did he know that Yakovlev didn't need his attention captured. Cohon's idea fascinated the ambassador. As Cohon got into the mechanics of the idea, he explained his fries and hamburgers would have to live up to certain quality standards in Moscow, just as they did in Ottawa. Bearing that in mind, Cohon explained he didn't intend to lob foreign-grown potatoes and beef over the Iron Curtain. Instead, he planned to use Soviet-grown produce. To ensure that the agriculture could meet McDonald's standards, Cohon would train Soviet farmers to plant and grow disease-free potatoes with the proper size and starch content. He would build processing plants that could slice the russet orbs into golden rectangular lengths, then freeze them; then he would develop the shipping operation that could transport the cartons to the proper location, where Cohon's people would train fry-cooks and other employees. In other words, Cohon's training would transport Western agricultural techniques and supply chains to Moscow.

Instead of throwing Cohon out of his office, as many other Soviet ambassadors might have done, Yakovlev listened. Perhaps he thought of the telegrams he'd been sending to Moscow for the past several years, with their descriptions of Canadian agricultural techniques. Cohon's dream of a Moscow McDonald's, if successful, stood to achieve a goal similar to what Yakovlev was attempting with his telegrams. If Cohon could serve Big Macs in the USSR, then perhaps party officials would see Cohon's success, and become more receptive to other innovations – innovations that might allow Soviet agriculture and industry to catch up to the West.

At this meeting, Yakovlev never came out and said to Cohon, "I believe Soviet communism could use a little capitalism." But Yakovlev's deeds spoke louder than his words. The ambassador reached forward and shook Cohon's hand. In his Russian-accented rumble, Yakovlev said exactly four words: "I will help you."

PERSONA NON GRATA

EARLY ONE TUESDAY MORNING in 1978, on January 23, a Soviet spy satellite fell from the sky and landed on Canada. It was unfortunate timing for Yakovlev, who had just sent out invitations for the opening reception of a museum exhibit at the Ontario Science Centre, in Toronto, marking the achievements of the Soviet space program. In fact, the reception was set to celebrate the arrival in Canada of 40,000 kilos of rocket modules, Earth orbiters, and cosmonaut suits. This satellite was considerably smaller than those items. It was also potentially lethal, since it was powered by a nuclear reactor.

The Canadians had been worried about the satellite for some time. Thanks to the tracking systems operated by North American Air Defence Command (NORAD), Ivan Head and key members of the Canadian government knew that the satellite was in trouble since shortly after its launch, a few months before. They also knew its orbit shot it from Africa across the Atlantic and then across Canada several times a day. Intelligence reports supplied its name, Cosmos 954, and its purpose, naval reconnaissance. Intelligence didn't provide any information about what would happen to its dense core of uranium-235 once it fell. No one was expecting Hiroshima or Nagasaki; still, no one really knew whether the radioactive material might make it to Earth, or what might happen if fragments fell in a Halifax kitchen, say, or in the waiting room of a Quebec City doctor's office.

Luckily, when it did come down, the satellite scattered pieces of itself along the barren taiga from Baker Lake to Great Slave Lake in Canada's Northwest Territories. It was the first time another country's satellite had fallen onto a foreign state. The Americans were the first to know. U.S. National Security Advisor Zbigniew Brzezinski called Ivan Head at home at 7 a.m. to give him the news. Head in turn called Yakovlev.

"Are you certain it's one of ours?" Yakovlev asked. "I don't have any instructions on this from Moscow. I can't even confirm it's a Soviet satellite." Yakovlev ended the call asking for time to consult with Moscow.

The initial response from the Soviet capital was "panic-filled telegrams" that at first lied about the satellite. It was the classic Soviet response: deny, then counter with accusations the matter was the fault of the West. But by this point Yakovlev had served as ambassador for almost five years. He had credibility with the Canadians, and he wasn't about to risk it by spouting the sort of absurd accusations that characterized the Nemtsanov affair. Yakovlev declined to pass on Moscow's initial response. Head and the Canadian government would wait a remarkable 36 hours before Yakovlev provided any reply from Moscow. It seems likely that during this time Yakovlev attempted to convince Moscow to provide a more level response. During the evening of Wednesday, January 25, Yakovlev called Head at home with a message from the "Soviet leadership." This message was reasonable and to the point. It didn't bother with any nonsense alleging Western conspiracies. Rather, it confirmed that the satellite was Soviet-owned. Cosmos 954 had been designed to prevent any radioactivity from spreading if it ever re-entered the Earth's atmosphere, Yakovlev told Head. Soviet experts had predicted it would fall into the Bering Sea.

Once the impact area had been analyzed – likely with the help of the American intelligence operatives – Canada claimed $6 million in costs relating to the retrieval of the radioactive debris. The Soviet Union eventually paid out half that amount. The episode is significant because it's an early example of Yakovlev's success in pushing the Kremlin to moderate its typically aggressive diplomacy. He would have more opportunity to do this in the future – much sooner than he expected.

BACK IN OTTAWA on Thursday, February 9, four days after the reception at the Ontario Science Centre, Yakovlev walked into the brown concrete building that housed the Department of External Affairs. It was shortly before noon, and the Soviet ambassador was heading to a hastily called meeting scheduled just that morning with the new under-secretary of state for External Affairs, Allan Gotlieb.

The last several weeks had been stressful for Yakovlev. In addition to the satellite incident, he was busy helping to organize a trip that Canada's secretary of state, Donald Jamieson, Gotlieb's political boss, was making to the Soviet Union beginning in seven days, on February 16. When Gotlieb asked for the meeting earlier that morning, Yakovlev probably thought the mandarin wanted to discuss the upcoming Jamieson trip, or some matter relating to Cosmos 954. The meeting began genially enough. Yakovlev and Gotlieb were neighbours in Rockcliffe Park. There was some small talk, inquiries about wives and their health, and other gossip.

Then the conversation turned serious. For most of the previous year, Gotlieb began, Canadian intelligence operatives had been investigating a spy ring based out of the Soviet embassy. The investigation began the previous April, after two Soviet diplomats approached a member of the Royal Canadian Mounted Police and pitched him on a deal. Gotlieb described how the Soviets wanted the RCMP officer to become what intelligence operatives referred to as a "mole" – a source of information, in this case about the Mounties' counterespionage operations. Instead, the target Mountie informed his superiors of the Soviet approach. The Mounties asked the target to cooperate and built an elaborate surveillance operation around him. The Mounties fed their man false information, which he passed to Soviet diplomats in exchange for cash – $30,500 all told. Meanwhile, other RCMP officers watched each meeting from afar, often with the help of eavesdropping equipment or video cameras.

Now, Gotlieb said, the Canadian government had decided to "PNG" the Soviet diplomats. The term PNG was an abbreviation that stood for the Latin phrase *persona non grata* – an unwelcome or unwanted person. In the diplomatic community, an embassy official declared persona non grata by the host government was banished from that country. Effectively, getting PNGed meant the end of a diplomatic career. Gotlieb swung his head back to peer through his reading spectacles at the list on his desk. He began reading: Igor Vartanyan, the embassy first secretary in charge of sports and cultural affairs; Vladimir Suvorov, a second secretary; Oleg Reztsov, embassy attaché. And Reztsov's wife, Vera.

Yakovlev blanched. This was a big deal. Over the whole of the last decade, only eight Soviet representatives had been expelled from Canada for spying. Now, in one day, four members of his 61-employee embassy were being PNGed.

He might have expected something like this. Despite the warmth with which Trudeau and Head regarded Yakovlev, and despite the Trudeau government's enthusiasm for bolstering trade relations with the Soviet Union, Canada had an aggressive, hard-bitten intelligence service quite out of character with the country's even-keeled self-image. This had a lot to do with the agency's culture. In other Western countries, intelligence operations were run by civilians. But in Canada it was the RCMP who handled counterespionage – in addition to acting as a federal law enforcement agency and to performing regional policing duties in less-populated provinces and territories. In America, a similar arrangement would have combined the duties of state police departments with those of the Federal Bureau of Investigation and the Central Intelligence Agency. The result was the concentration of considerable power in RCMP hands. In fact, after years of rumours, the Trudeau government had opened in December 1977, just two months before, a federal inquiry to investigate whether the Mounties had abused their considerable power. The inquiry had already established that the Mounties had committed break-ins without warrants and opened the mail of people they suspected harboured communist or Quebec separatist sentiments. For a force that could use some good publicity, a big Soviet spy bust must have represented an alluring option – particularly given the recent release of the tenth James Bond film, *The Spy Who Loved Me*.

Gotlieb explained that the four people whose names he'd read would have to leave the country within 48 hours. Then he continued reading:

Nikolai Talanov, an embassy counsellor.

"There are more?" asked Yakovlev.

Gotlieb kept his eyes on the list:

Anatoly A. Mikhailin, a trade official.

Vadim Borishpolets, the consular attaché.

"Borishpolets?" Yakovlev asked. "Are you certain?"

Gotlieb just kept going:

Vladimir Oshkaderov, a translator working at the International Civil Aviation Organization headquarters in Montreal.

Yevgeny Kablov, an embassy clerk.

Gennady Ivashavich, the embassy's third secretary.

And Pyotr Lillenurm, a second secretary.

These men, Gotlieb explained, were found by the RCMP to have supporting roles in the espionage operation. They would have to leave the embassy in two weeks, by February 23. Then he added two more names – Voldemar P. Veber and Andrei V. Krysin, both of whom were already in Moscow on business. Neither man would be allowed to return to Ottawa.

By the time Gotlieb finished Yakovlev looked as though he might collapse. Altogether the names came to 13 people. So far as diplomatic expulsions went, this one was the biggest in Canadian history. Secretary of State Jamieson would be cancelling his upcoming trip to the Soviet Union. It also endangered a trip Yakovlev had been trying to arrange for years for Prime Minister Trudeau. Trudeau hadn't visited the Soviet Union since 1971; a follow-up organized by Yakovlev would have opened the way for a return trip by Brezhnev, allowing Yakovlev to lobby for his return to the Soviet Union.

Yakovlev had Gotlieb go over the names again, more slowly this time. "Veber?" Yakovlev echoed after Gotlieb said his name. "Are you certain? And Borishpolets? It can't be. Are you sure?"

Gotlieb was sure. By the time Yakovlev left he was looking as troubled as Gotlieb had ever seen him.

ABOUT AN HOUR AFTER the end of Yakovlev's meeting with Gotlieb, as Yakovlev was still working on informing each of the listed diplomats of his impending banishment, Secretary of State Don Jamieson announced the details of the operation in the House of Commons. "Mr. Speaker, at noon today . . . the Soviet ambassador was informed that the Canadian government had irrefutable evidence that all 13 persons had been involved in an attempt to penetrate the RCMP Security Service." A press conference followed. Jamieson disclosed details that could have been lifted from a James Bond movie or a novel by John Le Carré. He described the way the Soviet agents passed messages in a hollowed-out stick hidden in a package of cigarettes. The Soviets wanted information on RCMP counterespionage tactics and character assessments of RCMP personnel. Instead, Jamieson said, "The RCMP member in return provided the Soviets with carefully screened nonsensitive information of completely fabricated material."

At meeting points as varied as Ottawa shopping centres, Montreal restaurants, and the wilderness of the Gatineau Hills, Jamieson continued, the Mountie mole was instructed by his Soviet handlers to hide messages in empty Coke cans. One signal for "message received" was a scattering of orange peels on a certain path in nearby Gatineau Park.

More details would trickle out over the years, particularly after Yakovlev's old friend from his Columbia days, Oleg Kalugin, penned his memoirs in the 1990s. According to Kalugin, who in 1978 was working as the KGB's chief of foreign counterintelligence, the KGB used for years a mole in the counterintelligence section of the RCMP's Security Service, which frequently shared information with American spy agencies. Over the years this mole provided the KGB with some useful information, verifying, for example, that a Soviet citizen named Nikolai Artamonov, who the KGB thought was working for them, was in fact working for the Americans – a discovery that led to Artamonov's kidnapping by the KGB, and eventual death. This mole in the RCMP was such a good source of information that the Soviets decided they wanted more sources inside the service. The mole provided them with several names, including a "dissident" member of the organization who had publicly criticized his employer. It was the approach to this dissident member of the RCMP, in Montreal, that triggered the round of PNGs currently aggravating Yakovlev.

Jamieson's press conference triggered a media sensation. Mobs of newspaper reporters and flying squads connected to all sorts of Canadian and American radio and television stations descended on the embassy and the ambassador's residence, as well as on the apartments of the deported officials, where, reporters related, the Soviets were packing their belongings into liquor store boxes bound up with rope. Yakovlev and his fellow embassy staffers felt as though they were under siege. Every television channel and radio station seemed to be discussing the spy story. The newscasters were calling this the biggest espionage scandal to hit Canada since the Gouzenko affair, the 1945 defection of a clerk in Ottawa's Soviet embassy whose debriefing had provided the first indication that Stalin was spying on the West. Gouzenko still remained in Canada, and the media dredged him up to get his take. He told one reporter that the number of Soviet spies working in Canada numbered 500. In fact, Gouzenko said, except for the ambassador himself, every Soviet employee in the embassy gathered information for the KGB. Other newspapers didn't even make that distinction; even Ambassador Yakovlev, they said, was a spy.

The first of the Soviet embassy officials, Borishpolets, left the country on Thursday, within hours of the news. Then on Friday afternoon the four alleged "ringleaders" assembled a convoy of vehicles at their homes in Ottawa's Sandy Hill neighbourhood for the 90-minute drive to Montreal's Mirabel Airport. They flew out that evening.

THAT THERE WERE SPIES in the Soviet embassy wasn't news to Yakovlev. Estimates on the fraction of the embassy's 61 staff members who were intelligence operatives ranged from one-half to two-thirds. Spotting all but those under the deepest of cover was simple enough. KGB agents usually had an air of entitlement – they thought they were the elite, and treated outsiders imperiously, as though they belonged to a lesser class. KGB budgets and salaries were far higher than those provided to most Soviet diplomats. Even some of the most senior of Yakovlev's staff might drive North American clunkers. Then, tellingly, some junior staffer – a security guard, perhaps, or a junior press attaché – would drive a new European sedan with power windows and A/C. There were other differences. Party doctrine discouraged regular Foreign Affairs workers from mixing with North American citizens because too much contact with the West was thought to corrupt one's ideological thinking. KGB operatives, in contrast, cultivated friendships with Canadian government officials by going to Ottawa cocktail parties or hanging around Parliament Hill cafeterias. Yakovlev felt he had a pretty good eye for even the most covert of KGB agents.

He was certain some of the people on Gotlieb's list weren't KGB agents. After a half decade in Ottawa he had become close with many of his staff, including several who were due to be deported. Their wives were friendly with Nina; their children were friends with Yakovlev's granddaughter, Natasha. Regardless of whether they really were working for the KGB, being outed as spies would wreck these people's careers. Cast out of Ottawa, they wouldn't be welcome as diplomats in other countries around the world.

Shortly after he returned to his office, Yakovlev placed a call to Ivan Head. The Soviet ambassador sounded disconsolate – "as though he was in mourning," Head would say later. A scandal as large as this one could doom Yakovlev's career as well. It didn't matter that Yakovlev had known nothing about this plot. Yakovlev argued strenuously with Head to convince the Canadian government to reconsider. The RCMP was just wrong about some of the people on the list, he said. "They couldn't possibly be engaged in this sort of business," he told Head.

"I know these people. They never get out of the embassy." Plus, it wasn't just 13 people who were being PNGed. It was their spouses, and their children. Their lives were being uprooted unjustly, Yakovlev felt.

Head's response to Yakovlev was unusually firm, at first. His tack portrayed Canada as the aggrieved party. This sort of large-scale operation, involving a significant fraction of embassy employees, wasn't the sort of thing that should happen between friends, said Head. Besides, it looked to him as if Yakovlev's diplomats got what was coming to them. They were adults. They understood the risks.

Gradually, though, Head softened. Either explicitly or through implication he made it clear that it had not been the intention of the Trudeau cabinet to air this revelation in public. They would have preferred to have dealt with the situation quietly, after Jamieson's Soviet visit. When the Mounties first informed the Trudeau government of their investigation several weeks before, on January 26, Head had argued against any deportations. The Jamieson visit was more important, he'd said. And aside from the fact that it would create some much-needed good publicity for the Mounties, there was no strategic reason to exile the diplomats. The information the "mole" was passing to the Soviets was false. Rather than declaring them PNG, the strategic thing to do would be to keep the alleged KGB agents under surveillance, in an attempt to discover whether they were involved in other espionage operations. But the Mounties were insistent. When the Trudeau cabinet didn't look as though it was going to do anything, the Mounties leaked information about the investigation to the media. It was the prospect of publicity that prompted the expulsions. Head made it clear to Yakovlev, that the RCMP could be a difficult organization to control.

They were at an impasse. Both men realized now this matter had little to do with Canada–Soviet relations. It was a problem caused by over-enthusiastic intelligence operatives on both sides. This game of espionage, these spies spying on other spies, stood to harm the good relations between their countries both men had worked for the past five years to build.

"Look, Ivan," Yakovlev said finally. "I'm going to try to do my best not to have this blow up into a major altercation. But I'll need constant access to you and the prime minister."

Head agreed.

ON THE MORNING of Saturday, February 11, newspapers throughout Canada reported on the ringleaders' departure, including the salient detail that the luggage of Oleg and Vera Reztsov's young son, Andrei, included a sombrero, three hockey sticks, and a stuffed-toy Saint Bernard. But Yakovlev had more important matters to deal with. He thought he might have new ammunition to save his friends. "I must see you, and I must see you right away," Yakovlev said during a telephone call to Head's home. "I apologize, but I must."

The two men met at Head's office in the Langevin Block, across the street from Parliament Hill. Yakovlev was carrying a file folder as he walked in.

"You have told me this isn't the way Canada functions, that this isn't what you do to us," Yakovlev said, holding the folder aloft. "But I want to show you this."

He handed the folder to Head. Inside was a report chronicling an attempt by an RCMP officer to turn a KGB agent. In other words, the RCMP was guilty of the same offences for which Head so sanctimoniously rebuked the Soviets. Just as the KGB was accused of doing in Ottawa, the RCMP had paid their KGB target thousands of dollars. The attempt failed, the KGB agent wrote up his account, and now a translated version of that account was in Head's hands. Yakovlev also would discuss the RCMP's approach to a Soviet consular worker in Montreal that had gone so far the Mounties had actually given the man a handwritten list of topics that interested them, such as attempts to penetrate Western intelligence agencies. The list was itemized by the price the Canadians would pay for the information, from $1,000 to $25,000. As Head acknowledged, in uncharacteristically colourful language, Yakovlev's information "blew the top of my head off."

"I'll have to look into this," Head said.

"You're not challenging the authenticity of what I'm telling you?"

"I'm not challenging it," Head said. "I've got to find out what all this is about."

Head called a meeting with Allan Gotlieb and the head of the Mounties, Commissioner Robert H. Simmonds; he also asked Simmonds to bring the officer in charge of the RCMP's Security Service, Director-General Michael R. Dare. The four men met in the Pearson Building in a special chamber called a "quiet room" that was supposed to be safe from surveillance. Once Head told the men what he'd heard from Yakovlev, Commissioner Simmonds turned to Dare for his reaction. "It's nonsense, of course," the commissioner said. "Right?"

"No, Commissioner," Dare said. "This is actually what happened."

Head nearly fell out of his chair. Immediately afterward Head went to Trudeau's house at 24 Sussex Drive to inform the prime minister. Trudeau and Head hoped they could prevent this information from getting out to the press. The RCMP was already under fire for spying on Canadian citizens. Now, it seemed, without the knowledge of the highest-ranking members of government, they were bungling attempts to spy on the Soviets as well. The recently begun governmental inquiry, the McDonald Commission, was already showing signs of turning up information that would portray the RCMP's intelligence arm as little better than Keystone Kops. This latest bungling was certain to darken the stain on the force, and possibly bleed over to the Trudeau Liberals. The greater implication also would have been clear to both men: the RCMP was out of control.

THE NEXT MORNING, a Sunday, Trudeau invited Yakovlev and Head to a meeting at 24 Sussex Drive. It is a measure of the informal relationship between Yakovlev and Trudeau that Trudeau passed most of the meeting getting dressed for a reception later that afternoon. The first order of business was following up on Yakovlev's accusation about the

RCMP's approach to a KGB member. Once Head established that the story had checked out, Yakovlev mentioned a series of other escapades the RCMP had conducted against the embassy. Yakovlev's staffers were perpetually finding microphones and other eavesdropping devices throughout their offices and other Soviet buildings in both Ottawa and Montreal – several dozen microphones, all told. This was fairly standard stuff, so far as Cold War-era espionage went; Yakovlev's Canadian counterpart in Moscow also found listening devices in his embassy, where the diplomats reserved their most sensitive conversations for specially constructed sound-impenetrable quiet chambers in the basement. After a fire incinerated an earlier incarnation of the Soviet embassy in Ottawa in 1956, the Canadians went so far as to install microphones within the embassy's windows, but Soviet countermeasures disabled them.

"If you can assure me, Mr. Prime Minister, that this episode won't affect our relations," Yakovlev, "then I think we can work our way through this in a way that won't be embarrassing to Canada."

"I'm not here to point fingers," Trudeau said. "We did what we felt we had to do. You must do what you feel you have to do. But I want you to tell your leadership that the relationship we've been trying to foster over the years will not be hindered or turned back because of this."

In such diplomatic banishments, the host country usually decreases the number of diplomats they permit at the offending embassy, similar to a red card decreasing a soccer team's permitted number of players on the field. Had the Canadians followed this custom with this case, permanent staff at the Soviet embassy would have decreased by 13 people, from 61 to 48 – a significant measure. Instead, Trudeau allowed Yakovlev to simply replace the staff that were banished.

Yakovlev also brought up his belief that some of the staff being expelled were not KGB operatives. To that, Trudeau smiled. "Mr. Ambassador, maybe I'm being deceived," he said to Yakovlev. "But maybe you are. Why don't you take a look at the evidence – the surveillance videos, for example. Or look, why don't we do this – why don't you give me the names of the people we're deporting without grounds, and I'll return them at once."

Yakovlev was now caught in a bind of his own making. The Soviet conceit said the USSR didn't spy. Not at all. By pointing out the handful of people he thought Canada to be wrongly expelling, Yakovlev would be implying that the others mentioned were rightfully being expelled. According to his memoirs, Yakovlev responded with a joke. He told the prime minister, "I can list all 13."

Worried about Yakovlev discovering state secrets apparently, the KGB declined Yakovlev's request to watch the tape. According to the official accounts that have appeared through the years, that's where the story ended. Trudeau offered to have his staff double-check the cases of the people Yakovlev was certain couldn't be spies, Yakovlev made his joke about all 13, and that was that.

Were that the case, this would be just another spy scandal, one among several that happened while Yakovlev was ambassador. However, according to a "top secret" memo written by Ivan Head shortly after these events, the account in Yakovlev's memoirs is fudging a bit. Head's account illustrates the trust that existed among Yakovlev, Head, and Trudeau. It's also an indication of Yakovlev contradicting official Soviet policy. Yakovlev's private reasoning had already disagreed with Soviet policy on many previous occasions. But this occasion is notable because it's a clear example of Yakovlev's behaviour contradicting the official Soviet line – of Yakovlev placing considerations of justice above his loyalty to the Communist Party. In other words, here Yakovlev did what he thought was right, rather than what the Communist Party wanted him to do. It's just this sort of behaviour that would trouble the party bureaucrats, years later, under perestroika.

Yakovlev's significant action was to provide Trudeau and Head with a list of the embassy employees who Yakovlev thought couldn't possibly be spying for the KGB. There were five names: Lillenurm, Kablov, Borishpolets, Mikhailin, and Veber. By naming these people, Yakovlev was indirectly confirming to Canadian government officials that the other eight Soviets actually *did* work for the KGB. It was a step many KGB agents might regard as treachery, this indirect outing of spies. Yakovlev was entrusting to Trudeau and Head information that would certainly cost the Soviet ambassador his job if the people back in Moscow ever heard he revealed it. That Yakovlev took this risk indicates the extent to which he trusted Trudeau and Head. It also shows how badly he wanted to save the careers of the embassy employees he figured were innocent.

Head agreed to consult the evidence against the five people Yakovlev named. Later, the three men strolled out to the stoop of 24 Sussex Drive. Yakovlev summoned his car, and as it approached, Trudeau noticed something. He smiled.

"You know, Mr. Ambassador," Trudeau said, nodding toward the car's front end, "in this context, I'm not sure whether you should be driving around town with such a licence plate number."

The three of them looked down at the spot on Yakovlev's bumper, where the license plate was. As in many other countries, diplomats in Canada received special plates to indicate their status – these were red instead of the white and blue plates sported by everyone else in Ottawa, and they began with the initials "CD" followed by three numbers.

Yakovlev groaned. "I have nothing to do with the way these plates are issued," he said.

Trudeau laughed, and the other two men joined in. It seemed absurd that, amid all this spy mania, the Soviet ambassador was driving around town with diplomatic licence plates that accidentally invoked Commander James Bond. Yakovlev's license plate read "CD 007."

ON TUESDAY, FEBRUARY 14, Head went to Yakovlev's residence to follow up on the spy scandal. He ended up staying nearly four hours, including lunch. "In years to come, journalists and politicians will be speculating about the nature of this conversation," Yakovlev said at the beginning, perhaps overstating the meeting's importance. Yakovlev started the discussion with a reference to Igor Gouzenko, the Soviet embassy defector who had been ubiquitous in the Canadian media lately as reporters struggled to find some apparent expert to comment.

Gouzenko was no expert, Yakovlev said. He'd defected more than 30 years ago. He had no idea what was happening lately. "Why do the newspapers continue to pay attention to him?" he wondered aloud.

Head shrugged. "He's a well-known name," he said. "But surely even the journalists should realize his information is more than 30 years out of date."

Then Yakovlev turned to business. His instructions, he told Head, were to continue to deny the involvement of any of the Soviets in "improper activities." He passed over his formal talking notes. It was an annotated list of Canadian spy operations against Soviets in Ottawa and Montreal; an indignant follow-up, in other words, to the protests he had made several days before. Yakovlev waited for Head to copy the note.

Then the ambassador broached the meeting's unofficial purpose – the results of Head's checking into the evidence behind the five employees on Yakovlev's list. No mention is made in the archives of measures the ambassador may have made to foil listening devices the KGB or other spy agencies may have placed in the ambassador's residence. However, Cold War paranoia, and the sensitivity of what they were about to discuss, make it likely the two men took precautions, possibly discussing the matter outside, in the residence's garden, or elsewhere.

Head pulled out a file folder he had brought – a narrative of the evidence against the Soviet embassy workers. This Voldemar Veber, Head said. He was the one who introduced the Mountie in question to the ringleader, Vartanyan. Then, not two months ago, on Christmas Eve at Ruby Foo's restaurant in Montreal, Veber attended a meeting with Vartanyan and the Mountie. Next was the embassy clerk Yevgeny Kablov, who the Mounties said had accompanied Vartanyan to a signal point last June. And similarly, Mikhailin, Borishpolets and Lillenurm each had visited signal points in the past; in fact, Lillenurm had visited one less than a month ago.

"Could the evidence have been fabricated?" the ambassador asked, deflated. Back in Moscow, and within the Soviet diplomatic community in Canada, the scuttlebutt ran that this was some American provocation, that the CIA had pushed the RCMP into manufacturing the scandal in an effort to embarrass Moscow. The second rumour going around had the RCMP engineering the scandal on its own, in a bid to repair its own sagging reputation.

Head said no. The evidence was real. "This was a carefully constructed exercise on the Soviet side," Head said, "and an equally carefully constructed Canadian response. . . Our prosecutors reviewed it."

"Yet Lillenurm cried when I spoke to him," the ambassador said. "Surely he's not guilty."

Head told Yakovlev how he had reviewed the evidence himself, on Trudeau's instructions. Head, a lawyer, had gone through the documents and files and satisfied himself that everything was in order.

Yakovlev switched subjects. This scandal would make things difficult for him, he said. "My so-called friends will cause trouble for me," he said, referring to the orthodox party bureaucrats back home. "And for Canadian–Soviet cooperation. They have opposed those policies from the beginning and will now use this as evidence – proof that their views were correct."

He then explained what Head probably already knew – that the typical Soviet response to a scandal like this was to retaliate with press coverage that aimed to embarrass the offending country. Thanks to old contacts he had within the Propaganda Department, Yakovlev had managed to hold the stories. But now, with all 13 of the Soviets still going home, Yakovlev warned Head to expect Soviet media to disclose the RCMP's intelligence failures. (In fact, in the coming weeks several attempts to embarrass the Canadian Mounties did run in the Soviet media, including an article in *Literaturnaya Gazeta* written by Yakovlev's friend Oleg Kalugin, under a pseudonym, describing the RCMP's attempts to turn Soviet diplomats in Canada.)

The ambassador wondered how the events of recent days would affect the Soviet visit he was trying to arrange for the prime minister. Head said the visit was out of the question now. Trudeau's mandate was coming to a close; shortly he would have an election campaign to contend with.

In the wake of the spy scandal, the prime minister couldn't afford to be seen getting friendly with the Soviet Union. For the moment, any hope Yakovlev had of engineering his return to Moscow was over.

AS THE DARKNESS of February in Ottawa made way for March and the hope of spring, the few remaining PNG-declared members of Yakovlev's staff packed up their lives and departed for Moscow. Still, the spy scandal affected Yakovlev's thinking long after its events had passed. In the following months and years, he would write at least four texts, two pseudonymously, related in whole or in part to the scandal and its after-effects. Each one provokes interesting questions about the Soviet ambassador's path toward perestroika.

The first text was what even the sometimes wordy Yakovlev describes as a "long-winded telegram" to Moscow providing an overview of the scandal, probably for the ostensible benefit of the Soviet Ministry of Foreign Affairs, although the telegram's consequences suggest it was disseminated among the members of the Politburo as well. The telegram reported what Yakovlev knew about the espionage operation – the signals the KGB used, and the fact that the Canadian spy service, one step ahead of the KGB, had bugged the restaurant table where the KGB officers were attempting to recruit the Mountie. Yakovlev also suggested operational changes to the structure of the Canadian embassy that would insulate the ambassador's valued diplomats from any implication in espionage affairs.

The airing of such an operational defeat would have embarrassed KGB chief Yuri Andropov and his chief of Foreign Intelligence, Vladimir Kryuchkov. Essentially, Yakovlev was trumpeting to the Politburo an instance in which the mighty KGB had been beaten at its own game by a comparatively puny Canadian counterintelligence service. In response, Andropov rebuked Yakovlev in a "top secret" telegram from Moscow charging that Yakovlev "underrated the goals of Soviet intelligence in North America." In the Politburo session where all this was discussed,

Andropov also attempted to have Yakovlev fired – not the sort of home-coming Yakovlev wanted. But the fanatically rules-oriented ideologue, Mikhail Suslov, stymied the attempt because the KGB didn't have any authority over foreign ambassadors. Kryuchkov would go on to become the KGB chief who led the August 1991 coup and accused Yakovlev of working for the Americans. Bearing in mind the KGB's long institutional memory, and instinctive yen for retribution, it's intriguing to wonder whether the 1978 spy fiasco played any role in fomenting the rivalry between Kryuchkov and Yakovlev – whether, even in 1978, Kryuchkov hoped he would one day have the opportunity to ruin the Soviet ambassador. Kryuchkov certainly expressed antipathy toward Yakovlev in the spy scandal's aftermath. On a subsequent trip to Moscow, the ambassador dropped by KGB headquarters for a standard briefing meeting in the presence of Kryuchkov. Afterward, Yakovlev mentioned to Kryuchkov his intent to visit the office of his old friend, Oleg Kalugin, then the head of KGB Foreign Counterintelligence. While Yakovlev was en route, Kryuchkov placed a call to Kalugin. "Please don't be too friendly with Yakovlev," Kryuchkov told Kalugin. "He's not the sort of man you can trust."

The second text Yakovlev wrote is a 16-page day-by-day summary of the spy scandal's press coverage. He titled the memo, "On the unfriendly actions of the Canadian government, carried out in February 1978 against staff of Soviet institutions in Canada." But the memo was about a lot more. It chronicled the virulent criticism Trudeau suffered in the scandal's aftermath from both sides of Canada's opposition, the right-wing Progressive Conservatives and the left-wing New Democrats. Conservative opposition members derided Trudeau for playing into the hands of the Soviets. Meanwhile, the NDP complained the Mounties were using the spy scandal to generate positive press for themselves. It was another example of Trudeau's inability to control the RCMP, they said, and more evidence that the Mounties' intelligence arm required wholesale reform. To Yakovlev, the contrast with the situation back home must have been striking. Under Moscow's one-party rule, the merest hint of disagreement with the Politburo could lead to imprisonment. Meanwhile, Canadian journalists and politicians were publicly accusing the country's leader of conduct bordering on treason. And still Canadian democracy continued to function. The *Globe and Mail* landed on door stoops across the nation each morning. Hockey games illuminated television tubes each night. It was evident to Yakovlev that the political system of a parliamentary democracy was robust enough to weather such criticism – unlike the Communist Party's one-party state.

The final two texts both involve the McDonald Commission, the inquiry that began two months before the spy scandal, in December 1977, and finally concluded several years later in 1981. The inquiry amounted to a slow-motion, microscopic examination of the Royal Canadian Mounted Police, in particular the habit of the Mounties' intelligence operation, the Security Service, to spy illegally on Canadian citizens. For several years the commission would regularly make front pages across the country as it unearthed hundreds of incidents when Mounties broke laws they were supposed to uphold, usually under the auspices of protecting Canadian security. They infiltrated and spied on groups thought to harbour separatist or communist sympathies, or agitate for the rights of women or minorities; in one famous instance the RCMP even burned down a barn thought to be used for meetings of the Black Panther Party. Other police burglarized left-wing news agencies. They stole membership lists of separatist political parties. And they conducted surveillance on thousands of otherwise innocent Canadian citizens suspected of harbouring political beliefs that differed from what the RCMP considered acceptable.

As it ground on, the McDonald Commission regularly featured prominently in Canadian newspapers, and eventually public revulsion over RCMP misconduct spurred Trudeau to carry out the commission's recommendation, to remove intelligence operations from the Mounties' mandate. Trudeau created a new civilian agency called the Canadian Security Intelligence Service, which was to be staffed with university-educated white-collar analysts. Overall, the reform amounted to a case study of the way opposition political parties, a free press, and a protracted and spirited public debate could trigger government reform.

The reform process fascinated Yakovlev to such an extent he wrote a 93-page pamphlet about the McDonald Commission and its discoveries of secret police misconduct, publishing it under the surname Agashin, a variation on Gasha, the diminutive form of his mother's first name of Agafya. Yakovlev also published an annotated, 10-page version covering much the same ground in a Russian political journal. The essays exposed to their Soviet readers the machinations of Canada's paranoid secret police force, corrupted by too much power and eager to stamp out the merest hint of dissidence. In an era when public criticism of the Soviets' own secret police warranted harsh retribution, it was lost on neither Yakovlev, nor on his readers, that such abuses were committed regularly by the KGB as well. Tellingly, in Yakovlev's memoirs, he notes that it was in the spy scandal's aftermath that he began wondering why it was necessary for the KGB to spy on Soviet citizens. "I was interested in getting a deeper understanding of what kind of organization this was that, together with the [Central Committee], was holding the entire country by its throat," Yakovlev writes in his memoirs. "I wanted to understand the mechanism of suppressing the intelligentsia, the mass media, and religion."

KILLING TIME

R USSIAN JOURNALIST Genrikh Borovik tells a story about Yakovlev that illustrates the complicated combination of frustration and inspiration that plagued the Soviet ambassador during his Canadian posting, particularly after 1978. The two men first met in the early 1960s, when Yakovlev was considered one of the few intelligentsia-friendly officials in the upper ranks of the Propaganda Department and Borovik was a naïve but up-and-coming journalist working for the Soviet journal *Ogonek*.

The two men hadn't seen each other for years when Borovik, working as a correspondent for the Soviet press in New York City, caught sight of Yakovlev in the lobby of the United Nations' Manhattan headquarters. Andrei Gromyko, the Soviet minister of foreign affairs, was in town, and he had invited Yakovlev to New York. Yakovlev was at loose ends when Borovik caught up to him, and after the typical Russian bear hug, Yakovlev suggested to Borovik that they head some-where where their conversation could be more frank. They ended up at Borovik's apartment. There wasn't much furniture – Borovik had only recently moved in – so the two men sat on the floor as they shared a bottle of vodka.

The Soviet ambassador told Borovik about Canadian life. He spoke of the similarities to home: two big northern countries where the cold climate caused a short growing season. Both sat on resource-rich territory. But the people of Canada were far better off than their Soviet counterparts, Yakovlev said, and he attributed this to the democracy of the Canadian system – to the free elections and power changeovers that acted as a check on corruption.

Yakovlev expressed, or was on the verge of expressing, similar sentiments to several people he trusted during his Canadian posting. Each time he described elements of capitalist democratic society he thought stood to benefit the Soviet Union. He tended to display excitement as he discussed these elements, exhibiting eagerness to improve the situation back home. There was also frustration. This last quality would grow markedly during his second five years in Ottawa.

He had the luxury of hope during his first years in exile. Yakovlev arrived in Ottawa as détente was in full bloom. Arms reduction talks were progressing, as was the Conference on Security and Cooperation in Europe, with the resulting Helsinki Final Act signed on August 1, 1975. Amid all this talk of cooperation and East–West relations, the ever-idealistic Yakovlev explored Canada and the West and developed a host of ideas for changes he thought might improve the Soviet system. By the time Yakovlev passed the five-year anniversary of his Canadian exile, in the summer of 1978, it was apparent to him that no one back home was interested in his advice.

Hence the frustration. By 1978, Yakovlev felt he had absorbed all he needed to know about the West. He was ready to return to Russia, to work in the Communist Party, where he figured his new perspective might do some good. But the Party didn't want him back. By the late 1970s Brezhnev's health was failing. Addicted to sleeping pills, suffering from a series of strokes, the general secretary was rumoured to have died a clinical death several times before being revived by doctors and restored to some semblance of awareness. Meanwhile the Politburo was poised in a complex balance of power among Brezhnev's rivals, such as Suslov, who preferred to stay behind the scenes, or Defence Minister

Dmitri Ustinov. Risk averse in the extreme, these men preferred a zombie of a leader to the uncertainty of the power struggle that would result from Brezhnev's ouster. It was fashionable for the era's Sovietologists to refer to the men atop the Soviet Union as an "ossified gerontocracy," and equally fashionable to point out their average age, in 1980, of 69. These men wanted stability, but what resulted was stagnation. Hypocrisy, corruption, and decay ruled most aspects of Soviet life. Workers left their jobs early to wait in queues at markets where there was no food because of lagging productivity – because workers left their jobs early, among other problems. In the provinces, people sustained themselves with food they grew in their own personal garden plots. Despite amounting to just 4 percent of the USSR's cultivated land, such plots contributed 30 percent of total agricultural production. Meanwhile the supposedly Marxist-Leninist Communist Party had strayed so far from Lenin's original ideals that a rumour had Moscow bookstores being discouraged from carrying Lenin's 55-volume complete works. "The key common goal of political leaders in the Kremlin was to minimize shifts of policy and avoid damaging internal controversy," noted one historian. And amid this mania for the status quo, a man like Yakovlev, already banished from Moscow for speaking his mind, stood little chance of being allowed to return. It seemed that Yakovlev would be stuck in Ottawa for as long as Brezhnev stayed the Soviet leader.

Now Yakovlev felt his exile. His posting had ceased to be a classroom, an opportunity to learn about an alternate way of life, and had become a jail – one where his stay was made interminable by his conviction that he could fix things, back home, if only they would give him the chance. Such a situation breeds cynicism in most men, and Yakovlev was no exception. "More and more frequently," he wrote in his memoirs, "my head was filled with bitter thoughts that my life was already behind me, while my country more and more obviously was becoming petrified and rapidly was falling behind world development. And I couldn't see an end to the darkness."

THEN MOSCOW RAISED THE STAKES. A little more than a year after the spy scandal, Trudeau asked to see Yakovlev. He hurried over to Trudeau's office and found the prime minister "somber and angry." Trudeau had just heard that the Soviet Union was placing a new, deadlier class of nuclear missile, the SS-20, along its borders with Western Europe. "What's going on, Sasha?" Trudeau asked.

Trudeau's puzzlement was genuine. Since the early 1970s, the Cold War had been neutralized by the concept of mutual deterrence thanks to strategic parity – the notion that a roughly equal capability to wipe out the other side deterred both sides from starting a world war. The tactical balance was particularly marked in Europe. By late in the decade, the Soviets' income from high oil prices had allowed them to build up a three-to-one edge in conventional weapons forces over the West, in Europe. This numerical superiority in infantry soldiers and tanks was balanced by American, French, and British nuclear weaponry.

But this new class of nuclear weapons the Soviets were deploying in Eastern Europe was deadlier than anything the continent had seen: blunt-nosed cylinders that packed three independently targeted nuclear warheads atop a two-stage solid-fuel rocket. Just 16.5 metres long and 1.8 metres in diameter, the missiles were able to be launched from a tractor trailer. Strung along the Warsaw Pact's western border, they could reach any European capital in minutes. Theoretically, the Soviets could use these new missiles to knock out strategic targets on the continent, then use their huge advantage in conventional forces to consolidate control. In Washington, the deployment of the SS-20s was forcing the Americans to contemplate whether they would risk the destruction of the continental United States to protect, say, Paris. It was now conceivable to think of a nuclear war that resulted not in global Armageddon, but in Soviet control of Europe.

The timing was horrible. Negotiators from both sides of the Cold War were about to agree to an arms limitation treaty, knows as SALT II. Trudeau tended to believe much of the Soviet rhetoric that coincided with the negotiations. He was conscious that the United States could behave aggressively. He blamed the Americans for many of the international tensions between Washington and Moscow. But now, with the introduction of the SS-20s, the Soviets seemed to be needlessly provoking their enemies at a particularly ill-advised time. Just as the world was about to make a positive and bold step toward peace, the Soviets were pulling everyone toward war. Trudeau asked Yakovlev whether this latest step was a rejection of Moscow's dove instincts. Was the Cold War entering a new phase?

Yakovlev blustered his way through the meeting. The standard Soviet defence of the SS-20s portrayed them as simple upgrades to an aging and outmoded arsenal. But privately he shared Trudeau's puzzlement. Trudeau asked Yakovlev to send a message back home, to convey the Canadian leader's dismay with the Soviet move. Yakovlev did. In fact, he sent several requests for clarification. Why was the military deploying these SS-20s? The only reply he received was an instruction from his superior in the Ministry of Foreign Affairs not to send any more telegrams.

OTHER CIRCUMSTANCES besides geopolitical events reduced Yakovlev's professional standing in Ottawa. Yakovlev's best friend in the Canadian government, Ivan Head, left Trudeau's office to lead Canada's International Development Research Centre, which aimed to assist the world's poorest economies. By now the mandarins at External Affairs trusted Yakovlev's ability to act as a middleman between Ottawa and the Moscow leadership. But in contrast to his friendship with Head, Yakovlev's relations with External's top bureaucrat, Allan Gotlieb, and the staff of the Soviet desk were considerably more professional.

Then Trudeau's fortunes faltered. He and his wife separated in March of 1977, and Margaret embarked on a travel-heavy schedule that saw her partying in Toronto with the Rolling Stones, shimmying in New York at Studio 54, and jetting off on shopping excursions to Paris and London. There were no more family dinners at 24 Sussex Drive for the Yakovlevs. Now his meetings with Trudeau happened one on one – not that Trudeau had much time anymore. As his mandate neared its end, Trudeau told advisors that his marital problems were sapping the mental strength necessary for a campaign. Nearing the last possible instant, Trudeau called an election on March 26, 1979, lost on May 22, and announced his resignation from politics on November 21. Worse for Yakovlev, replacing Trudeau as prime minister was Joe Clark, a young, green Progressive Conservative who aimed to patch up relations with the United States. In the binary politics of the Cold War, this meant distancing Canada from the Soviet Union – and from its ambassador.

More dispiriting news came from George Cohon, the McDonald's of Canada CEO trying to open a franchise beachhead at the fast-approaching 1980 Olympic Games in Moscow. When he visited Yakovlev's office one day in 1979, the entrepreneur's condition astonished the ambassador. Cohon was an avid tennis player and outdoorsman with the unfailing optimism of a Boy Scout. But he looked rundown and pale. The biggest surprise was his mood. Cohon seemed dejected.

Getting McDonald's into Moscow had become Cohon's life goal since he had first pitched Yakovlev on the idea. He averaged a half-dozen trips a year to Moscow to lobby party bureaucrats, many of them contacts Yakovlev assisted in arranging. Airfare, translator's fees, and promotional events cost McDonald's millions of dollars. In the course of their dealings, Cohon and Yakovlev had developed a remarkable friendship. Yakovlev became a resource for Cohon – an avuncular, engaging fount of advice on everything from ferreting out contacts in the Moscow party apparatus to crafting strategies in advance of Cohon's next transatlantic flight. Meanwhile, Cohon put Yakovlev through an informal version of McDonald's Hamburger University. The two men swung by an Ottawa franchise location where Cohon encouraged the Soviet ambassador to sample the cuisine and provided him with a tour behind the counter, telling Yakovlev of the mania for efficiency that allowed a dozen staff members to serve thousands of affordably priced hamburgers a day. Cohon also introduced Yakovlev to the restaurant's various success stories – a franchise owner who started at McDonald's as a fry-cook, say, or the cashiers making spare cash between classes toward their engineering degrees.

Days before he ended up in Yakovlev's embassy, Cohon was in Moscow shaking hands on a deal with a Soviet party official. The deal was a remarkably detailed affair, specifying the Soviet role in management and operation as well as the number of restaurants to be provided at which Olympic venues. It even specified the restaurants' opening hours. The agreement had only to be typed up and signed. It was supposed to be ready on a Wednesday morning at 10 a.m. That morning the Soviets called Cohon and told him the contract would be ready for 2 p.m. Then at 2 p.m. they said it wouldn't be ready until the next morning, at 10 a.m. This routine went on for days, then a week. It's a measure of how badly Cohon wanted to win this deal that he waited around for 17 days. It was only then that Cohon heard from the Soviets that the deal was off. They didn't provide a reason.

On his return to Canada Cohon went straight to Yakovlev's Ottawa office. "I thought the signing was just going to be a formality," Cohon said. "And then *poof*, up in smoke. Years of negotiations down the drain."

The ambassador said he'd look into the matter.

It was the conservative Politburo member Mikhail Suslov who killed it, Yakovlev discovered. Having McDonald's providing the food to the crowds and the athletes, Suslov said, would be an admission to the rest of the world that the Soviets weren't up to the task. Days later Yakovlev called back Cohon. "What I can say is that the deal was killed at a very high level," Yakovlev said. Then the ambassador explained a quirk of Soviet psychology to his capitalist friend: in the USSR, they never punished anyone for saying no; only the people who said yes were ever held responsible.

Cohon appeared ready to give up. Sensing this, Yakovlev did something that changed the course of Cohon's life: he encouraged him to keep trying – not for the Olympics, not anymore. Instead, to open a McDonald's in Moscow. To insert a bit of capitalism into the world's communist stronghold. "Don't be discouraged," said the Soviet ambassador. "You must not walk away. The ideology now is not right, but don't be pessimistic. The ideology will change. Something will happen."

Something *did* happen – but not the positive events Yakovlev foretold. In December 1979, the Soviet leadership opened another front in the Cold War by sending the Red Army into Afghanistan. The move set off a domino chain of events. Andrei Sakharov, the Soviet nuclear physicist, denounced the invasion to foreign media. Within days, the Politburo retaliated by forcing Sakharov to move to the industrial city of Gorky, which foreigners were barred from visiting – effectively, a state-provided laryngectomy to the best-known dissident still living in the USSR. The United States responded to the Afghanistan invasion with an embargo on wheat sales to the Soviets. They also pulled out of the Moscow Olympics. Prime Minister Joe Clark followed both measures. Canada restricted diplomatic relations with the USSR. Later the same year the U.S. elected perhaps the most militant Cold Warrior ever to occupy the presidency, a former California governor and Hollywood actor named Ronald Reagan, who was familiar to Yakovlev from their encounter during the ambassador's 1970 tour of America.

Events seemed to be spinning out of control. The Cold War was scary again. Reagan and his conservative advisors made the Soviet Union the focus of American foreign policy. They depicted the Cold War in messianic terms, as a conflict between God-fearing American capitalism and the "evil empire" of godless communism. Yakovlev had an opportunity to witness the Reagan phenomenon up close when the American president conducted his first foreign state visit to Ottawa, where Yakovlev delighted in the propensity of Canadian protesters to mock the U.S. president with comparisons to the chimp who costarred with him in *Bedtime for Bonzo*. Jibes aside, Reagan quickened the pace of an American arms buildup and spoke of a winnable nuclear war.

On top of all this, Yakovlev's father was diagnosed with stomach cancer. The family was close. Each year Yakovlev and his three sisters, and everyone's husbands and wives, returned to Nikolai and Agafya's house, sleeping on the floor and reminiscing about old times. Throughout his life, Aleksandr credited his father, Nikolai, with teaching him the principle of freedom, the edict that, within limits, people should be able to do as they please. On May 21, 1981, the phone rang at the ambassador's residence. Yakovlev took the call in the living room, next to the fireplace. The cancer had won. At 81, his father was dead. Once he set down the receiver Yakovlev stayed still in the chair, his cheeks wet, until 12-year-old Natasha came in and hugged him. Yakovlev returned to Yaroslavl for the funeral. He tried to convince his mother to return to Canada with him, or move to Moscow. She wouldn't. "There is no reason for me to live," she said. Agafya died the following spring, on April 21, 1982.

In such situations, a son's thoughts turn toward his own mortality. He analyzes his own life and examines the opportunity for long-term impact, for changes in the world. Yakovlev felt he still had the capability for great things, but circumstances were preventing him from living up to his potential. Rather than helping improve his country for younger generations, Yakovlev felt as though he was watching the USSR, and the world, lurch toward all-out nuclear war.

"Thus it was with me during my final years in Canada," Yakovlev wrote in his memoirs. "You pretend to be an active, smiling man, but in actuality you are being moved by some internal clockwork mechanism that is independent of your true state of mind. Life moves ahead as if in autopilot. You lose natural curiosity about life and events."

CLEARLY, THE YAKOVLEVS NEEDED A VACATION. And with little else to do in the spring of 1980, Aleksandr, Nina, and Natasha accepted an invitation to visit an unusual community of exiled Russian émigrés who lived in the Kootenay region of southeastern British Columbia. Known as the Doukhobors, the group split from the Russian Orthodox Church in the mid-nineteenth century. Because they emphasized a personal relationship with God they didn't have priests, nor did they worship in churches. In fact, they believed that *any* institution had the potential to compromise the individual's relationship with God, so they didn't recognize the legitimacy of political states or institutions. Private property was anathema to their belief in communal ownership, and as strict pacifists they subscribed to a vegetarian diet. Their refusal to be drafted into the Russian army in the 1890s had triggered reprisals by Tsar Nicholas II. The persecuted group appealed for help from Count Leo Tolstoy, the Russian hero and author of *War and Peace*, who admired their pacifism, and donated the proceeds from his novel *Resurrection* to finance their settlement in British Columbia and Saskatchewan. Once in Canada the group established insular communities that regarded the outside world with wariness, much like the Mennonites or the Amish. Eventually many settled just north of the United States border in the mountain valleys of the Kootenays, living communally in big brick homes that could house up to 50 people at a time, and subsisting on food they grew themselves. Persecution plagued them in Canada as well, thanks to their refusal to recognize the legitimacy of the Canadian government. They declined to register births, deaths, or marriages. Contrary to provincial law they didn't send their children to school. Many detractors disliked in particular the Doukhobors' idiosyncratic practice of registering displeasure by disrobing. Some of the group also had a propensity to protest government measures, or pretty much anything else, by setting fires. At various points through their history many Doukhobors served time in jail, including their long-time spiritual leader, John J. Verigin.

By 1980 the 20,000-strong Doukhobor community had made a fragile peace with the British Columbia government. Verigin had become a well-known figure among the leftist counterculture thanks to his community's practice of sheltering draft-dodging Americans during the Vietnam War – many of whom settled in the Kootenay region. One Doukhobor prophecy foretold an eventual return to their ancestral lands in the Soviet Caucasus, and throughout the 1970s Verigin had arranged several trips to the Soviet Union to investigate the possibility of a return. Yakovlev met Verigin when the spiritual leader required some help with visas. Shortly after, Verigin issued the invitation to visit the community during the highlight of the community calendar, an annual youth festival held during the Victoria Day holiday weekend in May. In accepting, Yakovlev made some requests. He wanted to experience how the Doukhobors really lived, and to stay with a family rather than in a hotel – a request that was happily granted.

The Yakovlevs made a road trip out of the holiday, opting to drive from Ottawa rather than fly into the British Columbia interior. Along with Nina and Natasha, and another family from the embassy, the Soviet ambassador set off west across the rugged glacier-scarred Canadian Shield, heading north of the Great Lakes, through North Bay and Nipigon and Sault Ste. Marie, then joining the lines between the prairies' provincial capitals the way constellations join the lines between stars. After Edmonton, they crossed the Continental Divide as they entered British Columbia, arriving in time for the Victoria Day holiday weekend in the small town of Castlegar, British Columbia, where the youth festival was to be held.

Abruptly and unexpectedly, Yakovlev found himself returned to the Russian countryside of his youth. The festival amounted to three days of singing and dancing. There were competitions and recitals, bake-offs and games and athletic contests, and when some event wasn't happening Yakovlev was off touring a museum or viewing an historic site. The first Soviet ambassador to visit this community of émigré Russians was the guest of honour through it all, of course, particularly after he told a meeting of the community's executive committee that he thought the Soviet Union would benefit from having such hard-working people in its midst.

What Yakovlev did in Castlegar was less important than the milieu in which he found himself. Through 80 years of exile, the Doukhobors had preserved their Russian traditions the way only an isolated religious community can. In a mountain valley in British Columbia, Yakovlev was astonished to find himself in an environment that felt more Russian than the streets of Moscow, that felt, in fact, like the Russia of his childhood. This was as it should be. After their exile beginning in 1899, the Doukhobors had held onto the only connection with home they could preserve – their Russian traditions. Their nostalgia for home preserved these traditions, so that as Yakovlev wandered the river shores and garden plots of Castlegar he found himself transported to the region around his parents home near Yaroslavl. Many of the Doukhobors dressed in traditional Russian costume, down to the babushkas the woman wore over their hair. To one another the Doukhobors spoke a rural Russian dialect, delighting Yakovlev because he heard words and phrases he hadn't come across since adolescence. A similar phenomenon happened during the

Doukhobor choir recital, when Yakovlev found himself able to sing along to many of the traditional songs.

This all prompted a nostalgia that was unexpectedly intense – it was surreal and exhilarating, this bizarre transportation to the Russia of his youth, and he seemed elated throughout his stay. (The sense of unreality increased on the Sunday, when on the other side of the American border, in Washington state, Mount St. Helens erupted, covering everything with a fine ash.) He and Nina and Natasha stayed in Castlegar at the home of Peter and Lisa Voykin, a Doukhobor couple who lived with their 16-year-old daughter on a rural road in the foothills above the town. In a situation similar to that of Yakovlev's parents years before, Peter Voykin worked at a trade – instead of a logger, as Yakovlev's father was, Peter Voykin was a plaster tradesman. On the side, however, the Voykins also farmed their own plot of land, a 1.5-hectare spread that provided them with most of their food. One morning Voykin was cutting brush with a scythe, and Yakovlev came over and asked to try out an implement he hadn't hefted in years. "Ah, that's how it's done," he said, as he swung the curved blade through the grass. At another point Lisa Voykin was in her kitchen preparing blinis and pirozhki for dinner when she noticed Yakovlev watching her hands. It was a little uncomfortable for her having this VIP's attention, until Yakovlev smiled. "You do that just like my mother used to," he said.

Yakovlev was impressed by the Doukhobors – by their lifestyle, the ethical tenets that guided them, and the way they preserved their Russian traditions. He clearly felt some affinity for these émigrés. Like him, the Doukhobors were ardent pacifists. They came from rural Russian stock and, perhaps most affectingly, their unwillingness to conform had led to their being cast from their homeland. When Yakovlev describes the group in his memoirs his prose turns florid, and the words he chooses perhaps unintentionally highlight the parallels he shared with the Doukhobors. "They were batted about the world by the ill will of those with whom they disagreed," Yakovlev wrote. "Unbelievably stout-hearted in the face of destiny's blows, steadfast in their faith . . . Driven by the wind of fate, hounded by the authorities, and tormented by the blows of tragic losses, these stubborn people, though at times naïve in their mis-conceptions, have sustained through all their ordeals an implacability toward deception, hypocrisy, and violence."

He would write a lengthy article about the Doukhobors, including it as the first piece in a collection of his perestroika-related writings. In the essay, he argues that the Doukhobor beliefs of pacifism, universal brotherhood, and equality for all are closely related to the ideals of com-munism. He emphasizes the community's care-taking of orphans, invalids, and the elderly. And he quotes a letter depicting the Doukhobors as "pioneers and fighters for the idea of communism."

Yakovlev would credit his visit to the Doukhobors with reawakening his idealism, and it's not difficult to see why. With their pacifist ways and their respect for the sanctity of the individual, the Doukhobors disproved a depressing line of reasoning that nevertheless had a lot of currency among Yakovlev's comrades in the Communist Party apparat, particularly his radical nationalist enemies in the *Molodaya Gvardiya* camp. This reason-ing says the people who trace their ethnic heritage to the land of the tsars are different from other nationalities. Russians, this reasoning proclaims, can endure extraordinary hardship. They are stubborn. They have a spirit that doesn't break under the most difficult conditions. In fact, this strength of character is so marked, and so incorrigible, that it explains the inabil-ity of foreign conquerors to win any battle for Russia. No invader, this group proclaims, has ever been able to hold the land of the Rus. And it's the character of the Russian people that makes their land indomitable.

A corollary to this line of thinking explains the *Animal Farm*-like polit-ical cycle that perpetually befalls Russia. Why does Russia keep ending up with dictators? Why *not* democracy? Ah, the Russian patriots pro-claim, it's because Russians are *different*. The character of the Russian people is so strong that they *require* dictators to keep them in line.

By the time Yakovlev was cruising with Nina and Natasha over thousands of miles of Canadian roadway, he had witnessed Canada's parliamentary-style democracy in action for seven years. During that period he had witnessed three federal elections. He had attended polit-ical conventions and watched countless hours of parliamentary debates.

He had discussed democratic theory with both Trudeau and Head. He had lots of ideas about how to humanize socialism in the Soviet Union. But he wouldn't have been Russian if one doubt didn't stick in his reformist's mind: What if Russia *was* different? Sure, performance-based incentives might encourage Saskatchewan farm workers to work harder and more productively than Yakovlev ever thought possible. And sure, perhaps in Charlottetown, the populace would tolerate changes in political leadership without any noticeable difference in day-to-day life. The *Globe and Mail* might criticize the government without seriously destabilizing the country – but could *Izvestia*? Was it possible that something in the Russian character prevented democracy from taking hold there?

And yet, the Doukhobor culture and traditions Yakovlev came across in Canada in the spring of 1980 were as Russian as any he'd ever seen. With the Red Army in Afghanistan and Soviet forces deploying deadly SS-20 missiles in Europe, with Brezhnev's cult of personality building and his own Canadian exile showing no signs of conclusion, Yakovlev might have been forgiven for losing some of the idealism that marked his career. Then, just as he was losing hope that Soviet socialism could ever be humanized, at the lowest point in his life, his visit to the Doukhobors reawakened the drive to change things.

AT ABOUT THE SAME TIME as the Doukhobor trip, Yakovlev received some intriguing reports on party politics from friends visiting from Moscow. Such prominent figures as the Soviet expert on North America, Georgi Arbatov, and the poet Yevgeny Yevtushenko whispered to him about the man who, in 1980, became at the age of 49 the youngest full member of the Politburo. His name was Mikhail Gorbachev. Yakovlev recognized the name; in the early 1970s, Yakovlev had heard about some of Gorbachev's experiments with agriculture when the younger man was party secretary in the southern Russian province of Stavropol. He had even suggested that Gorbachev become the head of AgitProp, but Gorbachev hadn't wanted the job.

As the buzz built around Gorbachev, Canada underwent its second election in as many years, thanks to the fall of the unstable minority government of Prime Minister Joe Clark. The threat to Canadian unity represented by Quebec nationalism convinced Trudeau to reconsider his retirement. Yakovlev watched Trudeau fight his third federal campaign, a majority win for the veteran, and noted in an article he published pseudonymously in *Novy Mir* that the prime minister "returned to his old hunting grounds more enriched in charisma, enjoying the backing of both the whole of his party and the whole of his nation" – an observation that reflected Yakovlev's admiration for Trudeau more than it did the Canadian situation. Trudeau was at this point occupied with fighting Quebec nationalism, assisting in the defeat of a referendum on independence, held just 10 weeks after he was sworn into office. Even against this backdrop, however, Trudeau found time for Yakovlev. He visited Yakovlev's home on a Sunday to inform the ambassador that Canada would sell wheat to a Soviet Union made desperate by the American embargo. The resulting deal drew little official recognition for Yakovlev, but it's certain to have gained the notice of the Politburo.

With Trudeau back, Yakovlev once again had access to Canada's corridors of power. He returned to lobbying senior government officials to pay visits to the Soviet Union. Rather than focusing on Trudeau, Yakovlev devoted much of his attention to the Canadian minister of agriculture, a southern Ontario farmer named Eugene Whelan, one of the most visible characters in Trudeau's cabinet thanks to his predilection for wearing enormous green Stetson cowboy hats. Even in the tense atmosphere following the war in Afghanistan, a visit by Whelan to the USSR wasn't such an outlandish notion, considering that Canadian grain sales to the USSR amounted to $1.8 billion a year in that era, almost single-handedly making the country Canada's fourth-largest trading partner. Whelan's visit was especially crucial now because Gorbachev happened to be the party secretary for agriculture. If Yakovlev could get Whelan to Moscow, the ambassador could use the excuse of diplomatic protocol to push Whelan into inviting Gorbachev on a reciprocal visit to Canada – where Yakovlev could lobby for an end to his exile in addition to showcasing the benefits to agricultural production of democracy and capitalist reform.

Whelan and Yakovlev would get together for lunches at Ottawa's Château Laurier Hotel where Yakovlev would pepper Whelan with all sorts of questions about agriculture, about productivity rates in livestock and oil seeds, or the volume of citrus fruits the country imported. Sometimes, just to bait Yakovlev, Whelan would point to the Russian's stiff left leg, and accuse him of faking his old war wound – was his knee fused that way to hide recording equipment for the Commies back home?

Bowing to Yakovlev's incessant badgering, Whelan finally conducted a week-long tour of the Soviet Union in the last week of September 1982. During the tour, Whelan had a four-hour meeting with Gorbachev that culminated with Whelan inviting Gorbachev to Canada. Gorbachev accepted in principle. Trouble was, with power in the Politburo so delicately balanced, the agriculture secretary's colleagues wouldn't allow their young associate to make such a profile-raising trip.

MEANWHILE, YAKOVLEV KILLED TIME. There was ice fishing, sledding parties, and openings for exhibits of Soviet art. The object of his study, Canadian politics, entered a fascinating period in the aftermath of the 1980 referendum on Quebec sovereignty, Trudeau was obsessed with patriating the Canadian constitution and amending it to secure individuals against rights abuses. This led to a nationwide conversation about constitutional issues that resulted in the April 1982 passing of a new Canadian constitution, including a new Charter of Rights and Freedoms. It was in this period that Yakovlev found the time to write his pseudonymous articles on Canadian political and cultural affairs for such Soviet journals as *Novy Mir*, about such topics as the McDonald Commission, the Doukhobors, and the Trudeau government's efforts to nationalize Canadian oil resources. He attended the twenty-fifth anniversary of the Pugwash Movement for nuclear disarmament, in Pugwash, Nova Scotia. In July of 1982 he became dean of Ottawa's diplomatic corps, an honorary position accorded to the capital's longest-serving ambassador, which required him to represent the embassies and their staffs to the Canadian government. The position helped him develop a friendship with Canada's nominal head of state, Governor General Ed Schreyer, a former Manitoba premier for the socialist New Democratic Party. Schreyer brought the writer Farley Mowat to the Yakovlevs' for dinner (along with Lily Schreyer and Claire Mowat); the couples had such a good time that Mowat and Schreyer opted for a shortcut as they returned to Rideau Hall. Rather than walk around to the main gate, Canada's head of state and the nation's most famous writer scaled the official residence's antique iron fence.

Yakovlev, the inveterate America watcher, also monitored Reagan's every pronouncement. The experience provided him with an understanding of the administration and its motives that would serve Yakovlev well in years to come. His observations about the Reagan administration during this period, delivered during a lunchtime address to Toronto's Empire Club, indicate that Yakovlev had even then moved past the binary, us-versus-them, black-white thinking of the Cold War. The speech was a sophisticated analysis of the American interplay between politics and culture. Yakovlev used the behaviour of characters played by John Wayne as a metaphor for the Reagan administration's conception of the Cold War. John Wayne characters, Yakovlev observed to the gathering of Toronto business leaders, "were familiar with two colours only, black and white, two types of people, good and bad, with two symbols dividing the world, Good and Evil. This might be viewed lightly if the subject was confined just to cinema. But regarded in terms of real life, the Wayne concept is a dismal and frightening one." Especially considering, Yakovlev said, the way Wayne's characters regarded those who dissented with American sentiments as "not quite human, as second-rate people who deserve extermination." For Yakovlev geopolitics was far more complicated.

Finally, the Kremlin's so-called ossified gerontocracy showed its first signs of fracture. The impetus was no spring chicken himself. KGB Chief Yuri Andropov was 68, with chronic kidney problems. Despite the battles he and his agents fought with Yakovlev over the years, Andropov was more intelligent, and less hypocritical, than many of his Politburo comrades. Yes, he was credited with popularizing the tactic of punitive psychiatry, which amounted to diagnosing hard-to-control elements with schizophrenia and then sending them to some out-of-the-way sanitarium. Still, his forebears had favoured more brutal methods. And he seemed to honestly want to cleanse the Soviet Union of its paralyzing corruption.

It was in the waning months of 1981 that Yakovlev first began hearing about corruption scandals tied to Brezhnev's friends and family. That Brezhnev's family was corrupt was no secret among the ranks of the Party. What was new was the fact the KGB was finally investigating the allegations – an indication, perhaps, of the frail state of Brezhnev's health, and the strength of Andropov's ambitions. The resulting scandal implicated Brezhnev's daughter, Galina, in a diamond-thieving scheme. The whispers that reached Yakovlev in Ottawa described $1 million in diamonds and $200,000 in cash found at the home of one of the couple's best friends, the director of the Soviet national circus. Such crimes were serious, with a possible maximum sentence of the death penalty.

But Andropov couldn't act alone. In January of 1982, Andropov showed the results of the investigation to Suslov. The resultant confrontations apparently were too much for the 79-year-old Suslov, who suffered a stroke that night and died a few days later. Galina's friends were rounded up and arrested on the morning of Suslov's funeral. To Yakovlev, it was clear what was happening: Andropov was attempting to discredit Brezhnev and push the long-serving and ailing general secretary into retirement. It was a power grab, a non-violent, slow-motion putsch.

Andropov replaced Suslov as the Party's second-most powerful figure. Soon after, Brezhnev suffered yet another stroke. Andropov's new role provided him a position from which to push finally for change. Soviet agriculture was approaching a crisis. More food than the Soviet Union imported rotted each year thanks to poor planning or inadequate storage facilities. After three consecutive poor harvests, the U.S. Department of Agriculture – the most reliable source of information on Soviet crops – forecast in June 1982 a fall harvest that was three-quarters of the official projections. Andropov began a drive to improve things that saw the secretary for agriculture, Mikhail Gorbachev, touring the countryside searching for solutions.

Yakovlev redoubled his efforts to get Gorbachev to Ottawa. Amid this climate of official interest in agricultural reform, Yakovlev was able to arrange a meeting with Gorbachev during one of his regular home visits. Gorbachev sounded interested in a visit to Canada. "You push it," Gorbachev told Yakovlev. "Write the telegrams and make Andropov agree."

Andropov's manoeuvring touched off skirmishes throughout the Party between the reformers and their orthodox opponents. One of the most reform-minded Moscow think tanks was IMEMO, the Institute of World Economy and International Relations, led by a courageous academic named Nikolai Inozemtsev. After Suslov's death such hard-line Politburo members as Moscow party boss Viktor Grishin targeted Inozemtsev's institute in an all-out campaign to silence its calls for a more open Soviet society. Grishin led an investigation into IMEMO that concluded Zionist elements were encouraging Inozemtsev and his associates to destabilize the leadership of the country. As it was calculated to do, stress related to the Grishin investigation caused Inozemtsev to suffer health problems. He died of a heart attack in August 1982, leaving vacant what must have been an alluring pulpit for any reform-minded political observer.

IN NOVEMBER 1982, Yakovlev was relaxing in his sauna when there was a knock on the door. Few people were allowed to bother Yakovlev in this wood-panelled chamber; only Nina, who worried about him setting the heat too high. When the door opened, though, Yakovlev saw the embassy's ranking KGB representative dressed in his overcoat and winter hat. The agent apologized. He said the matter was urgent. Yakovlev braced himself for news of some fresh hell. Which diplomats were exiled? What country had the Red Army invaded this time? The man leaned in close to Yakovlev's ear, and spoke.

"Brezhnev has died."

Yakovlev sat up and frowned. "Why are you whispering?"

The KGB chief straightened his posture. "It's frightening somehow."

"Why? You should be happy. Your man" – Yakovlev meant Andropov – "will take control now."

There was a silence as the agent considered Yakovlev's prediction. Then he brightened and left Yakovlev alone in the sauna to ponder the import of the news.

Brezhnev's death meant change.

Perhaps it could also mean an end to exile.

As Yakovlev predicted, Andropov succeeded Brezhnev, and Andropov's protégé, Gorbachev, received a boost in power. The new leader's first speech as party leader called for increased productivity and improved management in agriculture. Suddenly, rather than crowing about the achievements of the collective farmers, the Soviet media were criticizing their inefficiency. Stories chronicling waste in the transport system became commonplace; the December 17, 1982 edition of the daily newspaper *Izvestiya* featured three front-page stories depicting agricultural problems, with more features inside. Also suddenly, the obstacles to Gorbachev's travel disappeared.

With Gorbachev now eager to make the trip, Canada sent out an official invitation on January 25, 1983. By March the dates were finalized as May 16 to 26, including the spring holiday of Victoria Day.

The visit would be the biggest event of Yakovlev's Canadian posting, and it was approaching fast.

MISHA IN THE OTHER WORLD

THE WEEKS LEADING up to the trip were a flurry of anxious prepa- rations. Designing Gorbachev's itinerary was the dual rubric of the two Canadian ministries involved, External Affairs and Agriculture. But it was Yakovlev and his behind-the-scenes badgering that turned the trip into a primer on Canada and the West. Yakovlev wanted Gorbachev to witness in 10 days much of what Yakovlev had seen in 10 years. External Affairs asked whether Gorbachev should see a hockey game. No, Yakovlev replied. There was too much else to do. Yakovlev wanted Gorbachev to meet with the prime minister, and leaders of the opposition parties. Gorbachev should see Question Period, the bellicose, debate-laden sessions when opposition members of Parliament hurled loaded inquiries at the prime minister and his Liberal associates. As for the agricultural component, after one meeting with Yakovlev, Canadian bureaucrats noted, "Mr. Gorbachev should be exposed to our food chain from the fields right through to the supermar- kets." Yakovlev wanted Gorbachev to see beef-packaging facilities and vegetable storage methods. He wanted Gorbachev to see chicken farms, tomato-growing greenhouse operations, wheat fields and meat-process- ing plants. Detailed requests came from Gorbachev, too: animal-feed production techniques interested him, as did the growing of forage and automatic feeding techniques, among other subjects. Underlying all these requests was the encouraging sign that Gorbachev, different from his predecessors as the Party's agriculture secretary, understood there were benefits to understanding how farms worked in a foreign system – and rather than decrying that system as capitalist, or anti-Soviet, Gorbachev was receptive to learning from the experience. It was a profound cultural shift from the days when Yakovlev's telegrams went unread in Moscow.

Yakovlev consulted with Gorbachev during a February trip to Moscow. During the same visit, Yakovlev began discussing with associates his interest in the still-vacant director's position at the Institute of World Economy and International Relations. Once he was back in Ottawa, Yakovlev negotiated the size of the delegation Gorbachev was allowed to bring (18 people) and whether the accompanying Soviet security detail could carry firearms (no). By April 5, the program for the visit had been hashed out by all parties. Yakovlev got pretty much everything he wanted. The one thing External Affairs couldn't arrange was a meeting with Trudeau. This was supposed to be a parliamentary visit; it would have been unusual, in terms of protocol, for the delegation leader to be received by the prime minister. The best External could do was a meeting with Secretary of State Allan MacEachen, and even that was a little unusual. Because Gorbachev was the Party's agriculture secretary, he should have been happy to be received by his closest Canadian counterpart, Minister of Agriculture Eugene Whelan.

Even without the Trudeau encounter, the visit was shaping up to be a maelstrom of faces and meetings. The first two days were to be spent in Ottawa, where Canadian officials would provide Gorbachev with an education in parliamentary democracy, featuring Gorbachev's first public encounter with a Western political audience, an appearance before the federal government's Standing Committee on External Affairs and National Defence. Then Gorbachev, Yakovlev, Whelan, and the delegation of interpreters, diplomats, and Soviet parliamentarians would set out in an aged prop-driven plane Whelan had rented to shuttle them around Canada. Their first stop outside of Ottawa would be Essex County, where

Whelan lived, then on through the breadbasket of southern Ontario, to Niagara Falls and Toronto, and on to Alberta, where the attraction would be cattle-ranching operations. Saskatchewan's canola farming, Manitoba wheat fields, and dairy processing facilities in Montreal were to round out the trip. Then Gorbachev's people cut the trip short by three days, thanks to a conflict with a Communist Party gathering; Saskatchewan, Manitoba and Quebec would not be graced with his presence.

By mid-April, with barely a month before Gorbachev's arrival, a meeting between Trudeau and Gorbachev still wasn't certain. But Yakovlev kept up his lobbying. He thought it important to expose Gorbachev to Trudeau, and to his unconventional political mind. Also, arranging a meeting with the prime minister would prove to Gorbachev that Yakovlev had influence in Ottawa. Yakovlev could have simply called up his old friend to argue for the importance of meeting with Gorbachev. But this was no longer the era of détente. Official encounters with Soviet politicians came with political costs for Trudeau in the atmosphere of heightened East–West conflict.

In meeting after meeting with lower-ranking diplomats, Yakovlev pointed out the 52-year-old Gorbachev's position as the youngest full member of the Politburo. A close rapport existed between Andropov and Gorbachev, Yakovlev said, and there was a good chance Gorbachev would come bearing a personal message from Andropov for the prime minister. Finally, Yakovlev's badgering paid off. One day Trudeau called the Soviet ambassador. "Why do you insist that Gorbachev be received at the highest level?" he asked Yakovlev.

"Gorbachev is the future leader of our country," Yakovlev responded.

"Are you sure?"

"I'm sure."

Trudeau agreed to the meeting.

ON APRIL 25, Yakovlev began a 10 day visit to Moscow to prepare Gorbachev for the trip. These meetings would prove significant on several levels. Gorbachev's Canada trip was being discussed in Moscow as something of an acid test; his older colleagues in the Politburo were curious whether Gorbachev could manage diplomatic affairs. Soviet politicians tended to be nervous about the sort of unscripted, unpredictable encounters Gorbachev would face during his trip across Canada. Even a diplomat as skilled as Soviet Foreign Minister Andrei Gromyko cancelled a press conference during a 1975 trip to Canada because his aides didn't want him to be "humiliated by provocative questions." Provocative questions were what Gorbachev had to prove he could handle. For the first time, Gorbachev would be interrogated by Western politicians. In his encounter with Trudeau and his appearance before Canadian parliamentarians, Gorbachev needed to be able to defend himself and the Soviet Union without alienating potential allies. It was a tricky task to get the right tone. He had to appear strong without seeming scary, knowledgeable without appearing coached. He required enough command of the facts to be able to think on his feet. Gorbachev's success therefore rested on Yakovlev's ability to prepare him. If Gorbachev did well, Yakovlev gained the favour of the Party's heir apparent, a man with the ability to end the Soviet ambassador's exile. The two men were dependent on one another – the first such situation among many to come.

Their relations in these meetings would set the tone for their friendship. Gorbachev had the power and the charisma. Yakovlev had the knowledge. To an ambitious Gorbachev already assembling a brain trust of potential advisors, Yakovlev represented an attractive candidate. Among reform-minded party members, no one had more experience in the West than Yakovlev.

Over five or six meetings they had together while Yakovlev was in Moscow, the Soviet ambassador attempted to prepare Gorbachev for every contingency. The Canadians were certain to ask Gorbachev about Jewish emigration, KGB spying, and disarmament issues, including the insertion of SS-20s in Europe. Yakovlev helped Gorbachev develop responses that seemed upfront and frank, while spinning the issue to the Soviet advantage. "One could notice that Gorbachev was more tolerant, more practical. He trusted his own eyes rather than the writings of the classics," Yakovlev would say later. "During the preparation of his visit

I understood that this [was] to a certain extent a man of the new era. He was still slowed down by the chains of the old order, but his conscience was already different – more relaxed and more tolerant . . . I told him, of course, about agriculture, [the] judicial system, and elections, about what I liked and what I did not. He was listening very carefully. More and more confidence appeared in our conversations – he stopped being scared of me, and I stopped thinking of him as [a] member of [the] Politburo, and that I had to be afraid of him."

During this trip, too, Yakovlev is certain to have sounded party opinion on the race to succeed Inozemtsev as the director of IMEMO. Someone would have to be named to the position soon – IMEMO had been without a chief for going on nine months. But the latest news was disappointing. Yakovlev's name wasn't being mentioned among the front-runners. His exile had left him without much of a profile in Moscow, particularly among academic circles. Among the front-runners, one of whom was IMEMO's current deputy director, many had better ties to Andropov's circle.

On May 4, his last full day in Moscow, Yakovlev met with the Canadian ambassador to the Soviet Union, Geoffrey Pearson, to discuss the Gorbachev visit. Confessions of worry formed a significant portion of Yakovlev's contribution to the conversation. He said he was anxious about Gorbachev's appearance before Ottawa's External Affairs Committee. Gorbachev's encounters with the Canadian media worried him, as did confrontations with anti-Soviet demonstrations. The visit to Toronto stood the biggest chance of triggering some sort of protest. Was two nights in Toronto too long? Yakovlev asked. Perhaps they should switch where they were staying, from downtown to a lower-profile location in the suburbs (they did end up staying in an airport hotel). After almost a decade of waiting, Yakovlev clearly understood that he approached his best opportunity yet to return to the USSR.

YAKOVLEV'S TENSION matched what existed on the international stage between the United States and the Soviet Union. As Yakovlev prepared for Gorbachev's arrival, President Reagan was in the midst of using Soviet deployment of SS-20s in Europe, and the Afghanistan invasion, among other events, to justify an arms buildup that would nearly double the Pentagon's budget between 1980 and 1985. NATO was set to deploy in Western Europe its own super-accurate intermediate-range nuclear missiles, dubbed Pershing IIs, which could reach Moscow just 10 minutes after launch. Meanwhile, Andropov had the Soviet intelligence apparatus on heightened alert because he believed the Americans could be planning a surprise attack.

Just weeks before Gorbachev was to arrive in Ottawa, Reagan single-handedly brought the world closer to nuclear war with two speeches spaced 15 days apart. Before an organization called the National Association of Evangelicals, Reagan referred to Moscow's "evil empire" and portrayed the United States as "enjoined by scripture and the Lord Jesus to oppose it with all our might." Next he voiced his plan to fund a network of satellite-born lasers and "particle beams" that would defend the territorial United States from Soviet nuclear missiles. With *Return of the Jedi* about to be released in theatres, Reagan's Strategic Defense Initiative became known as "Star Wars." Reagan knew the United States spent much less on weaponry, proportional to the size of the economy, than the Soviet Union did, and such brinksmanship was calculated to push the Soviets into bankruptcy. Certainly, it risked the lives of every-one on the planet by worsening an already anxious nuclear standoff.

Popular culture reflected the anxieties of the age. One of the movie hits of the year was *WarGames*, a fable about the futility of nuclear war. Just months before, Canada's National Film Board won an Oscar for the era's version of *An Inconvenient Truth*, the short documentary *If You Love This Planet*. The film was such a powerful anti-war statement it was decried by the U.S. Justice Department as "foreign propaganda." Canadian cities hosted the biggest peace marches since the 1960s – 65,000 in Vancouver alone – as the nation debated whether to allow testing on Canadian soil of another new American weapon. The cruise missile was a 6.3-metre-long stubby-winged jet aircraft designed to sneak a nuclear warhead past Soviet radar by hugging the ground with navigation systems that recognized the terrain it flew over. A single battleship equipped with cruise missiles would reportedly contain more destructive power than all the bombs dropped in the Second World War. The Pentagon planned to deploy more than 7,000 across the world, and in test launches the missile's navigation system worked well enough over rugged California. But the flat, snow-covered, and nearly featureless landscape of Soviet Siberia was another matter, which explained the American desire to try the missiles in the similar territory of the Canadian Arctic. Still stung by Soviet deployment of SS-20 missiles, Trudeau was inclined to allow the testing, arguing the step was Canada's duty as a NATO member. And the Doomsday Clock, the symbolic timepiece used by the Bulletin of the Atomic Scientists at the University of Chicago to indicate the immediate threat of nuclear war, stood at four minutes to midnight – closer to Armageddon than at anytime since the aftermath of the Cuban missile crisis.

Amid this climate, Gorbachev flew into Ottawa on Monday, May 16, and arrived at 4 p.m. Yakovlev and Whelan were there to greet him. To mark the occasion Gorbachev recited the usual boilerplate on Canadian–Soviet relations, tweaked to reflect current anxieties. "The USSR and Canada are the two largest countries in the world with similar natural, climactic, and geographical conditions . . . We are neighbours separated from each other by only the Arctic Ocean," Gorbachev said. "The Soviet Union holds that no matter how complicated the situation may be, opportunities for overcoming the dangerous stretch in international relations do exist. It is essential to halt the drift to nuclear war, to end the arms race, to create at least a modicum of confidence in relations between states, and to renew the process of international détente."

A jet-lagged Gorbachev had a rejuvenating sleep at 7 Rideau Gate, a government residence just down the street from Yakovlev's home. Then the challenges began. The next morning, Yakovlev went with Gorbachev and an interpreter, among other Soviets, to room 253-D of the Centre Block on Ottawa's Parliament Hill to face Canada's Standing Committee on External Affairs and National Defence, composed of members from both the House of Commons and the Senate.

At 10:45, Committee Chairman Marcel Prud'homme called the meeting to order, made the usual administrative remarks, then invited Gorbachev to deliver his opening comments. He did quite a bit more than that. "Ladies and gentlemen," Gorbachev began, "allow me to take advantage of this meeting to share my thoughts with regard to what is disturbing the Soviet leaders and the Soviet people today." Gorbachev referred to the "tense international situation" and the "great uproar in the West about . . . Soviet military superiority." Then he did everything he could to humanize the Soviet side of the Cold War. "What possible motive could the Soviet Union have for bringing matters to the point of war?" he asked, invoking the carnage wreaked by the Second World War, and the pains Soviet citizens had taken to rebuild their society. "We have not done all that in order to have everything destroyed once again," he said. Time and time again, Gorbachev said, the U.S. had escalated the arms race, forcing the Soviet Union to respond by developing similar weapons. And now, Gorbachev noted, "The war machine is again gathering momentum, insatiably devouring huge resources; its sole product can only be new and still more horrible means of war." He ran through several arms limitation proposals the Soviets had made, such as Moscow's pledge not to be the first to use nuclear weapons – a pledge, he noted, that the West had not reciprocated. "We want to see all aspects of the strategic arms race stopped," he said, finally bringing up the cruise missile, which, he argued, both countries should agree not to deploy. Next came Reagan's Star Wars initiative. "This no-so-bright idea may create a most dangerous situation," Gorbachev said. "If it becomes a reality, then it will be still another move threatening escalation of both the offensive and defensive arms race . . . The arms race must be halted where it is and not permitted to start in areas where it does not exist." He finished with a passionate appeal for closer relations between Canada and the Soviet Union. "The distance between the continents should not be measured by the minutes of flight of ballistic missiles," he closed, "but by the closeness of our human values, the most basic of which is life itself."

Gorbachev had spoken for almost 20 minutes. It was a remarkable opening statement. Until now, Soviet politicians clogged their speeches with Marxist-Leninist dogma, with paeans to past leaders, with digressions on the evils of capitalism and the superiority of the Soviet system – all of which were wasted on Western ears. Gorbachev did none of that. His speech was attuned to the current concerns and sensibilities of a North American audience. He came off like a human being who realized he was speaking to other human beings. Given the tone, the fact the speech reflected an eyewitness's currency with North American affairs, and Yakovlev's experience as a speechwriter for Brezhnev, among other Politburo heavies, the Soviet ambassador probably played an important role in the drafting of Gorbachev's opening remarks.

Prud'homme opened the floor to questions. The first was from Allan McKinnon, an MP from the comparatively pro-U.S. Progressive Conservative Party. "I must say I found comfort in some of your remarks, but as so frequently happens when we try to understand the USSR, I found I was mystified by some of your other remarks." There was a pause. McKinnon asked Gorbachev to go back to 1979, after President Carter had signed SALT II, which was up for ratification by the U.S. Senate when the news about the SS-20s "chilled" those prospects. Then came the Afghanistan invasion. McKinnon asked whether the Soviet Union had stopped to consider they might endanger SALT II's ratification when they invaded Afghanistan?

Gorbachev responded as though he was expecting the question. "There is a widespread conception in the West that the process of détente and the fate of SALT II are tied to events in Afghanistan . . . We are not in agreement with that evaluation." What followed was a tidy chronology of recent Afghan history that employed the euphemisms and doublethink of a master propagandist. Gorbachev mentioned Afghanistan's 1978 Marxist revolt and the way the U.S. was supporting "counterrevolutionary forces" through such intermediaries as Pakistan and Iran. "By the end of 1979 we had essentially a situation where an undeclared war was being waged against the new regime." After repeated requests for help from the country's Marxist leaders, Gorbachev said, the Soviet Union decided to send "a limited contingent of armed forces" to assist "the legitimate representatives of the people . . . We want to see this problem resolved as soon as possible."

McKinnon's follow-up question attempted to catch Gorbachev in a logical fallacy. The Canadian politician observed how Brezhnev had said the U.S. and the USSR had about equal nuclear arms in 1979. And yet, McKinnon said, the Soviet Union had been deploying one SS-20 missile a week since then, totalling about 250 missiles. "Why do you keep on deploying these things if you had equality in 1979?"

Gorbachev's answer seemed to contradict McKinnon. "We undertook a unilateral commitment not to deploy missiles, you will remember, at one time. And we are not deploying these missiles . . . as of the beginning of negotiations." He repeated himself. "We committed ourselves unilaterally, to cease deployment . . . and after that, we have not been deploying these missiles."

"Since when?" McKinnon asked.

"My Soviet friends will help me with the date here," Gorbachev said, engaging in a round of consultation. "We have been observing this – 1981."

There was no opportunity for rebuttal; the committee chair said the volume of questions required him to move on to the next question, which was a gimme. A Canadian senator asked whether "Mr. Gorbachev" saw any "special role" for Canada, "given the fact that we are the meat in the sandwich between the two of you superpowers?" Gorbachev saw the opportunity to discuss cruise missiles and seized it. He first credited Trudeau and the Canadian government with a role in establishing détente – likely another Yakovlev plant referring to the line in Ottawa that cited Trudeau's 1971 trip to Moscow as opening the door for Nixon's détente-establishing visit in 1972. Now, though, Gorbachev said, he wanted to draw attention to the possibility of Canada testing cruise missiles. "This cannot but disturb us," he said. "Without meddling in your affairs . . . I would simply like to draw your attention to this problem."

"There are many of us who are quite disturbed about the cruise missile testing," observed the next questioner, Dr. Pauline Jewett, the External Affairs critic for the New Democratic Party, calling the cruise "a highly destabilizing escalation." She noted the Soviets also were guilty of destabilization, with the SS-20 deployments. "Why, really why . . . were these SS-20s introduced? Why are they continually added to, particularly in Soviet Europe and also Soviet Asia? As I say, I think that was the most destabilizing thing the Soviet Union has done."

It was exactly the sort of question Yakovlev wanted Gorbachev to have to confront. Jewett's question strived to reach Gorbachev as a human being, rather than as a hostile enemy. Her remarks were an appeal against escalation, a sober inquiry from a sober person alarmed by the indiscriminate way two superpowers were fooling around with the lives of every person on the planet. And Gorbachev met her on a similar footing. His response portrayed the Soviets as simply trying to match the number of weapons the West had in Europe. "But let us not talk about the arithmetic of the situation," Gorbachev said. "Because we both have these figures. The point is, we should be aiming at a situation where there are no missiles in Europe." Neither Britain nor France would give up their own nuclear arms, Gorbachev acknowledged. "Then we would have, on the Soviet side alone, enough missiles to offset those missiles. At any rate, we should aim at equality . . . but all the time bringing the levels down until we have finally gotten rid of them all.

"As far as the missiles stationed in Asia are concerned, what do you expect from us?" Gorbachev asked. "There are missiles in South Korea and on ships in the Pacific. The Nakasone government have agreed to turn Japan into an unsinkable missile carrier . . . What position are we to adopt? We cannot ignore the situation. Therefore, as far as the missiles in Asia are concerned . . . let us start work on limitation there as well." And limitation, Gorbachev said, should lead to "a total ban."

Such rhetoric had been issued before by the Soviets. But in the past the offers always seemed to be bluffs. When Gorbachev talked of total disarmament, he seemed to mean it. His response connected with Dr. Jewett; Gorbachev seemed to realize the insane situation the two superpowers had gotten themselves into, and to want to get out of it as much as anyone else.

Subsequent questions touched on Jewish refuseniks, the situation in the Middle East, the tensions in Poland, and North–South relations. Gorbachev demonstrated a facility with the facts. He cited the percentage of GNP the USSR contributed to international aid, the minutiae of statistics relating to Jewish emigration, and an awareness of Soviet problems with acid rain. Never mind that his figures were likely invented by distant party functionaries; he came off as well prepared. It helped, too, that the format favoured Gorbachev. Disallowing follow-up questions, as the committee chair had done, meant Gorbachev had only to talk around an uncomfortable issue, then wait for the next question.

As the committee was about to wrap up, Yakovlev was no doubt pleased with how things had gone. Gorbachev hadn't lost his temper, as Khrushchev had done in past decades. Nor had this jet-lagged Soviet minister committed Brezhnev's gaffe of drifting off at the microphone. The Politburo member was eloquent and empathetic. Like a stand-up comedian he was eager to get the room on his side. In fact, his ingratiating manner and obvious desire to charm resembled the conduct of a Western politician. "The thought ran through my mind that he could run for election – if they had elections," McKinnon quipped to one reporter.

"It was very clear that he had done his homework beforehand; he was extremely well briefed," recalls Jim Wright, who witnessed Gorbachev's performance as the Soviet desk officer in Canada's Department of External Affairs. "It was not something we expected from a Soviet Politburo representative. We expected someone who was going to be stoic, very Soviet, hard-line. We also expected that he was going to be a bit defensive. Because that was the style. When Soviets travelled in the West they always felt as though there was a bit of a chip on their shoulders, they were uncomfortable outside of their own setting. But Gorbachev was quite the opposite. He was charming. He was funny. People were genuinely impressed, that they were witnessing the performance of a new type of Soviet politician."

Five minutes after the committee was supposed to end, the chair recognized Allan Lawrence, a Progressive Conservative MP who had been signalling his intention to ask a question since the start of the meeting. "Be very, very brief," Prud'homme asked.

Lawrence ignored him. Speaking to Gorbachev, Lawrence said, "Obviously one of your purposes in being here, and we welcome it, is to knock down, to destroy, some of the distrust that exists in the Western world about the motivation and the long-term aims of the Soviet Union. I do not understand, sir, therefore, why the Soviet Union continues to place KGB agents . . . as it does in all the Western capitals. For instance, in the Ottawa embassy here it has been estimated that fully two-thirds of the staff of our genial ambassador here have had direct KGB training – "

"A question please," Prud'homme interrupted.

Lawrence quickened his pace. "If we are trying to break down this distrust, why do you find it necessary to have so many espionage agents, for instance, here in Ottawa?"

More than any time in the previous 90 minutes, Gorbachev bristled. "Without sufficient grounds you are accusing the Soviet Union of ill-intentioned things . . . I cannot agree with your characterization of the embassy in Canada." Gorbachev called Lawrence a prisoner of America's "spy mania."

Another good answer. In Canada less than a full day, Gorbachev had already figured out the most effective way to insult a Canadian was to accuse him of being too American. The final question was a lob about the state of the Soviet economy. "The situation with the Soviet economy is one of steady development," Gorbachev replied. And he was done. It was on to the next challenge.

AFTER LUNCH, Yakovlev, Gorbachev, and the rest of the Soviet delegation attended Question Period, where politicians who form the government are subjected to public questioning by opposition MPs. Gorbachev watched Prime Minister Trudeau being condemned by Progressive Conservative members for criticizing President Reagan's "warlike" attitude toward the Soviet Union. Yakovlev intended this stop on the tour to provide Gorbachev with an example of the way opposition politicians represented a check on government power. Gorbachev purported to be unimpressed; he called Question Period a "circus."

The next morning, a Wednesday, Gorbachev met with Trudeau for his first tête-à-tête with a Western political leader. Yakovlev was probably nervous. The previous day had gone well thanks to Yakovlev's coaching. But today was different. Trudeau could be unpredictable. Yakovlev's friendship with the Canadian prime minister was well known in Moscow. If Gorbachev and the prime minister failed to hit it off, then Yakovlev risked a fall in stature in Gorbachev's eyes.

Trudeau indicated with his opening sentences that he didn't intend to go easy on Gorbachev. He mentioned the friendly and productive relations of the early 1970s. Unfortunately, Trudeau said, the Soviet invasion of Afghanistan had forced Canada and her allies to "take some distance from earlier days . . . We are not happy with Afghanistan but it is there. Hopefully," Trudeau said, referring Andropov, "the new leadership will find ways to settle the issue."

Gorbachev responded as though he hadn't heard Trudeau. There were predictable platitudes and greetings from Andropov, Gromyko, and others. Then Gorbachev handed over a letter from Andropov, which contained an invitation to Moscow. The prime minister scanned it. Trudeau said he'd visit only under certain conditions, such as some significant Soviet step to decrease international tension over nuclear arms. "To make myself clear," the prime minister said, "I do not think Canadians would want me to visit the USSR unless I could . . . make a useful contribution to the cause of peace."

This was a different prime minister than Yakovlev had ever seen. Yakovlev dealt with the academic intellectual, the idealist who viewed the Soviet ambassador as an equally interested observer in global affairs. But this was Trudeau the statesman confronting a counterpart, one who bore culpability in an elevation of global tensions that greatly concerned him.

Trudeau brought up the SS-20s. Why did the Soviets need the SS-20s in the first place? What was the point? Put on the spot, Gorbachev acknowledged the criticism that the SS-20s introduced new elements to the European arsenals. But their deployment was a response to NATO missiles in Europe. Besides, he said, the SS-20s weren't anything new; they were just normal upgrades of old weapons. And the Soviets were still respecting Brezhnev's moratorium on deploying more weapons, which, he clarified, dated to March 1982 instead of 1981, as he had said the day before. In other words: Sure, people say the SS-20s are new and more dangerous missiles, but the West put us up to it. Besides, they're not *really* new. And besides, we're not putting any more in Europe. The Soviet Union only wants the two sides to have "approximate parity." To be equal, in other words.

Meanwhile, the United States wasn't budging in ongoing arms limitation talks, Gorbachev said. He wondered aloud: Were the talks merely designed as a smoke screen to allow the Americans time to build more weapons? Was Reagan participating in arms limitation talks only because, politically, he felt he had to? Gorbachev mentioned a press report in which one of Reagan's weapons negotiators criticized the president for not making European arms reductions a priority. How serious about the negotiations was the U.S., anyway?

Trudeau had just enough time to credit Gorbachev for understanding the political factors facing Reagan. And then the meeting had to end. There was a break for a few press photos – the two men would appear on the cover of the next day's *Globe and Mail*, shaking hands. But Trudeau wasn't done. Intrigued by this new Soviet politician, he joined Gorbachev and Yakovlev, among others, for a lunch given by the Department of External Affairs in the Pearson Building. There Trudeau transformed into his peacenik incarnation, bouncing ideas off Gorbachev on how to break the deadlock in arms negotiations between the United States and the Soviets. If arms control questions were so tough to agree on, Trudeau said, perhaps there were opportunities for the two superpowers to negotiate about *other* things – maybe something in the Third World, or something even more low-key, such as cultural exchanges. Once the two sides succeeded in agreeing to *something*, maybe then they could tackle more difficult problems.

Then Trudeau brought up the rhetoric used by both sides, which was inflaming the issue. Trudeau disclosed that he had been counselling the Reagan administration to ease their anti-Soviet rhetoric, and noted the president himself "perhaps recognizes some of the excesses which have occurred." Still, he said to Gorbachev, "It is not clear that you are prepared to lower the rhetoric vis-à-vis the U.S."

Now there was some friction. "Frankly, given the character and nature of the U.S. statements, our response has been much lower in tone than the arrogant statements of Reagan," Gorbachev said. "We would and could not employ such terminology." Gorbachev portrayed the Soviet Union as the hard-done-by partner of nuclear arms limitation talks, working for "constructive solutions" while there were indications "that the reduction of missiles in Europe is not an American priority."

Trudeau's response drew on discussions with the whole community of NATO leaders. Like some Canadians, he acknowledged that many Europeans didn't like Reagan's attitude toward arms negotiations. But there were similar problems with the Soviet deployment of SS-20s, he said. The Russians had to "make some move on the SS-20s or there will be no choice for us but to deploy," he said, referring to NATO's plan to place Pershing II missiles in Europe at the end of 1983. "I am speaking to you frankly, Mr. Gorbachev, so you will know there is a lot of criticism of the United States. But on the need for a reduction in the SS-20s, we are in agreement."

Then, as the talk approached its climax, Trudeau softened his message. He assured Gorbachev the Americans would change their tone, and soon. A U.S. election was coming up in the fall of 1984, he said, and Reagan's campaign would be strengthened if he could tell his voters he'd secured some breakthrough in the arms talks. "In this context, I am confident there will be an effort by the U.S. to unlock the situation," Trudeau said.

The prime minister wanted something else clarified. The previous day, Gorbachev had spoken to the External Affairs Committee repeatedly about the "unilateral moratorium" of missile deployment in

Europe. However, Trudeau said, a number of other sources indicated that the Soviets continued to put SS-20s in Europe. Gorbachev's reply came with confidence. "The number of carriers of medium-range missiles has not increased since the moratorium," he said, about the same thing he had told the committee, the day before. But Trudeau had the opportunity to ask follow-ups. The prime minister suggested the Soviets continued to deploy new SS-20 missiles. For each one they added, they removed an older missile – allowing the Soviets to claim they weren't adding to the number of missiles in Europe. But the SS-20s were MIRV missiles; that is, multiple independently targetable re-entry vehicles. Compared to the Soviets' older, single-warhead models, each SS-20 had three nuclear weapons on a single missile. By replacing an old missile with an SS-20, the Soviets could increase their destructive power at least threefold without adding to the overall number of missiles. At that point, Gorbachev changed the subject. "We do not want to get involved with all the details but we have not increased our weapons," he said.

If not strictly a lie, it was certainly semantic obfuscation, and both men knew Trudeau had caught Gorbachev at it. Having established that the Soviets weren't the peaceniks they purported to be, Trudeau let the matter go. He had more important things to discuss with this slippery Soviet politician – such as cruise missile testing. Trudeau said he'd heard the USSR was more worried about Pershing IIs, the American answer to SS-20s, than cruise missiles. Was that true?

Gorbachev responded with a story. Flying on his way toward Ottawa over Canadian terrain, he had looked out the window of his plane. "The land might well have been Siberia or Northern Kazakhstan," he said, observing that the similarity of terrain made it obvious why Canada was contemplating testing the cruise. Gorbachev told Trudeau he was aware of the "lengthy deliberations" surrounding the question of whether to test the cruise missile. The subject concerned the USSR, Gorbachev said. Testing and deploying the missile would be a destabilizing factor – an ominous term.

"Mr. Andropov has indicated he was testing the cruise," Trudeau recounted. "Why not us?"

"You do not have the cruise!" Gorbachev said.

"Agreed," said Trudeau. "We have no atomic weapons." But if the Soviet Union was testing it, he said, why should Canada feel guilty? Both sides saw the cruise as less destabilizing than an ICBM. The cruise was a side issue, Trudeau said, attempting to convince himself. Aloud, he mused that any decision to test the cruise would not contradict "my image as a dove – a peacemaker."

"In U.S. hands, the cruise is a strategic weapon," Gorbachev insisted. "The Americans cannot conduct business in any other manner."

Lunch wrapped up. The men exchanged thanks. Trudeau left Gorbachev with a bit of flattery. Members of Parliament had been impressed with Gorbachev's committee appearance, the day before, Trudeau said. Hopefully, the appearance would lead to increased understanding on both sides. Then he gave his best wishes to Andropov, and was gone.

The encounter lasted two and a half hours. It was testy, overall, but also frank – the sort of a dialogue East and West needed to have more often. Any concerns Yakovlev might have had were allayed that evening, at a party Yakovlev threw for Gorbachev with a guest list of 150 couples. Although Trudeau wasn't expected to attend, he dropped in halfway through dinner and plopped himself down next to Gorbachev. It was a public endorsement and an indication Trudeau thought Gorbachev had performed well in Ottawa. In other words, another challenge passed.

ON THE THURSDAY before Victoria Day weekend, May 19, 1983, the cross-country tour of the Canadian agricultural industry began. Their flying rattletrap of a plane was scheduled to leave once Whelan finished another session of Question Period. But by a coincidence that turned out to be fortuitous for Yakovlev, some inquiry on the part of the opposition, during Question Period, delayed Whelan in Ottawa. He wouldn't be able to leave with the Soviets at 3:45 p.m.; he'd have to catch a different flight later in the afternoon. The logistical tangle meant Yakovlev was able to sit next to Gorbachev during the approximately two-hour flight to their destination in the southwestern Ontario city of Windsor, across the river from Detroit.

Yakovlev and Gorbachev talked through the whole of the flight. Both men must have felt some relief. The stressful aspects of the trip were over and, thanks to the preparation they'd conducted together in Moscow, things had gone well, resulting in a certain mutual trust. As the plane bounced and sank through the clouds, the roar of the propellers afforded the two men some level of protection from other listeners. Here was their first opportunity to get acquainted at leisure, without the time pressure they faced during their Moscow briefing sessions, without the eaves-droppers likely to surround them in Ottawa. For Yakovlev, this was the chance to establish the personal relationship he hoped would secure an end to his dreaded exile. When inclined, both men had significant amounts of personal charm to deploy. With his warm brown eyes, quick smile, and fashionable personal style, Gorbachev had a charisma about him; in North American parlance, compared with other Soviet leaders, Gorbachev was *cool*. Meanwhile, from Gorbachev's perspective, Yakovlev was someone to admire. The two men were only seven years apart in age – Gorbachev's 52 to Yakovlev's 59 – but Yakovlev was from a different gen-eration. Gorbachev had been too young to fight in the Second World War. Citizens of his generation had been raised to look up to wounded veterans like Yakovlev. Even now, the ambassador's fused left knee forced him to perch on the edge of the aisle seat. In other respects, too, Yakovlev had participated in events that would have fascinated Gorbachev – he'd witnessed the Secret Speech, been on the first student exchange with America, and wandered the streets of Prague as Soviet troops crushed the Czechoslovakian Spring. He had participated in history.

It was after the plane ride that Canadians began noticing the friend-ship developing between the two men. Yakovlev was perpetually at Gorbachev's side, like a guide assisting a blind man's navigation. Whenever Gorbachev sat, Yakovlev chose the neighbouring spot; when-ever Gorbachev walked, Yakovlev paced alongside. After they landed at the airport in Windsor, they boarded a bus that drove a half-hour through Essex County farm fields to the town of Amherstburg, where Whelan lived in a large home set across the street from the shore of the Detroit

River. Aside from its view, Whelan's home was considerably less opulent than the Soviet visitors might have expected. It was a ranch-style split-level structure decorated according to suburban function. That was the Whelan style – unpretentious, plain folks. When the Soviets arrived at the Whelan home, they were greeted by Liz Whelan, Eugene's wife, who herded everybody downstairs into the wood-panelled basement, a low-ceilinged chamber where folding chairs and card tables were set to accommodate approximately 30 dinner guests. Whelan still wasn't there. He was said to be en route. So the 18 members of the Soviet delegation, and a handful of Whelan's Amherstburg friends – local politicians, mostly – stood around, sipping drinks and ogling the Soviet Politburo member.

It was a bit awkward. Yakovlev asked Liz Whelan whether they could go to the backyard, to get some air, and seconds later he and Gorbachev were strolling along a laneway out back, where the Whelan lot bordered fields of soybeans and corn. It was about 7:30 on a beautiful spring evening, with a light breeze riffling the new leaves on nearby trees. Gorbachev's Soviet security staff remained a watchful distance away.

"At first," Yakovlev recalls in his memoirs, "the talk was conventional, but suddenly, we could not contain ourselves, and a reckless conversation began." Gorbachev started things off, according to Yakovlev. "He talked about sore points in the Soviet Union, using such terms as the backwardness of the country, the necessity of cardinal changes, and dogmatism." The country's gold reserves were petering out, Gorbachev admitted, and the soils deteriorating because the crops hadn't been rotated. Production of tractors and other agricultural devices was lagging behind. And still the military gobbled the budget.

Such frank talk convinced Yakovlev that Gorbachev was a kindred soul – a reformer, like him. "Even then, he understood that what was going on in our country was leading to catastrophe," Yakovlev would say later. Yakovlev decided to take one of the risks that defined his career. He was about to do something that was only too rare when one Communist Party member spoke to another. Yakovlev was about to say what he really thought. This was the sort of conversation he'd had once or twice before – with Borovik in New York, for example, as well as with the International Department apparatchik, Anatoly Chernyaev, during a visit to Montreal. It was an uncorking of the inspiration and frustration that had been building since before Yakovlev arrived in Canada. The stakes were higher now. Unlike Chernyaev or Borovik, Gorbachev was a man who seemed likely to one day have the power to make the changes the Soviet Union required. And if it turned out that Gorbachev *wasn't* a reformer – if he turned out to be just another Communist Party functionary – then what Yakovlev was about to say could send the Soviet ambassador to an exile far less pleasant than Canada.

"I, too, broke loose from my chain, as it were," Yakovlev would say, later. "I spoke frankly about how primitive and shameful the USSR's policy looked from here, from the other side of the planet." He spoke disparagingly of the telegrams he received from Moscow ordering him to explain the "real intentions" and the "hostile actions" of the dissidents – Solzhenitsyn, Sharansky, Grigorenko. It was simply idiotic! Yakovlev said. What was the point of these stupid campaigns against dissidents? Why stage battles against people who were guilty only of thinking differently?

The ideas the Soviet ambassador had been storing up during his decade in Canada came spilling out. Yakovlev attended trials in Canada, he said, real trials, independent trials, where judges followed law and not the party's preference. We should move toward an independent judiciary, Yakovlev said. "The laws should be changed first," Gorbachev replied. "They should become real laws, and not arms in the hands of individuals or the Party."

Yakovlev moved on to agriculture. He described what he had seen in Canada, the way farmers worked their own land, beating Soviet communal farm labourers in productivity, and how that suggested the Soviets should reform their own system to move toward private ownership. "Yes, of course," Gorbachev replied, growing more cautious. "But we have to consider the psychology of a collective farmer, and party psychology." It was a way to stall Yakovlev. Gorbachev was in favour of radical change in the USSR, but there were limits to what he would support. Years later, Gorbachev would reminisce about the conversation for a CBC camera crew, "This was [a] free country, where people feel like people in the conditions of freedom and work in the conditions of freedom . . . People could show initiative, something that in our country was often punished. And it's from that point of view that our conversation with Yakovlev definitely took place. It was a conversation about the Canadian experience, about using it as an example."

Private ownership, an independent judiciary, allowing dissidents the free speech they wanted. Such ideas weren't particularly fresh. Many other Soviets also were calling for similar reforms. But most were doing it in whispers, during kitchen debates, in samizdat or in veiled language in obscure academic journals. They weren't blurting out such notions to the Party's number two man. The conversation exhilarated the Soviet ambassador. Gorbachev agreed! Recalling the incident years later, Yakovlev said, "The most important common understanding was the idea that we could not live this way anymore . . . We talked about absolutely everything, openly, and it was clear to me that this was a new kind of leader. It was a thrilling experience politically and intellectually." Later, Yakovlev would say that 80 percent of what came to be known as perestroika was mentioned in Eugene Whelan's backyard.

WHELAN FINALLY SHOWED UP around 8 p.m. Before the dinner of prime rib, baked potato, and Yorkshire pudding, Whelan gave a toast predicting that Gorbachev would become the next leader of the Soviet Union – quite a gaffe, given the Politburo's sensitivity to any sign of disloyalty or ambition. After dinner, the delegation piled into a luxury bus to make the half-hour trip to the hotel, the Windsor Holiday Inn, located on the bank of the Detroit River. Arriving at night, Gorbachev had a remarkable view of the Detroit skyline, across the river. Had he been able to cruise the American city's downtown, Gorbachev would have seen the empty storefronts and burned-out houses that testified to the economic hardships the global automotive capital had suffered since the 1967 riots. But long after sunset the view across 400 metres of river water was nothing but impressive – from the circular spires of the Renaissance Center to the tendril-hung suspension design of the Ambassador Bridge, Gorbachev saw a city built thanks to the enterprise and acumen of such industrialists as Henry Ford and Alfred Sloan. It was a compelling vantage from which to contemplate his and Yakovlev's discussion.

Next morning, a Friday, Gorbachev began his touring in earnest. Led by Eugene Whelan, Gorbachev, Yakovlev, and the entourage visited Hiram Walker's distillery, the source of Canadian Club rye whiskey, then drove from Windsor across Essex County to the tomato-growing region of Leamington. As their bus passed the brick postwar homes typical of the area, Gorbachev eyed the lawns and the automobiles and asked where the working people lived. Whelan gestured outside the bus and shrugged.

"They live where they please," he said.

Gorbachev proved to be an eager student. He asked dozens of questions – the questions of an agile mind attempting to grasp in a few days the realities of an alien economic system. They toured greenhouses, a vegetable-packing plant, and a Canadian processing facility belonging to Heinz, the food company, an eight-hectare site where 600 workers made many of the sauces and soups sold under the Heinz label – from ketchup to HP Sauce. Gorbachev was struck by the extent the factory was automated; from the unloading of trucks to the boxing of ketchup containers, the product went untouched by human hands, moved along instead with gleaming stainless steel arms and other, similarly clever mechanisms. Such automation was more advanced than what existed in Russia. As Gorbachev toured the plant, one of the Canadian diplomats caught him exchanging a look with Yakovlev. Gorbachev looked worried and Yakovlev's eyebrows were raised. See? Yakovlev seemed to be saying. Told you so.

That afternoon they flew to Toronto and had a dinner in the CN Tower's revolving restaurant. Staying at a hotel out in the middle of nowhere did seem to keep this leg of the trip low key. In any event, Yakovlev's fears proved unfounded: No protesters. Next morning, a Saturday, was a two-hour tour of a meat-packing plant, Kitchener's Schneider's Meats. Gorbachev intercepted the plant supervisor and peppered him with questions. How many people worked for him? Did they have health insurance? Did they have university degrees? The plant supervisor did; he'd begun working at Schneider's at 17, he said, but was able to pursue his post-secondary education thanks to a Schneider's program that paid for schooling for employees who maintained C averages.

After a tour of Bright's winery on the Niagara peninsula, Whelan was beginning to sense a little skepticism from his Soviet counterpart – an impatience, a feeling that all this was great, but he was eager to see the *real* operations, the regular plants, say, rather than the showcase facilities Whelan had shown him up to that point. Gorbachev, it seemed, suspected his hosts were providing him with a tour through a Potemkin Village. (The term refers to a court favourite of Empress Catherine II, who prepared for the monarch's visit to the Crimea by ordering the construction of sham villages to prevent her from having to confront the region's poverty.) Eager to disprove Gorbachev's Potemkin Village theory, Whelan pulled out the morning's newspaper and showed Gorbachev a supermarket flyer in an attempt to prove that the products he was seeing weren't only for the wealthy. When Gorbachev was not convinced, Whelan stood up and hollered to the bus driver to pull into the next supermarket they passed.

Minutes later, mid-afternoon shoppers were treated to the unusual sight of 18 Soviet politicians in suits and ties filing among the displays for laundry detergent and rump roasts. During the Cold War, few things symbolized the difference between the West and Soviet Russia as much as the countries' supermarkets. Senior members of the Communist Party had access to special stores with a large selection of products. But throughout the seven decades that the Soviets controlled Russia, the supermarkets accessible to most people were shoddy places where the shelves often were empty. Queues at the meat counter were common. Fruit sometimes seemed a pipe dream, and consumer choice was nonexistent. In contrast, supermarkets in the West were miracles of plenty.

Whelan found the manager, who gave the delegation a tour of the various sections – the butcher shop, the checkout lanes, the freezer aisle. Whelan played up the fact that the store wasn't some exclusive boutique; it was a run-of-the-mill market open to anyone who wanted to come in.

Gorbachev was obsessed with product prices. In the bakery, finally, he found one he liked. Bread in Canada was much more expensive than it was in the Soviet Union, he said. Whelan allowed him that point. Beside everything else it seemed the least he could do.

AFTER A SECOND NIGHT in Toronto, it was back on their tin can of an aircraft for a seven-hour flight to Calgary, which Yakovlev and Gorbachev passed deep in conversation. Once they landed, a bus took them to a ranch in the foothills of the Rocky Mountains, a family-run beef cattle operation. The owner showed them around the grounds; Gorbachev noticed the tractors, the grain silos, the houses and cars. Afterward, everyone sat on the front porch of the rancher's home while Gorbachev gleaned the operation's statistics, with Yakovlev sitting grinning behind him. How many heads of cattle did the ranch handle? Gorbachev asked. The owner gave him a number. Next Gorbachev asked how many people ran the ranch. At that, the owner scratched his head. He looked around, and he said, well, there's me, and my wife, and two or three others.

Gorbachev asked again about the number, through the translator. He got the same answer. And he tried again, clarifying this time he didn't mean, how many people were in the *family* – no, how many people worked the ranch. Where were the workers?

Yakovlev must have been delighted. This was exactly the sort of thing he wanted Gorbachev to see. There weren't any workers – the rancher, his family, and a handful of farmhands ran the farm by themselves – something like 8,000 head of cattle managed by about eight people. Gorbachev took some solace in the fact that government subsidies were necessary to make many Canadian farms profitable. In his memoirs, he dubs the workload of the Alberta ranchers "volunteer slavery." But it certainly didn't escape his comprehension that the same operation in the Soviet Union would have required many times the people to run it. This was Yakovlev's *point*: these farmers in the West, they executed feats of efficiency and labour – a wife running a combine operation all hours of a day, then replaced by her husband at night, the two of them running the combine machine around the clock – because they flourished as the farm flourished. It was a different form of the lesson George Cohon had been selling Yakovlev since the Montreal Olympics: the benefits of performance-based compensation.

That night, a Sunday, was Gorbachev's last in Canada. Their final destination was the ruggedly beautiful Rocky Mountain town of Banff, Alberta, where they stayed at the Banff Park Lodge. It was at the entrance to the hotel that Yakovlev got his first major scare. Gorbachev spied from his bus seat a gaggle of protesters waving placards and chanting. It was a situation similar to the one that confronted Yakovlev nearly 10 years before, just months into his Canadian posting, when Brezhnev walked down the gangway at the airstrip in Gander, Newfoundland, and spied the corps of demonstrators agitating in support of Jewish refuseniks. That time, Brezhnev, the Communist Party leader maligned by the West as a Stalinist, marched over to the demonstrators and had a discussion with them. In ironic contrast, Gorbachev, who would win a Nobel Prize for inculcating democracy in the Soviet Union, responded somewhat differently from his predecessor. He leaned over and said something in Russian to Yakovlev, who turned around and dutifully passed the message on to Jim Wright, the ranking diplomat on the bus. Yakovlev's demeanour, however, suggested he knew in advance the fruitless nature of the demand he was about to make.

"Mr. Wright, you must make these protesters leave right away," Yakovlev said in Russian. As the bus parked at the hotel entrance, Yakovlev explained Gorbachev was offended that his hosts would allow Canadian citizens to protest against an invited guest. Wright leaned over and peered through the bus window's smoked glass. He saw maybe a dozen Vietnamese Canadians demonstrating against Soviet policy toward North Vietnam. The protest was small, calm, and polite.

Wright pointed out to Yakovlev that the group didn't pose any danger to Gorbachev. This being Canada, Wright said, they had a right to demonstrate about whatever they liked. He shrugged. There wasn't anything he could do.

Yakovlev turned around and explained the situation to Gorbachev. Minutes later, a scrum of Soviet associates hustled their future leader into the hotel lobby. Gorbachev, clearly, had some evolving left to do. Nevertheless, the trip had an effect on Gorbachev. He realized how far ahead the Western world was, and he saw how the personal ownership of land and the proceeds of labour could motivate a work force. "The trip to Canada had a decisive impact in that it enabled [Gorbachev] to understand in much greater depth the processes occurring in the Western world, and to familiarize himself with a variety of options for the future development of the Soviet Union and with questions of democratization, freedom and glasnost," said Valery Boldin, Gorbachev's chief of staff.

There was one more detail to settle before Gorbachev's departure. The province of Alberta hosted a dinner that night for the delegation. Afterward, Yakovlev, Gorbachev, and Wright went for a stroll around the village of Banff. It was quite a setting – a mountain valley that saw pedestrians rendered inconsequential compared to the majesty of the surrounding peaks. Wright was struck by the light mood shared by his two Soviet companions. At the time, the Canadian diplomat attributed it to the beauty of their surroundings, and the exhilarating effect of the still frigid spring air. There was almost certainly another cause as well. At some point in the final few days, Gorbachev asked Yakovlev whether the ambassador wished to return to Moscow. "Would you head one of the Institutes at the Academy of Science?" Gorbachev asked, in a reference to the IMEMO job.

Yakovlev answered quickly. "Sure, no question!" he said. "I've been here already for 10 years."

The ambassador would speculate later that Gorbachev had decided to invite him during their conversation in the Whelans' backyard. Within days of Gorbachev's departure on May 23, 1983, the news was spreading on both sides of the Atlantic. "We have picked up a rumour that Yakovlev has been selected as head" of IMEMO, ran an External Affairs telegram dated May 26, 1983. "Decision was said to have been taken last week at Politburo level and will be announced shortly." Soon the appointment was generating significant amounts of controversy in Moscow party circles. Candidates passed over for the job complained that Yakovlev lacked academic prestige or sufficient stature; his new colleagues worried whether Yakovlev would be able to secure them access to leading party members, or protect their research from political influence. These were issues that Yakovlev could tackle later. A problem was solved that had plagued him for a decade. He was due to return to Moscow for good on July 14, 1983. His exile was over.

IN OTTAWA, Secretary of State Allan MacEachen advised against a black-tie farewell dinner for Yakovlev because he worried the occasion would be interpreted by media as symbolic of improved relations with the Soviets. Prime Minister Trudeau overrode those concerns and hosted Yakovlev's sendoff on June 27. "This is an occasion which I knew would come sooner or later," said Trudeau at the top of his toast. "But I am pleased that it has come later rather than sooner." He went on to say,

Sasha, you and I have met often. We have discussed everything from world peace to the health of your grandchildren and of my sons. We have, I hope, challenged each other intellectually; we have at times commiserated on the future of mankind and, at other times, looked together at a new horizon of cooperation and understanding between peoples.

Throughout your long and much-appreciated tenure in Canada, you have impressed me not only because you are a most able spokesman for your country, but also because you never failed to demonstrate your sensitivity to and interest in Canadian affairs and your love of this country and its people.

We have been through a lot. We have had some tough times to say the least. There was even a very difficult period when you did not have me as Prime Minister although that episode was blessedly short! We haven't seen eye-to-eye on everything, but that is natural. What we have done is far more important. We have found ways to work together to serve the interests of both our countries. We have been able to exchange views in a productive way, respecting our differences but more importantly capitalizing on broad areas of agreement such as that which comes from being two peoples who are products of the North.

You have always impressed me, Ambassador, by your love of life and your ability to make the best of any situation. You have known better than any of us the brutalities and losses of war. I have understood your desire for peace and your personal interest in greater understanding and cooperation between our two countries. While the road has not been even in the past, and we are bound to hit a few potholes in the future, it is reassuring to me to know that your voice will still be active in Moscow in your new and most important assignment. We wish you happiness and every success in your challenging responsibilities as director of one of the USSR's most prestigious academic institutions.

With my personal thanks for a job well done, I propose a toast to you and to Mrs. Yakovlev, who has assisted you so superbly, and to your continued success.

The Trudeau send-off was just one of dozens of goodbye dinners and farewell receptions in honour of the Soviet Ambassador. On his final evening in Canada, for example, Yakovlev and Nina dined with Ivan Head, Yakovlev's first real Canadian friend. After a meal full of reminiscing, Yakovlev handed his old friend a parting gift: a silver medal from the 1980 Moscow Olympics that Canada had boycotted. "We found we had a few of these left over," Yakovlev grinned.

But the encounter from this period that really foretold the singular role that Yakovlev would play in Soviet politics happened not in Ottawa but in northern Quebec. Yakovlev flew by float plane to a secluded fishing lodge owned by Coca-Cola. Yakovlev went at the invitation of George Cohon, the McDonald's of Canada founder who still wanted to open the golden arches in Moscow. This wasn't a business trip, however. Cohon invited Yakovlev as a friend, as a gesture of thanks for his help through the years. Cohon was struck by how preoccupied Yakovlev seemed as they fished. Rod in hand, Yakovlev seemed to be plotting strategy and formulating plans, as though he expected the battles history had in store for him.

The trip illustrates how different Yakovlev was from the figure who had arrived in Ottawa, a decade earlier. That figure would never have accepted the invitation of a capitalist like Cohon, certainly not to stay at a luxurious lodge owned by a corporation synonomous with America. This new Yakovlev was comfortable around capitalists and democrats. Rather than the suspicious, disgraced party official he seemed in 1973, he was now a confident friend to prime ministers and chief executives. Years later, Gorbachev would observe that Yakovlev returned to Moscow, "with a liberated thought process. In those days it was hard to find people like that." Indeed. In 1983 Yakovlev knew more about the West than virtually any other Soviet figure. Including the year at Columbia, Yakovlev had resided in the West for eleven years. Certainly not a Westerner, he was no longer wholly Soviet either. He was the rare figure in Soviet society with facility and insight into both Cold War systems. This was precisely why he was valuable to Gorbachev. Yakovlev's diplomatic posting may have ended, but his work as an ambassador between the poles of the Cold War was just beginning.

AFTERWORD

THE LIBERATED MAN

TWENTY MONTHS LATER, Yakovlev was in the KGB headquarters, the Lubyanka, eavesdropping on secret deliberations in the Politburo. It was March 11, 1985. The leader of the Soviet Union, Andropov's successor, Konstantin Chernenko, had died the day before. Now the top leaders of the Communist Party – the full and candidate members of the Politburo, and the secretaries of the Central Committee – had gathered in the Walnut Room in the Kremlin's government building. Soon they would move to the adjacent conference room, where the two dozen or so politicians would vote to decide the next leader of the Soviet Union.

Yakovlev was in the Lubyanka at the invitation of Vladimir Kryuchkov, head of the KGB's first chief directorate and as such responsible for all the agency's foreign intelligence operations. Kryuchkov had an informant who worked in the Walnut Room who would report to Kryuchkov on the Politburo's secret deliberations. Eager to ingratiate himself with a member of Gorbachev's inner circle, Kryuchkov had invited Yakovlev to KGB headquarters to listen in on the proceedings.

The previous year and a half had been tumultuous for Yakovlev and the Cold War. His return to Moscow made him "as happy as a child." Recalling this time, later, he would write, "When you're at home again, you feel reborn." He renewed friendships. With the luxury of time, he wandered areas he hadn't visited for a decade. And he worked.

His position as director of the Institute for World Economy and International Relations (IMEMO) put him atop the Central Committee's favourite think tank for difficult policy decisions. Equally important was his continuing friendship with Gorbachev, who stayed in constant contact; usually they spoke on the phone once a day. Both men were preparing the ground for Gorbachev's eventual leadership, which many expected to happen when Andropov died. They enlisted a third partner in Gorbachev's long-time friend, the party secretary in the Soviet republic of Georgia, Eduard Shevardnadze, who had a "burst" conversation with Gorbachev in 1984, one remarkably similar to Yakovlev's talk with Gorbachev in Whelan's backyard. This one happened while Gorbachev was vacationing in the Georgia resort town of Pitsunda. "We can't go on living like this," Shevardnadze exclaimed.

Inspired by the prospect of real social change, Yakovlev set about using his post atop IMEMO to establish an academic case for wholesale reform. At this point in his ongoing ideological evolution, he remained a socialist, albeit one subscribing to the liberal democratic ideals that inspired Harold Laski, or the activists of the Prague Spring in 1968, rather than the more militant strain of Marxism-Leninism to which his comrades in the Communist Party subscribed. He wanted to improve the Soviet system with democracy, with respect for human rights, market reforms, and an independent judiciary. According to fellow IMEMO academic Nikolai Kosolapov, among Yakovlev's first salient moves in this direction was research Yakovlev conducted with Kosolapov to analyze the implications of the USSR adopting a multi-party system – in other words, an end to the dominance of the Communist Party. When the State Planning Committee assigned IMEMO the lead position on a study of the Soviet economy, Yakovlev pushed for an honest report, ultimately handing in a document that predicted impending crisis. Another memo recommended joint ventures with foreign companies as a precursor to increasing participation in the global free market. With trusted associates, Yakovlev went even further. One old friend reacted with shock when Yakovlev advocated an end to one-party rule. Such a reform would provoke chaos, the friend said. It could even lead to capitalism – a prediction Yakovlev indicated would be fine with him.

Normally, such revolutionary talk would have drawn quick retribution from the Party – and Yakovlev did fight some battles. The worst of them were assaults from Viktor Grishin, a Politburo member and the corrupt boss of the Moscow Party committee, whose previous assaults against the former head of IMEMO, Nikolai Inozemtsev, had led to Inozemtsev's resignation and eventual death. Suddenly, speakers Yakovlev hosted were being investigated for anti-Soviet statements. Administrators in the Central Committee were accusing Yakovlev's academics of questioning communist doctrine. Yakovlev received some degree of protection from such harassment thanks to his association with Gorbachev. Rumours of Gorbachev's trip to Canada, and of the friendship developing between Yakovlev and Gorbachev, had spread among party circles. Andropov's kidneys were failing, and in his stead Gorbachev was chairing Politburo meetings. Few apparatchiks felt secure enough in their position to attack the trusted associate of the apparent successor to the general secretary.

Then, in the politicking following Andropov's death on February 9, 1984, the aging members of the Politburo installed Brezhnev's emphysema-afflicted comrade, Konstantin Chernenko, as party leader rather than Gorbachev. It was clear that Chernenko, too, was nearing the end of his life. Jockeying for succession intensified, with much of the momentum shifting Grishin's way. Gorbachev now had a rival as the leader of the Party's next generation.

A Soviet turn toward militant orthodoxy was the last thing the world needed. U.S. president Ronald Reagan's hostile rhetoric and reports of American troop exercises convinced the Soviet military of the imminent nature of a nuclear attack. Placed on high alert, Soviet fighter jets scrambled in September 1983 to intercept a Korean Air Lines passenger 747 that strayed off course. Apparently worried the airliner was an elaborate ruse, a test of their missile defences perhaps, Soviet fighters shot down KAL 007, killing all 269 passengers, including 63 Americans and 10 Canadians. Reagan in turn used the incident to justify further buildup of nuclear arms.

Yakovlev channeled his anger into the publication of a book about the United States, *On the Edge of an Abyss*, that followed in general terms the line he had argued in his Empire Club speech, depicting Reagan as a reckless cowboy. "The present Administration takes special pains to promote the idea of a 'resurgent America.' Alarmist methods . . . are used cynically to promote chauvinist attitudes," Yakovlev wrote. "The calculation is obvious: mass hysteria and fear in a society make it easier to get money for weapons."

Trudeau, by now the longest-serving leader in NATO, grew so concerned by all the sabre-rattling that he embarked on a mad dash to visit every world leader of any influence, attempting to get the two sides together, to talk, to ratchet down the rhetoric before the two superpowers destroyed the world. His "peace mission" stop in Moscow coincided with Andropov's funeral. He wrangled an ineffectual thirty-five-minute meeting with an almost incapacitated Chernenko. While in Moscow, Trudeau also attended a lavish dinner party at Yakovlev's apartment – one of several times the two men would get together in subsequent years. The Canadian ambassador to Moscow, Peter Roberts, who also attended, was astonished at how relaxed Trudeau seemed at Yakovlev's. Roberts noted Trudeau even had a glass of vodka, something Trudeau rarely did in Ottawa. Yakovlev's notes of the dinnertime conversation indicate the fraught atmosphere of the times and the candid relationship that existed between the two men. Characterizing Reagan, with whom Trudeau had met just weeks previously in another peace mission encounter, the prime minister said the president "is obviously not a deep person . . . [Reagan] is more interested in the 'play for the public' than the essence of the matter." Interestingly, however, Yakovlev noted that Trudeau discounted the pressure exerted on Reagan by such figures as Secretary of Defense Caspar

Weinberger. "Not so long ago in conversation with me," Yakovlev quotes Trudeau as saying, "[Reagan] agreed that the U.S. and the USSR should 'live with each other and cooperate.'" Whether Reagan actually said that is open to discussion; what is interesting based on later events is, that's how Yakovlev understood it.

When Chernenko died in March 1985, the Communist Party was divided in two opposing camps. Chernenko himself had seemed to favour Grishin, to whom the Party leader had awarded the Order of Lenin, the state's highest honour, just months before his death. Gorbachev too had his supporters, particularly after his December 1984 trip to London, when Yakovlev's typically impeccable briefings and Gorbachev's own innate gifts allowed him to charm the British press and Prime Minister Margaret Thatcher, who exclaimed, "I like Mr. Gorbachev. We can do business together."

Then Yakovlev's old boss from his days as ambassador, Soviet minister of foreign affairs Andrei Gromyko, asked Yakovlev to act as an intermediary in negotiations with Gorbachev. Gromyko was one of the old men of the Politburo. His opinion would be among the most influential in the coming deliberations. Yakovlev agreed, with Gorbachev's assent. It turned out Gromyko had his eye on a new post. The foreign minister wanted to become chairman of the Presidium of the Supreme Soviet – that is, the nominal head of state for the USSR, a role not unlike that of the Canadian governor-general. If Gorbachev could guarantee that, Gromyko would provide his support.

Gorbachev agreed, of course. Whether the rest of the Politburo would fall in line was still in dispute, however. So when Kryuchkov offered to let Yakovlev listen in on the deliberations, Yakovlev accepted. Updates arrived, likely by phone, every few minutes. The members were in the Walnut Room. They were gathered at the conference table. They were sitting, with Gorbachev at one end, but to the side, to avoid sitting exactly at the head. "Now," Gorbachev said, "we must decide the question of the general secretary." Yakovlev couldn't have seen it while sitting in KGB headquarters, but he is certain to have heard about how Andrei Gromyko stood, almost before Gorbachev had finished speaking. "Allow me to speak," he said. "I have thought a great deal, and would like to make a motion to consider as candidate for the post of the general secretary of the Communist Party, Mikhail Sergeyevich Gorbachev."

There was more. Gromyko went on for quite some time, describing Gorbachev as a man of great potential, arguing the case, and the crucial moment came when he ran out of gas. The second person to speak was another old man. He, too, supported Gorbachev. From there the others fell in line. In time for a more public meeting two hours later, the Politburo voted unanimously, as was the custom. Minutes later in the Lubyanka, a relieved Yakovlev drank to the health of the new general secretary, Mikhail Gorbachev. An opportunity anticipated by Yakovlev since the thaw of the 1960s had finally arrived.

At first the changes came slowly. They were hints rather than the historic events that would come later. Stage-setting, in other words. Many involved changes in personnel. Gorbachev replaced outgoing foreign minister Gromyko with Eduard Shevardnadze. He turfed his rival, Moscow party boss Viktor Grishin, and installed in his place a reformer named Boris Yeltsin. He installed Yakovlev as the official holder of the job he'd previously held on an interim basis: propaganda chief. Yakovlev's ascent through the party ranks would continue as Gorbachev promoted his friend to the extraordinary post of Central Committee ideology secretary in 1986.

In these early years of perestroika, Yakovlev's best-known reform was the policy of glasnost, which amounted to a wholesale freeing of the press. He turfed tired establishment hacks who had spent decades echoing the Party's lies; fired them, and installed energetic, honest replacements eager to depict Soviet society as they saw it. "Write about everything but do not lie!" Yakovlev told them. Then, when upset party members demanded the firing of one or another scandal-exposing journalist, Yakovlev sided with the journalists. It was a gambit similar to what he'd done surreptitiously in the 1960s and early '70s. But this was much more public. And Yakovlev's support extended to virtually all honest journalists. This policy of glasnost alone may have brought about the Soviet collapse eventually, since for the first time in seventy years newspapers were allowed to report on separatist sentiments in such Soviet republics as Latvia, Lithuania, and, to the south, Azerbaijan. The exposure provided the separatists with their first momentum. Even when that became apparent, Yakovlev refused to censor the Soviet media.

Aside from his work on the media front, Yakovlev also played a crucial behind-the-scenes role in perestroika. Six months after Gorbachev became general secretary, Yakovlev wrote him a memo that suggested splitting the Communist Party into two political parties, paving the way for democratic elections. Gorbachev ignored the memo. Months later, Gorbachev convened a series of brainstorming sessions at Zavidovo to formulate a new foreign policy. Before Shevardnadze, Raisa Gorbachev, and other reformers, Yakovlev beseeched the rest to think in revolutionary terms. As already noted by Robert English, both Shevardnadze and Gorbachev recalled the difficulty of these sessions. Shevardnadze worried their ideas were "heading into dangerous, uncharted waters." Gorbachev recalled how the group quarrelled, not speaking to one another for a day and a half. It's reasonable to assume Yakovlev's badgering played a major role in these difficulties.

Similarly, as Gorbachev's behind-the-scenes strategist, Yakovlev played a leading role in every democratic reform of the perestroika era. For example, Yakovlev was the most radical member of the quartet that supported Gorbachev during the historic arms limitation negotiation that happened in Reykjavik, Iceland, over three days in mid-October, 1986. Gorbachev presented a proposal that would have significantly curtailed the number of existing nuclear warheads. Reagan balked at the last second. But thanks to the trusting relationship built between the two men, the two sides agreed the following year to ban all intermediate-range nuclear weapons, such as SS-20 missiles. Also in 1986, Yakovlev had a hand in pushing Gorbachev to free from his internal exile the world-renowned Soviet physicist Andrei Sakharov.

In 1987, Gorbachev promoted Yakovlev to full membership in the Politburo, making the former ambassador the first member of that body to have lived in the West for any length of time since the early days of

Stalin – a measure of the insular nature of Soviet society. It was in this capacity that Yakovlev came to occupy the role of the Party's best-known democrat, which had its disadvantages. Many in the Party disliked perestroika's reforms. They regarded the faltering steps toward Cold War peace as capitulation to the West. They were alarmed by discussions of democratic voting for political leaders, because such a measure would imperil the power they exerted over the country. Still reluctant to criticize Gorbachev as party leader, party members who disliked perestroika began targeting Yakovlev and, to a lesser extent, Shevardnadze with their displeasure. Then Gorbachev, at Yakovlev's encouragement, promoted Kryuchkov into the KGB's top spot. Whether for the sake of ambition or party loyalty, Kryuchkov set to breaking the partnership that spawned perestroika by bad-mouthing Yakovlev to Gorbachev.

Epoch-making changes were becoming regular occurrences. Orthodox forces in the Party ordered the violent suppression of separatist demonstrations in Tbilisi, Georgia, killing 19 people. Following months saw a wave of public activism spread across Eastern Europe, culminating in the toppling of the Berlin Wall on November 9, 1989. The month after that saw the Communist Party leader in Czechoslovakia resign to be replaced by a former participant in the Prague Spring, Václav Havel. Romanian Communist Party Leader Nicolae Ceauşescu fared worse: he was executed by firing squad on Christmas Day. On a happier note, in January 1990 George Cohon finally realized his dream, with Yakovlev's continuing help, opening – after 14 years and an investment of $50 million – the first Russian McDonald's on Moscow's Pushkin Square, just a few metres from the spot where demonstrators protested the Sinyavsky–Daniel trial of 1966.

Then Gorbachev faltered. Disagreement over perestroika was threatening to break the party in two. Yakovlev wanted to see a split; then, he thought, Soviet citizens could vote for whether they wanted the country run by reformers or orthodox communists. Meanwhile Kryuchkov and other neo-Stalinists wanted perestroika to stop. This book's introduction chronicled the way the Soviet leader, facing the collapse of the Soviet Union and the dissolution of the Communist Party, allied himself with Kryuchkov's orthodox forces in an attempt to stave off the Party's demise. In the aftermath, both Yakovlev and Shevardnadze resigned from the Party and worked together to create the Movement for Democratic Reform, an organization designed to counter the strength of the Communist Party's orthodox wing. Meanwhile, with independence movements in such republics as Lithuania, Latvia, and Estonia gaining momentum, Gorbachev did nothing after the KGB repressed protests – most egregiously, resulting in the deaths of 13 people in Vilnius, Lithuania. Finally, Kryuchkov and the other hard-liners with whom Gorbachev had aligned himself betrayed the Soviet leader with the coup of August 1991, triggering the end to 70 years of Soviet rule over Russia and its federated republics.

KRYUCHKOV CALLED YAKOVLEV "one of the most ominous figures of our history." But if Yakovlev's influence was so large, why does he remain almost unknown to Westerners for whom Gorbachev is a single-monikered celebrity?

While other first-hand witnesses to perestroika's power dynamics lack Kryuchkov's choler, they corroborate Yakovlev's influence on perestroika, and on Gorbachev. In one of the first memoirs published after the collapse of the Soviet Union, orthodox Politburo member Yegor Ligachev portrayed Yakovlev at the least as Gorbachev's *éminence grise*. As Ligachev portrayed it, the relationship between Gorbachev and Yakovlev wasn't all that dissimilar from the symbiotic partnership of George W. Bush and onetime deputy chief of staff Karl Rove. "Gorbachev was not the only one who gave instructions," Ligachev wrote. "Often it was Yakovlev . . .Yakovlev . . . stood invisibly behind many of the unexpected turns and zigzags in the policies." Ligachev posed a question many Soviet loyalists have wondered since: "Who was echoing whom – Yakovlev, echoing Gorbachev, or vice versa?"

Western Kremlinologists missed Yakovlev's zeal for democracy and market reform, at first. Taken aback by the pace and direction of the changes happening in the Soviet Union, American policy analysts examined Gorbachev's brain trust to discover which members were pulling for the "new thinking." They dismissed Yakovlev as one of the Communist Party's conservative dogmatists because American foreign policy analysts examined Yakovlev's political writing, including the anti-Reagan diatribe, *On the Edge of an Abyss*, and concluded not only that Yakovlev hated America, but that he also opposed freedom and democracy. Apparently, it didn't occur to the analysts that one could simultaneously support freedom and democracy while also disliking the way America wielded its power during the Cold War.

The current executive editor of the *New York Times*, Bill Keller, was one of the first Western observers to recognize Yakovlev's influence. As the paper's Moscow bureau chief in 1988 he observed that Yakovlev was widely regarded as the second most influential man in the Soviet Union, behind Gorbachev. "Other men have made their way into Gorbachev's inner circle and contributed to the upheaval called perestroika, but none has been so indispensable as Yakovlev," wrote Keller the following year. His colleague, the *Washington Post*'s David Remnick (who is now editor of *The New Yorker*) was similarly complimentary; in his Pulitzer Prize-winning account of the Soviet collapse, *Lenin's Tomb*, Remnick observed: "From the moment Gorbachev took power, Yakovlev was an essential, if not lead, player in every progressive idea, policy, or gesture coming from the Kremlin." Elsewhere, Remnick called Yakovlev "Gorbachev's good angel."

Today such renowned Sovietologists as Mark Kramer, Timothy Colton, Stephen F. Cohen, and Archie Brown recognize Yakovlev's singular role in perestroika. His name is often preceded by such descriptive phrases as "architect of perestroika" and "godfather of glasnost." In the best account of the way "new thinking" gave rise to perestroika, *Russia and the Idea of the West: Gorbachev, Intellectuals and the End of the Cold War*, Robert D. English depicts Yakovlev as "Gorbachev's preeminent domestic and foreign policy advisor" and "the strongest proponent of democratization in Gorbachev's circle." Yakovlev's story is regarded by such men as the former dean of Harvard's Kennedy School of Government Joseph Nye Jr. and former U.S. deputy secretary of state

Richard Armitage as a case study for the efficacy of soft power – that is, the tactic of responding to enemy states with dialogue and engagement. Yakovlev is also recognized as one of the era's most tragic of figures, thanks to the fervour with which he rejected the system he once championed. After the Soviet collapse, he seemed obsessed with righting the crimes of the Communist Party. He chaired a commission that rehabilitated victims of repression – that is, he and his team dug through the Soviet archives, examining the evidence that caused people to be found guilty of "anti-Soviet" behaviour and other misdeeds. His work cleared the names of hundreds of thousands.

Yakovlev's ideological evolution continued throughout the perestroika era, and beyond. By the Soviet collapse there are indications he rejected even the democratic socialism favoured by such figures as Harold Laski. He would go on to write a book-length indictment of Marxism, *A Century of Violence in Soviet Russia*, using language that wouldn't have been out of place in a speech by Reagan, circa 1983. Today, inside an increasingly autocratic Russia, many citizens consider Yakovlev a traitor who corrupted Soviet strength with foreign ideas, triggering the Soviet collapse, the loss of the Cold War, and the bankrupt, hungry years of the 1990s. In some circles, his name elicits the sort of invective some Americans reserve for Nixon. In other circles, it elicits a lot worse.

Amid the credit and the blame, it's easy to lose sight of what Yakovlev actually did. First, Yakovlev didn't "father" the ideas of perestroika. By the time Gorbachev came to power in March 1985, such Soviet dissidents and radical academics as Andrei Sakharov, Tatyana Zaslavskaya, Abel Aganbegyan and Petr Kapitsa had been advocating for years a wholesale humanization of Bolshevik Communism in the form of market and democratic reforms, among other ideas. Reforms along similar lines had been attempted before in the Soviet bloc, only to be curtailed by the Party's hard-line, conservative side: during Czechoslovakia's Prague Spring; by Khrushchev after the 20th Party Congress; and, in a lesser form, during Lenin's New Economic Policy in the 1920s. Second, so far as Communist Party officials went, Gorbachev was an unusually reform-minded politician long before Yakovlev got to him; thanks in part to his coming of age at thaw-era Moscow State University and his friendship with Prague Spring leader Zdeněk Mlynář.

Today academics recognize that Yakovlev acted as a crucial conduit into the previously dogmatic upper aerie of the Communist Party for the creative "new thinking" of the dissident Soviet intelligentsia. Crucially, he also proved a steadying influence on Gorbachev, whose method of policy development involved consulting a wide range of opinions before making a decision. Throughout Gorbachev's six and a half years in power, Yakovlev was the radical counterbalance to the conservatives among this mix of advisors, ever pulling the whole lot toward reform and revolution. Had a stubborn, uncompromising figure like Yakovlev not existed, Gorbachev's tendency toward consensus might have corrupted his reformist bent in the face of hard-line communist opposition, before perestroika had time to develop – if it started at all.

Yakovlev was not the traitor his opponents accused him of being. He was a patriot who wanted his country to realize its potential for greatness by shrugging off the corruption and repression that resulted from Communist Party rule. He strongly believed that democratic reform was the best way for his country to achieve its potential. Unfortunately his goal contained a paradox. The Soviet Union existed by using its populace as a means to an end – a means to perpetuate the power of the ruling Communist Party. Saving the Soviet Union with just reforms was a logical impossibility, because justice and the Soviet system couldn't coexist. Yakovlev came to this realization during Gorbachev's leadership. To his credit, when forced to choose between justice and the Soviet system, Yakovlev sided with justice. Whether Gorbachev joined him is a matter of some debate; certainly, Yakovlev's detractors in the Communist Party did not.

FEW MINDS HAVE CHANGED as much as Yakovlev's did over the course of his lifetime. When his exile ended on July 14, 1983, his political thinking included the zeal for democracy and market reform that would prove integral to the Soviet collapse and the end of the Cold War. Somewhere between adolescence and the end of his exile, Yakovlev went from Stalin's acolyte to Stalinism's nemesis, from zealous communist to enthusiastic endorser of democratic free-market reform. Mapping the transformational terrain that is Yakovlev's biography is difficult because Yakovlev never experienced a conversion similar, say, to that of Saul on the road to Damascus, when the non-believer suddenly became an ardent adherent to Christianity. Yakovlev's evolution was gradual and it happened in unsteady, irregular lurches. Charting this evolution is difficult, too, because Communist Party members lied about what they believed. Yakovlev's characterization of his views changed depending on his audience until shortly before he resigned from the Party in August 1991.

Still, Yakovlev spoke frankly and comparatively frequently in the last 14 years of his life; he also wrote extensively about his ideological conversion, particularly in his fascinating memoirs. With such clues, along with press interviews, articles, and pseudonymous papers, as well as the writings of his peers and rivals, it's possible to knit together, with what seems a reasonable amount of certainty, the arc of Yakovlev's transformation – as I have attempted to do in this volume.

It is worth noting here that Yakovlev sometimes denied the influence of the West on his political thinking. At various times, in various ways, he insisted his time in the West did not change him. "It simply did not," he said on one occasion. This attitude seems like revisionism. Yakovlev acknowledged, in more conciliatory moods, that his time in the West influenced his reformist convictions. He was particularly reluctant to discuss America's influence on him. However, his year at Columbia seems certain to have helped forge the unusually democratic sentiments that defined his 1960's work in Propaganda. Before he went to Canada, Yakovlev wrote, "I had read thousands of books, defended two theses on America, lived for a year in Columbia University with students. In a political sense, there was nothing new for me there. But one thing is to have read, and quite the other, to watch for a long time how it worked, or not worked."

Canada was singularly well suited to encourage Yakovlev to re-examine the Communist Party's guiding precepts, and not just because it was a democracy that wasn't the United States. There was, for example, the country's relative unimportance in world affairs, which made Yakovlev's embassy in Ottawa a comparatively sleepy outpost on the Soviet diplomatic circuit. This gave Yakovlev time to think and to indulge his curiosity in pet projects, such as the study of agriculture. Also, Canada was a much more hospitable place for a Soviet exile than other Western democracies might have been. Thanks to such socialist-inspired innovations as state-provided medicare, Canada's system was a mix of capitalism and communism. In Canada, too, Yakovlev experienced his first national elections and witnessed examples of democratic political change, such as the institution of the Canadian Charter of Rights and Freedoms and the McDonald Commission that led to the reform of the nation's secret police operations. He also discovered a colony of Russian expatriates, the Doukhobors, who disproved the notion that his country required autocratic rulers to keep its citizens in line.

Ultimately it may have been the people he met as the Soviet ambassador who most encouraged him to examine the precepts of one-party rule. Through Ivan Head, Yakovlev formed his first sympathetic contacts in the Canadian government, leading him to a friendship with Prime Minister Pierre Elliott Trudeau, whose contrarian intellectualism combined a zeal to protect human rights and a long-standing fascination with, and sympathy for, the Soviet experiment. This unusual combination of interests and enthusiasms led Trudeau to attempt to position Canada as the intellectual bridge between the Soviet Union and the United States. In the short term, the policy did little to affect global affairs; in the long term, it may have helped end the Cold War.

Other Canadians also proved integral to Yakovlev's evolution. George Cohon, the McDonald's restaurateur, helped show Yakovlev the positive aspects of capitalism through the prism of Big Macs and chocolate shakes. And Agriculture Minister Eugene Whelan provided Yakovlev with a mechanism to lure Gorbachev to Canada. Significantly, each of these men interacted with Yakovlev outside of the enemy-friend moral dichotomy that dominated relations between Moscow and Western capitals during the Cold War. In wide-ranging conversations on politics and philosophy with these engaged but non-judgmental men, Yakovlev moved away from the hyper-competitive interplay between (American) capitalism and (Soviet) communism and grew confident that the best system involved some blend of the two. It was this confidence that proved influential to Gorbachev and his brain trust.

"Canada gave me a chance to breathe other air, to study in a new environment, meet with the people and freely talk to them and open my heart," Yakovlev wrote. Specifically, Yakovlev acknowledged that in Canada he became more convinced of the necessity for free and competitive elections, private land ownership, and an independent legal system. "I strengthened my beliefs in these three positions mainly because I saw them successfully implemented in Canada," he said. "I visited courts as a spectator, I went to the farms, and many times I observed elections both federal and local." Such observations, Yakovlev wrote, "confirmed my convictions that we have to move in this direction."

By exiling Yakovlev to Ottawa in 1973, the Communist Party intended to neutralize a dangerously subversive force within its ranks. Thanks to Pierre Elliott Trudeau and a whole host of other factors, that exile helped Yakovlev evolve subversive theories into radical convictions. The irony is compelling: if the Party wanted to render Yakovlev harmless by exiling him, they sent him to exactly the wrong place.

THE END OF AN EMPIRE is a mushy business. When, exactly, did the Soviet era conclude? By the end of 1991 it had been more than 70 years since the October day in 1917 when Lenin and his Bolsheviks declared themselves the rulers of Russia. They went on to establish a corrupt mechanism that allowed Communist Party officials to exploit a populace who would come to number more than a quarter-billion people. Lenin, Stalin, and the system they created are unrivalled in homicidal productivity. Depending on your source and how, exactly, one defines "murder," estimates on the number of victims range from 8 million to upwards of 20 million for Stalin alone – and he was in complete control for just 25 of those years. The living suffered as well, from famine, certainly, but also from a system that punished the ambitious and stifled the creative, that regarded individuality with suspicion and treated honesty as a capital crime. In other words, a system that asphyxiated the bright, peculiarly human qualities that make life interesting, leaving behind a vast, secretive, and hypocritical empire of monotony.

Did that system end on August 23, 1991, at the Russian parliamentary session where Yeltsin suspended the Communist Party's Russian branch? Did it happen the next day, as Gorbachev resigned as the Party's general secretary and dissolved its ruling Central Committee? Did the end occur while Russian crowds cheered the toppling of the statue of Felix Dzerzhinsky, founder of the Soviet secret police, which stood in front the storied headquarters of the KGB? At that point the Soviet hammer-and-sickle flag still hung over the Kremlin. And Gorbachev, as the Soviet president, retained his hold on the "button" that controlled the Soviet store of nuclear warheads.

One of the moments more likely to qualify as the malevolent empire's conclusion happened shortly after the meeting on December 23, 1991, when three men negotiated the final transfer of power from Gorbachev to his arch-enemy, the Russian president, Boris Yeltsin. Yakovlev was the third man present. He was there to smooth relations between the two leaders, who despised one another to such an extent that they apparently didn't trust themselves to be alone, in the same room, without their relations descending into an ugly display of acrimony. There also was some symbolism to Yakovlev's presence; he was the link between Gorbachev and Yeltsin, the person who pushed Gorbachev into the reforms that triggered the old system's collapse, clearing the way for Yeltsin to attempt to build a more just and democratic replacement. "It so happened," wrote Yakovlev in his memoirs, "that I became a witness not only to the beginning, but also to the end, of the lofty career of Mikhail Gorbachev."

The meeting happened on the third floor of the Kremlin's government building, one floor up from Stalin's old office. Gorbachev had moved his staff there after he was voted the Soviet president in

March 1990. Set on the opposite side of a reception area from the Walnut Room, Gorbachev's office was a dome-ceilinged rectangular chamber, twice as long as it was wide, illuminated by massive chandeliers and decorated in cherrywood furnishings imported from Italy – a conference table and Gorbachev's desk, from behind which he could look down at Yeltsin and Yakovlev, seated in two matching leather armchairs.

The meeting began at noon. Friction snagged the proceedings even before Yeltsin's arrival. Gorbachev had given permission to a TV crew to record Yeltsin's entrance; when Yelstin stepped off the elevator he refused to be recorded, and the crew was banished. Once in the office, the haggling began. That Gorbachev would transfer his power to Yeltsin was a given, at this point. But before his rival officially resigned, Yeltsin wanted to exact a promise from Gorbachev to stay out of politics; he didn't need a hostile ex-leader criticizing him or rallying opposition. In exchange for staying out of Yelstin's blow-dried white hair, Gorbachev aimed to negotiate a lucrative package of perquisites – a pension, drivers, a security detail, use of a state dacha, and funding to create a research foundation.

Gradually, the men worked through the details. Gorbachev would resign publicly in two days, on December 25, with a televised speech. They'd transfer the control of the nuclear button – actually, a small, cell-phone-like device – on the same day. Yeltsin agreed to give Gorbachev a majestic Moscow building, a former academic institute, to use as the new headquarters for the Gorbachev Foundation, which would be staffed by academics and some of his former associates. (Yakovlev would become the organization's vice-president.) Gorbachev wanted to devote the foundation to the study of economics and politics. Here, Yeltsin halted their progress. The foundation couldn't study politics – that would violate Gorbachev's pledge. The men argued. Temperatures rose. Finally, Yakovlev suggested changing the wording of the foundation's purpose from the study of "politics" to "political science." That, apparently, was enough of a concession for Yeltsin.

By the time the men finished their negotiations, it was dinnertime. They retired to the Walnut Room for a meal. Soon Gorbachev realized the import of what had just passed. He offered an excuse, that he wasn't feeling very well, and retired to the chambers that, thanks to the papers he'd just signed, were no longer his. An aide reported that Gorbachev appeared flushed. British Prime Minister John Major called to say goodbye. During the call Gorbachev acted "dazed," an aide said.

Yakovlev and Yeltsin lasted another hour in the Walnut Room. The mood lifted once Gorbachev left. Neither Yakovlev nor Yeltsin maintained emotional ties to the Party that had once dominated their lives. Yakovlev considered it a vast criminal apparatus; he would never get over his participation in its crimes. Yeltsin, less apt to philosophize, just saw the Soviet Union as a barrier to progress. Thanks to its imminent dissolution, Yeltsin had just become sole leader of what remained the world's most massive slab of land. In a fit of emotion, Yeltsin toasted Yakovlev and told him he would officially recognize the older man's contributions to the country's democratic movement, and provide him with financial security forever – a promise, Yakovlev would one day note, that Yeltsin didn't keep.

Yeltsin also wanted to know why Yakovlev would continue to work with Gorbachev. "He's betrayed you repeatedly," Yeltsin said. "Let's find a job worthy of you." But Yakovlev declined because, he said, he felt sorry for his old friend.

After dinner, Yeltsin and Yakovlev parted in the hall outside the Walnut Room. Yeltsin strode off toward his fate, his heels clicking on the polished parquet floor in a cadence that sounded to Yakovlev like a triumphal march. Moments later Yakovlev found Gorbachev lying on a couch in what was no longer his office. Yakovlev could see that his friend had been crying.

"There, you see, Sash," Gorbachev said, using the diminutive of "Aleksandr" to refer to his old friend. "That's how it is."

Yakovlev understood Gorbachev's statement as an admission of both his grief and his embarrassment over his inability to stave off the signs of that grief. Yakovlev realized he was witnessing a man at his life's darkest moment.

Yakovlev couldn't help but be affected by the pathos of Gorbachev's position. He attributed his sadness to the injustice of Gorbachev's fate; he felt his friend deserved better than this ignominious early departure. How far this was, Yakovlev felt, from the dreams they'd originally described to one another during their first discussions of perestroika on Whelan's farm. Yakovlev said a few comforting words. Gorbachev was sure to have a glorious retirement; the Gorbachev Foundation was bound to become a world-renowned research institute, he told his friend. Gorbachev asked for a glass of water. Yakovlev brought it to him; the last leader of the Soviet Union drank and then he asked to be left alone.

During the next several years the tumult in their relationship would continue. Soon after Yakovlev began working as the Gorbachev Foundation's vice-president, he discovered through Yeltsin's opening of confidential Soviet archives that Gorbachev had, via Kryuchkov, been monitoring Yakovlev's private telephone conversations. Feeling betrayed, Yakovlev left Gorbachev's organization and eventually started one of his own, the International Democracy Foundation, committed to righting the injustices of the Soviet era through voluminous research in the Soviet archives.

Once the Soviet empire collapsed, the country was forced to declare bankruptcy, a profoundly humiliating process for the former superpower. Billions of dollars in state resources ended up in the hands of a few oligarchs. Although these events happened in the 1990s, under Yeltsin's watch, many Russians blame perestroika, Gorbachev, and especially Yakovlev, for this chapter in Russian history.

Yakovlev lived well into the reign of Vladimir Putin as Russian president, when high energy prices helped return Russia to its former prominence as a world power. He witnessed the Russian national economy growing at nearly 7 percent a year. He also witnessed Putin's consolidation of power, supposedly to safeguard that growth. Yakovlev died of a blood clot, possibly related to his wartime wound, in the upstairs office of his dacha on October 18, 2005. Shortly before, he told friends he thought Russia's reversal of perestroika was a natural relapse for a country struggling to shrug off the influence of a thousand years of authoritarianism. Gorbachev waited almost to the end of Putin's reign to criticize the autocratic president. Yakovlev despised the backsliding from the start and was confident the pendulum would swing once again toward perestroika's democratic freedoms. He died proud of his public service. In his memoirs, he writes, "Of utmost importance in my life remains not my doubts, grievances or dissatisfactions in the reaping-time of freedom. But the fact that Mikhail Sergeyevich and I, arm in arm, even though stumbling along, made our way toward this freedom, giving no thought to how it would end for us – in glory or in curses."

Yakovlev wrote extensively about his life as well as Soviet history. He enjoyed mixing the two, often at incongruous moments, and he was apt to recycle the raw material in slightly different forms. The fullest version of his memoirs is *Sumerki* (2003). An earlier version, *Omut Pamyati* (2000), is almost as comprehensive. A third incarnation exists in English translation that has some fresh material not found in either edition – although the text was commissioned by an American publisher and the book may not ever be published. Where possible I've cited *Sumerki* in the following source notes. Interested readers who aren't fluent in Russian can glean much about Yakovlev's life, and his ideological evolution, by reading the shorter, translated volumes, *A Century of Violence in Soviet Russia* (2002) or *The Fate of Marxism in Russia* (1993). In the following notes I've abbreviated several frequently used citations. **FBIS–SOV** refers to translations of Russian media published by the CIA's Foreign Broadcast Information Service. **LAC** indicates a document found in Ottawa's Library and Archives Canada. **BBC–BLA** indicates the source is unpublished transcripts of several interviews Yakovlev conducted for the documentary series, *The Second Russian Revolution*, produced by Brian Lapping Associates Ltd. and aired on BBC in May/July 1991 with two additional post-coup documentary episodes aired in November 1991. These transcripts are stored in the library at the London School of Economics. **CBC** indicates the source is unpublished interview transcripts conducted by Yakovlev, Gorbachev and at least seven others for the Canadian Broadcasting Corporation's Jan. 14, 2003, documentary, *Aleksandr Yakovlev: The Commissar of Glasnost*.

1. THE TARGET

3   **One clear summer day** Oleg Kalugin's *The First Directorate*, 347–48, and Yakovlev's *Omut Pamyati*, 483, both describe the encounter between the two men. The men differ about the number of counterintelligence agents assigned to monitor the encounter. I also spoke with Mr. Kalugin extensively about this encounter when I interviewed him in Washington in March 2007.

    The younger man Details on Kalugin's career are found throughout his memoir, *The First Directorate*, particularly 148 and following. On dissident Georgi Markov, see ibid., 178–186.

4   **By August 1991** Ibid., 330–333.

    His companion On blaming Yakovlev, see two former Communist Party insiders who display remarkable bitterness when they discuss Yakovlev: Yegor Ligachev, *Inside Gorbachev's Kremlin: The Memoirs of Yegor Ligachev*, 112, and Vladimir Kryuchkov, *Lichnoe delo: tri dnia i vsia zhizn*, 286

    They picked the street On the planned assassination, see Yakovlev, *Sumerki*, 537.

5   **"I put it in a safe"** Kalugin, *First Directorate*, 148.

    Before the men parted Yakovlev was vocal in his predictions of an impending coup that summer. For another view of the climate in Moscow from a reporter describing a Yakovlev meeting at the same point, consult David Remnick's *Lenin's Tomb*, 448–49. Remnick also has an excellent short summary of Kalugin's life, 354–56.

2. THE TRAITOR

6   **Gorbachev preferred not to work** Andrei Grachev, *Final Days*, 185.

    One day about a year The Kryuchkov / Boldin / Gorbachev meeting is recounted at length in Kryuchkov, *Lichnoe Delo*, 294–297. Yakovlev also discusses it in *Sumerki*, 536–37. I've also drawn from Kryuchkov's comments to the Russian press when he went public with these allegations in 1993. See *Current Digest of the Post-Soviet Press* 45, No. 8 (1993): 5–6.

7   **In addition to running** For an interesting look at the nomenklatura as a social tier, consult Voslenskii's *Nomenklatura: The Soviet Ruling Class*, particularly 69–111.

"The nomenklatura is another planet" Len Karpinsky quoted by Remnick, David. Letter from Moscow. *New Yorker*, Mar. 23, 1992, 69.

8   **Gorbachev and Yakovlev** The Soviet collapse spawned stacks of books, but for an entertaining chronology that provides a reader with an accurate sense of the pace of the changes, consult the chronology following the *Memoirs* of Mikhail Gorbachev, 697–712.

By the time Boldin Antipathy toward perestroika persists in Russia. One interesting reflection of this is former Russian president Vladimir Putin's demonstrated distaste for the Soviet collapse, which Putin has called the greatest geopolitical catastrophe of the 20th century. See for example Leon Aron, "Putin's Cold War," *Wall Street Journal*, Dec. 26, 2007, A11. For more on KGB spying on senior Party members, see *Sumerki*, 535–37 and 623, as well as Kryuchkov, *Lichnoe Delo*, 296–97.

"One of the most ominous" Kryuchkov, *Lichnoe Delo*, 283.

9   **"His main feature is"** Ibid., 286.

"foremen" Ibid., 292.

Yakovlev's "anti-Soviet" influence Ibid., 287, although the former KGB chair depicts Gorbachev as behaving under Yakovlev's influence throughout Kryuchkov's section on Yakovlev, *Lichnoe Delo*, 282–97.

Once in Gorbachev's Meeting account in Kryuchkov, *Lichnoe Delo*, 294–97.

white crow Nina Yakovleva also used this term to describe her husband. Personal interview, December 2006.

Kryuchkov's investigation Kryuchkov, *Lichnoe Delo*, 294–97.

10   **Ring of Five** Interesting exposition on the astonishing nature of the Ring of Five case is to be found in Philip Knightley, "Turning the Philby Case on Its Head," *New York Review of Books*, April 26, 2007, 51–54.

Kryuchkov told Gorbachev Interestingly, Kryuchkov is easier on Kalugin than he is on Yakovlev. For Kryuchkov on Kalugin see *Lichnoe Delo*, 420–25.

Gorbachev's reaction Kryuchkov, *Lichnoe Delo*, 297. For his part, Yakovlev believes Kryuchkov is dishonest about Gorbachev's reaction. See *Sumerki*, 536.

3. THE DOOMSAYER

12   **Shortly after Kryuchkov** This encounter is based on an account found in Anatoly Chernyaev, *My Six Years With Gorbachev*, 245–47.
Yakovlev's exterior demeanour Anatoly Yakovlev (Aleksandr's son) interview, December 2006.
Yakovlev was the longest-serving Chernyaev, *Six Years*, 246.
Gorbachev gave it to Kryuchkov Ibid.

13   **The tirade illustrates** To get a sense of the ups and downs in the Yakovlev–Gorbachev relationship, see Yakovlev, *Sumerki*, 459–520. Interestingly, Yakovlev also had a friendly relationship with Raisa Gorbacheva. See *Sumerki*, 606–7.
"What are you afraid of?" Chernyaev, *Six Years*, 250.
"I didn't even feel" Ibid., 245–46.
"If you leave now" Ibid.
That, at least, was On Kryuchkov's machinations, see Yakovlev, *Sumerki*, 535–39.

14   **Did Gorbachev believe?** Ibid., 472.
There was a powerful irony See ibid., 372.
"If I had known" Yakovlev, *Sumerki*, 472.
As Gorbachev cozied Yakovlev writes of Gorbachev's developing paranoia ibid., 535. For more examples, see Boldin, *Ten Years*, 258–59.

15   **The covert campaign against** Anatoly Yakovlev recounted to me the shooting incident and his father's reaction during several interviews in December 2006.
All of these episodes On accusations against Yakovlev, see *Sumerki*, 533.

16   **The situation grew** The Vilnius bloodshed is recounted well in Remnick, *Lenin's Tomb*, 387–90. My source on statistics for deaths and number of wounded, as well as the aftermath, is John B. Dunlop, "The August 1991 Coup and Its Impact on Soviet Politics," *Journal of Cold War Studies* 5, No. 1 (Winter 2003): 97.
"What should we do?" Chernyaev, *Six Years*, 257–58.
He was hospitalized Personal communication with Anatoly Yakovlev, April 20, 2007.
Gorbachev didn't listen Yakovlev's best account of the behind-the-scenes turmoil triggered by the demonstration is found in BBC–BLA,

Sept. 14, 1991, 5. Number of protestors and the police response from Dunlop, "August 1991 Coup," *Cold War Studies*, 98.

17   **By mid-1991** Yakovlev warned Gorbachev about an impending coup several times. See his *Sumerki*, 531.

"These are toadies" Remnick, *Lenin's Tomb*, 447.

"Yakovlev characterized" Yakovlev, *Sumerki*, 426.

"The people around you" Remnick, *Lenin's Tomb*, 447.

Finally, Yakovlev did Yakovlev, *Sumerki*, 427, 614.

4. THE PUTSCH

Few events in recent history have generated more literature, academic, journalistic or personal, than the August 1991 coup. Much of it is self-serving. It's rare to find observers who even attempt, let alone achieve, objectivity. For on-the-ground reporting from a knowledgeable eyewitness, see Remnick's *Lenin's Tomb*, 451–490. When not specifically noted the Yakovlev-specific material in this chapter is drawn from *Sumerki*, 614–18.

18   **One week after** That Kalugin alerted Yakovlev to the coup is in Yakovlev, BBC–BLA, Sept. 14, 1991, 1–5. Kalugin also provides his account of this conversation in his *First Directorate*, 348–49.

19   **The radio was broadcasting** One interesting subtext is that many learned of Kryuchkov's anti-democratic coup from Radio Mayak, the broadcasting station Yakovlev founded during Khrushchev's thaw. For a fascinating insider account of events during the coup at Gorbachev's dacha, consult Chernyaev, *Six Years*, 402–23.

The irony was Many have noted the coup perpetrators were onetime Gorbachev loyalists. One eloquent recounting of the line of thinking is in Remnick, *Lenin's Tomb*, 455–56. Details on Kryuchkov's bugging of the Union Treaty negotiations found in Gorbachev's *Memoirs*, 643.

At Yakovlev's apartment For his account of the first minutes of the coup, see Yakovlev, *Sumerki*, 615. Also see BBC–BLA, Sept. 14, 1991, 1–4.

"I feel shame" Lapping's Sept. 14, 1991, interview with Yakovlev, 1.

21   **The crowd recognized him** BBC-BLA, Sept. 14, 1991, interview with Yakovlev, 15.

Later, people would debate Yakovlev says he thought the coup failed during the night of August 20, 1991, in BBC–BLA, 17–18, during which he also speaks of the food-bearing babushkas.

22   **"You have given"** Remnick, *Lenin's Tomb*, 495.

He mentioned only two Gorbachev, *Memoirs*, 644.

5. "THE BLOW THAT EXPLODED MY HEAD"

Yakovlev spoke frequently and candidly about his youth, and his experiences in the Great Patriotic War. The most comprehensive accounts are to be found in *Sumerki*, 35–59, from which I've drawn most of my colour. For a fascinating and comparatively concise alternate view of Yakovlev's life, including his early years, consult the chapter on him in Remnick's *Lenin's Tomb*, 290–305.

25   **"It is hard to think"** Paul Hollander, foreword to Yakovlev's *A Century of Violence*, viii.

What happened in between? Kryuchkov persisted in his attempts at slandering Yakovlev, going public with his accusations after the collapse by writing an article titled, "The Ambassador of Misfortune," *Sovetskaya Rossya*, Feb. 13, 1993. See also Remnick, *Resurrection*, 86, where one of Kryuchkov's associates says that Yakovlev was such an effective agent of the CIA there should be a statue of him at the agency's headquarters in Langley, Virginia.

26   **"We hid our sense of doom"** From an unpublished English translation of the Yakovlev memoirs by Kathleen Luft called *The Maelstrom of Memory* and commissioned by New York–based Encounter Books, ch. 2, pg. 26.

Eight weeks after Probably the best description of his early life by Yakovlev himself is featured in an interview that appeared in the June 5, 1990, edition of *Komsomolskaya Pravda*, 1–2. My source is translation found in FBIS–SOV–90–122, June 25, 1990, 44–53.

28   **Conditions for Soviet infantry** Robert Service, *A History of Twentieth–Century Russia*, 264.

Yakovlev belonged to a brigade Yakovlev resisted glorifying his war experiences in type. In conversation with friends he was more candid. Details on his brigade's reputation and his shouting "For Stalin!" are to be found in the chapter on him in Loren Graham's *Moscow Stories*, 223–36. Also see *Komsomolskaya Pravda* interview, FBIS–SOV–90–122, June 25, 1990, 46.

29   **"Who sent them to their death?"** Yakovlev, *Sumerki*, 45.

32   **"dancing yet to do"** Yakovlev, *Omut Pamyati*, 43.

During surgery On Yakovlev's war decorations, see the long article by Vil Dorofeev, "Aleksandr Yakovlev: uyti, chtoby ostatsya," *Dialog* no. 17 (November 1990): 89–103.

Yakovlev left the hospital Source on Yakovlev's father pleurisy is personal communication with Anatoly Yakovlev, Feb. 17, 2007.

33 **Like everyone except** For more on conditions for Soviet civilians during and after wartime, see Service, *A History of Twentieth–Century Russia*, 296. See also Robert Service, *Stalin: A Biography*, 482–83.

Once the first flush of their reunion Excellent colour on Yakovlev's post-front activities in Dorofeev, "Yakovlev," *Dialog*, 89–103. Personal communication with Anatoly Yakovlev also provided date of Communist Party membership and other context.

34 **He began dating a young woman** Nina Yakovleva provided valuable colour on the early years of her relationship with her husband during two long interviews in December 2006.

The war exacted Service, *Stalin*, 482.

As bad as things were Details on marriage provided by author interview with Nina Yakovleva, December 2006.

35 **But the injustice that most troubled** A particularly vivid description of this anecdote, which Yakovlev mentions in several interviews, is found in Yakovlev, CBC, tapes 8–11, 1. Also good is the version in *Century of Violence*, 4–5.

36 **Crowded into these freight cars** Anne Applebaum's *Gulag: A History*, 435–38.

But then Stalin decided For an interesting look at the democratic effects fighting in foreign lands had on Russian soldiers, see Service, *Stalin*, 485.

37 **"first serious cracks"** Yakovlev, *Sumerki*, 58.

6. THE SECRET SPEECH

38 **Crises of faith** Many former communists have written about the wrenching experience represented by their loss of idealism. As one can tell from the quote that precedes the book, I'm partial to Arthur Koestler's *Darkness at Noon*, which is justifiably praised for its clear description of one man's falling out with Bolshevik communism.

For Yakovlev, the decade The reasoning in this paragraph is a synthesis of impressions gathered from Yakovlev's *Sumerki*, specifically, 59–66, 249–55.

39   "What was I like" Yakovlev, *Sumerki*, 254.

frontoviki Find an excellent character sketch of the frontoviki, and their tensions with the intelligentsia, in Ludmilla Alexeyva and Paul Goldberg's *The Thaw Generation: Coming of Age in the Post-Stalin Era*, 56–58.

40   **Soon after the war** On selection to Higher Party School see Yakovlev, *Sumerki*, 59.

One year, for example Ibid., 63.

41   **Another incident** Yakovlev frequently mentioned his encounters with the Committee for Party Control. One recounting is found in *Century of Violence*, 207–09. See also *Komsomolskaya Pravda* in FBIS–SOV–90–122, June 25, 1990, 48. The following discussion of the repressive climate of the time is found throughout the latter half of the chapter on anti-Semitism in *Century of Violence*, 202–212. For more on the Doctor's Plot, and Stalin's increasing paranoia, see Service, *Stalin*, 571–80.

43   "I interpreted everything" Yakovlev, *Omut Pamyati*, 117.

Like any member Yakovlev's attitude toward Stalin was typical. For an excellent exposition of this "old thinking" see Robert D. English's *Russia and the Idea of the West*, 17–48.

44   **The event, for Yakovlev** On the move, see Yakovlev, *Sumerki*, 249. By personal communication, Anatoly Yakovlev provided useful context on his father's job description in this period, as well as key details of family history.

Stalin died For detail on popular response to the dictator's death see Service, *Stalin*, 588–90

45   "Everyone was silent." Yakovlev, *Omut Pamyati*, 58.

"I felt quite uncomfortable" Ibid., 249.

Stalin's successor For a gripping account of the Secret Speech and its aftereffects consult William Taubman's *Khrushchev: The Man And His Era*, 270–99.

46   **Yakovlev was one of the few** Yakovlev, *Sumerki*, 251–52.

this was pretty dull stuff Taubman, *Khrushchev*, 271.

47 **Khrushchev's speech** Compared to speeches at most Party Congresses,
    a profoundly readable document. I've quoted from the version
    posted online and annotated by Jonathan Bone at
    http://www.uwm.edu/Course/448-343/index12.html.
48 **"Everything was shattered"** Yakovlev, *Sumerki*, 254.
49 **Copies of Khrushchev's speech** Taubman, *Khrushchev*, 283–84.
    It caused heart attacks Ibid., 290.
    It touched off revolutions Ibid., 294–99.

7. THE PARANOID STYLE

50 **Soviet attitudes toward their leaders** On Yakovlev's difficulty processing
    the implications of Khrushchev's speech, see Yakovlev's *Century of
    Violence*, 5–13.
    "The speech turned my" Yakovlev, *Sumerki*, 255.
51 **Across the world** For further effects of the speech on Communists see
    English's *Idea of the West*, 67–70.
52 **"I sensed a need"** Yakovlev, *Century of Violence*, 8.
    Soviet society was changing For more on the climate of the time see
    Alexeyeva and Goldberg's *Thaw Generation*, 71. Background on
    Eisenhower's idea, and the resulting Lacy–Zarubin agreement, which
    opened the way for the first student exchanges of the Cold War, found
    in Yale Richmond, *Cultural Exchange and the Cold War: Raising the
    Iron Curtain*, 23–27.
53 **"kow-towing to bourgeois culture"** This quote, as well as valuable
    detail on the insularity of Soviet society, found in Robert F. Byrnes's
    Soviet–American Academic Exchanges 1958–1975, 32–33.
    Khrushchev's first trip there Taubman, Khrushchev, 419–21.
54 **Yakovlev is bound** Valuable context to Yakovlev's participation in the
    exchange provided during two interviews with Nina Yakovleva,
    December 2006.
    In early September of 1958 Orientation session colour found in
    Kalugin's *First Directorate*, 25–27. On Yakovlev's quarters at Columbia,
    and other background, see Harry Schwartz, "U.S. and Soviet Students
    Praise Exchange," *New York Times*, May 11, 1959, 1. The newspaper story
    also provides the names of the other two Soviet exchange students,

besides Yakovlev and Kalugin. Additional details found in an untitled sidebar on page 7 of the same edition, "Harmony at Columbia."

They weren't scholars That Yakovlev was the only non-spy among the Soviet exchange students at Columbia, see Kalugin, *First Directorate*, 26.

55 **One dark evening** Yakovlev's relationship with Loren Graham is recounted well in Graham's *Moscow Stories*, 223–36. Graham kindly provided additional details, particularly about the night Yakovlev dined at his apartment, in several personal communications in the summer of 2007.

56 **This was exactly the sort** Kryuchkov, *Lichnoe Delo*, 294–95. On the psychology of encirclement and its siege mentality, see English's *Idea of the West*, 37–43.

57 **This manic suspicion** Kalugin shared with me the Soviet exchange students' impressions of New York, and America, author interview, Washington, DC, March 2007.

The communist explorer On Yakovlev feeling as though he was being watched, see ibid. However, I should note that I first encountered the notion that the FBI considered Yakovlev to be the leader of the Soviet spies studying at Columbia in Yale Richmond's *Cultural Exchange*, 28.

58 **Then, in October** Background on the Pasternak affair provided by the second volume of Christopher J. Barnes's *Boris Pasternak: A Literary Biography*, 342–47.

In Yakovlev's Manhattan Yakovlev, *Sumerki*, 175–77.

59 **Some American students** In conversation, both Graham and Kalugin recounted the attention the Soviet students drew from their American counterparts.

Even among the other Kalugin describes how stodgy he considered Yakovlev in those days in Kalugin, CBC, 1–3.

60 **Loren Graham managed** Throughout the recounting of Yakovlev's dinner at Graham's apartment I've drawn on my personal communication with Loren Graham as well as Graham's *Moscow Stories*, 223–36.

62 **"Loren, I've been reading"** Graham, *Moscow Stories*, 224.

64 **Just before his American** Yakovlev recounts his impressions of the American tour in *Sumerki*, 333–34, which is the source of the anecdote about dinner at the Iowa homestead. Kalugin, who also went on the trip, discussed the trip in conversation with me as well.

66 **Yakovlev flew home** In later years, Yakovlev discussed candidly his continuing belief in the superiority of Soviet communism to American capitalism in the wake of his first trip to the United States. See Bill Keller, "Moscow's Other Mastermind," *New York Times Magazine*, February 19, 1989.

Yes, Yakovlev thought For fascinating examinations of Soviet technical prowess, consult Richard Rhodes's *Dark Sun: The Making of the Hydrogen Bomb* as well as *Sakharov: A Biography* by Richard Lourie.

67 **"My first year in New York"** Kalugin, *First Directorate*, 32.

68 **Yakovlev remained critical** Yakovlev, *Pax Americana*, 9.

America changed Yakovlev In Moscow in December 2006, Yakovlev's old friend and colleague in the Central Committee apparat, Albert Belyaev, told me that Yakovlev's associates in the 1960s attributed to his year in America his comparatively liberal nature on such topics as limited pluralism in the press. On a tangent, it is worth noting that few commentators have attempted to rank in print the relative importance of Yakovlev's foreign experiences to his ideological evolution, which seems appropriate, given its tortuous nature. However, on page 29 of *Cultural Exchange*, Yale Richmond sources translator Antonina Bouis sourcing a conversation with Yakovlev in describing his year in Columbia as "more meaningful" than his decade in Canada. "Meaningful" is a frustratingly vague term. If Richmond is arguing that the year in America was more important to Yakovlev's ideological evolution than his decade in Canada, I have to disagree based on a number of considerations, particularly Yakovlev's own tone in writing about his foreign experiences in his memoirs, which, notably, Richmond does not use as a source. Yes, foreign experience can be formative early in life. But Yakovlev was an adult of 34 during his months as a graduate student at Columbia in 1958–59; he was also wary of being corrupted by America's alien political system. In contrast, during his residence in Canada for the ten years from 1973–83, Yakovlev was open to new ideas as an engaged diplomat interacting, debating, observing, and befriending idealistic, committed democrats and capitalists. Richmond's conclusion strikes me as that of a patriot overreaching evidence to claim for his own country an historic achievement. Because my Canadian citizenship leaves me open to the same criticism, I consulted with the comparatively impartial Anatoly Yakovlev on this matter, who responded by e-mail on Jan. 23, 2008. He believes that the Columbia experience proved to his father that America wasn't as bad as Soviet propaganda depicted it to be. Meanwhile, Anatoly writes, "what he had mastered in Canada, was a very clear understanding of a principle of freedom in [the] Lockean sense, a formula that a man is free by nature, and also that he has to, he must, and he is obligated to implement his freedom if he wants to stay a man. . . And for that reason you also have to live in a law-abiding society, thinking of other people and founding your actions on their consent. . . Canada made him conscious of a possibility that a free society can exist, and that I think, was [a] more meaningful experience than a semi-conscious feeling of being brainwashed by Stalinist paranoic propaganda" – which was what Yakovlev attained at Columbia.

"the example of Roosevelt" Graham, *Moscow Stories*, 224.

8. POWER STRUGGLE

70 **In 1960, after four years** Source on dissertation topic is personal communication with Anatoly Yakovlev. Translated title of the dissertation is, "The criticism of the American bourgeois literature on U.S. foreign policy, 1953–57." Personal communication, Anatoly Yakovlev.
     He soon found himself Other widespread practices for analysis of Soviet power dynamics included analyzing lists of leaders in Party newspapers, where your proximity to the leader indicated greater power, and monitoring the size of welcome committees at airports, where bigger was better.

71 **That was nonsense.** For an excellent, if dry, description of the mechanics of power among the Central Committee apparat, see Hough and Fainsod, *How the Soviet Union is Governed*, 409–48.

72 **To what extent** Bukovsky is quoted in Jamie Glazov's May 9, 2001, article referencing an extensive dialogue with Bukovsky in *FrontPage Magazine*, http://www.frontpagemag.com/Articles/ReadArticle.asp?ID=3263. Source on Borovik is author interview, December 2006.

73 **When he rejoined** Yakovlev, *Sumerki*, 275.

74 **It was the warmest period** Such books as Taubman's Khrushchev biography and Alexeyeva and Goldberg's *The Thaw Generation* contain

excellent descriptions of the spirit of this period. On *Novy Mir's* role
see *The Thaw Generation*, 95–96.

"so indigestible, you feel like screaming" Dina Spechler, *Permitted
Dissent in the USSR: Novy Mir and the Soviet Regime*, 21.

Tvardovsky followed See Solzhenitsyn's memoir, *The Oak and the Calf*,
and the response to the memoir, *Solzhenitsyn, Tvardovsky and Novy Mir*
by Vladimir Lakshin. For a more objective view on the magazine, see
Michael Scammell's excellent biography, *Solzhenitsyn*.

Yakovlev, too, felt Yakovelv, *Sumerki*, 296.

"Probably the students" Lev Kopelov, *Ease My Sorrows*, 245. I first
came across this quote in Robert English's *Russia and the Idea of the
West*, 78.

75 **Inspired by the thaw** On his radio shake-up, see Yakovlev, *Sumerki*,
278–79. Great background on Soviet radio provided by Gayle Durham
Hollander, "Recent Developments in Soviet Radio and Television News
Reporting," *The Public Opinion Quarterly* 31, No. 3 (Autumn 1967),
359–65.

The media also were Valuable context on Soviet life and culture
provided in Hedrick Smith's book, *The Russians*, where I found the
airplane anecdote on 345–346.

76 **Such policies perpetuated** Material on the Novocherkassk uprising
found in Taubman, *Khrushchev*, 519–23.

But for a perverse reference On Yakovlev's boss mentioning
Novocherkassk, see *Sumerki*, 259–61.

9. IRON SHURIK

78 **Soon after rejoining** Informative background on Shelepin in Robert M.
Slusser's entry on the politician in Simmonds, *Soviet Leaders*, 87–95;
Roy Medvedev, *Khrushchev*, 133; Arbatov, *The System*, 119–21. Also see
the following items from *New York Times*: "A Moscow Bureaucrat:
Aleksandr Nikolaevich Shelepin," Nov. 17, 1964, 4; "Soviet Said To Cut
Shelepin's Power," Dec. 7, 1965, 3; "Brezhnev's Authority Enhanced
By Soviet Party Reorganization," April 9, 1966, 2; "Shelepin's Role A
Kremlin Riddle," June 5, 1966, 22; "Shelepin Named To A Lesser Post,"
July 12, 1967, 20.

79   **"humbuggery, spoilage, bureaucratism"** "Shelepin Named To A Lesser Post," *The New York Times,* July 12, 1967, 20.

    "How can these people" The quote, and Shelepin's condemnation, are from Michel Tatu's *Power in the Kremlin,* 197ff. Roy Medvedev's 1982 book, *Khrushchev,* also provided valuable background and context.

    "to be nimble" "A Moscow Bureaucrat," *New York Times,* Nov. 17, 1964, 4.

    Indeed, while publicly disavowing Details on the Bandera murder, and more helpful context on Shelepin's stint as KGB leader, provided by John Barron's *KGB: The Secret Work of Soviet Secret Agents,* 313–316. Also see Vladislav M. Zubok's "SPY vs. SPY: The KGB vs. the CIA, 1960–1962," *Cold War International History Project Bulletin,* no. 4 (Fall 1994), 22–33.

    It's not clear That Stepakov was a Shelepin man is found in Yakovlev's *Sumerki,* 322. The "awaken" quote from Yakovlev, *Omut Pamyati,* 188. As Yakovlev portrays it, his association with Shelepin was almost accidental. However, other accounts suggest Yakovlev consciously aligned himself with the Shelepin faction. See, for example, the memoirs of fellow Central Committee apparat G.L. Smirnov, *Uroki Minuvshego,* 163, in which Smirnov recounts the way Yakovlev admonished a member of the Brezhnev faction for backing the wrong man. Yakovlev also is characterized as a Shelepin man in Vadim Medvedev's book, *V Komande Gorbacheva,* 20. My December 2006 interviews with Albert Belyaev and Georgi Arbatov also provided additional context on this matter.

80   **Khrushchev's fate is relevant** See Yakovlev, *Omut Pamyati,* 114–15.

    One of Khrushchev's reforms I drew context on Khrushchev from throughout Taubman's *Khrushchev.* For valuable information on his increasing unpopularity with Party cadres, see 578–619. Information on the leader's toppling is taken from 3–17. And the Brezhnev-as-ballerina quip is to be found in Taubman, 614.

81   **Other grand schemes** On Yakovlev helping to prepare Brezhnev's first speech as leader, see *Sumerki,* 299.

    With Shelepin On staff turnover following Khrushchev's ouster, and Yakovlev's own promotion, see ibid., 300–301.

82   **He also helped Shelepin's** Yakovlev's question to Bovin and Arbatov from *The Diary of Anatoly Chernyaev: 1986,* trans. Anna Melyakov, ed.

Svetlana Savranskaya, entry for February 22, 1986, 24, http://www.gwu.edu/-%7Ensarchiv/NSAEBB/NSAEBB220/Chernyaev_1986.pdf. Key details from the anecdote about the Captain Solyanik corruption scandal drawn from Yakovlev's *Sumerki*, 306–308. Helping to fix the date the anecdote occurred is the *Time* article, "Revisions in Russia," July 30, 1965, http://www.time.com/time/magazine/article/0,9171,834056,00.html.

83 **Once the meeting began** Context on this meeting provided by Yakovlev's fellow member of the Central Committee apparat, Albert Belyaev, during our December 2006 interview.

So most of the Secretariat Valuable context on Suslov that informs the whole of the book is drawn from Roy Medvedev, "The Death of the 'Chief Idealogue'," *New Left Review* 36 (November/December 1982): 55–65. Translated for publication by A.D.P. Briggs.

84 **"Everyone here was correct"** Quotes on this page and next are drawn from Yakovlev's *Sumerki*, 307–308.

Amid all these power games The Shelepin "tightening up" quote is from Solzhenitsyn, *The Oak and the Calf*, 98–99. Additional context for this section is drawn from earlier cited *New York Times* stories as well as from Zhores Medvedev's *Andropov*, 47–53.

85 **A month after Shelepin** Information about the moves against *Novy Mir* found in Spechler's *Permitted Dissent*, 214.

Vladimir Stepakov Information for this paragraph drawn from December 2006 interview with Albert Belyaev.

86 **Tvardovsky was a big** The poet's poignant story drawn from Mary Chaffin's "Alexander Tvardovsky: A Biographical Study," in *Solzhenitsyn, Tvardovsky and Novy Mir* by Vladimir Lakshin, 91–137. Yakovlev's respect for Tvardovsky is clear throughout Yakovlev, *Sumerki*, 312.

"era of Tvardovsky" See Cohen, *An End to Silence*, 62.

In September of 1965 See Spechler, *Permitted Dissent*, 217, as well as Scammell's *Solzhenitsyn*, 526–530, Service's *A History of Twentieth-Century Russia*, 381, and Yitzhak M. Brudny's *Reinventing Russia: Russian Nationalism and the Soviet State, 1953–1991*, 64.

87 **This business put Yakovlev** That Yakovlev wriggled out of the Sinyavsky-Daniel trial, and the parallel to the Pasternak episode, is found in Yakovlev, *Sumerki*, 177–78.

88 **The Sinyavsky–Daniel trial** Source on Yakovlev's defence of Tvardovsky and other members of the intelligentsia is author interview,

Albert Belyaev, Moscow, December 2006. See also Markwick, *Rewriting History*, 200.

Truth, Tvardovsky wrote Spechler's *Permitted Dissent*, 217–20.

How could the reform-minded Yakovlev Excellent context on the unconventional alliances found in Russian opposition factions provided by Smith's *The Russians*, 292. See also similar point made in David Remnick's "The Tsar's Opponent," *New Yorker*, Oct. 1, 2007, 65–78.

10. A FIST TO THE JAW

90   **In June 1966** Source of the anecdote is Yakovlev, *Sumerki*, 321, which I've fixed in time thanks to a page 19, June 6, 1966, *New York Times* story, "Shelepin Off To Mongolia."

In a society Timing on the moves against Semichastny and Shelepin provided by Service's *A History of Twentieth-Century Russia*, 384–85. That Shelepin was having abdominal surgery during his demotion is from Dusko Doder's *Shadows and Whispers*, 154. For the Semichastny–Allilueva connection see Zhores Medvedev, *Andropov*, 55.

91   **"The country swam with the current"** Yakovlev, *Omut Pamyati*, 164–65.

92   **Yakovlev kept busy** Background on the "doktor nauk" degree provided in personal communication from Anatoly Yakovlev, who provided the dissertation's full name: "U.S. Political Science and the Main Foreign Policy Doctrines of American Imperialism: A Critical Review of the Post-War Political Literature on the Problems of War, Peace and International Relations, 1945–1966." On having fun with the absurdities of the Soviet system, see Yakovlev, *Sumerki*, 303.

On August 20, 1968 Yakovlev recounts his experiences in Prague in *Sumerki*, 326–31, from where I've drawn much of the material for this section that is personally related to Yakovlev's experiences, including quotes.

According to the rhetoric Source on Czechoslovakian history in H. Gordon Skilling's comprehensive *Czechoslovakia's Interrupted Revolution*. Source on manner the Prague Spring was covered by the Soviet press is Alexeyeva and Goldberg's *Thaw Generation*, 210–220.

93   **There was another take** Source for much of the background context on perceptions of the Prague Spring among the Moscow intelligentsia

is English's *Russia and the Idea of the West*, 109-13. See also *Thaw Generation*, 210-220.

Yakovlev and his team On invasion death toll of 50, see Skilling, *Interrupted Revolution*, 775.

94 **Here's what the Czech people did** Source on all slogans is Josef Josten's *Unarmed Combat as Practised in Czechoslovakia since 1968*.

95 **The liberal party member** The Karpsinky quote is in the essay he wrote as L. Okunev, "Words Are Also Deeds," first published in Roy Medvedev's samizdat *Political Diary* and included in the compilation edited by Stephen F. Cohen, *An End to Silence: Uncensored Opinion in the Soviet Union*, 306–310. I first came across the quote in Robert English's book, *Russia and the Idea of the West*.

Yakovlev is certain Many different translations exist of the "Two Thousand Words." I've quoted from the version in Josten, *Unarmed Combat*, 71–79.

"proceeding from the principles" Ibid., 31.

96 **Acting "from the principles"** Source on tactics on both sides, particularly related to the battle waged over radio propaganda, is Philip Windsor's *Czechoslovakia 1968*, 120, and Skilling's *Interrupted Revolution*, 778.

"They have guns and rockets" Skilling, *Interrupted Revolution*, 776.

97 **They did try to print the newspaper** Yakovlev, *Sumerki*, 327–28.

After a week in Prague On publication of *Zpravy* and other Soviet propaganda-related machinations, see Skilling, *Interrupted Revolution*, 817n10.

98 **Yakovlev's entreaties** On troop levels, see Windsor, *Czechoslovakia 1968*, 107. Source on text of Palach's note is Josten, *Unarmed Combat*, 34.

11. ONE TRAGEDY LIKE ANY OTHER

99 **In certain quarters** On the militant patriotism, see, for example, Arbatov, *The System*, 136–63. Also see Service's *Twentieth–Century Russia*, 387–8, where he describes the regime's "siege mentality."

Even before the Soviet tanks On the inexorable penetration of communication technology into Soviet society, see Hollander's "Recent Developments in Soviet Radio and Television News Reporting," *The Public Opinion Quarterly* 31, No. 3 (Autumn 1967): 359–65.

100 **In response, the ever-present undercurrent** On xenophobia, see
Brudny, *Reinventing Russia*, 69.

Three weeks after the invasion Viktor Chalmaev's essay appeared in
the September 1968 issue of *Molodaya Gvardiya* 9 (1968). Of the
wealth of academic literature written about the phenomenon of
radical nationalism from 1968–73, easily the most entertaining
accounts reside in the body of work created by Alexander Yanov, whose
writing has been compiled in a number of different volumes. See, for
example, chapters 10 and 11 in his book, *The Russian Challenge and the
Year 2000* – and in particular, pages 105–113. More valuable guidance
provided by John B. Dunlop's book, *The Faces of Contemporary Russian
Nationalism*, particularly 218–33. Brudny's already cited volume also
was extremely helpful.

101 **Although they didn't say so** For the climate of the era and
Trapeznikov's anti-intellectual leanings, see, for example, English,
Russia and the Idea of the West, 122–23, 136–38. Note that English refers
to the radical nationalists as "neo–Slavophiles." Also see Arbatov, *The
System*, 127, 146–47. That Shauro and Stepakov sympathized with the
radical nationalists is from Brudny, *Reinventing Russia*, 94–97; with
additional context on Trapeznikov, Shauro, and Stepakov provided in an
interview with Albert Belyaev, December 2006. The "educated shopkeepers" essay is by Mikhail Lobanov, *Molodaya Gvardiya* 4 (1968).

Yakovlev especially was disgusted Yakovlev, *Sumerki*, 312–313, with additional context provided in interviews with Yakovlev's wife, Nina, and his
son, Anatoly, in December 2006. On the background of the radical
nationalists, see Brudny, *Reinventing Russia*, 73.

102 **Aside from writing the odd** In a memo dated October 1969 found in
his personal papers by his son, Anatoly, Yakovlev argued against any
special celebration for the upcoming 90th anniversary of Stalin's supposed birth, celebrated on December 21, 1879, although the dictator is
thought to have falsified both the year and the day. The Trapeznikov
anecdote recounted in Yakovlev, *Sumerki*, 258. For more on Yakovlev's
protection of lesser–ranked liberal Soviets, see English, *Russia and the
Idea of the West*, 113, 135 and 290n83. In addition, Yakovlev is said to
have protected the unrelated writer and editor, Yegor Yakovlev, in
G.L. Smirnov's *Uroki Minuvshego*, 132–33. Also, additional context on

this point provided during December 2006 interviews with Albert
Belyaev and, to a lesser extent, Georgi Arbatov.

103 **Tvardovsky, too, was barely hanging on** English, *Russia and the Idea of
the West,* 79.

   It came in the form The Dementyev essay, title translated by Brudny
   in *Reinventing Russia,* 83–85, as "On Traditions and Nationalism,"
   was in *Novy Mir,* 4 (1969). My commentary is informed by the opinions
   featured in Yanov, *Russian Challenge,* 113–14, which is the source of the
   quote translation, as well as Scammell, *Solzhenitsyn,* 670 and Dunlop,
   Faces, 221–23.

104 **Yakovlev and the other liberals** See the discussion of the May 1969
   Literaturnaya Gazeta article in Brudny, *Reinventing Russia,* 85–6.
   Although Yakovlev doesn't explicitly mention in his memoirs his participation in the preparation of this article, he does say in *Sumerki,* 315, that
   he helped prepare and edit the similar article in *Kommunist* (no. 17,
   1970) that also appeared under the byline "V. Ivanov," which leads me
   to believe he also participated in the earlier version. Along similar lines,
   Yanov in *Russian Challenge,* 117, speaks of "the Propaganda
   Department's point of view."

   Typically, when the Party That Brezhnev's wife was Jewish, see Service,
   Twentieth–Century Russia, 382.

   So that July The letter was published in *Ogonek* 30 (1969). My source
   on the translation of the "Letter of the Eleven" is Yanov, *Russian
   Challenge,* 115.

105 **On another level** On Solzehnitsyn expulsion, see the writers' *The Oak
   and the Calf,* 257–64.

   Meanwhile, *Novy Mir*'s Tvardovsky Zhores Medvedev, *10 Years After
   Ivan Denisovich,* 125.

106 **"Faced with the facts of the past"** Source of the translation for
   Tvardovsky's poem is Spechler, *Permitted Dissent,* 226. Many of the
   above mentioned publications chronicle this attempt by the Party to
   force Tvardovsky out of *Novy Mir;* see, for example, Scammell,
   Solzhenitsyn, 684.

   "How are things?" Medvedev, *10 Years,* 125.

12. INSPIRATION FROM AMERICA

Source on much of the eyewitness accounts in this chapter were provided in several personal communications by Nicholas Daniloff, at the time the UPI wire service reporter who acted as the trip's tour guide. Daniloff also wrote a day-by-day account shortly after the visit's end for the February 21, 1970, edition of *Editor & Publisher* magazine, 12. Finally, Daniloff also provided me with the relevant excerpt from a draft version of his memoirs, *Of Spies and Spokesman: My Life as a Cold War Correspondent*, which in my version is paginated 190–202 but could be numbered differently in the actual memoirs. Unless noted below, details related to the trip are culled from one of the above sources.

107 **As the Moscow intelligentsia** Yakovlev's account of the trip is found in *Sumerki*, 331–33.

111 **California, too, had its problems** See Jane Fonda's fascinating autobiography, *My Life So Far*, 217–46. For more context on Fonda, see Rex Reed's *New York Times* profile, "Jane: Everybody Expected Me to Fall on My Face," Jan. 25, 1970, 87; also see Mary Hershberger's *Jane Fonda's War: A Political Biography of an Antiwar Icon*, particularly 1–25.
But at the party That McQueen was voted America's favourite film star found in Christopher Sandford's biography, *McQueen*, 464.

112 **At some point in the evening** The Khrushchev–Monroe connection is in Taubman's *Khrushchev*, 430. That Yakovlev refers to Fonda as "Jane," along with further dialogue and details about Yakovlev's interaction with Fonda, found in Yakovlev, *Sumerki*, 331–32. On Fonda's nascent activism, see "Indians Seized in Attempt to Take Over Coast Fort," *New York Times*, March 9, 1970, 22.

113 **By this point** On Hoover's surveillance of Fonda, see her memoirs, 235, 239, 255–57.

114 **Upon their return to the Soviet Union** Daniloff monitored what the Soviet journalists published after their return, as he mentions in my draft of his memoirs, 201–202. Lev Tolkunov's collected writings, *Mify i Realnost*, also provide an account of the trip. The item about Fonda portraits in U.S. military base urinals is from Hershberger, *Jane Fonda's War*, 2–3.

13. ACTING CHIEF OF AGITPROP

116 **On February 10** Description of the encounter between Tvardovsky and Solzhenitsyn drawn from Solzhenitsyn's *The Oak and the Calf*, 275, and Scammell's *Solzhenitsyn*, 684–88.

118 **The experience broke Tvardovsky** See Zhores Medvedev, *Denisovich*, 129–30.

"That's our prize, too" Ibid., 138.

"There are many ways" Solzhenitsyn, *The Oak and the Calf*, 285.

The setup with the poem Yakovlev's dismay at the Party's treatment of Tvardovsky is evident as he recounts the poet's tale in his memoirs, *Sumerki*, 314–15. Additional context provided in December 2006 interview with Albert Belyaev.

119 **Much of Yakovlev's time** Valuable context on this point provided by Georgi Arbatov during our December 2006 interview, as well as in Arbatov's memoir, *The System*, 134–36. Another source on what it was like to work closely with Brezhnev is found in Petr Cherkasov's "The Twilight of the Brezhnev Era," *Russian Politics and Law* 43 no. 6 (November–December 2005): 76–95.

Among the most impressive Source on Zavidovo description is Kissinger, *Years of Upheaval*, 228–35.

121 **"Stepakov's just been dismissed"** Yakovlev recounts the scene in the billiards room, and events of the following day, in *Sumerki*, 322–24, with further details provided during the interview with Arbatov. Yakovlev says in his memoirs that this happened in 1969. However, the *New York Times* mentioned that the dismissal happened "last week" in the un-bylined sidebar, "Propaganda Aides Shifted," April 10, 1970, 10. Citing Arbatov, Brudny says the departure happened in March 1970 in *Reinventing Russia*, 87.

123 **Yakovlev waited anxiously** G.L. Smirnov's *Uroki Minuvshego*, 163, and Vadim Medvedev's *V Komande Gorbacheva*, 19–20, both contend that Yakovlev's earlier affiliation with Shelepin prompted Brezhnev's reluctance to confirm Yakovlev's appointment as head of the Propaganda Department. Albert Belyaev and Georgi Arbatov also subscribed to this line of thinking in our December 2006 interviews.

He asked his associates Yakovlev recounts how he recommended Gorbachev for the post of propaganda chief in BBC–BLA, July 14, 1990, 1.

124 **At this point Yakovlev decided** Yakovlev, *Sumerki*, 323. Yakovlev's antipathy toward "toadying" is apparent in *Sumerki*, 324, where one of Brezhnev's advisors informs Yakovlev that Yakovlev stands a chance at being confirmed to the post of Propaganda chief if he appeals to KGB chief Yuri Andropov, a strategy Yakovlev declines to take because he doesn't like Andropov or what he stands for.

He could leave the Central Committee That Yakovlev considered attempting to lead a research institute is from my December 2006 interview with Georgi Arbatov.

The last course Yakovelv, *Sumerki*, 323.

125 **With such choices** Ibid., 316–17.

Bringing up Simonov On Simonov friendship see ibid. 335.

126 **Yakovlev never says so** For similar analysis of the import of Yakovlev's elevation to acting head of Propaganda, see Brudny, *Reinventing Russia*, 90. On the Rumyanstev putsch, see English, *Russia and the Idea of the West*, 134.

127 **In this fight with the Stalinists** Source of anecdote about Yakovlev protecting the poet Yevgeny Yevtushenko is Bill Keller's profile, "Moscow's Other Mastermind: Aleksandr Yakovlev, Gorbachev's Little-Known Alter-Ego," *New York Times Magazine*, Feb. 19, 1989, 30 and following. Also, on collaborating with Trapeznikov on the firing of the Institute of Russian History chief, see Markwick, *Rewriting History in Soviet Russia*, 228. I'm grateful to University of Toronto history professor Robert E. Johnson for pointing out this item.

Such complicity was necessary See, for example, Arbatov's *The System*, 146. For a great overview on the attacks against liberal Party members and outspoken intelligentsia see English, *Russia and the Idea of the West*, 133–41. On Polyansky's anti-Semitism, see for example, Yanov, *Russian Challenge*, 122, where Polyansky is referred to as *Molodaya Gvardiya's* "patron." In Service, *Twentieth–Century Russia*, 390, Polyansky's ideas are said to be "virtually those of a Russian nationalist." On Andropov's tolerance of nationalism, see Yanov's discussion of the *Veche* affair, in which the KGB is portrayed as allowing continued publication of the virulently nationalist samizdat journal. *Russian Challenge*, 128–54. On the *Sovetskaya Rossiya* affair see Yakovlev,

Sumerki, 318–20. Brudny, *Reinventing Russia*, 90, contains material linking this affair to the Shevtsov novel.

129 **"The topic of Stalin"** In a memo found by Anatoly Yakovlev in his father's personal papers, dated June 19, 1970, and titled (in translation), "About some publications on Stalin."

But that summer The Semanov essay, "O tsennostyakh otnositelnykh i vechnykh," appeared in *Molodaya Gvardiya* 8 (1970): 308–20.

130 **"The turning point"** Source on translated quote is Yanov, *Russian New Right*, 53. Yanov's work also provided valuable direction for my analysis of the Semanov article, although Yakovlev provides similar analysis in *Sumerki*, 315.

"The adherents of chauvinism" Yakovlev, *Sumerki*, 315, which is also the source of Yakovlev sending letters of complaint to party leaders.

"the long-awaited salvo" Ibid. features Yakovlev discussing the article, which is clearly the one that appeared in *Kommunist* 17 (1970). The "member of the intelligentsia" is Yanov, whose quotes appear in *Russian New Right*, 54.

131 **Finally, it seemed** Article under Yakovlev byline is in *Kommunist* 10 (1971). The quote is from page 53, and the source on the translation is Roy Medvedev's *On Socialist Democracy*, 208–9. I'm grateful to Anatoly Yakovlev for providing context on his father's article.

132 **He kept at it.** I came across this Yakovlev article in *Kommunist* in Brudny, *Reinventing Russia*, 95. The article, "XXIV siezd K.P.S.S.: problemy ideino-vospitatelnoi raboty," was published in *Kommunist* 10 (1971), 40–56. For more about *On Literary Criticism*, see Brudny, *Reinventing Russia*, 95.

There were reasons for hope Source on Yakovlev's participation in preparations for the 1972 Summit Series is Yakovlev, CBC, tapes 8–11, 7.

133 **To silence the nationalists** On the *LitGaz* article, see *Sumerki*, 324–26. Additional context to the article's lead-up provided in December 2006 interviews with Anatoly Yakovlev, Nina Yakovleva, Georgi Arbatov, and Albert Belyaev. Also see Yanov, *Russian Challenge*, 121.

The article appeared I've quoted from the translation provided in *The Current Digest of the Soviet Press* 24 No. 47 (December 20, 1972): 1–7.

134 **"the harshest criticism"** Brudny, *Reinventing Russia*, 98.

Its appearance caused Context on the response provided during interviews with Sergei Semanov, Anatoly Yakovlev, Albert Belyaev, and

Georgi Arbatov, December 2006. See also Arbatov's *The System*, 147, as well as previously cited volumes by Yanov, Brudny, and Dunlop.

135 **That didn't happen.** For an artifact of intelligentsia antipathy toward this Sholokov see the fascinating theory set forth in Roy Medvedev's *Problems in the Literary Biography of Mikhail Sholokov*.

Shortly after the article appeared This encounter is described in Yakovlev, *Sumerki*, 325, as well as in Arbatov, *The System*, 147. Also, Georgi Arbatov animatedly acted out Brezhnev's actions and provided further description during our December 2006 interview.

Much of the speculation was correct Yakovlev lists the people who read the article in *Sumerki*, 324. That Yakovlev realized the article would be controversial is implied in G.L. Smirnov, *Uroki Minuvshego*, 127.

136 **Yakovlev had regrets** Quote from *Sumerki*, 335. Source on the meetings with the writers he criticized is interview with Sergei Semanov, Moscow, December 2006. See also Brudny, *Reinventing Russia*, 99.

Yakovlev was relieved On the Secretariat meeting, see *Sumerki*, 325.

137 **Yakovlev went straight** The Demichev meeting is described in *Komsomolskaya Pravda*, FBIS–SOV–90–122, June 25, 1990, 49–50, as well as in *Sumerki*, 325–26.

138 **The next morning** Interview with Anatoly Yakovlev and Nina Yakovleva, December 2006.

While he was in hospital Leaders' machinations to remove Yakovlev described in *Sumerki*, 324–25.

14. THE RELUCTANT DIPLOMAT

141 **The Party officially named** Background context for the hectic run-up to the Yakovlevs' departure from Moscow provided in a series of interviews with Anatoly Yakovlev and Nina Yakovleva, December 2006. That Yakovlev was named to his post in mid-May, 1973, is confirmed by a letter found in LAC, RG25 vol. 16521, file 22–10–USSR–1 pt. 2, signed N. Podgorny and dated May 16, 1973. The letter informs the Canadian government of the recall of Yakovlev's predecessor as ambassador to Canada, Boris Miroshnichenko.

142 **A few managed charitable** Gromyko's unconventional language acquisition advice mentioned in *Sumerki*, 326. That friends warned Yakovlev about KGB agents in foreign embassies is ibid., 337. Ratio of

KGB-linked embassy staff members from interview with Oleg Kalugin, Washington, D.C., March 2007.

Sympathy came from Barvikha Sanitarium anecdote source is Yakovlev, *Sumerki*, 274–75.

Back in Yaroslavl Interviews with Anatoly Yakovlev and Nina Yakovleva, Moscow, December 2006.

143 **Yakovelv and Nina arrived** In his *Komsomolskaya Pravda*, FBIS–SOV–90–122, June 25, 1990, 50, Yakovlev said he arrived in Canada on the date of July 21. In fact, he arrived on July 19 as indicated by Soviet embassy diplomatic note no. 173 dated Aug. 16, 1973, in LAC, RG25 vol. 16521, file 22–10-USSR, pt. 2. Most details and descriptions of the circumstances of Yakovlev's arrival from interview with Nina Yakovleva, Moscow, December 2006, with some context provided by Yakovlev, *Sumerki*, 337.

145 **The early days in Ottawa** Source of details on Yakovlev's visit with the protocol chief as well as his presentations of credentials found in LAC RG25, vol. 16521, file 22–10–USSR, pt. 2; in memos and schedules dated July 24, 1973, and in an undated transcript of Yakovlev's short speech.

147 **It was during** The Chrétien musk oxen anecdote found in *Sumerki*, 338–39. Additional context provided in interview with Anatoly Yakovlev, Moscow, December 2006.

148 **By the autumn of 1973** Interviews with Nina Yakovleva and Anatoly Yakovlev, Moscow, December 2006.

Then, still more humiliation LAC RG25 vol. 9218, file 20–USSR–9 pt. 8, in a Sept. 18, 1973, memo written by J. Halstead, subject heading "Suslov visit."

The fact that Yakovlev's boss Description of October Revolution anniversary party as well as, in following paragraphs, Nina Yakovleva's homesickness and difficulties adjusting to diplomatic life, provided by Yakovlev family interviews, December 2006. Additional context provided by Anatoly Yakovlev in personal communication dated May 31, 2007.

150 **Midway through that first** Quite a bit of documentary evidence exists in LAC recording this remarkable, bizarre and mostly forgotten episode of Canadian-Soviet relations. Although Yakovlev does mention this episode in the Canadian chapter of his *Sumerki*, 339, I've drawn most of my details from RG25 vol. 9218, file 20–USSR–9 pt. 8. See below for more specific sources from this file.

151 **Preparing for the visit** Source on Alfa–66 is a Jan. 23, 1974 secret memo titled "Brezhnev Stop-over at Gander: Security" and an identically titled secret memo dated Jan. 24, 1974, by V.G. Turner, the director of the Department of External Affairs Eastern European Division. RG25 vol. 9218, file 20–USSR–9 pt. 8.

Brezhnev was scheduled Source of most details on Brezhnev's first visit is LAC RG25 vol. 9218, file 20–USSR–9 pt. 8. See a confidential four-page account by External Affairs' diplomat O.A. Chistoff, "Brezhnev Stop-over at Gander, January 28, 1974," and dated Jan. 29. 1974, as well as an unclassified memo by O.A. Chistoff, "Leonid Ilich Brezhnev's Stopover at Gander . . ." dated Feb. 4, 1974 detailing Chistoff's meeting with I.F. Kovalenko, Soviet embassy counselor. Note that in Yakovlev's memoirs he puts Don Jamieson at the first meeting; in fact, Jamieson arrived only at the second meeting, and in contrast to Yakovlev's description, he wasn't yet the Canadian Secretary of State.

153 **Brezhnev would touch down again** Source on one of the more unusual protests of the Cold War, as well as other aspects of Brezhnev's return visit, is a series of confidential memos by O.A. Chistoff, found in LAC RG25 vol. 9218, file 20–USSR–9 pt. 8, namely: "Brezhnev's Stopover at Gander on Feb. 3, 1974: Sequence of Events," dated Feb. 5, 1974; "Brezhnev's Stop-over at Gander on February 3, 1974: Side issues," dated Feb. 6, 1974; and "Brezhnev's Stopover at Gander on February 3, 1974: Questions about Jews, Fishing Questions, Civil Aviation," dated Feb. 7, 1974. The inconsistency of "stopover" spelling is Chistoff's.

15. THE NEW CANADA

158 **"It is difficult"** English, *Russia and the Idea of the West*, 75.

159 **A little more than a year** See Ivan Head, "The Foreign Policy of the New Canada," *Foreign Affairs* 50, no. 2 (January 1972): 237–52. In a personal communication dated Jan. 20, 2008, Anatoly Yakovlev says it was Georgi Arbatov who suggested Yakovlev meet Ivan Head.

Head occupied a role See, for example, historian Robert Bothwell's illuminating interview with Ford in the Bothwell papers at the University of Toronto's Thomas Fisher Rare Book Library. Ford also alludes to the friction between Trudeau's office and External Affairs, and External Affairs' anti-Soviet bent, in *Our Man in Moscow*,

113–17. Further context on differing perspectives toward the Soviets in the prime minister's office and External Affairs provided in interview with Landon and Geoffrey Pearson, Ottawa, June 2007. Canadian diplomats speculating about Yakovlev is in LAC RG 25 vol. 16521, file 22–10–USSR–1 pt. 2, in an Oct. 2, 1974 letter by O.A. Chistoff.

160 **But Pearson stepped down** See Granatstein and Bothwell, *Pirouette*, 3–35. See also Mitchell Sharp, *Which Reminds Me . . .* , 171–75. "'New Guys with New Ideas' – 1968–1984," *Our Past: The History of the Department of Foreign Affairs and International Trade*, http://www.dfait-maeci.gc.ca/hist/history-11-en.asp.

161 **Thanks to his experience** I'm grateful to Ralph Lysyshyn, the Canadian ambassador to Russia, for making this point in an interview at his home near Ottawa, November 2007.

In his gruff Details on the relationship between Head and Yakovlev are drawn from a telephone interview I conducted with Head in October 2002, when I was researching a feature story about Gorbachev's 1983 tour of Canada, "The Walk That Changed The World," *Saturday Night* (April 2003): 39–42. Also valuable was Head, CBC, 1–3. Head described Kissinger as his "counterpart" in my interview with him. That Trudeau wanted to establish Head as the Canadian Kissinger, see Granatstein and Bothwell, *Pirouette*, 50.

Yakovlev met with Head Description of embassy study provided in personal communication by Anatoly Yakovlev, June 16, 2007.

162 **To explain this** Context of growing nationalism provided by William Borders, "Un-Canadian Talk About Fuel For the U.S.," *New York Times*, Nov. 18, 1973, 187.

163 **So "the new Canada"** The Newman quote is from "A Leading Editor Sees Canada Coming Into Her Own," *New York Times*, Oct. 14, 1973, 3. *The Times* is quoting Newman's book, *Home Country*. The Fulford quotes are from Robert Fulford, "Canada wants out (of the United States)," *New York Times Book Review*, Apr. 21, 1974, 28.

164 **Another fact of the new Canada** My interviews with such Canadian diplomats as Allan Gotlieb and Si Taylor provided context on Head's agnosticism in the Cold War. Also see the tone in the section on the Soviet Union and China in Ivan L. Head and Pierre Elliott Trudeau, *The Canadian Way*, 217–263. Quote is from 221.

166 **Their first encounter** Head makes similar points in both my interview and the CBC interview, and also describes Yakovlev as different from other Soviets in *The Canadian Way*, 259–60.

167 **So, after the first encounter** On Head and Yakovlev's burgeoning relationship see, for example, Head's files in the Trudeau papers, LAC MG26 O11 vol. 136, which features numerous letters exchanged between Head and Yakovlev on such matters as the Ukrainian dissident Valentyn Moroz and alleged Soviet war criminal David Geldiaschvilli.

"I am concerned" Quote from confidential memo by E.P. Black, "Soviet Ambassador's Contacts with the Prime Minister's Office," Feb. 26, 1975, LAC RG25, vol. 16521, file 22–10–USSR–1 pt. 2. See also the diligence with which Head informs External about his contacts with Yakovlev throughout numerous documents in LAC MG26 O19 vol. 136.

16. THROWING SNOWBALLS AT LENIN'S TOMB

168 **The idea behind** Background on the Summit Series provided by Scott Young's *War on Ice*, particularly 168–191.

169 **Watching the series** Yakovlev comments on his hockey attendance in *Sumerki*, 336. On watching the game with Trudeau, see *Sumerki*, 342.

170 **The Summit Series** Quote from Yakovlev, CBC, tapes 8–11, 7.

Pierre Trudeau picked up Ibid.

Trudeau affected The Reston quote is from a column in *New York Times*, Mar. 3, 1976, 29.

171 **The Canadian leader's** Most facts about Trudeau's early life are drawn from John English's impressively comprehensive biography, *Citizen of the World*, particularly 14–15.

172 **"Canada and Canadians want"** Details from the 1971 trip from Granatstein and Bothwell's *Pirouette*, 191–96.

Canada's prime minister Another prominent leader who seemed agnostic in the Cold War was West Germany's Willy Brandt, whose chancellorship concluded in 1972. Trudeau's attempt at rapprochement can nevertheless be interpreted as similar to Brandt's *ostpolitik*.

"the great material inequalities" English, *Citizen*, 195.

173 **Trudeau's thesis advisor** Details on Laski's well-known mentorship of Trudeau from English, *Citizen*, 170–74. That Laski influenced Joe Kennedy Jr. is from Nigel Hamilton's *JFK: Reckless Youth*, 108–9, 139–43.

Central to Laski's appeal Further background on Laski provided by Michael Newman's *Harold Laski: A Political Biography*, 258–309. Quotes are from 289 and 291.

174 **"[Laski] became a major"** Quote from English, *Citizen*, 171–3.
By the time Details from Trudeau's travel experiences in the Soviet Union and elsewhere, from ibid., 177–90, 262–72, 336.

175 **Later in life** Head and Trudeau, *Canadian Way*, 217. Trudeau's stance on the Soviet invasion of Czechoslovakia and "military threat" from Gwyn, *Northern Magus*, 304.
"a rapprochement with Moscow" See Ford, *Our Man in Moscow*, 134–35.

176 **"He could not see"** Granatstein and Bothwell, *Pirouette*, 8.
One key advisor Confidential at request of source.
"The sovereignty of the individual" Gwyn, *Northern Magus*, 53–54. On the demonstration shenanigans, see Gerald Clark, "From Trudeaumania to political maturity," *New York Times Book Review*, Nov. 3, 1974, 319.
What matters is that On Trudeau's stance toward the United States, see Mark MacGuigan's *An Inside Look At External Affairs in the Trudeau Years: The Memoirs of Mark MacGuigan*, 10.

177 **"his position . . . neutralist-idealist"** English, *Citizen*, 265.
Once Yakovlev befriended Gotlieb quote from August 2007 interview in Toronto.
"He would refuse" Ford, *Our Man in Moscow*, 135.
"The new Soviet ambassador" LAC, Ivan L. Head papers, Box 15, "Memorandum for the Prime Minister" dated Sept. 12, 1973.

178 **Yakovlev and Trudeau's relationship** The blini invitation from interview with Igor Zakharov, November 2007.
Their families also got along Interview with Nina Yakovleva, December 2006, which is also the source of the quote that concludes the paragraph.
"Margaret treated my wife" Yakovlev, CBC, tapes 8–11, 4.
In fact, one legend Alexandre Trudeau, Nov. 14, 2007, personal communication.

179 **The two families grew closer** Context provided by Natasha Lobanova, Yakovlev's granddaughter, over the course of 2006–7, as well as interview with Alexandre Trudeau, March 2007. The "staff member" from External is Si Taylor, author interview, June 2007.

Still, this was the Cold War On External's concern about the relationship, see E.P. Black, "Soviet Ambassador's Contacts with the Prime Minister's Office," Feb. 26, 1975, LAC RG25, vol. 16521, file 22–10–USSR–1 pt. 2.

180 **It seems more likely** Context on experience of conversing with Trudeau provided in interview with James Coutts, November 2007, Toronto.

As time passed Information for context on following characterization of Trudeau-'Yakovlev relationship gleaned from literally dozens of primary and secondary sources. However, my most valuable source was my only contact with Yakovlev when he was alive. To research my feature on the 1983 Gorbachev trip, "The Walk That Changed The World," *Saturday Night* (April 2003): 39–42, I faxed Yakovlev a long list of questions in the autumn of 2002. He responded with 5,000 words of answers by e-mail through his executive assistant, Gennady Zolotov, in February 2003 – too late for me to use much for the *Saturday Night* piece, but a valuable resource for this book. Yakovlev spoke of his relationship with Trudeau on page four of that document. In addition, Head's interviews with me for the same article, and his interview with the CBC, provided valuable context on the ambassador-PM relationship, as did Trudeau's interview with Robert Bothwell, Bothwell papers, Thomas Fisher Rare Book Library, University of Toronto.

181 **In the early days** On Geldiaschvilli, see the LAC's Ivan L. Head papers, confidential Memorandum for the Prime Minister by Ivan Head, "Subject: Foreign Relations," Dec. 30, 1974, in which Yakovlev asks Head to inform the prime minister of the unprecedented nature of the commuting of Geldiaschvilli's sentence. Also see the Oct. 12, 1976, letter from Alexandra Geldiaschvilli to the "Rt. Hon. Pierre Elliott Trudeau," MG26 O7 vol. 535, file 12/U56. Most External Affairs documents spell the name "Geldiashvilli." However, in the letter to Trudeau, the wife herself spells it "Geldiaschvilli," which is the spelling I've used. On Brezhnev, see the secret Memorandum for the Prime Minister by Ivan Head, "Subject: Canada–Soviet Relations," Jan. 21, 1975, in MG26 O11 vol. 25, file 840/U56.

The relationship could work The Yakovlev quote from *Sumerki*, 349. On Solzhenitsyn see *Omut Pamyati*, 218–19.

182 **Trudeau and Yakovlev** That Trudeau insulated his relationship with Yakovlev from External is in MacGuigan, *External Affairs*, 9. Yakovlev's

quotes on Trudeau from *Sumerki*, 349–51. Yakovlev quote on the "shrewd intellectual" from Yakovlev's pseudonymous article as S. Potapov, "Canada's dilemma," *Novy Mir* 7 (1982), 1. Translation provided by Anatoly Yakovlev.

Yakovlev's behaviour Details on Yakovlev's salons provided by Ralph Lysyshyn, interview, November 2007, as well as Trudeau's interview by Robert Bothwell in Bothwell papers, Thomas Fisher Rare Book Library, University of Toronto.

183 **There is some evidence** Zakharov interview by author, November 2007. **Even without their** Context on 1974 provided by numerous newspaper and magazine sources, particularly William Borders, "Canada's 'Trudeaumania' is Dissolved by Inflation," *New York Times*, May 10, 1974, 4.

184 **Among the biggest** Margaret Trudeau quote, "Now Margaret Trudeau Is A Campaign Regular," *New York Times*, June 23, 1974, 13.

186 **It is surely significant** Quote from Editorial, "Decision in Canada," *New York Times*, July 10, 1974, 36.

17. A TIME OF REST AND MANY THOUGHTS

187 **Ottawa wasn't just** Details of Yakovlev's growing comfort in Ottawa as well as Yakovlev family life from family interviews, particularly Nina Yakovleva in Moscow, December 2006, and granddaughter Natasha Lobanova at various points throughout 2006 and 2007.

189 **Regardless, Canada became** In fact, Yakovlev actually says, "I made a careful study of Canadian life." *Sumerki*, 356. Some details of farm visits from personal communication to author by Aleksandr Yakovlev, February 2003, 1–3, as well as Yakovlev, CBC, tapes 8–11, 3–5. In Whelan, CBC, 1, Whelan details Yakovlev's fascination with the Canadian political process, describing how the ambassador "would go to political conventions." Additional context provided in interviews with former Yakovlev embassy employees Gennady Zolotov and Nikolai Pleshanov (agricultural attaché), December 2006. Also see the comprehensive knowledge of Canadian life Yakovlev displayed in the half-dozen or so articles he wrote about Canada, including Yakovlev writing as S. Potapov, "Canada's dilemma," *Novy Mir* 7 (1982), and Yakovlev writing as N.N. Agashin, "Dosye na 800 tisyach kanadtsev (k itogam

raboti komissii Macdonalda)", *USA: Economika, Politika, Ideologia* 6
(1982): 49–59. On Yakovlev's book-writing efforts and assistant procure-
ment, see LAC RG24, vol. 16521, file 22–10–USSR–1, Confidential
memo "Courtesy Call by Soviet Ambassador," dated Mar. 9, 1976.

191   **"It was a time of both rest"** Personal communication to author by
Aleksandr Yakovlev, February 2003, 2.

The job had its inconveniences Most background on Moroz from
Arnold Bruner, "Moroz imprisoned with psychopaths," *Globe and Mail*,
Dec. 19, 1977, 5. See also Ivan L. Head, Secret Memorandum for the
Prime Minister, "Subject: Canada-Soviet Relations," Jan. 21, 1975, 2,
LAC MG26 O11 vol. 25, file 840/U56.

There were other irritants In addition to the above secret memo, which
also mentions Gresko and features the Prime Minister's scrawled reply,
"Tell the Ambassador I was not really embarrassed," see MG26 O11 vol.
26, file 840/U56, secret memos dated Nov. 22 and Nov. 26, 1974, which
illustrate the flap the incident caused in External Affairs before the story
broke. Also see Richard Cleroux, "Soviet spy in U.K. becomes attaché at
Montreal Games," *Globe and Mail*, Dec. 7, 1974, 1.

192   **There was friction** See Yakovlev, *Sumerki*, 348–49. Embassy background
provided by interview with Yakovlev friend and longtime member of the
Soviet diplomatic colony in Montreal, Marietta Stepanyants, Moscow,
December 2006.

18. WAR MINUS THE SHOOTING

194   **In 1976, Montreal** Details and statistics relating to the hyper-politicized
nature of the Montreal Olympics in Andrew Strenk, "Back to the Very
First Day: Eighty Years of Politics in the Olympic Games," *Journal of
Sport and Social Issues* 2 no. 1 (Spring/Summer 1978): 24–28.

195   **So athletic supremacy** Yakovlev's concern in the run-up to the Montreal
Olympics is reflected in a letter Ivan Head wrote after a meeting with
Yakovlev to Basil Robinson, the then-Undersecretary of State for External
Affairs, June 21, 1976. LAC MG26 O19 vol. 136, USSR file.

196   **As soon as the Games** See Yakovlev's account of the 1976 Olympics in
Sumerki, 342–43.

For Yakovlev, the Olympics Most of the background on Sergei
Nemtsanov provided in author interview with Skip Phoenix, Toronto,

November 2007. Also see "A Soviet Swimmer Defects In Canada," *New York Times*, July 30, 1976, 2.

197 **When they discovered** Immediate diplomatic aftermath of the defection provided by External Affairs telegram GEA0677 and GEA0676, both by O.A. Chistoff, both headed "Soviet Olympic Diver: S. Nemtsanov" and dated July 30, 1976. LAC RG25 vol. 9338 file 20–15–3.

198 **Yakovlev at this point** Telegram GEA0681, July 30, 1976; also, another excellent chronology from the point of view of Canada's External Affairs found in O.A. Chistoff's Confidential Memorandum for the Minister, "Subject: Soviet Olympic Diver: Sergei Nemtsanov," Aug. 3, 1976. Along with Yakovlev's diplomatic note, all documents found in LAC RG25 vol. 9338 file 20–15–3.

The assistant under-secretary Details on Nemtsanov's activities from Skip Phoenix interview.

200 **With his job hanging** The PM's letter plus those of Nemtsanov's mother and grandmother are in LAC RG25 vol. 9338 file 20–15–3.

201 **"As I mentioned"** Trudeau's follow-up letter dated July 31, 1976, also in LAC RG25 vol. 9338 file 20–15–3.

So it was that Details of this meeting provided in the annex to O.A. Chistoff's Confidential Memorandum for the Minister, "Subject: Soviet Olympic Diver: Sergei Nemtsanov," Aug. 3, 1976. LAC RG25 vol. 9338 file 20–15–3.

And that was it On press conference, see "Defector Abducted, Soviet Aide Charges," *New York Times*, Aug. 3, 1976, 3. On Yakovlev comment to MacEachen, see telegram GEA–712 by O.A. Chistoff, "Soviet Olympic Athlete Nemtsanov," Aug. 12, 1976. LAC RG25 vol. 9338 file 20–15–3.

202 **It was not to be** Telegram GEA0726, Aug. 17, 1976, LAC MG26 O7 vol. 535, file 12/U56/9.2.

Once behind the Iron Curtain See "Drugged in Canada, defector says," *Globe and Mail*, Sept. 11, 1976, 1. On the Ivan Head memo, see Confidential memo for the Prime Minister by Ivan L. Head, "Soviet Defector," Sept. 17, 1976, LAC MG26 O7 vol. 535, file 12/U56/9.2.

The Soviet ambassador was Yakovlev, *Sumerki*, 342–43, as well as Yakovlev, CBC, tapes 8–11, 3.

203 **Yakovlev's Olympic experience** Meeting details from author interview, George Cohon, several times through 2006 and 2007, as well as the entertaining Cohon memoirs, George Cohon with David Macfarlane,

To Russia with Fries, 21, 27. See Yakovlev's recounting of the meeting in CBC, tapes 8–11, 8.

19. PERSONA NON GRATA

206 **Early one Tuesday** The Cosmos 954 incident is mentioned in Head and Trudeau, *The Canadian Way*, 256–59, as well as in Head, CBC, 15–18. Also see Yakovlev, *Sumerki*, 354–55. Details on the Soviet space exhibit in Zena Cherry, "Science centre spaceship display celebrates Sputnik 1," *Globe and Mail*, Feb. 7, 1978, 13.

208 **Back in Ottawa** See the host of articles led by the misleadingly titled Jeffrey Simpson and Mary Trueman article, "Ottawa expels 11 Russians for trying to infiltrate RCMP," *Globe and Mail*, Feb. 10, 1978, 1. Gotlieb provided valuable context in an August 2007 interview in Toronto to bolster his short account in *The Washington Diaries 1981–1989*, 510–11.

209 **He might have expected** See Richard Cleroux, *Official Secrets: The Story Behind The Canadian Security Intelligence Service*, 31–64.

211 **About an hour** See *Globe and Mail*, Feb. 10, 1978, 1, for a description of the press conference. Number of embassy employees from LAC RG24, vol. 16521, file 22–10–USSR–1, Confidential memo "Courtesy Call by Soviet Ambassador," dated Mar. 9, 1976.
More details would trickle See Kalugin, *The First Directorate*, 152–57. My Washington interview with Kalugin also provided context here.

212 **Jamieson's press conference** How events were perceived inside the Soviet diplomatic colony provided in interviews with former members Nina Yakovleva, Natasha Lobanova, and Marietta Stepanyants. That Yakovlev, too, was accused of spying, see "Envoy ouster Canadian plot, Russians say in Tass report," *Edmonton Journal*, Feb. 10, 1978, A6.

213 **That there were spies** Interview with Oleg Kalugin, March 2007.
Shortly after he returned Head speaks on his dealings with Yakovlev during the spy scandal in Head, CBC, 6–12. See also in Head and Trudeau, *The Canadian Way*, 260–62.

215 **On the morning of** Details on Reztsov's young son, see Mary Trueman, "PM scoffs at suspicions on spy coup's timing," *Globe and Mail*, Feb. 11,

1978, A12. Details also drawn from *Ottawa Citizen* front-page story published same day. Dialogue and anecdote about weekend contact with Head is from Head, CBC, 11–12.

216 **The next morning, a Sunday** Yakovlev describes this meeting, and his impressions of the spy scandal, in *Sumerki*, 346–48. Further details in a seven-page Top Secret memo, "Notes of Conversation between U.S.S.R. Ambassador A.N. Yakovlev and Ivan L. Head, February 14, 1978," dated Feb. 17, 1978, in the LAC's Ivan L. Head papers.

219 **"You know Mr. Ambassador"** License plate anecdote from Head, CBC, 9.
On Tuesday, February 14 See previously cited Top Secret memo dated Feb. 17, 1978, Ivan L. Head papers.

222 **The first text** Yakovlev, *Sumerki*, 347. That Kryuchkov warned Kalugin away from Yakovlev on a subsequent home leave is from my Kalugin interview as well as Kalugin, CBC, 7.

223 **The second text** Text provided by Anatoly Yakovlev from his father's personal archives. Undated. In English, the memo is called, "On the unfriendly actions of the Canadian government, carried out in February 1978 against staff of Soviet institutions in Canada."

224 **The final two texts** Again, provided by Anatoly Yakovlev from his father's personal archives. The abbreviated version is N.N. Agashin, "Dosye na 800 tisyach kanadtsev (k itogam raboti komissii Macdonalda)," *USA: Economika, Politika, Ideologia* 6 (1982): 49–59. The longer version is N. Agashin, *Bednyi Santa Klaus: ili Politseikoye oko demokratii* (Moscow: Agentstvo Pechati Novosti, 1983). The title, in English, *Poor Santa*, refers to a joke about a young boy who writes a letter to Santa asking whether his red suit means Santa's a Communist. The punch line has the boy being investigated by the RCMP on suspicion of harbouring subversive beliefs.

225 **The reform process** Concluding quote from Yakovlev, *Sumerki*, 372.

20. KILLING TIME

226 **Russian journalist Genrikh Borovik** Interview with author in Moscow, December 2006. Borovik also recounts this anecdote in the Yakovlev tribute, "Three Conversations," *Grazhdanin* 5 (2003).

227 **Yakovlev expressed** That Yakovlev referred to such experiences
as "bursting," see Yakovlev, CBC, tapes 8–11, 6. For similar "burst"
conversations that feature Yakovlev voicing desires to reform the
Soviet Union, see *The Diary of Anatoly Chernyaev: 1985*, trans. Anna
Melyakov, ed. Svetlana Savranskaya, entry for November 11, 1985, 153.
http://www.gwu .edu/~nsarchiv/ NSAEBB/NSAEBB192/Chernyaev-
_Diary_translation_1985.pdf, in which Chernyaev describes an "ultra-
democratic" talk with Yakovlev on the streets of Montreal. Yakovlev was
also tempted to have a similar conversation with Soviet premier Alexei
Kosygin at Kosygin's dacha in Pitsunda on the Black Sea, during the
November 1973 visit to the USSR of Canadian Secretary of State for
External Affairs Mitchell Sharp. See *Sumerki*, 321.
Hence the frustration Conditions in the USSR from Service,
Twentieth–Century Russia. The "key common goal" quote, 425, average
age stat, 402.

228 **Now Yakovlev felt** See Yakovlev, *Sumerki*, 349. Quote is from ibid., 360.

229 **Then Moscow raised** Ibid., 239. For a remarkable account of this tense
moment in history, see Richard Rhodes, *Arsenals of Folly: The Making
of the Nuclear Arms Race*, particularly 134–153. Additional Cold War
context provided by John Lewis Gaddis, *The Cold War: A New History*,
195–236. For discussion of the game-changing nature of SS–20s see
Matlock, *Reagan and Gorbachev*, 38–41.
The timing was horrible For Trudeau on America, see Head and
Trudeau, *The Canadian Way*, 168–69.

230 **Other circumstances** Considerable documentation on Head's
departure from the Prime Minister's Office to the IDRC exists in
LAC, Ivan Head papers. On new relationship with External Affairs,
Gotlieb interview, Toronto, August 2007. On Trudeau, see
Stephen Clarkson and Christina McCall, *Trudeau And Our
Times* vol. 1, 134–59.

231 **More dispiriting news** Cohon interviews, Toronto, 2006 and 2007 as
well as *To Russia With Fries*, 31–36, 81–83, 182, and Yakovlev, *Sumerki*,
343–44.

232 **Something *did* happen.** On Sakharov, see Lourie, *Sakharov*, 301–3.

233 **Events seemed to be spinning** Yakovlev mentions Reagan's visit in
Sumerki, 351. On Reagan's foreign policy and the context of the times

see Jules Tygiel, *Ronald Reagan and the Triumph of American Conservatism*, 149–52 as well as Gaddis, *Cold War*, 199–214 and Rhodes, *Arsenals of Folly*, 147–53.

On top of all this Interviews with Natasha Lobanova, Toronto, 2006 and 2007. Further context provided by Yakovlev's interview in *Komsomolskaya Pravda*, June 5, 1990, trans. in FBIS–SOV–90–122, June 25, 1990, 50.

234 **"Thus it was"** Yakovlev, *Sumerki*, 359–60.

Clearly, the Yakovlevs On the visit with the Doukhobors, see ibid., 351–53. Additional material on following pages on Doukhobors, and Yakovlev's visit, from interviews with Natasha Lobanova, Toronto, 2006 and 2007, in addition to Nina Yakovleva and Nikolai Pleshanov, Moscow, December 2006. Yakovlev also wrote quite a long article on Doukhobor history first published in *Druzhba narodov* 12 (1984) and then republished with a new perestroika-relevant introduction in his 1989 book, *Realizm – zemlya perestroyki: Izbrannye vystupleniya i stat'i*, 40–69. For background on the Doukhobors and details of Yakovlev's activities in the British Columbia interior I relied heavily on interviews with J.J. Verigin, Jr., along with Dmitri (Jim) Popoff and his father, Eli, in Grand Forks, BC, December 2007, as well as Peter and Lisa Voykin, in Castlegar, BC, December 2007. See also Hubert G. Mayes, "Resurrection: Tolstoy and Canada's Doukhobors," *The Beaver* (October/November 1999): 38–44 and the entertaining book by Gregory J. Cran, *Negotiating Buck Naked: Doukhobors, Public Policy & Conflict Resolution*, particularly 1–45.

239 **At about the same time** Personal communication to author by Aleksandr Yakovlev, February 2003, 2–3. On earlier relationship with Gorbachev see Yakovlev, BBC–BLA, July 14, 1990, as well as *Komsomolskaya Pravda* Yakovlev interview, FBIS–SOV–90–122, June 25, 1990, 50.

240 **As the buzz built** Yakovlev publishing pseudonymously as S. Potapov, "Canada's dilemma," *Novy Mir* 7 (1982). Translation provided by Anatoly Yakovlev. On wheat embargo, see Yakovlev, *Sumerki*, 304, as well as "Canada to Sell Grain to Russia," *New York Times*, Mar. 3, 1980, D5.

With Trudeau back Context on Yakovlev from author interview with Eugene Whelan, Amherstburg, Ontario, October, 2002. Also see

Whelan, CBC, 3–5. On $1.8 billion grain sales see LAC RG25 vol. 8704, file 20–USSR–9 pt. 14, "Visit of Mikhail Gorbachev: Notes for the Prime Minister," dated May 16, 1983.

241 **Meanwhile, Yakovlev killed time** See Yakovlev as S. Potapov, "Canada's dilemma," *Novy Mir* 7 (1982). On Pugwash see Flora Lewis, "Punishing the Soviets," *New York Times*, Jul. 22, 1982, 23, in which Yakovlev is quoted. On Schreyer friendship, interview with Ed Schreyer, October 2006 and December 2007. On dinner, source is Dec. 30 and 31, 1980, diary entry graciously provided by Claire Mowat. According to author's personal communication with Farley Mowat, Yakovlev in 1986 played an important role in the arrangements for the Siberia location filming for Mowat's documentary, *The New North*.

242 **Yakovlev, the inveterate America watcher** Feb. 3, 1983, speech to Toronto's Empire Club, Aleksandr N. Yakovlev, "Idols and Dangers of a Complex World: Notes from an address. . . ."
Finally, the Kremlin's Details on Andropov's machinations, the Brezhnev corruption scandal, strokes of Suslov and Brezhnev, and Andropov's resultant push for agricultural reform, see Medvedev, *Andropov*, 9, 15, 88–98, 131–32.

244 **Yakovlev redoubled** Personal communication to author by Aleksandr Yakovlev, February 2003, 2.
Andropov's manoeuvring Grishin v. Inozemtsev from English, *Russia and the Idea of the West*, 170–71.
In November 1982 See Yakovlev, *Sumerki*, 571.

245 **As Yakovlev predicted** On *Izvestia* stories, Medvedev, *Andropov*, 131–32.
With Gorbachev now eager Dates in this paragraph from various memos, LAC RG25 vol. 9218, file 20–USSR–9 pt. 13.

21. MISHA IN THE OTHER WORLD

246 **The weeks leading** Excellent documentation on the Gorbachev trip exists in the External Affairs records at Library and Archives Canada, particularly in LAC RG25 vol. 9218, file 20–USSR–9 pt. 13 and vol. 8704, file 20–USSR–9 pt. 14. See confidential memo GEA–0445, A.P. McLaine, "Visit to Canada: CPSU Politburo Member M. Gorbachev," Mar. 8, 1983.

247 **Yakovlev consulted with** Among the people with whom Yakovlev discussed his interest in the IMEMO position was Canadian ambassador to
the Soviet Union, Geoffrey Pearson. See LAC RG25, vol. 16521,
22–10–USSR–1 pt. 2, telegram "Possible promotion of Yakovlev," dated
May 27, 1983. On Yakovlev's negotiations see RG25, vol. 9218, file
20–USSR–9, pt. 13, memos GEA–0675, Apr. 7, 1983, and GEA–0541,
Mar. 22, 1983.
  Even without the LAC RG25, vol. 9218, file 20–USSR–9, pt. 13, "Draft
Program for the Visit to Canada by . . ."

248 **In meeting after meeting** Yakovlev discussed his efforts, and the
Trudeau call, in personal communication to author by Aleksandr
Yakovlev, February 2003, 4.
  On April 25 Date is from LAC RG25, vol. 9218, file 20–USSR–9, pt. 13,
memo GEA–0860, April 27, 1983.

249 **Over five or six** Meeting number and quotes from personal communication to author by Aleksandr Yakovlev, February 2003, 3.

250 **During this trip** For background on the race to succeed Inozemtsev at
IMEMO see the flurry of memos and telegrams sent between Ottawa
and Moscow in LAC RG25, vol. 16521, file 22–10–USSR–1 pt. 2.
  On May 4 See LAC RG25, vol. 9218, file 20–USSR–9 pt. 13, confiden-
tial telegram XYGR1749, "Gorbachev Visit," dated May 4, 1983, 1–2.
  Yakovlev's tension See Gaddis, *The Cold War*, 225–27.

251 **Just weeks before** Frances FitzGerald, *Way Out There In The Blue:
Reagan, Star Wars and the End of the Cold War*, 19.
  Popular culture On the cruise, and the climate of the times, John Hays,
"Testing the Cruise," *Maclean's*, May 30, 1983, 22–26.

252 **Amid this climate** "Statement on Arrival in Canada," LAC RG25, vol.
9218, file 20–USSR–9 pt. 13.

253 **At 10:45 . . . Prud'homme** "Respecting: Visit to Canada of the Soviet
Parliamentary Delegation," *Minutes of Proceedings and Evidence of
the Standing Committee on External Affairs and National Defence* 95
(May 17, 1983): 1–34.

258 **After lunch, Yakovlev** Oct. 21, 2002, author interview with Nikita Kiriloff.

259 **The next morning** Account of the Trudeau/Gorbachev encounter
based almost entirely on confidential – Canadian eyes only memo,
"Prime Minister's Discussions with Mr. Gorbachev, May 18, 1983,"

dated May 20, 1983, 1–9, LAC RG25, vol. 8704, file 20–USSR–9 pt. 14.
Also helpful in the same file was A.P. McLaine, "Mikhail Gorbachev:
Personal Reflections," dated Dec. 3, 1984, and apparently written at the
request of British diplomats in advance of Gorbachev's encounter with
Margaret Thatcher.

263 **On the Thursday** Details on circumstances and events during the plane
ride and at Whelan's house later drawn from interviews in October 2002
with Jim Wright, Nikita Kiriloff, Eugene Whelan and Susan Whelan, as
well as May 27, 1983, memo GEA–1050, "Cdn-Soviet Relations: Visit of
Mikhail Gorbachev," LAC RG25, vol. 8704, file 20–USSR–9 pt. 14.

265 **"At first," Yakovlev recalls** Yakovlev spoke candidly in interviews about
this conversation. For this account, I relied most heavily on personal
communication to author by Aleksandr Yakovlev, February 2003, 3, and
Yakovlev, CBC, tapes 8–11, 6. Also see Yakovlev's *Sumerki*, 354.

266 **Yakovlev moved on to agriculture** First Gorbachev quote counseling
caution in agriculture reform from personal communication to author
by Aleksandr Yakovlev, February 2003, 3. Second Gorbachev quote from
Gorbachev, CBC, 2.

267 **Private ownership** Quote in this paragraph from Remnick, *Lenin's
Tomb*, 295. The "80 percent" stat is from Yakovlev, CBC, tapes 8–11, 6.

268 **Next morning, a Friday** Question about where the workers live is from
author interview with Whelan, October 2002.
Gorbachev proved Author interview with Jim Wright, Ottawa, and
Eugene Whelan, Amherstburg, Ontario, both October 2002.

269 **After a tour of Bright's** Grocery anecdote, ibid.

270 **After a second night** Ranch anecdote, ibid.
Yakovlev must have "Volunteer slavery" is from Gorbachev, *Memoirs*, 195.

271 **That night, a Sunday** Protest details, ibid., as well as Oct. 21, 2002,
author interview with interpreter Nikita Kiriloff.

272 **There was one more detail** Walking in Banff from Wright interview,
Ottawa, Oct. 7, 2002, 6. Gorbachev's request from personal communica-
tion to author by Aleksandr Yakovlev, February 2003, 4.
The ambassador would Yakovlev's speculation is ibid. "We have picked
up a rumour" from secret telegram GEA–1046, "Possible Promotion of
Yakovlev," May 26, 1983, LAC RG25 vol. 16521, file 22–10–USSR–1, pt. 2.
On controversy generated by Yakovlev appointment, see ibid., secret
telegram dated June 6, 1983, "Promotion of Yakovlev to be director of

IMEMO." Additional context provided in interview with IMEMO faculty member Nikolai Kosolapov, Moscow, December 2006.

273 **In Ottawa** See LAC RG25 vol. 16521, file 22–10–USSR–1, pt. 2. MacEachen's reluctance is discussed in confidential telegram, "Departure of Soviet Ambassador," June 9, 1983, which notes, "SSEA has reservations about suggestion for black tie dinner proposed, keeping in mind that the level of farewell entertainment could be taken as a signal regarding the state of our bilateral relations." Also see in same file, "Toast For Dinner Given By The Prime Minister In Honour Of Dr. Alexander N. Yakovlev, Ambassador of the USSR, And Mrs. Yakovlev," dated June 24, 1983, 1–2.

274 **On his final evening** Last dinner, Head, CBC, 14. Date of Yakovlev departure from LAC RG25 vol. 16521, file 22–10–USSR–1, pt. 2, letter from Yakovlev to SSEA MacEachen dated July 14, 1983. Cohon fishing trip source is Cohon himself, author interviews through 2006 and 2007.

AFTERWORD: THE LIBERATED MAN

279 **The previous year** "Happy" quote, Yakovlev, *Sumerki*, 360. "Liberated," Gorbachev's, CBC, 3.

280 **His position as director** IMEMO activities, author interview with Nikolai Kosolapov, Moscow, December 2006. On Shevardnadze's conversation with Gorbachev see Ekedahl and Goodman, *The Wars of Eduard Shevardnaze*, 29–30. Also, on the tense climate of this era in the Cold War, see Rhodes, *Arsenals of Folly*, 154–167.
Inspired by the prospect Soviet economy study, Yakovlev, *Sumerki*, 364–65. Old friend shocked, G.L. Smirnov, *Uroki Minuvshego*, 169.

282 **Trudeau, by now the longest-serving** On Trudeau and the peace mission, see Granatstein and Bothwell, *Pirouette*, 363–76. On Trudeau's visit with Yakovlev, see Roberts, *Raising Eyebrows*, 135–38. Yakovlev notes from the dinnertime conversation are from his personal archives, note dated Feb. 14, 1984, titled, "A record of the conversation with the PM of Canada Trudeau."

283 **When Chernenko died** Context on Grishin's political machinations as well as perspective on the transfer of power provided by Ligachev, *Inside Gorbachev's Kremlin*, 66–80.

Then Yakovlev's old boss On Gromyko and Gorbachev using Yakovlev as an intermediary in the succession negotiations, see Yakovlev, *Sumerki*, 459–461.

Gorbachev agreed, of course. Source on Soviet leaders' succession deliberations is Ligachev, *Inside Gorbachev's Kremlin*, 75–77.

284 **In these early years** For Yakovlev's role in glasnost see Remnick, *Lenin's Tomb*, 296–7.

285 **Aside from his work** For more on the Zavidavo sessions see English, *Russia and the Idea of the West*, 193–200.

286 **Epoch-making changes** Details on McDonald's from Bill Keller, "Of Famous Arches, Beeg Meks and Rubles," *New York Times*, Jan. 28, 1990, 1.

287 **While other first-hand** Yegor Ligachev, *Inside Gorbachev's Kremlin*, 112.
Western Kremlinologists For a concise summary of how the Americans missed Yakovlev and his liberal influence, see Matlock, *Autopsy of an Empire*, 76.

288 **The current executive** Second most influential, Bill Keller, "Riding Shotgun on Gorbachev's Glasnost Express: Aleksandr N. Yakovlev," Oct. 28, 1988. Quote is from Bill Keller, "Moscow's Other Mastermind," *New York Times Magazine*, February 19, 1989. Remnick first quote is from *Lenin's Tomb*, 296. Good angel, Remnick, CBC, 1.
Today such renowned English, *Russia and the Idea of the West*, 208. Joseph S. Nye, Jr. writes of Yakovlev in his *Soft Power: The Means to Success in World Politics*. And Armitage mentioned Yakovlev's story in a congressional hearing devoted to soft power on November 6, 2007.

291 **It is worth noting** Quotes in this paragraph from Yakovlev, CBC, tapes 8–11, 4.

293 **"Canada gave me a chance"** Personal communication to author by Aleksandr Yakovlev, February 2003, 1.
The end of an empire As the chair of the Commission for the Rehabilitation of Victims of Political Repression, Yakovlev was one of the foremost experts on the Soviet death toll. "My own many years of experience in the rehabilitation of victims of political terror allow me to assert that the number of people in the USSR who were killed for political motives or who died in prisons and camps during the entire period of Soviet power totaled 20 to 25 million," he wrote. "And unquestionably one must add those who died of famine – more than 5.5 million during

the civil war and more than 5 million during the 1930s." Yakovlev,
A Century of Violence in Soviet Russia, 234.

294 **One of the moments** Unless otherwise specified, my source for details
in this chapter's encounter between Yakovlev, Yeltsin and Gorbachev,
can be found in Yakovlev's *Sumerki*, 516–18. Why Yeltsin and Gorbachev
wanted Yakovlev there is my own speculation. For his part, in what is
likely an episode of false modesty, Yakovlev professes in his memoirs not
to know why they wanted him there.

"It so happened" Yakovlev, *Sumerki*, 516.

The meeting Description of Gorbachev's office from Boldin,
Ten Years, 162.

295 **The meeting began at noon.** On bickering between Yeltsin and
Gorbachev, see Grachev, *Final Days*, 181.

Gradually, the men The snag in negotiations over whether the
Gorbachev Foundation could study politics is from Yakovlev, *Sumerki*,
517. See also Grachev, *Final Days*, 184.

By the time British Prime Minister John Major's farewell call is from
Grachev, *Final Days*, 182.

297 **During the next several years** Yakovlev's discovery that Gorbachev knew
Kryuchkov and the KGB were eavesdropping on Yakovlev is featured in
Sumerki, 623.

Yakovlev lived well into the reign Yakovlev's opinion on Putinesque
backsliding from author interview, Anatoly Yakovlev, December 2006.

298 **"The main thing in my life"** Yakovlev, *Omut Pamyati*, 513.

BIBLIOGRAPHY

Alexeyeva, Ludmilla and Paul Goldberg. *The Thaw Generation: Coming of Age in the Post-Stalin Era.* Boston: Little, 1990.

Applebaum, Anne. *Gulag: A History.* New York: Doubleday, 2003.

Arbatov, G. A. *The System: An Insider's Life in Soviet Politics.* New York: Times Books, 1992.

Barron, John. *KGB: The Secret Work of Soviet Secret Agents.* New York: Reader's Digest Press, 1974.

Boldin, V. I. *Ten Years that Shook the World: The Gorbachev Era as Witnessed by His Chief of Staff.* New York: Basic Books, 1994.

Brown, Archie. *The Gorbachev Factor.* New York: Oxford University Press, 1996.

Brudny, Yitzhak M. *Reinventing Russia: Russian Nationalism and the Soviet State, 1953–1991.* Cambridge, Mass.: Harvard University Press, 1998.

Byrnes, Robert Francis. *Soviet-American Academic Exchanges, 1958–1975.* Bloomington: Indiana University Press, 1976.

Checkel, Jeffrey. *Ideas and International Political Change: Soviet/Russian Behaviour and the End of the Cold War.* New Haven: Yale University Press, 1997.

Chernyaev, Anatoly. *My Six Years with Gorbachev,* edited by Elizabeth Tucker, Robert English. University Park: Pennsylvania State University Press, 2000.

Clarkson, Stephen and Christina McCall. *Trudeau and our Times.* Toronto: McClelland and Stewart, 1990.

Cleroux, Richard. *Official Secrets: The Story Behind the Canadian Security Intelligence Service.* Montreal, Que.: McGraw-Hill Ryerson, 1990.

Cohen, Andrew and J.L. Granatstein, eds. *Trudeau's Shadow: The Life and Legacy of Pierre Elliott Trudeau.* Toronto: Random House of Canada, 1998.

Cohen, Stephen F. *Voices of Glasnost: Conversations with Gorbachev's Reformers*, edited by Katrina Vanden Heuvel. New York: Norton, 1989.

Cohen, Stephen F., ed. *An End to Silence: Uncensored Opinion in the Soviet Union*. New York: Norton, 1982.

Cohon, George and David Macfarlane. *To Russia with Fries*. Toronto: McClelland and Stewart, 1997.

Cran, Gregory. *Negotiating Buck Naked: Doukhobors, Public Policy, and Conflict Resolution*. Vancouver: University of British Columbia Press, 2006.

Daniloff, Nicholas. *Of Spies and Spokesmen: My Life As a Cold War Correspondent*. Columbia, MO: University of Missouri Press, 2008.

Doder, Dusko. *Shadows and Whispers*. New York: Random House, 1986.

Dunlop, John B. *The Faces of Contemporary Russian Nationalism*. Princeton, N.J.: Princeton University Press, 1983.

English, John. *Citizen of the World: The Life of Pierre Elliott Trudeau*. Toronto: Alfred A. Knopf Canada, 2006.

English, Robert. *Russia and the Idea of the West: Gorbachev, Intellectuals, and the End of the Cold War*. New York: Columbia University Press, 2000.

Ekedahl, Carolyn McGiffert and Melvin A. Goodman. *The Wars of Eduard Shevardnadze*. University Park, Penn.: Pennsylvania State University Press, 1997.

Fainsod, Merle. *How the Soviet Union is Governed*, edited by Jerry Fincher Hough, Merle Fainsod. Cambridge, Mass.: Harvard University Press, 1979.

FitzGerald, Frances. *Way Out there in the Blue: Reagan, Star Wars, and the End of the Cold War*. New York: Simon & Schuster, 2000.

Fonda, Jane. *My Life so Far*. New York: Random House, 2005.

Ford, R. A. D. *Our Man in Moscow: A Diplomat's Reflections on the Soviet Union*. Toronto: University of Toronto Press, 1989.

Gaddis, John Lewis. *The Cold War: A New History*. New York: Penguin Press, 2005.

Gorbachev, Mikhail Sergeevich. *Memoirs*. New York: Doubleday, 1996.

Gotlieb, Allan. *The Washington Diaries, 1981–1989*. Toronto: McClelland & Stewart, 2006.

Grachev, A. S. *Final Days: The Inside Story of the Collapse of the Soviet Union*. Boulder, Co.: Westview Press, 1995.

Graham, Loren R. *Moscow Stories*. Bloomington: Indiana University Press, 2006.

Granatstein,J.L. and Robert Bothwell. *Pirouette: Pierre Trudeau and Canadian Foreign Policy.* Toronto: University of Toronto Press, 1990.

Gwyn, Richard J. *The Northern Magus: Pierre Trudeau and Canadians,* edited by Sandra Gwyn. Toronto: McClelland and Stewart, 1980.

Hamilton, Nigel. *JFK, Reckless Youth.* New York: Random House, 1992.

Head,Ivan L. and Pierre Elliott Trudeau. *The Canadian Way: Shaping Canada's Foreign Policy 1968–1984.* Toronto: McClelland and Stewart, 1995.

Hershberger, Mary. *Jane Fonda's War: A Political Biography of an Antiwar Icon.* New York: W.W. Norton, 2005.

Hofstadter, Richard. *The Paranoid Style in American Politics, and Other Essays.* Chicago: University of Chicago Press, 1979.

———. *The Age of Reform: From Bryan to F.D.R.* New York: Alfred A. Knopf, 1955.

Josten, Josef. *Unarmed Combat as Practised in Czechoslovakia since August, 1968.* Delhi: D.K. Pub. House, 1973.

Kaiser, Robert G. *Why Gorbachev Happened: His Triumphs and His Failure.* New York: Simon & Schuster, 1991.

Kalugin, Oleg. *The First Directorate: My 32 Years in Intelligence and Espionage Against the West,* edited by Fen Montaigne. New York: St. Martin's Press, 1994.

Kissinger, Henry. *Years of Upheaval.* Toronto: Little, 1982.

Koestler, Arthur. *Darkness at Noon.* Harmondsworth, Middlesex, England: Penguin Books in Association with J. Cape, 1964.

Kopelev, Lev. *Ease My Sorrows: A Memoir.* New York: Random House, 1983.

Kramnick, Isaac. *Harold Laski: A Life on the Left,* edited by Barry Sheerman. London: H. Hamilton, 1993.

Kryuchkov, Vladimir. *Lichnoe Delo: Tri Dnia i Vsia Zhizn.* Moskva: Izd-vo Olimp, 2001.

Lakshin, V. *Solzhenitsyn, Tvardovsky, and Novy Mir,* edited by Mary Chaffin, L. Aldwinckle. Cambridge, Massachusetts: MIT Press, .

Ligachev, E. K. *Inside Gorbachev's Kremlin: The Memoirs of Yegor Ligachev.* Boulder, Colo.: Westview Press, 1996.

Lourie, Richard. *Sakharov: A Biography.* Hanover, NH: University Press of New England, 2002.

MacGuigan, Mark. *An Inside Look at External Affairs during the Trudeau Years: The Memoirs of Mark MacGuigan*, edited by P. Whitney Lackenbauer. Calgary: University of Calgary Press, 2002.

Markwick, Roger D. *Rewriting History in Soviet Russia: The Politics of Revisionist Historiography, 1956–1974.* New York: Palgrave, 2001.

Matlock, Jack F. *Reagan and Gorbachev: How the Cold War Ended.* New York: Random House, 2004.

——. *Autopsy on an Empire: The American Ambassador's Account of the Collapse of the Soviet Union.* New York: Random House, 1995.

Medvedev, Roy Aleksandrovich. *Khrushchev.* Oxford: B. Blackwell, 1982.

Medvedev, Vadim Andreevich. *V Komande Gorbacheva: Vzgliad Iznutri.* Moskva: 1994.

Medvedev, Zhores A. *Andropov.* Oxford: Blackwell, 1983.

——. *10 Years After Ivan Denisovich.* London: Macmillan, 1973.

Medvedev, Zhores Aleksandrovich. *A Question of Madness*, edited by Roy A. Medvedev. London: Macmillan, 1971.

Newman, Michael. *Harold Laski: A Political Biography.* Basingstoke: Macmillan, 1993.

Newman, Peter Charles. *Home Country: People, Places, and Power Politics.* Toronto: McClelland and Stewart, 1973.

Nye, Joseph S. *Soft Power: The Means to Success in World Politics.* New York: Public Affairs, 2004.

Pearson, Landon. *Letters from Moscow.* Manotick, ON: Penumbra Press, 2003.

Remnick, David. *Resurrection: The Struggle for a New Russia.* New York: Vintage Books, 1998.

——. *Lenin's Tomb: The Last Days of the Soviet Empire.* New York: Vintage Books, 1994.

Rhodes, Richard. *Arsenals of Folly: The Making of the Nuclear Arms Race.* New York: Alfred A. Knopf, 2007.

——. *Dark Sun: The Making of the Hydrogen Bomb.* New York: Simon & Schuster, 1995.

Richmond, Yale. *Cultural Exchange & the Cold War: Raising the Iron Curtain.* University Park: Pennsylvania State University Press, 2003.

Roberts, Peter. *Raising Eyebrows: An Undiplomatic Memoir.* Ottawa, ON: Golden Dog Press, 2000.

Rohmer, Richard H. *Ultimatum.* Toronto: Clarke, 1973.

Sandford, Christopher. *McQueen: The Biography*. London: HarperCollins Entertainment, 2001.

Sawatsky, John. *Men in the Shadows: The RCMP Security Service*. Toronto: Doubleday Canada, 1980.

Scammell, Michael. *Solzhenitsyn: A Biography*. New York: Norton, 1984.

Service, Robert. *Stalin: A Biography*. Cambridge, Mass.: Belknap Press of Harvard University Press, 2005.

——. *A History of Twentieth-Century Russia*. Cambridge, Mass.: Harvard University Press, 1998.

Sharp, Mitchell. *Which Reminds Me—: A Memoir*. Toronto: University of Toronto Press, 1994.

Simmonds, George W. *Soviet Leaders*. New York: T. Y. Crowell Co., 1967.

Skilling, H. Gordon. *Czechoslovakia's Interrupted Revolution*. Princeton, N.J.: Princeton University Press, 1976.

Smirnov, G. L. *Uroki Minuvshego*. Moskva: ROSSPEN, 1997.

Smith, Hedrick. *The Russians*. New York: Quadrangle/New York Times Book Co., 1976.

Solzhenitsyn, Aleksandr Isaevich. *The Oak and the Calf: Sketches of Literary Life in the Soviet Union*. New York: Harper & Row, 1980.

Spechler, Dina. *Permitted Dissent in the USSR: Novy Mir and the Soviet Regime*. New York, N.Y.: Praeger, 1982.

Taubman, William. *Khrushchev: The Man and His Era*. New York: Norton, 2003.

Tolkunov, Lev Nikolaevich. *Mify i Realnost: [Ocherki]*. Moskva: Izvestia, 1971.

Trudeau, Margaret. *Margaret Trudeau: Beyond Reason*. New York: Paddington Press, 1979.

Trudeau, Pierre Elliott. *Memoirs*. Toronto: McClelland & Stewart, 1993.

Truman, David Bicknell. *The Congressional Party, a Case Study*. New York: Wiley, 1959.

Tygiel, Jules. *Ronald Reagan and the Triumph of American Conservatism*. 2nd Ed. New York: Pearson Longman, 2006.

Voslensky, M. S. *Nomenklatura: Anatomy of the Soviet Ruling Class*. London: Bodley Head, 1984.

Whelan, Eugene F. with Rick Archbold. *Whelan: The Man in the Green Stetson*. Toronto: Irwin, 1986.

Yakovlev, Aleksandr N. *Sumerki*. Moskva: Materik, 2003.

———. *A Century of Violence in Soviet Russia*, edited by Anthony Austin, Paul Hollander. New Haven, Conn.: Yale University Press, 2002.

———. *Omut Pamyati: Ot Stolypina do Putina*. Moskva: Vagrius, 2001.

———. *The Fate of Marxism in Russia*. New Haven, Conn.: Yale University Press, 1993.

———. *On the Edge of an Abyss: From Truman to Reagan: The Doctrines and Realities of the Nuclear Age*, edited by Yakovlev. Moscow: Progress Publishers, 1985.

———. *Pax Americana*. Moskva: Molodaia gvardiia, 1969.

———. *Realizm – zemlia perestroiki: izbrannye vystupleniia i stati*. Moscow: Izdvo politecheskoi litry, 1990.

———. *The Maelstrom of Memory: From Stolypin to Putin*. Unpublished English manuscript trans. Kathleen Luft. (New York: Encounter Books).

Yanov, Alexander. *The Russian Challenge and the Year 2000*. New York, NY: Basil Blackwell Inc., 1987.

———. *The Russian New Right: Right-Wing Ideologies in the Contemporary USSR*. Berkeley: Institute of International Studies, 1978.

Young, Scott. *War on Ice: Canada in International Hockey*. Toronto: McClelland and Stewart, 1976.

The following people assisted in the researching of this book by contributing personal communications or interviews. In-person interviews denoted by place the interview occurred. Names not followed by a place name occurred by telephone, post or e-mail. Asterisk (*) denotes that the interview was conducted in 2002/2003 for my article on the 1983 Gorbachev trip, "The Walk That Changed The World," *Saturday Night* (April 2003): 39–42. The remainder were conducted in 2006/2007 period.

Leon Aron, Washington, D.C.
Vadim Bakatin, Moscow
Albert Belyaev, Moscow
Genrikh Borovik, Moscow
Archie Brown
George Cohon, Toronto
Timothy Colton*
Jim Coutts, Toronto
Nick Daniloff
Charles Doran*
Bob Fowler
Allan Gotlieb, Toronto
Loren Graham
Ann Head
Ivan Head*
Robert E. Johnson, Toronto
Oleg Kalugin, Washington, D.C.
Bob Kaiser
Nikita Kiriloff *

Nikolai Kosolapov, Moscow
Marc Lalonde
Natasha Lobanova, Mississauga
Ralph Lysyshyn, Ottawa
Claire and Farley Mowat
Landon and Geoffrey Pearson,
    Ottawa
Skip Phoenix, Toronto
Nikolai Pleshanov, Moscow
Eli and Dorothy Popoff, Grand
    Forks, BC
Jim Popoff, Grand Forks, BC
Ed Schreyer
John Smiley*, Ottawa
Si Taylor, Ottawa
Alexandre Trudeau, Montreal
J.J. Verigin, Jr., Grand Forks, BC
Peter and Lucy Voykin, Castlegar, BC
Eugene Whelan*, Amherstburg, ON

Susan Whelan*, Windsor, ON
James Wright*, Ottawa
Anatoly Yakovlev, Moscow
Nina Yakovlev, Moscow

Nataliya Ushatskaya, Moscow
Aleksandr Yakovlev*
Igor Zakharov
Gennady Zolotov, Moscow

ACKNOWLEDGEMENTS

This book would not have been possible without the cooperation of the Yakovlev family, in particular, Aleksandr Yakovlev's widow, Nina, his daughter, Nataliya, his son, Anatoly, and his grand-daughter Natasha. In every sense of the word they were ideal sources. Early in my research they tolerated my ignorance and helped me to gain my footing on the mountain of written material that exists on perestroika and its origins. They helped to arrange interviews. They were available for consultation whenever I needed while at the same time avoiding attempts to influence my analysis or conclusions. Well into her eighties, Nina shrugged off a bout of the flu to sit for one of several interviews with me. Whenever I needed, Anatoly dug through his father's personal archives to locate documents that provided valuable context to the events depicted in the memoirs. Whether my inquiries came in person, over the telephone or by e-mail, he always responded promptly regardless of his own workload. He also provided feedback on several drafts of the book.

To me, one of the book's most intriguing images was the fifty-something Aleksandr walking hand in hand in Ottawa's Rockcliffe Park with Natasha, his grand-daughter. Early in my research I learned that Natasha Lobanova still lives in Canada, outside of Toronto, where she is raising her daughter, Anna. Natasha turned out to enjoy reminiscing about her grandfather. She was unfailingly interested in hearing how my research was going and was always ready to sit at her kitchen table and discuss elements of Aleksandr's personality over a cup of tea. She also spent several days assisting on matters of translation. Natasha started out as a source; by the end of the book she had become a friend.

McDonald's of Russia founder George Cohon continues to display loyalty and gratitude to Yakovlev and the Yakovlev family. These qualities motivated him to contribute numerous hours of interviews. He was always willing to place telephone calls to his impressive network of friends to assist in arranging interviews in both Russia and Canada, and his infectious enthusiasm contributed to my own for this project. Cohon benefited from Yakovlev's encouragement at key periods in Cohon's quest to open the first McDonald's in Russia; in the same manner, I benefited from Cohon's at key periods in my quest to finish this book.

Research involved travelling from Moscow to Montreal, from Ottawa to Washington, DC, and from Essex County in southwestern Ontario to the mountain valleys of the British Columbia interior. In each place I relied on others' hospitality and kindness. Thanks to Tereza, George, Ash and Ilya in Moscow, Bob and Annette Anderson outside of Ottawa, and Jim Popoff and the Popoff family as well as J.J. Verigin, Jr., in Grand Forks, British Columbia.

Archie Brown and Robert Kaiser provided valuable advice in the early stages of research. At Library and Archives Canada, archivists Paulette Dozois and Christian Rioux responded promptly to requests and demonstrated interest in the project. Svetlana Savranskaya at George Washington University's National Security Archive willingly scanned unpublished Anatoly Chernyaev diaries at my request. CBC's Alex Shprintsen provided a veritable treasure trove of research materials when he pointed me toward the interview transcripts from the television documentary, *Aleksandr Yakovlev: The Commissar of Glasnost*, featuring interviews not just with Yakovlev but also Ivan Head and Mikhail Gorbachev, among others. At the University of Toronto's Centre for European, Russian and Eurasian Studies, Peter Solomon and Robert E. Johnson were generous with advice and time, as was their U of T colleague, Robert Bothwell. I am grateful to Solomon as well for offering comments on an early draft as well as directing me to my two Russian-speaking research assistants, Ph.D. candidates Auri Berg and Olga Kesarchuk, whose adroit translation and background knowledge assisted in providing context for the book. J. Larry Black and Greg Donaghy also provided research direction.

This book happened because literary agent Anne McDermid tracked down an untested writer and asked him whether he had any book ideas. Also thanks to Martha Magor in Anne's office. McClelland & Stewart senior editor Chris Bucci displayed early faith in the project and contributed shaping advice throughout. My friend Jeremy Busch also took the time to provide shaping advice and valuable editorial comments.

Thank you to the Canada Council for the Arts. This project was made possible with its generous support.

I am lucky to be surrounded by supportive family members who are, if anything, more confident than I am of my abilities as a writer. My siblings and their significant others – Mark and Jody Shulgan, Julie Shulgan and Isaac Junkin – never failed to look fascinated during our weekly Sunday dinners as I recounted my latest epiphany about Soviet history. Julie Shulgan was always ready with diverting conversation during late-night work breaks. Mark Shulgan was an engaging listener during early-morning runs and was always ready with champagne when I passed some significant waypoint.

I wouldn't have been able to become a writer without the support of my parents, who remain as encouraging of me today as they were when I was writing science-fiction stories at the age of 12. Any writer would do well to have as enthusiastic a fan as my mother, Nancy Shulgan. My father, Myron W. Shulgan, was the first to encourage me to do a book on Yakovlev. His editorial judgment is impeccable.

Most of all, thanks to Natalie Tregaskiss and Myron F. Shulgan. Writing a book is far tougher on the writer's family than on the writer. The writer is motivated by plaudits and accolades hoped-for upon completion. The family, meanwhile, just pines for the return of the husband and father. Completing this work was complicated by the birth of Myron the same week I signed the book deal. Natalie has borne the ensuing emotional and financial sacrifices without complaint. She has assumed more than her share of child-rearing responsibilities. She has tolerated my stress and cheered me out of grumpiness. In other words, she has been my redemption, as typically has been the case.

INDEX